I have known Mark Ballard for over 30 years and have been blessed to preach in his church in New England before he founded Northeastern Baptist College. He was a trustee when I served as president of LifeWay. He and his wife Cindy are remarkable leaders who have made an indelible impact upon New England. These pages confront issues that every Bible believing and Christ honoring believer must face. These are the critical issues for our day, and we must find a way to confront them in a way that is consistent with God's Word! God was not surprised by the 21st century. He gave us His inerrant Word to guide us as we navigate the stormy waters of contemporary culture biblically and effectively. Every believer will find encouragement and clarity in this volume. This is a strong statement for all who desire to be true to the principles found in these pages. One thing for sure as you read these chapters, you will find them faithful to the Word of God and edifying for all the churches in our land.

JIMMY DRAPER
President Emeritus,
LifeWay

You will consult *Does it Still Matter?* often. Each chapter is written by someone knowledgeable in the particular subject matter of that chapter. Read it and be encouraged and blessed.

JERRY VINES
Pastor–Emeritus,
First Baptist Church, Jacksonville, FL
Two-time President,
Southern Baptist Convention

Mark Ballard and Timothy Christian brought together a stellar team of essayists and compiled a work that is much needed. As Southern Baptists and evangelicals in general currently struggle to find a way forward that is faithful to Scripture, this book takes a sobering look at the place from whence we have come to offer a path forward for the future. Under the guise of the dominant question set forth in the title, *Does It Still Matter?*, multiple contributors mine the richness of biblical truth and Southern Baptist heritage to address an array of issues. This is a work illustrative of the scriptural fidelity needed to address the serious challenges facing believers today. *Does It Still Matter?* belongs in the hands of the pew member, preacher, pupil, and professor, for it offers great perspective on the Conservative Resurgence while issuing a challenge to hold a biblical line on each topic addressed in the book.

LEE E. BRAND JR.
Vice President and Dean,
Mid-America Baptist Seminary
First Vice President,
Southern Baptist Convention

In a day and age of cultural confusion and biblical compromise, even within the churches, this book, written by warriors of the faith who have invested their lives for the Gospel, answers prophetically the most pressing questions of our day. It is a must read for every pastor and lay leader.

EMIR CANER
President,
Truett McConnell University

Some men and women lived it, some prayed for it, and some were the products of the Conservative Resurgence of 1979. The basic foundational question for the CR is the issue of inerrancy. Would Southern Baptist decide to be people of the book or would we reject the God who communicates in favor of neo-orthodoxy? The question is still relevant. Over 40 years later, the question is once again, at the forefront of theological institutions, churches, and ministries. The contemporary issues of hermeneutics, meaning, gender issues, transgender issues, gospel content are all up for grabs as the Conservative Resurgence seems to be but a whisper on history books. Eleven masters work their way through these 21st century issues that present a formidable challenge to inerrancy. They peel back the layers of contemporary thought and expose them for undermining the very fabric of the Conservative Resurgence-inerrancy. These eleven masters deal with problematic issues by demonstrating that the God who speaks is still relevant to humanity's problems. The Conservative Resurgence still matters!

MARVIN JONES
President,
Yellowstone Christian College

With so many changing winds in our culture, there are now a variety of pressure points that pastors and churches must navigate. This new resource from Dr. Ballard is tremendously helpful for anyone who strives to stay strong in Biblical truth and stand for what pleases God.

BRAD JURKOVICH
Senior Pastor,
First Baptist Church, Bossier City, LA
Spokesman,
Conservative Baptist Network

The title of the book asks *"Does it Still Matter?"* The answer is yes. The issues deftly addressed in this short, readable resource are among the most important of our day. But the Conservative Resurgence itself matters as well, forty years later, as we face a new leftist threat from within and without, seeking to co-opt the church and assert a false gospel. The church must win this battle of ideas: it matters now more than ever.

ROD D. MARTIN
Founder and CEO,
The Martin Organization, Inc.

In every generation the Christian message of the gospel is under attack. Understanding the importance of the conservative resurgence within the Southern Baptist Convention will serve to remind the future generations of faithful men and women how important it is to fight strenuously for the defense of the faith. This work is written by a coterie of scholars addressing a wide range of critical theological issues which matter! Many of the key leaders of the conservative resurgence are contributors.

ANTHONY ALLEN
President,
Hannibal-Lagrange University

This superb volume will make a significant contribution to resolving the current crisis of identity that is roiling practically every facet of the Southern Baptist Convention. Grounding their work in rigorous study of the Bible, the authors provide answers to many of the identity-shaping questions we are asking ourselves forty years after our battle for the Bible. Anyone who wants to understand what is at stake and how we must answer the question of who we are as Southern Baptists must read this book.

BARRETT DUKE
Executive Director,
Montana Southern Baptist Convention

Dr. Ballard and his team have accomplished what very few are able to do in writing. Their work, *Does It Still Matter?* is richly theological, deeply devotional, and accessibly readable for every follower of Jesus. I highly recommend this book to pastors, church leaders, deacons, Sunday School teachers, and anyone committed to biblical orthodoxy. This work is a great contribution to the local church.

TIMOTHY PIGG
Senior Pastor,
Fellowship Church, Immokalee, FL

In a time in which secular ideologies embedded in social and cultural frameworks are challenging the foundations of the church while many evangelical institutions have begun to dwindle in their commitment to the truth of the Gospel, it is encouraging to read a book that reminds us of who we are, what we believe, and why we believe. *Does It Still Matter?* calls us to an unequivocal adherence to those Baptist distinctives that have defined us through the years as a people on a mission.

JAVIER CHAVEZ
Senior Pastor,
Iglesia Bautista Amistad Cristiana International
Visiting Professor of Global Studies,
Truett-McConnell University

If I may use the voice of Amos in chapter 7…"And the Lord said unto me, Amos what seest thou? And I said, A plumb line." That's what I see in this very timely book - a pertinent reminder of the biblical plumb line of righteousness because it still very much matters and should be heeded **today**!

LORINE HEARNE SPRATT
Executive Assistant to Dr. Brad Jurkovich,
First Baptist Church Bossier City, LA

In an age marked by apathy and indifference in a sea of information inundation, the question "Does it still matter?" should shake readers out of an autopilot reverie and back to the biblical command to "not grow weary in well doing" (Gal. 6:9). *Does It Still Matter?* presents nearly a dozen subjects worthy of contemplation, providing even the most disillusioned and distracted a point from which to re-engage and rediscover the satisfaction of not only spending time on worthy endeavors (Eph. 5:16) but also of simply obeying Scripture's admonition to work "heartily, as to the Lord, and not unto men" (Col. 3:23). This volume, compiled by refined-as-gold Christian leaders, will encourage your heart and provoke you to God-honoring action in areas of life that do indeed still matter a great deal.

H. SHARAYAH COLTER
Founder,
Colter & Co.

DOES IT STILL MATTER?

Essays in Honor of
the Conservative Resurgence

Edited by
MARK H. BALLARD
& TIMOTHY K CHRISTIAN

DOES IT STILL MATTER?

Essays in Honor of the Conservative Resurgence

Edited by
MARK H. BALLARD
& TIMOTHY K CHRISTIAN

BENNINGTON, VT

Does it Still Matter?
Essays in Honor of the Conservative Resurgence
Copyright © 2022 by Mark H. Ballard & Timothy K. Christian

Published by Northeastern Baptist Press
Post Office Box 4600
Bennington, VT 05201

Scripture taken from the New King James Version®, unless otherwise indicated. Copyright © 1982 by Thomas Nelson. Used by permission.
All rights reserved.

Cover design by Leason Stiles

Hardcover ISBN: 978-1-953331-08-3

Does It Still Matter: Essays in Honor of the Conservative Resurgence is dedicated to the thousands of Southern Baptist Pastors and People in the Pew who at great personal cost stood firm on the inerrancy of Scripture. These amazing folks dedicated their lives, their resources, and their reputations to stand firm on the Word of God. Many traveled hundreds of miles, slept in their cars, and ate peanut butter and jelly sandwiches to serve as messengers at the SBC annual meetings from 1979-2000. Many were attacked verbally, threatened physically, and suffered the loss of pay and/or loss of ministry positions to take a stand. Yet, year after year, no matter the costs, they stood firm. These faithful servants of the Lord handed off to a new millennium a SBC fully committed to the Inerrancy of Scripture. With these essays, we pay honor to each of them.

TABLE OF CONTENTS

CONTRIBUTORS, QUALIFICATIONS, AND CHAPTERS

Introduction
DOES IT STILL MATTER?
Timothy K. Christian

Timothy K. Christian (B.A., Tennessee Temple College; M.Div., D.Min. Mid-America Baptist Theological Seminary; Th.D., University of South Africa) was a pastor for twenty-seven years and a college and seminary administrator and Professor of Theology for 20 years. He retired at the end of 2020 to be a part-time writer and the full-time caregiver for Judy, his wife of 45+ years, who battles Advanced Secondary Progressive Multiple Sclerosis. They enjoy their two married children and their spouses, Trina (Shane) and Marcus (Sarah), and their seven grandchildren.

Christian pastored Baptist Churches in TN, AR, IN, Italy (English speaking), GA, FL, NH, NY, and CT. He is a conference speaker, author, coauthor, or editor of thirteen books, several theological journal articles, and dozens of sermon booklets. He participated in the Conservative Resurgence from its inception, and is a member of the Conservative Baptist Network. He has served the Southern Baptist Convention as: Member—Committee on Committees representing New England; Chairman—Credentials Committee; Chairman—Committee on Committees representing New York.

Chapter 1
DOES INERRANCY STILL MATTER?
Mark H. Ballard

Mark H. Ballard (B.A. Criswell College; M.Div., Ph.D. Southeastern Baptist Theological Seminary) faithful pastor, diligent church planter, passionate evangelist, innovative educator, creative and prolific author, and pacesetting Baptist leader—is the Founding President of Northeastern Baptist College in Bennington, Vermont. He and his wife Cindy have a teenage son, Benjamin. Ballard has served as a church planter and pastor in New York, New Hampshire, Virginia, Florida, North Carolina, and Texas. He has filled pulpits, held revival services, and served as a conference speaker in numerous states for 30+ years.

Ballard was involved in the Conservative Resurgence from its early years and is a member of the Steering Council of the Conservative Baptist Network. He has served the Southern Baptist Convention as a Baptist Convention of New England representative: Member—Committee on Committees; Trustee—LifeWay Christian Resources; Member—SBC Executive Committee; President and Vice President—Baptist Convention of New England.

* * * * *

Ballard and Christian have collaborated on numerous projects, including Bible conferences, evangelism training events, regional church-planting strategies, nationally published articles, and previous books, including *Normal's Journey*; *Open Doors: The Pathway to God-Sized Assignments*; *Priorities: Reaching the Life God Intended*; and *Words Matter: What is the Gospel?*

Chapter 2
DOES THE GOSPEL STILL MATTER?
Johnny Hunt

Johnny M. Hunt (B.A. Gardner-Webb College, M.Div. and D.Min. South-eastern Baptist Theological Seminary) is a member of the Lumbee Native American Indian tribe based in North Carolina. Hunt's father left the family when he was seven. Johnny became an alcoholic and gambler at a young age, dropping out of school at 16 and managing a poolroom. Jesus Christ radically transformed Hunt's life during his late teens, after someone shared the gospel with him. He detailed the story in his book, *Out of the Poolroom.* After his conversion, several men from his home church in Wilmington, North Carolina, mentored him. He realized not only that God was calling him into the ministry but that he must also prepare himself to fulfill God's calling. Therefore, he went to college and seminary.

Hunt's first pastorate was in North Carolina, his home state, but he became nationally known as the pastor of the dynamic, fast-growing First Baptist Church of Woodstock, GA. Under Hunt's leadership the church grew to be one of the larger churches in America with over 19,000 members. Hunt was a leader in the Conservative Resurgence. He served the SBC in many capacities, ultimately being elected to two terms as President of the SBC. He pastored FBC Woodstock for 42 years before transitioning to be the Senior Vice President for Evangelism and Leadership of the North American Mission Board. Since his conversion, Johnny Hunt's passion for the gospel of Jesus Christ and for mentoring other men have been well-known driving forces in his life. He authored 10 books and is in constant demand as a speaker across the US.

He and his wife, Janet, have two daughters and four grandchildren.

Chapter 3
DOES BAPTISM STILL MATTER?
Chuck Kelley

Dr. Chuck Kelley served as President of the New Orleans Baptist Theological Seminary (NOBTS) from 1996 until his retirement in 2018. He is now President Emeritus and Distinguished Research Professor of Evangelism at NOBTS, and also Director and Founder of Innovative Evangelism. He was a leader among leaders in the Conservative Resurgence and was on the Baptist Faith & Message 2000 revision committee.

Kelley describes himself as a follower of Jesus, husband to Rhonda, and Distinguished Research Professor of Evangelism at New Orleans Baptist Theological Seminary. Born in Beaumont, Texas, in 1952, Kelley grew up in First Baptist Church of Beaumont. He was ordained as a minister in February 1972 at the age of 19. Kelley earned a Bachelor of Arts in Philosophy from Baylor University in 1974. While there, he met Rhonda Harrington, whom he married in June 1974. Kelley holds two degrees from NOBTS: M.Div. (1978) and Th.D. (1983).

Kelley began teaching evangelism at NOBTS in 1983. From 1989 to 1996, he was the Roland Q. Leavell Professor of Evangelism, and from 1993 to 1996, he directed the Leavell Center for Evangelism and Church Health. In addition, he was chair of the Pastoral Ministries Division at NOBTS from 1993 to 1995.

Kelley has authored, edited, and contributed to seven books. He has also written multiple articles for journals and magazines, as well as Sunday School curriculum and Evangelism curriculum for local churches.

Chapter 4

DOES THE TERM BAPTIST STILL MATTER?

Michael W. McDill

Dr. Michael W. McDill (B.A. Portland State University; M.Div., Th.M., & Ph.D. Theology and Church History, Southeastern Baptist Theological Seminary) is Professor of Church History and Theology at Northeastern Baptist College (NEBC). Previously, he was Associate Professor of Church History and Theology at Mid-America Baptist Theological Seminary.

Dr. McDill has served as a pastor, interim pastor, supply preacher, and Bible teacher for various churches in New York, North Carolina, Virginia, Oregon, New Hampshire, Massachusetts, Vermont, and Connecticut. He also served as Pastor of the Deep Springs Baptist Church, Stoneville, NC from 1991-1997. He served on the trustee board of NEBC from 2013-2015. His writings include "Balthasar Hubmaier and Free Will," a chapter in *The Anabaptists and Contemporary Baptists: Restoring New Testament Christianity.* Michael and his wife Becky have four children and two grandchildren.

Chapter 5

DOES THE LOCAL CHURCH STILL MATTER?

Ronnie W. Rogers

Ronnie Rogers (B.A., Biblical Studies, Criswell College; M.S., Counseling, Henderson State University) has been a pastor for 35+ years. He currently serves as Senior Pastor of Trinity Baptist Church in Norman, Oklahoma.

He has served his denomination in multiple capacities. He served as: Chairman - Nominating Committee of the Southern Baptist Convention; Chairman - Board of Trustees for Midwestern Baptist Theological Seminary; President - Arkansas Baptist State Convention; and Member - Committee on Committees of the Southern Baptist Convention.

Pastor Rogers is a seasoned pastor, prolific author and blogger. He has presented four papers at conferences in Oxford, England. He has authored seven books, including three on various aspects of the life and ministry of a local church. He is uniquely qualified to write the chapter, "Does The Local Church Still Matter?" He has also contributed chapters and essays to several other books.

He and his wife Gina have two married daughters, Natalie and Nancy, two sons-in-law, Rocky and JR, and seven grandchildren.

Chapter 6
DOES GRAMMATICAL-HISTORICAL INTERPRETATION STILL MATTER?
Paige Patterson

Paige Patterson has more than four decades of experience in educating pastors and missionaries. After almost 18 years as president of the Criswell College in Dallas, Patterson served for 11 years as president of Southeastern Baptist Theological Seminary in Wake Forest, North Carolina, and then 15 years as president of Southwestern Baptist Theological Seminary in Fort Worth, Texas. Patterson's leadership focus is on an intense commitment to evangelism and global missions with a foundational component of challenging research and rigorous academic preparation. He continues his influence on Christian Education today through his role as the President of the Sandy Creek Foundation and his work with colleges and seminaries around the globe.

After graduating from Hardin-Simmons University, Patterson completed the Th.M. and Ph.D. degrees at New Orleans Baptist Theological Seminary. Patterson, along with his long time friend Paul Pressler, served as the architects and key leaders of the Conservative Resurgence at great personal sacrifice. Southern Baptists elected him to serve as President of the Southern Baptist Convention for two terms (1998–2000). During those years, he appointed a committee to revise the Baptist Faith & Message. He also presided over the historic Southern Baptist Convention session that adopted the revised statement of faith.

Paige and Dorothy Patterson have traveled to and ministered in more than 138 countries of the world, sharing Christ with various heads of state, including Yasser Arafat of the Palestinian Authority and Menachem Begin of Israel. He led church planting movements in several states and also pastored churches in Arkansas, Louisiana, and Texas.

Patterson has penned numerous books and articles, including commentaries on Song of Solomon, 1 Corinthians, Titus, 1 Peter, and most recently the Revelation volume in The New American Commentary Series.

Chapter 7

DOES EXPOSITORY PREACHING STILL MATTER?

David Allen

David L. Allen is the Distinguished Professor of Preaching, holds the George W. Truett Chair of Pastoral Ministry, and is the director of the Southwestern Center for Text-Driven Preaching at Southwestern Baptist Theological

Seminary. He was married to Sherri for 37 years. She died of cancer in 2015. They had four children and five grandchildren. God in his grace brought Kate Finley into his life and they married in October 2016.

Allen earned the B.A., Criswell College, M.Div., Southwestern Baptist Theological Seminary, and Ph.D. in Humanities with a Major in Linguistics from The University of Texas at Arlington.

During his ministry he served as senior pastor of two churches for a total of 21 years, and has served as interim pastor of a dozen churches. Allen has led or been a part of over 400 revivals, Bible conferences, and lecture series, including study tours in the Philippines, Israel, Oxford, and Germany. Along with numerous articles and chapters in multi-author volumes, he is the author of *Hebrews* in the New American Commentary Series; *Lukan Authorship of Hebrews*; *1-3 John: Fellowship in God's Family* in the "Preaching the Word" Series; *Preaching Tools: an Annotated Survey of Commentaries and Preaching Resources for Every Book of the Bible*; and *The Extent of the Atonement: History and Critique*. He is currently working on a commentary on Job (*Exalting Jesus in Job*) in the Christ-Centered Exposition Commentary Series, edited by David Platt and Danny Akin.

David Allen served as the co-editor and contributor to *Whosoever Will: A Biblical-Theological Critique of Five-Point Calvinism*; *Text-Driven Preaching*; *The Return of Christ: a Premillennial Perspective*; and *Preach the Word: Essays on Biblical Preaching in Honor of Jerry Vines*.

Chapter 8
DOES GENDER IDENTITY STILL MATTER?
Candi Finch

Candi Finch holds a B.A. in Communication, M.Div. in Women's Studies, and Ph.D. in Systematic Theology and Church History. She has served on the Resolutions Committee and the Women's Ministry Advisory Council for the Southern Baptist Convention. Candi currently serves as a Trustee of Northeastern Baptist College. She is the Dean of Women, the Director of Admissions, and an Associate Professor of Women's Studies in Theology at Mid-America Baptist Theological Seminary.

Finch's life with God has been an adventure—she has been on mission trips both stateside and internationally, worked on a church staff doing girls ministry, served as a seminary professor teaching classes in the US and overseas, spent several summers working with teenagers both in the US and overseas, and even led a travelling drama group to raise money for missions.

Candi Finch has contributed to books for women and youth. She speaks at women's conferences and has a passion to see women of all ages come to know the Lord and be discipled in their faith. Several people invested in her life when she was in high school and was a new believer. Their impact reminds her daily of the positive influence we can have on others for Christ.

Chapter 9
DO GENDER ROLES STILL MATTER?
Dorothy Patterson

Dorothy Kelley Patterson is a self-described homemaker. She has been a lifelong helper to her husband, Paige Patterson, former President of three Christian institutions of higher education and of the Southern Baptist Convention. She has served as professor of theology in women's studies for almost four decades. She earned graduate and postgraduate degrees in theology, and teaches, speaks, and writes for women. She is a member of the Evangelical Theological Society, served on the founding board for the Council for Biblical Manhood and Womanhood, and attends First Baptist

Church of Dallas. She is a prolific author and contributor to more than fifteen books. She is also a blogger.

Dorothy Patterson has been active in theological education for women, serving as professor of theology in women's studies at both Southeastern and Southwestern Baptist Theological Seminaries, but she sees her most critical roles as that of wife, mother, and grandmother. Their son Armour is a writer and lives in Melissa, Texas, with his wife Rachel. Their daughter Carmen is married to Mark Howell, President of E2initiative. The Howells presented the Pattersons with two granddaughters, Abigail and Rebekah.

The Pattersons reside in the Dallas, Texas area but travel extensively to preach, teach, and evangelize throughout the world.

Chapter 10
DOES THE RAPTURE STILL MATTER?
Mark H. Ballard

Chapter 11
DOES THE CONSERVATIVE RESURGENCE STILL MATTER?
Z. Scott Colter

Scott Colter earned a B.A. and M.Div. from Southwestern Baptist Theological Seminary, and a Ph.D. from Mid-America Baptist Theological Seminary. He has been married to Sharayah for ten years. Scott and Sharayah are the proud parents of a four-year-old son and a one-year-old daughter.

He now serves as Director of Strategic Initiatives at Mid-America Baptist Theological Seminary and as the Executive Director of the Conservative Baptist Network.

Prior to serving at Mid-America, Dr. Colter was the Executive Director of the Sandy Creek Foundation in Dallas, Texas. He helped facilitate international and domestic ministry, mission work, evangelism, theological publications, and cultural engagement. Before leading the Sandy Creek Foundation, he served for more than a decade at Southwestern Baptist Theological Seminary where he worked ultimately as the Chief of Staff to the President and served in the institution's executive cabinet. Scott also oversaw the work of the research doctoral office and later served as the Director of Institutional Advancement. In ministry, he served as an associate to the senior pastor at Birchman Baptist Church in Fort Worth, Texas.

Epilogue
WHERE DO WE GO FROM HERE?
Timothy K. Christian

Introduction

DOES IT
STILL MATTER?

TIMOTHY K. CHRISTIAN

"Can you believe it?" the pastor said as he hugged his wife. "It's finally over!"

"At last," she said. "I wasn't sure it would ever happen."

"Me either. It took 21 years, but the truth finally won."

Such was the sentiment of the vast majority when the gavel sounded concluding the Southern Baptist Convention's (SBC) annual meeting in Orlando, Florida, on June 14, 2000. The hum of jovial camaraderie among the more than 11,000 messengers filing out of the Orlando Convention Center was palpable. They had represented their home churches and the 15-million+ members of the SBC churches spread across North America. They had publicly debated and voted overwhelmingly in favor of a newly revised "Baptist Faith and Message" (BF&M)—the SBC's statement of faith. The messengers believed their vote had settled the controversy for the foreseeable future.

Through the BF&M 2000, Southern Baptists spoke decisively. Article 1, "The Scriptures," affirmed the Bible's full inerrancy, though it did not use the term. The 111-word statement declared:

> The Holy Bible was written by men divinely inspired and is God's revelation of Himself to man. It is a perfect treasure of divine instruction. It has God for its author, salvation for its end, and truth,

1

without any mixture of error, for its matter. Therefore, all Scripture is totally true and trustworthy. It reveals the principles by which God judges us, and therefore is, and will remain to the end of the world, the true center of Christian union, and the supreme standard by which all human conduct, creeds, and religious opinions should be tried. All Scripture is a testimony to Christ, who is Himself the focus of divine revelation.[1]

What led to the climactic vote?

MOTIVATION FOR THE CONSERVATIVE RESURGENCE

Theological concerns had been brewing in the Convention at least since the 1960s. Subsequent chapters will describe some of the specific concerns. Here we summarize.

The Theological Issue: Inerrancy

The primary issue was whether or not the Bible is fully inerrant. Why does this issue matter?

One's view of the Bible ultimately determines how one answers all faith and practice questions. For example, is the Genesis creation account history or legend? Were Adam and Eve real people in an historic narrative, or representative characters in a symbolic narrative? Are the Old and New Testament miracles facts or myths? Was Jesus the promised Messiah—the Christ? Was He virgin born, God incarnate? Was Jesus Christ's death vicarious, substitutionary, and redemptive? Did He literally, physically rise from

---

1. "Article 1: The Scriptures," Baptist Faith and Message 2000, accessed 3 September 2021, https://bfm.sbc.net/bfm2000/#i-the-scriptures.

the dead? And what about baptism, church membership, or the role and gender of a pastor? Is the Bible true? Does it mean what it says? Is it worthy of careful exegesis and exposition? Is it the authoritative source for a pastor's sermon preparation and delivery? Is the Bible the final, trustworthy foundation that definitively answers all such questions?

A grassroots effort to clarify and reaffirm Southern Baptists' long-standing belief in the verbal-plenary inspiration of the 39 Old Testament books and the 27 New Testament books, gathered momentum in the late 1960s and 70s. A majority of the SBC pastors, along with the people in the pews, firmly believed the Bible and the Bible alone is the inspired, authoritative, infallible, and inerrant Word of God. It is the final authority for the faith and practice of all believers and every local church. Not every SBC pastor was a seminary graduate, but a majority of the pastors and people expected that SBC seminary graduates would believe the Bible wholeheartedly.

From time to time, however, reports surfaced that an increasing number of recent seminary graduates were answering the questions above with a veiled, spiritualized, "No." Some leaders of Baptist agencies, as well as some professors at Baptist colleges and seminaries, were redefining biblical terms and doctrines. Publication of books and articles by such leaders furthered these concerns.[2]

Pastors and laypeople published letters of concern in the Baptist papers of their various state conventions. They went to the annual Conventions to express sincere concerns. Leaders promised to investigate and, if needed, correct any problems. But year after year, nothing changed.

Respected agency executives and seminary presidents denied that any problem existed. Repeatedly they reassured Convention Messengers that no

---

2. For the perspective of a pastor and Baptist historian, see "Theological Inadequacy" in Jerry Sutton, *The Baptist Reformation: The Conservative Resurgence in the Southern Baptist Convention* (Nashville: Broadman & Holman Publishers, 2000), 6-30. For the perspective of an active laymen, see "Seeds of Dissension" in, Paul Pressler, *A Hill on Which to Die: One Southern Baptist's Journey* (Nashville: Broadman & Holman Publishers, 1999), 49-55.

liberals had infiltrated the SBC fortress. "Fear not. All is well," they said. "The problem is not in our agencies or classrooms. The problem is with those sounding the alarm." The leaders portrayed them as libelous fear mongers, worse than "Chicken Little," agitating the uninformed, alerting them to a non-existent danger.

The Beginning

Nothing changed until the 1979 Convention in Houston, Texas. The SBC elected Dr. Adrian Rogers as President. The dynamic 47-year-old pastor of the fast-growing Belleview Baptist Church in Memphis, TN, was fearless. In spite of harsh criticism, he used the little authority the SBC's Constitution granted to its President. The President appoints members to one key committee in the Convention's structure: the Committee on Committees.

Beginning with Rogers, and continuing for the next twenty-one years, the Convention elected bold, theologically conservative presidents. These men, in turn, appointed only like-minded inerrantists to the Committee on Committees. The Committee members nominated inerrantists to serve on the Committee on Nominations. The Committee on Nominations nominated inerrantists to serve as Trustees or Committee members of the various SBC Boards and Agencies. Subsequent Southern Baptist Conventions elected those nominees to serve. Thus, over time, the Boards of all SBC agencies were solidly committed to the Bible's practical authority and inerrancy. The Trustees held their agency to the Convention's Statement of Faith and the guiding principles near and dear to Baptists in the pews. We call this process and its results, *The Conservative Resurgence of the Southern Baptist Convention.*

If, however, the above process sounds easy, such was not the case. There were many controversial, tense, and even volatile moments and meetings along the way. Both sides made mistakes. Both sides, at times, misunderstood and misjudged one another's motives. No one knew how it would turn out.

The Pivot Point

The denials and reassurances—"Trust me; no liberals here"—continued, intensified, and culminated at the 1985 SBC annual meeting in Dallas. That year, at the urging of the moderates, President Charles Stanley appointed a Peace Committee to interview leaders of the agencies and the leadership and faculties of all six Southern Baptist seminaries. When the completed report was presented to the convention two years later, to the surprise of none of the conservatives, but perhaps to some of the moderates, all of the conservative's theological concerns over the years were confirmed.

The Peace Committee members represented both the moderate and conservative sides in the SBC controversy. The Committee's report revealed a glaring theological divide, even among the committee members. The report stated:

> In meeting after meeting of the Peace Committee, talk turned to the nature of inspiration of the Scriptures, often to the point of preempting the committee's established agenda. Gradually, it became clear that while there might be other theological differences, the authority of the Word of God is the focus of differences. The primary source of the controversy in the Southern Baptist Convention is the Bible; more specifically, the ways in which the Bible is viewed.
>
> All Baptists see the Bible as authoritative; the question is the extent and nature of its authority....
>
> Early in its second year, the Peace Committee continued to discuss theological concerns, including the fact that there are at least

two separate and distinct interpretations of Article I of the Baptist Faith and Message Statement of 1963, reflective of the diversity present in the Convention. One view holds that when the article says the Bible has "truth without any mixture of error for its matter," it means *all* areas—historical, scientific, theological and philosophical. The other holds the "truth" relates only to matters of faith and practice.[3]

The Peace Committee's interviews were revealing. In reality, several of the 'so called' moderates, especially among seminary professors, were much closer to theological liberals than they had previously admitted. The report stated:

> We have found significant theological diversity within our seminaries, reflective of the diversity within our wider constituency. These divergencies are found among those who claim to hold a high view of Scripture and to teach in accordance with, and not contrary to, the Baptist Faith and Message Statement of 1963.
>
> Examples of this diversity include the following, which are intended to be illustrative but not exhaustive.
>
> 1. Some accept and affirm the direct creation and historicity of Adam and Eve while others view them instead as representative of the human race in its creation and fall.
> 2. Some understand the historicity of every event in Scripture as reported by the original source while others hold that the historicity can be clarified and revised by the findings of modern historical scholarship.

---

3. SBC in St. Louis, Missouri, June 16, 1987, "Report of the Southern Baptist Convention Peace Committee," accessed 31 August 2021, http://www.baptist-2baptist.net/b2barticle.asp?ID=65.

3. Some hold to the stated authorship of every book in the Bible while others hold that in some cases such attribution may not refer to the final author or may be pseudonymous.
4. Some hold that every miracle in the Bible is intended to be taken as an historical event while others hold that some miracles are intended to be taken as parabolic.[4]

Further, many SBC missionaries had embraced the moderate-liberal teaching and had exported it to most of the 125 international mission fields where they served. Some, though thankfully not all, were primarily religious social workers. Many of these never shared the gospel with a single person from their appointment through their retirement.[5]

As a result of the Peace Committee report, it became clear that there was no room for compromise. The moderate and conservative views of the Bible were incompatible. One side or the other had to hold sway. Through the committee and trustee process, the conservative movement won the day. They accomplished what had never been done before. A denomination that was well down the road toward liberalism repented. It turned 180 degrees to become a thoroughly conservative denomination. Those involved were convinced the Conservative Resurgence was indeed the handiwork of God.

The Culmination

The impact of the Conservative Resurgence on the boards and agencies became transformative a few years before the 2000 Convention in Orlando. Yet, June 14, 2000, is considered the culminating event. That day the Convention Messengers overwhelmingly adopted a revised and updated version of the BF&M.

---

4. "Report of Peace Committee"; http://www.baptist2baptist.net/b2barticle.asp?ID=65.

5. Mark H. Ballard with Timothy K. Christian, *Words Matter: What is the Gospel?* (Bennington, VT: Northeastern Baptist Press, 2020), 19-20.

Throughout the controversy, the moderates claimed fidelity to the BF&M 1963. All seminary professors signed the BF&M when they were hired. They confessed to believe it and promised their teaching would remain consistent with it. Yet, as the Peace Committee report confirmed, many rejected the Bible's infallibility and inerrancy.

From June 1998-June 1999, Paige Patterson, credited with being one of the architects of the Conservative Resurgence, served his first of two terms as the SBC President. He appointed a committee to revise and update the BF&M. Adrian Rogers was the chairman. The committee reported their work and officially presented the document for approval at the 2000 SBC. Specifically, the document closed the gap on inerrancy. As noted above, the messengers believed the affirmative vote on the BF&M 2000 had settled the controversy for decades to come.

Such were the happy thoughts of most who left the Orlando Convention Center on that hot, June day in 2000. The co-editors of this volume, Mark H. Ballard and Timothy K. Christian, were present to give their affirmative votes. In fact, they were active participants in the Conservative Resurgence.

Leading up to the 2000 Convention, Ballard had served on the SBC Committee on Committees. At the 2000 Convention he was elected to the Board of Trustees of LifeWay Christian Resources. He was near the platform when the scheduled business session to debate the BF&M began. He and his wife sat about ten rows from the President's podium for the historic debate and vote.

Christian was the Chairman of the Credentials Committee at the 2000 SBC. The Committee registered messengers, confirming that each was a duly elected representative of a local Southern Baptist Church in good standing with the Convention. After completing a frenzy of late registrations shortly before the scheduled time for the BF&M business session, Christian and his wife found seats at the back of the convention hall. The debate was interesting and revealing. Finally, the question was called. The raised-ballot vote was overwhelmingly affirmative. The Ballards and Christians joined the spontaneous thunderous applause and standing ovation. Many in the hall cheered; others wept for joy.

"We were convinced," Ballard later said, "that the BF&M 2000 securely tethered the SBC to an unwavering commitment to the Bible's full inerrancy, infallibility, and absolute authority. We thought it was settled for at least 50 years. Our conviction was based on more than the strength of the vote or the clarity of our new statement of faith. It was also based in a simple fact. Nearly all of the several dozen churches whose pastors and messengers voted against the BF&M 2000 withdrew their memberships from their local Baptist Associations, State Conventions, and the Southern Baptist Convention. Most, in protest, aligned themselves with the leftward leaning Cooperative Baptist Fellowship. We thought the opposing army had abandoned the battlefield, leaving us to freely and harmoniously work our mission fields. Of course, I now realize our confidence was naïve."

Some leaders noted that Baptists must be eternally vigilant. We must always "contend earnestly for the faith which was once for all delivered to the saints" (Jude 3). While everyone agreed, in reality most of us believed that any challenge to Baptist beliefs in at least the next two or three decades would come from outside the Southern Baptist camp. Challenges would arise within our ranks—someday. No doubt about it. Scripture and church history affirm the leftward tendency of spiritual and theological drift. Few thought internal challenges could arise within the first 20 years following the BF&M 2000's overwhelming adoption. But again, we were naïve.

Attendance at the annual conventions slowly declined over the next few years. The average Baptist was confident that the SBC's theological issues were settled. Our new agency and seminary leaders were unwavering inerrantists. We could trust them to ensure that those supported by the Cooperative Program, the denominational funding mechanism, would operate within the BF&M 2000. They would gladly adhere to the guiding principles set forth by the Convention.

WHY THIS BOOK?

For many of us who supported and participated in the Resurgence, it is shocking to realize that it began more than 40 years ago and the BF&M 2000 has been in use for more than 20 years. The editors of this volume were young pastors in the Resurgence days. Their present day gray hair and beards affirm this is no longer true. We, however, do not look back on those days with shame or embarrassment, but with joy. We believe both the Conservative Resurgence and the BF&M 2000 were necessary and God honoring. Now, however, we have a growing concern.

The theological focus of the Conservative Resurgence seems to be waning. We sense a growing indifference toward the BF&M, and an even greater antipathy for self-identifying as a Baptist. Our concern, however, is not for a movement, or even for our denomination. Our passion is for the Bible's God-revealed truth.

We are concerned for the health and future of biblical, pastoral local church ministry. Particularly, we are concerned about the chosen trajectory of several leading Southern Baptist pastors and churches. At times, we are more than concerned; we are alarmed. They influence many. The trajectory, in our understanding, already is having a debilitating influence on some of our Convention's agencies and schools.

Therefore, we have asked a simple question. Does it still matter? Do the doctrinal issue that inspired the Conservative Resurgence still matter? What about the Baptist Faith and Message 2000? Does it still matter?

In the summer of 2019, Ballard and Christian discussed the need for this volume. "First, we consider writing the entire volume. But as we began," Ballard notes, "we discovered we were not alone. Concern was growing among pastors across the SBC. Looking back, I believe Resolution 9 [discussed below] that was passed at the 2019 Convention became the boiling point. As we prayed and talked, I identified crucial key issues, not only in SBC life, but also in the larger evangelical community. Through my contacts at the college, the Executive Committee, and the Conservative Baptist Network, I identified a distinguished panel of authors who were theologically passionate and uniquely knowledgeable about their individual topics. They are also skilled writers. Nearly all have first hand knowledge of the Conservative Resurgence; they were active supporters and participants in part or all of the Conservative Resurgence years."

Thus this book was born: *Does It Still Matter? Essays in Honor of the Conservative Resurgence of the Southern Baptist Convention*. Each essay answers the question with a resounding, "Yes!" The essayists are convinced the issues that inspired the Conservative Resurgence remain relevant and urgent today. In light of recent drastic changes in our culture and the Convention's drastic decline in baptisms [discussed below], each chapter addresses a different area of concern for SBC life and ministry. Most of the chapters also speak to issues faced by all conservative evangelical churches and denominations.

The plans for this book were largely completed in the fall of 2019. Yet, the dawn of a new decade only increased the need for the book. As this volume went to press in 2021, the SBC was engaged in controversy over issues related to the ERLC, Critical Race Theory, Intersectionality, LGBTQ+ issues, and more. In addition, on Friday, February 14, 2020, a group of pastors announced the launch of the Conservative Baptist Network of Southern Baptists. Within hours of the announcement more than 2,000 Southern Baptists joined the network. Since that first day, the network has grown steadily. The growth rate demonstrates that thousands of Southern Baptist pastors, lay leaders, and churches are concerned about the future of the SBC. Many believe the gains of the Conservative Resurgence are now eroding, if not being totally jettisoned.

We the editors thank those who invested their valuable time to research and write these enlightening chapters. In doing so, the authors had no desire to be critics cursing the darkness. Anyone can complain and criticize. Rather, they sought to be helpful discerning analysts, shining the Scriptures' illuminating light on their topic. Discernment is directly connected with accurately interpreting and applying the Bible (Heb 4:12; 5:14). Also, it should be motivated by love (Phil 1:9), and lead us to prayer. "God never gives us discernment in order that we may criticize," observed Oswald Chambers, "but that we may intercede."[6]

Each writer longs to encourage the saints, bless the churches, and glorify God. We are committed Baptists and unashamed. We are committed to our local churches and deeply concerned for the lostness evident in our culture. Above all, we are confident of our Savior's power to save, forgive, cleanse, and revive. We are therefore not ashamed of the biblical gospel (Rom 1:16).

Finally, we thank you, the reader, for investing your valuable time to read, pray, and consider the challenges in the following chapters. May these pages grow your discernment and prayer life.

---

6. Oswald Chambers, *My Utmost for His Highest* (New York: Dodd, Mead & Co., 1965), 328.

Baptist Faith
and Message

Article 1, "The Scriptures," through the years

1925

We believe that the Holy Bible was written by men divinely inspired, and is a perfect treasure of heavenly instruction; that it has God for its author, salvation for its end, and truth, without any mixture of error, for its matter; that it reveals the principles by which God will judge us; and therefore is, and will remain to the end of the world, the true center of Christian union, and the supreme standard by which all human conduct, creeds and religious opinions should be tried.

Luke 16:29-31; 2 Tim. 3:15-17; Eph. 2:20; Heb. 1:1; 2 Peter 1:19-21; John 16:13-15; Matt. 22:29-31; Psalm 19:7-10; Psalm 119:1-8.

1963

The Holy Bible was written by men divinely inspired and is the record of God's revelation of Himself to man. It is a perfect treasure of divine instruction. It has God for its author, salvation for its end, and truth, without any mixture of error, for its matter. It reveals the principles by which God judges us; and therefore is, and will remain to the end of the world, the true center of Christian union, and the supreme standard by which all human conduct, creeds, and religious opinions should be tried. The criterion by which the Bible is to be interpreted is Jesus Christ.

Ex. 24:4; Deut. 4:1-2; 17:19; Josh. 8:34; Psalms 19:7-10; 119:11,89,105,140; Isa. 34:16; 40:8; Jer. 15:16; 36; Matt. 5:17-18; 22:29; Luke 21:33; 24:44-46; John 5:39; 16:13-15; 17:17; Acts 2:16ff.; 17:11; Rom. 15:4; 16:25-26; 2 Tim. 3:15-17; Heb. 1:1-2; 4:12; 1 Peter 1:25; 2 Peter 1:19-21.

2000

The Holy Bible was written by men divinely inspired and is God's revelation of Himself to man. It is a perfect treasure of divine instruction. It has God for its author, salvation for its end, and truth, without any mixture of error, for its matter. Therefore, all Scripture is totally true and trustworthy. It reveals the principles by which God judges us, and therefore is, and will remain to the end of the world, the true center of Christian union, and the supreme standard by which all human conduct, creeds, and religious opinions should be tried. All Scripture is a testimony to Christ, who is Himself the focus of divine revelation.

Exodus 24:4; Deuteronomy 4:1-2; 17:19; Joshua 8:34; Psalms 19:7-10; 119:11, 89, 105, 140; Isaiah 34:16; 40:8; Jeremiah 15:16; 36:1-32; Matthew 5:17-18; 22:29; Luke 21:33; 24:44-46; John 5:39; 16:13-15; 17:17; Acts 2:16ff.; 17:11; Romans 15:4; 16:25-26; 2 Timothy 3:15-17; Hebrews 1:1-2; 4:12; 1 Peter 1:25; 2 Peter 1:19-21.

1

DOES INERRANCY
STILL MATTER?

MARK H. BALLARD

As people attended the Southern Baptist Convention Pastor's Conference in Houston on June 1, 1979, tension filled the room. Decades of frustration among conservative pastors and laymen were coming to a head. After repeated attempts to deal with a perceived theological drift to the left among Southern Baptist Seminaries and entity personnel, pastors and laymen felt they were deceived and ignored by entity leadership.

While seminary and entity leaders proclaimed their respective organizations held to the Baptist Faith and Message, last updated in 1963, pastors and laymen were repeatedly hearing of professors, missionaries, and authors, who taught, wrote, and did things contrary to their understanding of the Convention's statement of faith. The primary concern related to the nature and authority of the Bible.

Nearly everyone purported to stand by the Baptist Faith and Message's statement on Scripture. However, clearly there was serious disagreement over what the article on Scripture actually meant. Note the wording of Article I in the 1963 statement.

The Holy Bible was written by men divinely inspired and is the record of God's revelation of Himself to man. It is a perfect treasure of divine instruction. It has God for its author, salvation for its end, and truth, without any mixture of error, for its matter. It reveals the principles by which God judges us; and therefore is, and will remain to the end of the world, the true center of Christian union, and the supreme standard by which all human conduct, creeds, and religious opinions should be tried. The criterion by which the Bible is to be interpreted is Jesus Christ.[1]

The average Baptist in the pew held on to phrases like "perfect treasure," "God for its author," "truth, without any mixture of error," and "the supreme standard." To most pastors across the Southern Baptist Convention, and certainly to most of the people in the pew, these statements ensured that anyone hired to teach at a Baptist seminary, write Baptist literature or books, or serve as a Baptist missionary, were men and women who united around the inerrancy of Scripture and the importance of getting the Gospel message to everyone on earth. In fact, to most, the commitment to the Bible resulted in the urgency of presenting the Gospel and therefore the need for the churches to unite and cooperate to fulfill the Great Commission.

The Southern Baptist seminary leaders and employees affirmed the same statement that messengers from the churches adopted in 1963. Yet, evidence seemed to be mounting that things were being taught in the classroom that went against the common understanding of what the above-mentioned phrases actually mean. Reports were being heard that some professors in the seminaries taught that the first eleven chapters of Genesis were not factual, that Jonah was not swallowed by a great fish, and that many miracles recorded in the Bible were not actual historical events.

---

1. "Comparison Chart," The Baptist Faith and Message, accessed August 28, 2021, https://bfm.sbc.net/comparison-chart/.

The leaders in question, and those who supported them, emphasized the phrase that refers to the Bible as "the record of God's revelation." To many in this group the Bible *contained* the Word of God, but was not in and of itself, the Word of God. The last sentence of the statement was also key for those who believed and taught that the Bible contained "factual errors." The sentence reads, "The criterion by which the Bible is to be interpreted is Jesus Christ." Based on this phrase some argued that the true meaning of a passage points to Jesus, while the actual events described may or may not be real events. Some found here a loophole that allowed them to affirm the document and still deny the inerrancy of certain passages of Scripture. They argued that their personal experience with Jesus Christ led them to interpret the text in ways other than the natural meaning of the text.

Thus, while most Southern Baptists in the pew, the pulpit, the seminary, and the entities ascribed to the Baptist Faith and Message and used the same vocabulary to speak of the Bible (authority, inspiration, and even infallibility), they used a vastly different dictionary. For a decade or more, evidence of this divide had been mounting. Several works, noted below, provide a full discussion of the issues and events leading up to the 1979 Houston Convention.[2] The tension was palpable throughout the Pastors Conference held on the first of June.

Leading up to the Pastor's Conference, Paige Patterson and Paul Pressler, along with a group of Southern Baptist pastors, had spent months holding meetings among Southern Baptists across the country. The meetings informed both pastors and the people in the pew how change could actually take place in the Convention. Electing a Conservative President was

---

2. James C. Hefley, *The Conservative Resurgence in the Southern Baptist Convention* (Garland, TX: Hannibal Books, 1991); Jerry Sutton, *The Baptist Reformation* (Nashville: B&H Publishing, 2000); Paul Pressler, *A Hill on Which to Die* (Nashville: B&H Publishing, 1999); and Paige Patterson, *Anatomy of a Reformation: The Southern Baptist Convention 1978-2004* (Fort Worth, TX: Seminary Hill Press, 2011).

key. Having a Conservative President did not ensure change; that president must use his limited power to ensure change.

The President would have to carefully choose those whom he appointed to the Committee on Committees. Those appointed to this committee must carefully choose the ones whom they nominated to serve on the Committee on Nominations. The members of this committee would have to nominate people to serve on the boards of the seminaries, agencies, and commissions who unwaveringly held to the inerrancy of Scripture and who would demand that their organizations do the same. This process would have to be repeated over several years. Eventually, all the Boards would insist on Biblical fidelity. The question was who the first presidential nominee should be.

On the afternoon of Sunday, May 31, Paul and Nancy Pressler held a dinner for about thirty leading pastors from around the Convention in their home. The dinner included times of fellowship and discussion about the upcoming convention.[3] On Monday, following the afternoon session, Pressler arranged for another dinner meeting with more in attendance. This meeting included not only a time of prayer and fellowship, but also an open discussion about who the group thought should be nominated to serve as president of the Convention. Pressler reports, "No candidate had arisen prior to the meeting, although three names were prominently mentioned. They were Adrian Roger, Jerry Vines, and Bailey Smith."[4]

Another meeting was held on the eve of the '79 Convention with about 350 people in attendance. The attendees were asked to write down their top three choices to serve as president in the order of preference. Adrian Rogers was the clear choice. The problem was Rogers that was not willing to be nominated. James Hefley reports that as late as 6:00 pm that evening, Rogers told Paige Patterson that "God hadn't told him to be a candidate."[5] Following

3. Pressler, *A Hill on Which to Die*, 100.

4. Pressler, *A Hill on Which to Die*, 100.

5. Hefley, *Conservative Resurgence*, 38.

the vote of the 350 gathered participants, Pressler informed Rogers of the will of the gathering. Rogers once again indicated that he had not heard from God that he was to be nominated.[6] Nearly everyone, except Adrian and his wife Joyce, was convinced that Rogers should be the next president.

Joyce had generally been opposed to the idea of Adrian allowing his name to be placed in nomination. However, Monday evening, in their hotel room, Joyce told Adrian her heart was beginning to change on the matter. After 11:00 pm Monday night Rogers went down to the hotel lobby to walk, pray, and think about what he should do. He ran into Jerry Vines and Paige Patterson in the Lobby. They spoke for a few minutes and then the three of them returned to the Roger's hotel room to pray. The three men and Joyce prayed for the Lord to lead Adrian Rogers as to His will in the matter. After an extended period of prayer, Rogers received confirmation that it was indeed the will of God that he be nominated.[7]

The next day, Rogers was one of five nominees. Most expected a split vote with the need for a run-off election. However, a second ballot was not required. Rogers was elected President with 51.36% of the vote on the first ballot. The next closest candidate, Robert Naylor (also a conservative theologically), received 23.39% of the vote.[8] Adrian Rogers had been elected as president and the Conservative Resurgence had begun.

The issue was clear. The Inerrancy of Scripture cannot be compromised. Rogers would only appoint people to serve who were committed to the inerrancy of Scripture. His appointments to serve on the Committee on Committees would not only be committed to inerrancy but would only nominate people who would then nominate those who held an unwavering commitment to requiring the seminaries, entities, and commissions to unashamedly hold to the inerrancy of Scripture. Without question, one's view of the inerrancy of Scripture mattered!

---

6. Pressler, *A Hill on Which to Die*, 101.

7. Hefley, *Conservative Resurgence*, 38.

8. Pressler, *A Hill on Which to Die*, 104.

A Twenty-Year Battle
over Inerrancy

The Inerrancy of Scripture was the prominent theme in Southern Baptist life over the next 20 years. No one had the luxury of avoiding the question. Every Southern Baptist involved in the Convention had to take a stand for or against using the term inerrancy. While many attempts were made to downplay the controversy in the early days, reality set in and most people realized the need to stand on one side or the other.

Early in the battle, conservative Baptists recognized several problems of serious concern. Patterson notes:

> There were uncertainties about where some denominational leaders and professors stood on the nature of the atonement, creation, the resurrection of Christ, abortion, the sanctity of marriage, and a host of other issues. However, early in the contest the decision was made to focus on only one issue. That decision was the most strategic one made by conservatives ... only one issue, i.e., the inerrancy of the Bible, would take center stage.[9]

Public conflict continued through the 1980s with the focus remaining on the inerrancy of Scripture.

For a brief introduction to the conflict within the convention, one can read Paige Patterson's summary in *The Southern Baptist Conservative Resurgence: The History. The Plan. The Assessment.*[10] More detailed treatments can be found in books written by James C. Hefley, Jerry Sutton, and Paul Pressler.[11] In Patterson's short presentation, he notes two significant events

---

9. Paige Patterson, *The Southern Baptist Conservative Resurgence: The History. The Plan. The Assessment.* (Fort Worth, TX: Seminary Hill Press, 2012), 22.

10. Patterson, *Conservative Resurgence*, 22.

11. See note 2, above.

toward the end of the "open conflict." This chapter will only note the first event, which arose during the Dallas Convention where 45,519 messengers registered to do business.[12]

Tensions were high at the largest recorded meeting of Southern Baptists to date. The meeting was held June 11-13, 1985 in Dallas. Just prior to the Convention, W. A. Criswell preached his famous sermon, "Whether we Live or Die." Charles Stanley was elected to serve as president for a second term. But the most significant thing coming out of that convention was the formation of The Peace Committee. Two years later, the Committee brought their final report. The Committee affirmed that the cause of the conflict was indeed a doctrinal concern over the inerrancy of Scripture. Additionally, this group acknowledged the need for the seminaries and entities to hire professors and employees who fit within the overwhelming Baptist belief in the inerrancy of the Bible.[13]

By the time The Peace Committee's work was completed, the majority of the seats on the various Southern Baptist Boards were held by inerrantists. Over the next few years, SBC boards held their presidents and employees accountable to the Baptist Faith and Message and to the fact that they worked for Baptists in the pew who strongly held that the Bible was completely true, "without any mixture of error." By the mid-1990s everyone realized that Conservatives had won the day.

Toward the end of the millennium, attention turned to re-examine the Baptist Faith and Message and to close the loopholes moderates and liberals had used to deny the inerrancy of the Bible. At the 1998 Southern Baptist Convention, Paige Patterson was elected to serve as Convention President. In 1999 not only was he re-elected, but also a motion was adopted requesting Patterson to appoint a "Blue ribbon committee to review the Baptist Faith and Message statement with the responsibility to report and bring any recommendations to this (Convention) meeting next June in

---

12. Patterson, *Conservative Resurgence*, 27.
13. Patterson, *Conservative Resurgence*, 28-29.

Orlando."[14] Patterson appointed a fifteen-member committee with Adrian Rogers serving as the Chair.

The Committee brought their recommendations to the Convention meeting in Orlando, FL in June of 2000. While several items were addressed, of significance to this chapter is the wording of Article I: The Scriptures.

> The Holy Bible was written by men divinely inspired and is God's revelation of Himself to man. It is a perfect treasure of divine instruction. It has God for its author, salvation for its end, and truth, without any mixture of error, for its matter. Therefore, all Scripture is totally true and trustworthy. It reveals the principles by which God judges us, and therefore is, and will remain to the end of the world, the true center of Christian union, and the supreme standard by which all human conduct, creeds, and religious opinions should be tried. All Scripture is a testimony to Christ, who is Himself the focus of divine revelation.[15]

The committee had closed the loopholes that had previously been used by moderates and liberals to affirm the statement while teaching and writing from perspectives that denied the inerrancy of Scripture. I, together with many others, stood and applauded as shouts of "Amen!" "Praise the Lord!" and Hallelujah!" were heard all across the room. The messengers overwhelmingly adopted the new language.

Thousands of Southern Baptists in the room breathed a sigh of relief. The "Battle for the Bible" was over and those willing to stand on the inerrancy of Scripture had won the day. Inerrancy mattered! It mattered to Bap-

---

14. "Report of the Baptist Faith and Message Study Committee to the Southern Baptist Convention," The Baptist Faith and Message, accessed August 31, 2021, https://bfm.sbc.net/preamble/.

15. "The Baptist Faith and Message 2000," The Baptist Faith and Message, accessed August 31, 2021, https://bfm.sbc.net/bfm2000/.

tists in the pew! It mattered to preachers in the pulpit! Inerrancy mattered to the professor in the Seminary! It mattered to the curriculum writers at LifeWay! It mattered to the missionary on the international field! It mattered to the North American Missionary! It mattered to those serving at the Ethics and Religious Liberty Commission. Inerrancy even mattered to those serving at the Annuity Board of the Convention. The battle was over, and Baptists once again stood firm on the inspiration, infallibility, inerrancy, and authority of the Bible.

RENEWED CONCERNS OVER INERRANCY

A Front Line View

Having been a student at the Criswell College for six years in the late 1980s and early 1990s as well as a student at Southeastern Seminary from 1992-1995, I had a front-line view during the latter half of the controversy. At Criswell College, I was taught to carefully examine every side of an issue, be fair in assessing arguments, but never compromise the truth. My college experience further prepared me for the battles over the Bible I would face.

At seminary, an Old Testament Professor constantly challenged the accuracy of the Bible. As a young student I respectfully, but forcefully, defended the inerrancy of Scripture. During my seminary days, I served as pastor of a rural congregation where a deacon denied the deity of Christ. As I concluded seminary, I assumed the pastorate of a church in Virginia. I offered a resolution on "Partial-Birth Abortion" at my first Baptist General Association of Virginia Annual Meeting. The Resolutions Committee not only refused to recommend the resolution to the Convention, but they refused to print it with the other resolutions presented. After extensive discussion and procedural maneuvers, the motion to allow my resolution to be read and voted on was defeated.

The following year, I was privileged to be part of the founding meeting of the Southern Baptist Conservatives of Virginia Convention. This joyous occasion set the stage for serious growth for the conservative cause in Virginia and became an example for the Southern Baptists of Texas Convention, which formed a short time later. With each victory, more joy, more peace, and more sighs of relief were uttered. Yet, the greatest sense of relief came for me that moment I stood to applaud the adoption of the Baptist Faith and Message 2000.

A Nagging Thought

As I walked out of the Convention Hall filled with joy on that hot Florida day, a nagging thought emerged from the recesses of my mind. Throughout the final years of the controversy I had heard various Conservative Resurgence leaders say, "Every generation must stand for Scripture." That thought echoed in my mind as I walked toward the parking garage. "I wonder, when will the next attack on inerrancy come? Surely not in our lifetime. I know I entered this battle mid-way through, and I am young. But, surely, surely, this issue is settled among Southern Baptists for my lifetime."

On occasion the nagging thoughts returned, but soon they were pushed aside. Everything was going well. There were still a few small skirmishes here and there. In 1998 the Lord led me to move to New England where there were still vestiges of moderate influence. A few unforgettable battles on the floor of the regional convention had to be fought. However, the Lord was faithful and within a few years, things were moving in the right direction. Nearly everyone acknowledged the Baptist Faith and Message 2000, including the inerrancy of the Bible, as the doctrinal position of the regional convention.

Soon the battles over the Bible seemed to be long over. They were a distant memory. All the SBC Seminaries were solid. Not one professor could be found who would not sign the Baptist Faith and Message 2000 and the Chicago Statement on Inerrancy. The leaders of all the SBC entities stood firm on the Bible. Now was the time to focus on increasing Cooperative Program giving and taking the Gospel to the ends of the earth.

Speeches for the nomination of presidents occasionally tipped their hat to inerrancy, but it was heard less and less. What was the need? Every Baptist believes in inerrancy, right? Presidents began asking other questions of the people they nominated to serve on the Committee on Committees. The Committee on Nominations put less emphasis on inerrancy. To many it no longer seemed necessary to ask the inerrancy question. After all, the conservatives had won the Battle for the Bible.

Occasionally, back in the recesses of my mind, that nagging question returned. "I wonder if we will ever have to stand strong for the inerrancy of Scripture again?" Each time, ministry demands pushed the nagging thought out of his mind for days, months, even years; but it always returned.

An Unexpected Reality

In May of 2017, I was serving my second four-year term on the Southern Baptist Convention's Executive Committee. That spring had been a tumultuous time to serve on the Committee with the sudden resignation of the President of the EC due to a moral failure. The EC, under the godly leadership of Stephen Rummage, had managed to handle the issue well.

Chairman Rummage was rotating out of the leadership role and it was time to elect a new chair to lead the Executive Committee during the search for a new President. Three men were nominated for the position. The day before the June Convention, the EC was to meet. One of the items on the agenda was to elect the new Chair.

That nagging thought had returned to my mind several times over the previous few years. In 2013 I had returned to Southeastern Seminary to pursue a PhD. I saw several things that raised concerns during my time in the program. I even addressed some of the concerns to my long-time friend and the President of the Seminary, Daniel Akin. I was beginning to suspect that there were those among our Southern Baptist Seminaries and Entities who signed off on the BF&M 2000 but somehow did not hold to the inerrancy of the Bible.

As the election for the Chair of the Executive Committee drew closer, the nagging thought moved from the recesses of my mind to the forefront. I determined that I could not have it on my conscience to have accidently voted for someone who did not unashamedly hold to the inerrancy of the Bible to lead the Executive Committee of the Southern Baptist Convention. I also knew that if there were indeed leaders among the convention's entities who did not hold to the inerrancy of Scripture, they would likely still be unwilling to openly admit such a thing. After praying about the situation, I wrote an email that was sent to all the candidates. I asked five questions, two of which are relevant to this chapter and are included here.

1. Could you briefly state your view of Biblical Authority?
2. Could you briefly state what you mean by the term Gospel?

Two of the candidates used the term inerrancy and provided a strong statement on the Bible. However, the third candidate caused surprise with his response. He not only failed to use the term inerrancy, but his response also sounded more like the moderates of 1980 than those who affirm the Baptist Faith and Message 2000. This response was so shocking, that I wrote the candidate back seeking permission to reveal his views to the full Executive Committee. This request led to additional emails, phone calls, and an in-person conversation.

In the end, the candidate offered to allow tme to share his statements only if he could rewrite the statement and include the word, inerrancy. However, he would prefer not to do so. He further expressed he did not like the term, but if the author would vote for him and encourage others to do so, he would use it. He had hoped the Southern Baptist Convention had moved beyond concern about whether someone held to inerrancy or not. He simply did not, and does not, believe that inerrancy really matters.

A Renewed Concern

Just a little over forty years after the Conservative Resurgence began among Southern Baptists, and just twenty years after Southern Baptists adopted the Baptist Faith and Message 2000, the doctrine of the inerrancy of Scripture is once again under attack. Before directly addressing the question of whether inerrancy still matters today, this chapter must first seek to understand the contemporary attacks on inerrancy. The next section of this chapter will demonstrate that those who hold to the inerrancy of the Bible can no longer be silent. Inerrantists can no longer pretend that the battle for the Bible is over. Examining the current attacks on inerrancy should cause Baptists in the pew to arouse from slumber with a renewed concern to stand unwaveringly for the inerrancy of the Bible.

CONTEMPORARY ATTACKS ON INERRANCY

Is the doctrine of inerrancy threatened today? If so, what are the threats and where do they come from? While researching this chapter, I discovered at least four current threats to the doctrine of Biblical Inerrancy. While it is not common to find someone in the Southern Baptist Convention or in the larger Evangelical world who will outright deny the inerrancy of Scripture, there are those among us who downplay the issue. One of the most dangerous attacks on inerrancy comes from those who affirm the term but redefine it in a way that overturns the concept altogether. Some hermeneutical approaches undermine the inerrancy of the Bible. Additionally, one's view of the sufficiency of Scripture can ultimately lead to a demotion of the inerrancy of Scripture.

Downplaying Inerrancy

As the youngest of nine children, I grew up knowing only eight siblings. My oldest sister died of leukemia prior to my birth. The age span between me and my siblings provided for many interesting moments. My oldest living sibling is 18 years older than me. Consequently, I became an uncle at the ripe old age of five. Try explaining to your kindergarten class that you are an uncle. Many such moments provided for an interesting early life.

While in Middle School, my dad and I traveled to an older sister's house for a visit. While there, a niece and a nephew decided to return to stay at Granddad's house for a week. On the three-hour ride home, I became frustrated. My niece and nephew spent the majority of the trip asking questions of me. Frustration with the inquisition mounted as the inquisitive youngsters repeatedly voiced one question: WHY? Why is the sky blue? Why is the grass green? Why are the clouds white? In frustration with the constant questions I began to say, "Because that is the way God made it!" Without a moment's hesitation the youngsters would retort, "WHY?"

While asking *why* is part of the learning process for every child, often the *why* questions are impossible to answer satisfactorily. Often *why* questions have to do with the motivation of one's heart. This becomes a problem for the issue at hand. When evidence suggests that a Christian leader is downplaying the inerrancy of Scripture, the immediate tendency is to ask *why*. Unless the leader openly states or explains the reason why he or she would downplay such a crucial issue, it becomes impossible to know why. Yet, when one sees evidence that a fellow believer downplays inerrancy, to ask the *why* question is altogether natural.

Motivation is a tricky thing. The Bible clearly teaches that our motivation matters. However, the Bible also demonstrates that motivation is deceptive. For instance, the Bible says, "The heart is deceitful above all things and desperately wicked, who can know it?" (Jeremiah 17:9). This implies that we may struggle to know our own motivation, much less to know someone else's motivation.

The difficulty of knowing *why* may explain Jesus statements in the Sermon on the Mount. In Matthew 7:1 Jesus said, "Judge not, that you be not judged." However, in the same chapter Jesus warns of false prophets saying, "Therefore, by their fruits you will know them" (Matthew 7:20). The warning of the first verse may be a warning against assigning motivation. The fact is that we really do not know someone else's heart. We cannot be certain of the *why* question. What we can observe are the actions one exhibits.

Consequently, this section of the chapter will not primarily seek to answer *why* some downplay inerrancy. Rather, the emphasis will be a demonstration that this action definitely exists today. Further, one can argue that to downplay this crucial doctrine not only diminishes the doctrine but also in reality, constitutes an attack on the doctrine. Let's take a closer look at the example mentioned earlier.

A Candidate for Executive Committee Chair

Earlier in this chapter I recounted a personal experience leading up to the election of the immediate past chairman of the SBC Executive Committee. In the exchange one candidate really did not want to answer the questionnaire the author presented to the three candidates. When he did so, he failed to use the term inerrancy. Sensing that the author may not vote for him, he continued to engage on the subject after the author had already decided who would receive his vote. You will recall the candidate offered to amend his questionnaire to include the word inerrancy to gain votes. However, the candidate also indicated he did not believe inerrancy to be an important issue and would rather Southern Baptist never talk about inerrancy again.

The candidate essentially affirmed inerrancy as his personal doctrinal position but downplayed the importance of the doctrine. He was willing to use the term if it was necessary to gain votes, but his preference was to ignore the term all together. The candidate was certainly not willing to go on record as denying inerrancy, he simply wanted to downplay the importance of the concept.

Having been involved in SBC life on every level since 1984, I have been privileged to serve in various roles in eight different local associations, five state/regional conventions, on the Committee on Committees, as a Trustee of LifeWay Christian Resources, and most recently as a member of the SBC Executive Committee. Throughout the first 25 years of my denominational service (1984-2009) the word *inerrancy* could be heard in nearly every meeting of any size. Emphasis was placed on the importance of inerrancy, candidates for various offices were screened by their position on inerrancy, and nearly everyone championed the Bible as the verbal-plenary inspired Word of God.

Over the last 12 years, the term *inerrancy* has been rarely mentioned at Baptist gatherings. Many assumed that the question need not be asked any longer. However, as the previous example demonstrates, when inerrancy is not part of the conversation, people who downplay the importance of the doctrine can rise to key leadership roles. Downplaying inerrancy actually becomes an attack on inerrancy, because it opens the door for individuals to rise to leadership who re-define inerrancy, or possibly even deny it altogether.

Re-Defining Inerrancy

One of the most dangerous attacks on inerrancy today is a redefining of the term. Among conservative evangelicals, some refuse to jettison the term inerrancy, but they redefine it. This is particularly dangerous. One who takes this approach can sign off on statements of faith that use the term inerrancy, while denying certain aspects of the nature of Scripture that were intended by the authors of the document. One example of this can be seen with a popular member of the Evangelical Theological Society, particularly when one considers his treatment of the Chicago Statement on Biblical Inerrancy.

Craig Blomberg

In 2014 Craig Blomberg published his work, *Can We Still Believe the Bible?* with Brazos Press. In the opening pages of the monograph Blomberg states, "What this book does address is why I still believe the Bible as I write these words in 2013."[16] In chapters four and five Blomberg deals directly with the issue of inerrancy. He adopts Paul Fienberg's definition in chapter four. "Inerrancy means that when all facts are known, the Scriptures in their original autographs and properly interpreted will be shown to be wholly true in everything that they affirm, whether that has to do with doctrine or morality or with the social, physical, or life sciences."[17] Following this "working definition," Blomberg seeks to unpack what the definition entails.

Regarding this definition, Blomberg emphasizes four points. First, he notes the importance of the phrase, "when all facts are known."[18] Second, he discusses the importance of the phrase, "the Scriptures in their original autographs."[19] Third, Blomberg examines the phrase, "properly interpreted."[20] Fourth, he contemplates the phrase, "in everything they affirm."[21] While most scholars who hold to the inerrancy of the Bible would desire to speak to all four of these areas, Blomberg's emphasis on "properly interpreted" opens the door for a new concept of inerrancy than what has been typically understood by members of the Evangelical Theological Society. This con-

---

16. Craig Blomberg, *Can We Still Believe the Bible? An Evangelical Engagement with Contemporary Questions* (Grand Rapids: Brazos, 2014), 5.

17. Blomberg, *Still Believe*, 123.

18. Blomberg, *Still Believe*, 123.

19. Blomberg, *Still Believe*, 124.

20. Blomberg, *Still Believe*, 124–125.

21. Blomberg, *Still Believe*, 125.

cern becomes more prominent in the closing paragraph of chapter four and throughout chapter five.

Consistent with his writing style in this book, Blomberg uses the final paragraph of chapter four to introduce the reader to the topic of chapter five. Notice the author's questions.

> The rhetoric and passion seem to become even more intense when one turns to the question of acceptable literary genres in the Bible. Must Genesis be interpreted as affirming a historical Adam and Eve? Are the books of Job and Jonah factual or theological fiction? Can Isaiah be viewed as a composite of two or three documents? Might Daniel have been written in the second century BC because it prophesies so explicitly about events that span several centuries all the way up to the desecration of the Jerusalem temple in 167 BC? Can any parts of the Gospels and Acts be properly labeled myth or legend, and what would those labels mean? Can the pseudonymity of New Testament Epistles ever be consistent with inerrancy? Chapter 5 turns to these kinds of questions.[22]

Asking these questions does not mean that one has abandoned a traditional understanding of inerrancy. Good scholarship asks such questions. The answers one gives to such questions reveals whether or not one has abandoned a traditional understanding of inerrancy.

Building on his discussion of Fienberg's phrase "properly interpreted" in chapter four, Blomberg turns his attention to discussing the interpretation of various genres in chapter five. To support his understanding of these issues, he turns to the Chicago Statement on Biblical Inerrancy.[23] In particular, he quotes from two sections: Articles 8 and 13. Blomberg writes, "Article 8 includes the clear statement 'We affirm that God in His Work

---

22. Blomberg, *Still Believe*, 145.

23. R. C. Sproul and Norman L. Geisler, *Explaining Biblical Inerrancy: Official Commentary on the ICBI Statements* (Matthews, NC: Bastion Books, 2013).

of inspiration utilized the distinctive personalities and literary styles of the writers whom He had chosen and prepared.'"[24] Blomberg then quotes Article 13 as follows.

> We deny that it is proper to evaluate Scripture according to standards of truth and error that are alien to its usage or purpose. We further deny that inerrancy is negated by Biblical phenomena such as a lack of modern technical precision, irregularities of grammar or spelling, observational descriptions of nature, the reporting of falsehood, the use of hyperbole and round numbers, the topical arrangement of material, variant selections of material in parallel accounts, or the use of free citations.[25]

The key phrase for Blomberg is "standards of truth and error that are alien to its usage or *purpose*" (emphasis added). Throughout the balance of chapter five, he takes this phrase to allow a wide variety of interpretations related to the questions posed at the end of chapter four.

Blomberg walks through several biblical issues where there is wide disagreement among evangelicals today. He begins with the first eleven chapters of Genesis. In the end he concludes that one could hold to a variety of interpretations of these chapters based on disagreements of genre and still hold to inerrancy. Specifically, he suggests that one could believe that Adam and Eve are not real names of real people but only Hebrew words representing all humans, and still hold to the inerrancy of the Bible as defined by the Chicago Statement.[26]

Blomberg continues to demonstrate his allowance of interpretive diversity among self-proclaimed inerrantists by examining questions concerning the book of Job. He asserts, "It almost defies imagination that one

---

24. Blomberg, *Still Believe*, 149.
25. Blomberg, *Still Believe*, 49. See also Sproul and Geisler, *Biblical Inerrancy*, 47.
26. Blomberg, *Still Believe*, 149–152.

person should suffer such extreme loss, one misfortune at a time, each in a neat sequence, as happens to Job in the rhythmically narrated parallelism of the opening chapter. That he would gain all of this and more back at the end of his misery is even less lifelike."[27] While not denying that a man named Job lived, Blomberg clearly opts for an inerrancy of purpose when it comes to Job rather than an inerrancy of historical fact. He argues that what is inerrant is the theological purpose of the book, not its history.[28]

The scope of this chapter will not permit a thorough examination of all that Blomberg discusses in his fifth chapter. However, it should be noted that he addresses each of the questions presented at the end of chapter four in a similar fashion. In the end, under the guise of being consistent with the Chicago Statement, Blomberg vigorously argues that evangelicals cannot give up inerrancy, but must redefine it as an inerrancy of purpose. He argues that we must allow the interpreter to apply the tools of higher criticism and modern scholarship to determine that what is naturally presented as narrative in the Bible is not necessarily historical fact.[29]

Blomberg's understanding of the Chicago Statement stands in direct opposition to the authors of the Chicago Statement. In evaluating Blomberg's view, the reader should consider the commentary on the Chicago Statement on Biblical Inerrancy as well as the commentary on the Chicago Statement on Hermeneutics. These two commentaries were written by two of the framers of the statements: J. I. Packer and Norman Geisler.[30]

---

27. Blomberg, *Still Believe*, 155.

28. Blomberg, *Still Believe*, 156.

29. On May 5, 2021, I received a promotional email from B&H Academic announcing the coming release (July 1, 2021) of a Second Edition of *From Pentecost to Patmos: An Introduction to Acts through Revelation*, by Craig L. Blomberg and Darlene M. Seal. While the book is only available for pre-order at the time of this writing, it is concerning that a Southern Baptist owned entity would publish an author that clearly redefines inerrancy to a view that allows for one to deny the historicity of Adam and Eve, Job 1, Jonah 2 and still call himself an inerrantist.

30. Sproul and Geisler, *Biblical Inerrancy*.

Another work worth considering is the 2011 monograph *Defending Inerrancy: Affirming the Accuracy of Scripture for a New Generation.*[31] One of the most telling works that must be read is the 2015 work *Vital Issues in the Inerrancy Debate*, in which Geisler and others directly demonstrate serious problems with Blomberg's approach.[32] While a thorough refutation of Blomberg's position is beyond the scope of this chapter, these three resources should go a long way in aiding the reader's evaluation.

The biggest danger of Blomberg's position may come in his definition of inerrancy. Some in the Evangelical Society join the scholarly group thinking they are using not only the same vocabulary as other members, but also the same dictionary. One may read the Chicago Statement on Biblical Inerrancy and the Chicago Statement on Biblical Hermeneutics and believe that every member holds to an inerrancy consistent with Packer, Geisler, and the other framers of those two important documents. Yet clearly, Blomberg has exchanged an inerrancy of historical fact for an inerrancy of purpose in regard to several crucial texts throughout the Bible. The unsuspecting member of ETS may be surprised to discover that while the vocabulary of inerrancy remains in vogue in the society, there is more than one dictionary in use.

SBC Life

The danger of Blomberg's approach to an inerrancy of purpose, rather than an inerrancy of historical fact, may be one reason recent discussions in the Southern Baptist Convention has left many pastors and people in the pew scratching their heads in confusion. If Blomberg's view of inerrancy is held by individuals teaching in SBC seminaries or working for SBC entities, it may explain how they can sign off on the Baptist Faith & Message 2000

---

31. Norman L. Geisler and William C. Roach, *Defending Inerrancy: Affirming the Accuracy of Scripture for a New Generation* (Grand Rapids: Baker Books 2012).

32. F. David Farnell and Norman L. Geisler, *Vital Issues in the Inerrancy Debate* (Eugene, OR: Wipf and Stock, 2016).

and put forth views that are contrary to the views of the thousands of pastors and church members across the SBC who believe the issue of inerrancy was settled long ago. It is at least conceivable that we may have people who use the same vocabulary of the average pastor or church but use an altogether different dictionary who are working for SBC entities. If this is the case, it is no wonder that the SBC has found itself facing one internal crisis after another in recent years.

In the Spring of 2020, The Southern Baptist Theological Seminary fired Professor Russell Fuller. Fuller later reported that he was asked to sign a non-disclosure agreement in exchange for a severance package, which he refused to do. Shortly after the firing, three video interviews were posted on YouTube, allowing Fuller to tell his side of the story.[33] In the three videos, Fuller alleges that he was fired because he objected to a liberal drift that was clearly evident in the seminary. His charges included issues related to the inerrancy and sufficiency of Scripture, along with concerns over a shift in biblical hermeneutics.[34] While some of this information will be briefly discussed in the next two sections of this chapter, one issue Fuller raised relates to Blomberg's inerrancy of purpose view regarding the book of Job.

In the first video, Fuller expresses concern over the hiring of Dominick Hernández at Southern Seminary. He describes the interview process and his involvement in questioning Hernández formally, and later his personal conversation with Hernández during a lunch break. Fuller alleges that Hernández

---

33. Russell Fuller, "Downgrade at Southern Seminary: Higher Criticism (Part I)," interview by Jon Harris, *Conversations That Matter*, May 18, 2020, video, 23:20, https://www.youtube.com/watch?v=vMfiRWgobOU; Russell Fuller, "Downgrade at Southern Seminary: Postmodernism (Part II)," interview by Jon Harris, *Conversations that Matter*, May 21, 2020, video, 27:54, https://www.youtube.com/watch?v=Y-uZUcR7tN0; and Russell Fuller, "Downgrade at Southern Seminary: Critical Theory & Al Mohler (Part III)," interview by Jon Harris, *Conversations that Matter*, May 25, 2020, video, 25:59, https://www.youtube.com/watch?v=Z4Wc3nGPGyY.

34. Fuller, "Downgrade (Part II)," and Fuller, "Downgrade (Part III)."

believes and teaches that the author of the book of Job intentionally used and possibly believed in Canaanite mythology.[35] Shortly after the release of Fuller's three video interviews, Southern Seminary responded with their own set of videos. In the first response video, a conversation is held with Hernández and the assertion is that he simply believed that Bildad believed in mythology, but that he never claimed the author of Job believed it.[36] In the interview Hernández never specifically rejected the idea that the author of Job believed mythology. In order to discover his actual view on the topic, I determined to review the evidence presented by Fuller personally.

Fuller presented two lines of evidence. First, he referred to a paper Hernández presented to the Society of Biblical Literature at the Boston Conference in 2017.[37] Fuller also claimed a close examination of Hernández's dissertation further revealed his view that the author of Job intentionally used mythology and likely believed it himself.[38] Both of these documents are readily available to the public. Therefore, this writer read both documents in order to reach an understanding of the claims alleged by Fuller.

The opening paragraph of Hernández's SBL paper presents the question at hand:

> Terror, calamity, the devouring of human flesh—these are the themes that pervade mythical literature, in which the entities performing these types of actions are figments of the author's creative ingenuity. However, what if this imagery were to, in fact, reflect

---

35. Fuller, "Downgrade (Part I)."

36. Dominick S. Hernández, "An Interview with Dominick S. Hernández," interview by Jim Hamilton, *Southern Seminary*, May 19, 2020, video, 17:14, https://www.youtube.com/watch?v=yx10NOTO8uw.

37. Dominick S. Hernández, "Mythopoetic Imagery Relating to the First-born of Death and the King of Terrors," (SBL Paper, Boston, 2017).

38. Dominick S. Hernández, "Will the Lamp of the Wicked Wane: The Prosperity of the Wicked as a Theme in Job and the Ancient Near East" (PhD diss., Bar-Ilan University, Ramat Gan, Israel, 2016).

genuine personages within the cognitive environment of the writer, and simply a figment of his imagination? What if the writer were to actually believe that such characters exist and that they carry out retribution upon the impious?[39]

In his second paragraph, Hernández specifies his area of concern: "Could this have been the case of the author of Job, in which the 'Firstborn of Death' and the 'King of Terrors' engage in violence, contributing to the downfall of the wicked?"[40] Having caught the attention of his readers, Hernández expresses his purpose: "This paper will evaluate the relationship of the mythological 'Firstborn of Death' and the 'King of Terrors' to the Ugaritic deity *Mot*, and consider to what extent these personages may have emerged within the ancient Israelite milieu."[41] Hernández proceeds with his paper by comparing Bildad's speech in relationship to "The Firstborn of Death" and "The King of Terrors" in relationship to Canaanite and Ugaritic mythology. Just prior to concluding his paper, Hernández writes, "Considering the mythopoetic images stemming from ancient cultures, as well as the context of Bildad's retributive claim, a direct correspondence has been proposed between the King of Terrors and the Canaanite deity *Mot*."[42] There is no question that Hernández believes that Bildad believed in mythology.

The question that remains is whether Hernández believes the author of Job was simply reporting Bildad's belief, or if he thinks that the author of Job actually believed in the mythological personages of the "Firstborn of Death" and the "King of Terrors" himself. To discover the answer to this question, one need not look any further than the concluding paragraphs of the SBL paper.

---

39. Hernández, "Mythopoetic Imagery," 1.
40. Hernández, "Mythopoetic Imagery," 1.
41. Hernández, "Mythopoetic Imagery," 1.
42. Hernández, "Mythopoetic Imagery," 8–9.

On page 10 of his paper, Hernández writes, "The Israelites—and thereby, the poet of Job—were part of the ancient Near Eastern thought world in which Death was personified, considered to be a voracious entity, and in which there was a ruler over the netherworld. Thus, personified Death in Job, though admittedly could have been derived from the Ugaritic deity, *Mot*, could have also quite naturally emerged within the ancient Israelite milieu."[43] These two sentences clearly demonstrate that Hernández argues that the Israelites and the "poet of Job" believed in both a personified "Death" and a "ruler over the netherworld" that consumed the wicked. Whether in the end Hernández assigns the belief in mythology as having arisen from the Canaanite false god *Mot*, or from the suggestion that Israel and the author of Job lived in a culture that believed in these mythical figures, the bottom line is that he suggests the author of Job believed in mythology.

The final paragraph of Hernández's SBL paper should be noted:

> Whether or not these characters of personified death came from the same source of cultural consciousness, we see that one can gain a better understanding of the text of Job through study of similar ancient Near Eastern entities. The author of Job was operating well within the common understanding of his cognitive environment when he warned (through Bildad) of these terrors and calamities that would befall the impious. If the author of Job believed that horrific beings such as the Firstborn of Death and the King of Terrors truly existed, it is easy to understand why he would include these characters in a speech urging someone to turn from wickedness.[44]

In his conclusion, Hernández clearly puts the speech of Bildad as far more than simply a speech reported by the author. He places the emphasis not on Bildad, but on the author of Job. He states that "the author of Job ...

---

43. Hernández, "Mythopoetic Imagery," 10.
44. Hernández, "Mythopoetic Imagery," 11.

warned (through Bildad) …"[45] He then suggests that if the author actually believed in the mythical figures, it would be "easy to understand why he would include these characters in a speech urging someone to turn from wickedness."[46] Any straightforward reading of Hernández's SBL paper must recognize that Hernández is arguing at least the likelihood that the author of Job believed mythology and intentionally used mythology in his writing.

An examination of Hernández's dissertation mentioned above is beyond the scope of this chapter. However, I did read the dissertation. Just as Fuller was correct in his assessment of Hernández's SBL paper, I believe he was correct in his assessment of the dissertation as well.[47] The reader of this chapter would do well to read both the SBL Paper and the dissertation and conduct his/her own careful assessment.

Having described the concerns of Dominick Hernández's writing, the larger question of this section of the chapter relates to how one could sign *The Baptist Faith and Message 2000* and *The Chicago Statement on Inerrancy* and believe that the author of Job believed and wrote mythology. As previously noted, it is impossible for one man to know another man's motivation, beyond what one clearly states. However, there appears to be only a few options: 1. One could intentionally sign a statement of faith, agreeing to teach within its limits, that is opposed to one's belief. 2. One could sign a statement of faith, agreeing to teach within its limits, without paying attention to the statement. 3. One could sign a statement of faith, agreeing to teach within its limits, but define a word like "inerrancy" in a different way than was intended by the drafters of the statement.

One explanation may be that, like Craig Blomberg, Dominick Hernández has adopted the "inerrancy of purpose" approach. If this is the case, it should be stated. If this is not the case, then Hernández should clearly state how he believes he can simultaneously hold to the inerrancy of the

---

45. Hernández, "Mythopoetic Imagery," 11.
46. Hernández, "Mythopoetic Imagery," 11.
47. Fuller, "Downgrade (Part I)."

Bible *and* believe that the author of Job intentionally wrote myth into the Bible and likely believed myth himself. One further question that must be answered but is once again beyond the scope of this chapter, is why Russell Fuller would be fired and Dominick Hernández would be retained as a professor at The Southern Baptist Theological Seminary.[48]

As we have seen some among us downplay inerrancy, some also re-define inerrancy. However, some attacks on inerrancy today are more subtle. Such is the case with the next two sections of this chapter. We now turn our attention to one of those subtle attacks: Hermeneutics and Inerrancy.

Hermeneutics and Inerrancy

Since at least 1982 Evangelicals have recognized the fact that there is a clear connection between hermeneutics and inerrancy. As a follow up to *The Chicago Statement on Biblical Inerrancy: Articles of Affirmation and Denial (1978)*,[49] the framers of the statement recognized the need for a statement on hermeneutics. It was understood that one could claim inerrancy and effectively undermine the term as had been done earlier in the twentieth century with the term *infallibility*. One way inerrancy could be undermined is through hermeneutics. Therefore, a group of Evangelical leaders produced *The Chicago Statement on Biblical Hermeneutics: Articles of Affirmation and Denial (1982)*.[50]

---

48. On the eve of publication, I checked SBTS's website and did not see Dominick Hernández listed under current faculty. However, several news articles on the site referenced him as a celebrated member of the faculty. On June 7, 2021, Hernández posted on his personal blog that he would soon be transitioning to Talbot School of Theology at Biola University. The timing of his transition is uncertain. However, this does not negate the question of why Russell Fuller was fired, and Dominick Hernández was defended, when Hernández was the one with views outside of the Baptist Faith and Message 2000.

49. Sproul and Geisler, *Biblical Inerrancy.*

50. Sproul and Geisler, *Biblical Inerrancy.*

Earlier in this chapter, it was noted that Blomberg argued that Article 13 of the Chicago Statement on Inerrancy allowed for one to have an interpretation of the genre of Genesis 1-11 that would deny these chapters as being historical narrative. This would then allow the interpreter to deny that Adam and Eve were real names of real people and yet still claim to be an inerrantist.[51] While this is an extreme example of how hermeneutics can impact one's view of inerrancy, it clearly demonstrates how Blomberg used the field of biblical hermeneutics to provide a means for him to redefine inerrancy, contrary to the *Official Commentary on the Chicago Statements*.[52] However, the field of biblical hermeneutics offers other, more subtle, ways to harm the long-standing view of inerrancy held by both Evangelicals in general and Southern Baptists in particular.

Southeastern Baptist Theological Seminary

I was privileged to pursue a PhD at Southeastern Baptist Theological Seminary, graduating in 2017. The week of May 27-31, 2013 was spent participating in a seminar titled, *Integrative Seminar I*. Four professors led the seminar, including the leader of the PhD program, Heath Thomas, who led both the introduction and a segment toward the latter part of the week. In the final portion of the week, Thomas, along with another professor led us through a discussion of Theological Method and Hermeneutics.[53] While Kenneth Keathley primarily led the section on Theological Method, Heath Thomas led the discussion on Hermeneutics. Our discussion centered on the book *Deep Exegesis* by Peter Leithart.[54]

---

51. See note 26.

52. See Geisler's commentary on Articles XI, XII, and XIV in Sproul and Geisler, *Biblical Inerrancy*.

53. Heath Thomas and Kenneth Keathley. *PHD 9201 Integrative Seminar I: Course Syllabus*, 2013, Southeastern Baptist Theological Seminary, Wake Forest, NC.

54. Peter Leithart, *Deep Exegesis: The Mystery of Reading Scripture* (Waco,

Leithart's work is composed of six chapters. Each of the chapters were discussed and examined in light of various authors who agreed and disagreed with Leithart's perspective. An examination of *Deep Exegesis* is beyond the scope of this chapter. However, this brief description of the seminar is provided to establish the backdrop of one of our discussions. Often throughout the discussion, I found myself feeling like a fish out of water. Of course, we found much agreement among the seminar participants, but there were often disagreements over basic hermeneutical principles. One example demonstrates the concern.

The concept of the clarity (perspicuity) of Scripture has been a long-standing hermeneutical principle that Evangelicals in general, and Baptists in particular, have championed. Further, Baptists, and many other evangelical groups, have traditionally held that because of the clarity of Scripture, a person who has the Holy Spirit living within is not dependent on the expertise of scholars to understand the Bible. While a knowledge of Hebrew, Greek, Church History, ancient historical studies, etc., provide nuances that are helpful, it is understood that any literate person who has a Bible in hand and the Spirit residing internally, can read, understand, and apply the Scripture. This principle is reflected in the Chicago Statement on Biblical Hermeneutics. Consider the affirmations of Articles XXIII and XXIV.

ARTICLE XXIII

We affirm the clarity of Scripture and specifically
of its message about salvation from sin.

We deny that all passages of Scripture are equally clear
or have equal bearing on the message of redemption.

TX: Baylor University Press, 2009).

ARTICLE XXIV

We affirm that a person is not dependent for understanding
of Scripture on the expertise of biblical scholars.
We deny that a person should ignore the fruits of the
technical study of Scripture by biblical scholars.[55]

These two articles work together to avoid two extremes. One extreme
seeks to so emphasize the scholarly study of Scripture that the layman is left
completely dependent on the scholarly expert to know anything about the
Bible at all. As one of the framers of the Chicago Statements noted, "For if
the understanding of the laity is contingent on the teaching of experts, then
Protestant interpretive experts will have replaced the teaching magisterium of
Catholic priests with a kind of teaching magisterium of Protestant scholars."[56]

The second extreme these two articles seek to avoid is the view that
the scholarly study of Scripture is of no value. Some passages of Scripture
are more readily understood than others. Often further clarity can be found
when one understands historical studies, language studies, genre studies, etc.
The literate interpreter can both understand the basic message of a text, and
at the same time benefit in his or her depth of understanding from some of
the scholarly works on the text.

The balanced view described in the previous two paragraphs and stated in the two articles above, has been the long-standing view of evangelicals. Baptists have championed this view throughout their entire history.
The clarity (perspicuity) of Scripture, is a core principle of hermeneutics
that must not be jettisoned.

Yet, the perspicuity of Scripture was questioned directly by Heath
Thomas in the *Integrative Seminar I*, in which I participated in May 2013. As

---

55. "The Chicago Statement on Biblical Hermeneutics: Articles of Affirmation and Denial" (International Council on Biblical Inerrancy, 1982).
56. Sproul and Geisler, *Biblical Inerrancy*, 84–85.

the seminar participants were discussing one of the areas of hermeneutical disagreement described above, Thomas responded to a statement made by this author. He said, "Mark, you remind me of a person with whom I recently discussed these issues. He said that he actually believed that a person who could read English could take an English translation of the Bible, read it, and understand it. I told him he was wrong. I said, that unless that person has a working knowledge of the biblical languages, church, and ancient history, he/she has no way of comprehending the Bible."[57] Thomas' statement in this seminar is in direct conflict with the doctrine of the perspicuity of Scripture and the Chicago Statement on Biblical Hermeneutics.

Other hermeneutical concerns arose during the present writer's years pursuing a PhD at Southeastern. However, just one more will be presented as an illustration of the problem being discussed in this section of the chapter. During another seminar in May of 2014, the participants were engaged in another discussion over hermeneutical concerns. Toward the end of the week, the President of the seminary dropped by to visit and go to lunch with the seminar participants. He engaged in the conversation. Soon, to my surprise, the President began to speak of a shift that had taken place in his own hermeneutical approach. Having known the President for many years, the statement garnered my curiosity.

As I listened intently, I could not believe what I was hearing when the President provided a description of a recent sermon he preached. The sermon focused on the story of David and Goliath from 1 Samuel 17. As President Akin described the sermon, it became clear that he had supplemented an allegorical approach to the text for a grammatical-historical interpretation approach. In fact, as described in the seminar, he had almost completely supplanted the grammatical-historical approach by claiming the "true meaning of the text" was to be discovered only in a comparison

---

57. Heath Thomas, PhD Seminar at Southeastern Baptist Theological Seminary, May 27–31, 2013.

with Genesis 3:15, Goliath's armor, and the death, burial, and resurrection of Jesus.

Akin's argument hung on the meaning of the Hebrew word, *qasqeset*, translated into English as a coat of *mail*. Akin correctly argued that the word means, "scaled."[58] He suggested that this is the same word that would be used to describe the scales of a snake. He further suggested that coming toward David in the sunlight, Goliath would have looked like "a gigantic snake man." Connecting this concept back to Genesis 3:15, Akin argued that "the snake man" was a representative of Satan and that David, being in the line of the Messiah, was representative of Jesus. He drew further parallels to David cutting off Goliath's head and the crushing of the head of the snake described in Genesis 3:15. It is important to note, that this was not argued to be an application, but in fact the primary meaning of the text.[59]

I sat in shock as I listened to my long-time friend explain how he and the others in the room had completely misunderstood the story of David and Goliath all these years. Push back ensued, particularly in regard to the grammatical-historical approach to interpretation and the immediate grammatical and historical context of the chapter. Akin indicated that he did not deny the historical realities but continued to insist that the true meaning of the text, and that which should be preached was the connection of "the snake man" and Genesis 3:15. I pointed out that if one were to push the issue of "scales" a fish might be the more appropriate description. The discussion concluded with Akin inviting the seminar participants to listen to his sermon on the text, which can be accessed via his personal website.[60] In

---

58. According to BDB, *quaqeset* may be defined as "scale, as of a fish, of water animals having fin and scale" (*The Brown, Driver, Briggs Hebrew and English Lexicon* [Peabody, MA: Hendrickson, 1996]).

59. Danny Akin, personal conversation, May 2014.

60. "God's Unlikely Champion (The Shepherd Boy Who Made His Name Famous in All the Earth) – 1 Samuel 17:1-58," Danny Akin, last modified August 23, 2013, https://www.danielakin.com/gods-unlikely-champion-the-shepherd-

researching for this chapter, the present author returned to the website and listened to the sermon. While Akin does deal with some of the grammatical-historical context, he clearly emphasizes the allegorical interpretation over and above the plain reading of the text.

The Relationship Between
Faulty Hermeneutics and Inerrancy

For many years Evangelicals, including Baptists, have noted a connection with one's view of the inerrant nature of Scripture and one's view of biblical hermeneutics. In the introduction to a *Short Exposition of The Chicago Statement on Biblical Hermeneutics*, Norman Geisler notes, "The work of Summit I had hardly been completed when it became evident that there was yet another major task to be tackled. While we recognize that belief in the inerrancy of Scripture is basic to maintaining its authority, the values of that commitment are only as real as one's understanding of the meaning of Scripture."[61] If one holds to the inerrancy of Scripture, based on a view that the Bible is the verbal-plenary inspired Word of God, then care must be given to interpret Scripture in accordance with the author's intended meaning. The reader is not allowed to infuse meaning into a text, damaging the grammatical-historical context in favor of a deduced theological "meta-narrative." If the reader supplies meaning via a deduced theological perspective, the authority now resides in the interpreter, rather than in the text of Scripture. If the authority rests in the interpreter, the Bible itself is no longer the "final authority for faith and practice."[62]

One may claim to hold to the inerrancy of Scripture, but if one's hermeneutical practices replace the natural meaning of the text within its

---

boy-who-made-his-name-famous-in-all-the-earth/.

61. Sproul and Geisler, *Biblical Inerrancy*, 13. The reference to "Summit I" refers to the 1978 Council on Biblical Inerrancy which produced the Chicago Statement on Inerrancy.

62. "The Baptist Faith and Message 2000."

grammatical-historical context with a reader infused meaning from a single verse in a different context, one's view of inerrancy has been damaged. The danger of the current hermeneutical practices described above is not a frontal assault on the Bible, denying inerrancy. Rather, the danger of these practices is a subtle attack on inerrancy by replacing the grammatical-historical meaning, with a reader infused meaning.

One final concern needs to be noted. If the grammatical-historical meaning of a text is not "the real meaning," then by what standard can we judge someone's claim to interpretation? I suggested to Akin that rather than seeing Goliath as "the snake man," maybe we should see him as "the fish man." There is more grammatical and historical evidence for this possibility. We could connect the scales of Goliath's armor to Dagon the fish god of fertility. We could create a whole scenario of how David was not at all concerned about a snake, but about a competing god worshiped by the Philistines. How are we to know which interpretation is correct?

Please allow me to submit that the way to determine the interpretation is not by overusing the semantic range of a single Hebrew word. Nor is it to immediately run to ancient Near Eastern studies, or to Genesis 3:15. Rather, it is to recognize that First Samuel chapters fifteen through thirty-one is demonstrating two things: (1) Saul has been rejected as king over Israel because of his unbelief and disobedience. (2) David has been chosen as king over Israel because of his faith and obedience. One can preach the whole counsel of God without misusing David as an allegorical representation of Jesus or as a moralistic example devoid of a focus on God as deliverer and hero. One can preach the text for what it is and still make solid application to both the saved and the lost. To do otherwise subtly removes the authority from the inerrant Scripture and places the authority in the hands of the elite academic reader. This is a subtle attack, albeit a real attack, on the inerrancy of Scripture.

The Sufficiency of Scripture & Inerrancy

Making the Connection

Just one year after the Southern Baptist Convention adopted the Baptist Faith and Message 2000, Jimmy Draper and Ken Keathley saw the need to write a book calling believers to renew their commitment to Biblical Authority.[63] Many had declared the "Conservative Resurgence" over, having believed it came to a victorious conclusion. Yet, Draper and Keathley saw that the issue of Biblical Authority remained a concern.

The book begins by describing how even a small step away from Biblical Authority is a tragic step that leads one down a slide that can end with a complete rejection of the Bible's authority. In the first chapter, the authors identify issues that have challenged the authority of Scripture. They argue that sometimes well-meaning people sub-consciously take a step away from Biblical Authority without wanting to abandon Biblical Doctrine altogether. For instance, while using the term inerrancy may not be absolutely necessary, compromising on its use "could end in spiritual disaster."[64] The following chapters of the monograph address several major concerns the authors saw in play twenty years ago which they believed could lead the way to derail the accomplishments of the Conservative Resurgence.

In chapter seven, "The Next Big Issue for Christians," the authors address concerns over the Sufficiency of Scripture. Early in the chapter they define the concept: "The ability of the Word of God to address every area of human existence is called the sufficiency of Scripture."[65] In describing the importance of the doctrine the authors argue, "Just as the doctrine of the inerrancy of Scripture logically leads to belief in its authority, even so the doctrine of authority of the Bible necessitates the confidence that the Scriptures

---

63. James T. Draper and Kenneth Keathley, *Biblical Authority: The Critical Issue for the Body of Christ* (Nashville: B&H Publishers, 2001).

64. Draper and Keathley, *Biblical Authority*, 9.

65. Draper and Keathley, *Biblical Authority*, 80.

are sufficient."[66] While it would likely be difficult to find a Southern Baptist working at one of our entities that would deny the inerrancy of Scripture, another way inerrancy is damaged, even by those who do not directly attempt to redefine inerrancy as described above, is to deny its sufficiency.

A Current Concern in SBC Life

Draper and Keathley's concern rests in the fact that today the sufficiency of Scripture is being "disavowed in a number of subtle ways."[67] In the balance of chapter seven, the authors discuss three ways they observed in 2001 that believers were beginning to undermine the Bible's sufficiency. They discussed the way some confuse the illumination of the Spirit with the inspiration of the Spirit, by addressing the concept of private revelation. Draper and Keathley express concern regarding some modern counseling techniques that challenge the sufficiency of Scripture. They also address Worship Techniques that tend to displace the importance of the preaching of the Word.

Since the 2019 Southern Baptist Convention held in Birmingham, AL, many Southern Baptist pastors and members in the pew have observed another subtle threat to the sufficiency of Scripture. In his book, *A Corruption of Consequence: Adding Social Justice to the Gospel*, Pastor Ronnie Rogers chronicles the problem. Not only does Rogers provide a clear, respectful, and charitable examination of the issues that threaten to usurp the inerrancy and authority of the Bible by attacking its sufficiency, he also provides helpful appendices to aid his readers.

Appendix 4 was written by Stephen Feinstein, a messenger to the 2018 Convention who submitted Resolution 9.[68] Following three introductory

---

66. Draper and Keathley, *Biblical Authority*, 80.

67. Draper and Keathley, *Biblical Authority*, 81.

68. Ronnie W. Rogers, *A Corruption of Consequence: Adding Social Justice to the Gospel* (Eugene, OR: Resource Publications, 2021), 138-142.

paragraphs, Feinstein provides the reader with the Resolution he submitted to the 2019 Resolutions Committee. The original resolution condemns Critical Race Theory and Intersectionality for the unbiblical philosophies that they are.[69]

In Appendix 2, Rogers provides the resolution as presented to the Convention after the Resolutions Committee altered the contents of original submission.[70] Rogers offers commentary on the resolution as presented by the Resolution Committee in Appendix 3.[71] The author correctly notes the confusion caused by the lack of clarity coming out of the Resolutions Committee. In the body of the book, Rogers explicitly describes and documents the reality that while some leaders within our SBC have publicly spoken against Critical Race Theory and Intersectionality, they have also permitted, and even encouraged, its influence within the entities they lead.

A full discussion of the issues surrounding this problem is beyond the scope of this chapter, it should be noted that by adopting CRT/I as an analytical tool, one is essentially rejecting the sufficiency of Scripture. CRT/I is a worldly philosophy, based in Marxism, and is diametrically opposed to Scripture on several fronts. For a complete discussion of the issues related to CRT/I, please see Rogers's work.[72] Those who insist on the necessity of CRT/I essentially suggest that the Bible's teaching on ethnic relations and reconciliation is not sufficient. Specifically, the philosophy speaks against the Bible's teaching on justice, reconciliation, forgiveness, restoration, etc. Furthermore, CRT/I attacks the Gospel by at best, confusing it, and at worst, completely replacing it.

---

69. Rogers, *Corruption of Consequence*, 138-142.
70. Rogers, *Corruption of Consequence*, 129-131.
71. Rogers, *Corruption of Consequence*, 132-134.
72. Rogers, *Corruption of Consequence*.

More Direct Attacks on the Sufficiency of Scripture

Recently, more direct attacks on the sufficiency of Scripture have taken shape. One of the more direct attacks on the sufficiency of Scripture has come in relationship to Bible translation. Increasingly calls are going forth for diverse translation teams, suggesting that without diversity on the team, a translation is somehow flawed. Another different, but similar, attack comes in what can be called, *standpoint hermeneutics*. Together these two concepts are gaining in popularity but ultimately devalue the long-standing Baptist doctrine of the sufficiency of Scripture.

On September 23, 2019, Esau McCaulley, an Anglican priest and professor at Wheaton College, published an article in the Washington Post titled, "Why it mattes if your Bible was translated by a racially diverse group."[73] In his article, McCaulley argues that future Bible translation committees should include a diverse ethnicity and gender membership. He argues that the diverse cultures will provide a more accurate translation. However, if cultural diversity is required to translate the Bible from Hebrew and Greek, then we are placing a higher value on the translator's culture than we are the culture of the Biblical text itself. If the modern interpreter is to bring his or her culture into the translation process in a way that yields a different meaning, then the question must be asked, "How did anyone at anytime in church history have a possibility for an accurate understanding of the text of Scripture without the benefit of the current diverse cultures that are now able to render the true meaning?"

The fact is that no culture should change one's translation of a text of Scripture. Certainly, we must recognize our cultural limitations. But we should not base our translation of a text on our culture. We should base

---

73. Esau McCaulley, "Why it matters if your Bible was translated by a racially diverse group," *The Washington Post*, September 23, 2019, https://www.google.com/amp/s/www.washingtonpost.com/religion/2019/09/23/why-it-matters-if-your-bible-was-translated-by-a-racially-diverse-group/%3FoutputType%3Damp.

our translation of a text on the grammatical-historical context of the passage under consideration. If a translator from a western culture finds one meaning, while an Asian translator finds another meaning, and an African translator finds yet another meaning, then all three translators are prioritizing their own culture over the culture of the Biblical author. The authority shifts from the text to the translator. While this may fit very well into our post-modern reader response world, it replaces the sufficiency of Scripture with the sufficiency of the culture of the translator(s).

On June 16, 2020, Southeastern Baptist Theological Seminary posted a YouTube video titled, "Southeastern Symposium – Elizabeth Mburu."[74] Dr. Mburu is a PhD graduate of Southeastern and serves as an Associate Professor of New Testament and Greek at International Leadership University and Pan-Africa Christian University in Nairobi, Kenya. She is also on the board of the African Bible Commentary and the editorial coordinator and New Testament editor for its revision. Mburu also serves as the Africa Regional Coordinator for Langham Literature.

In her lecture, Mburu argues for an "African Hermeneutic." Her basic premise is that there needs to be an "African Hermeneutic" that is distinct from the hermeneutics that most African Christians have inherited from western missionaries and colonization. She does affirm two crucial hermeneutical principles: (1) There is only one meaning to a text, though there may be many applications. (2) The author's meaning must carry the day. These two principles stand in contrast to much of what we see in modern hermeneutics and Mburu should be commended for taking this stand.

However, the basic premise of Mburu's lecture is that African Culture requires an African Hermeneutic to truly understand the Bible. She states, "People sometimes think of hermeneutics as if it has principles set in stone.

---

74. Elizabeth Mburu, "Southeastern Symposium - Elizabeth Mburu," *Southeastern Baptist Theological Seminary*, June 16, 2020, video, 44:41, https://youtu.be/7VrKFWnjRPs.

But is hermeneutics static or dynamic in the sense that it can change as methods of interpretation adapt to different cultural contexts?"[75] This statement seems to open the door to counter her two stated principles of meaning being singular and residing in the author, rather than in the reader. If one's culture determines meaning in "dialogue with the culture of the Bible,"[76] then one brings something to the interpretive decisions as to the meaning of the passage. This confusion can be observed throughout the lecture.

The model of interpretation for which Mburu argues for is built as a four-legged stool. She describes the four legs in the order of priority: (1) The interpreter must first look for parallels to African Culture. (2) The interpreter must seek a theological understanding of the passage. (3) The interpreter must consider the literary context of the passage. (4) The interpreter must consider the historical context of the passage. Mburu then connects all this with the seat of application, arguing that application pulls it all together and in many ways is the beginning point of African Hermeneutics.[77] While she treats each of the four legs as separate concepts, she continually weaves African culture as the priority in understanding each of the other legs. In essence, Mburu argues that African culture has a better possibility of understanding the text of Scripture than other, particularly western cultures.

As noted above, this approach is commonly called *standpoint hermeneutics*. The approach places more emphasis on the cultural context of the reader than on the grammatical-historical context of the passage. In the end, this approach diminishes the Sufficiency of Scripture by arguing that certain modern cultures have a better possibility of truly understanding the text of Scripture than others. Thus, the Bible itself is not sufficient. For one to understand the Scripture, one must be versed in the various modern cultures of our day. Once again, the Sufficiency of Scripture is replaced with the sufficiency of the interpreter's culture.

---

75. Mburu, "Southeastern Symposium."
76. Mburu, "Southeastern Symposium."
77. Mburu, "Southeastern Symposium."

If in the end one must have a cultural knowledge beyond the grammatical-historical context of Scripture to translate or interpret the Bible, the sufficiency of Scripture is replaced by the sufficiency of one culture or another. If Scripture is not sufficient in and of itself, then the doctrine of inerrancy is diminished. There is no sure word from God, if my white, American, maleness keeps me from understanding the real meaning of the Bible. I may claim God's Word is inerrant, but in a translation or interpretation of the Bible from a certain culture or cultures. Thus, social justice, critical race theory, and intersectionality become the authority, rather than the inerrant Word of God.

DOES INERRANCY STILL MATTER?

The messengers gathered for the Southern Baptist Convention in 1979 decided that inerrancy matters, and Adrian Rogers was elected the first president in a series of presidential candidates to emphasize its importance. The messengers gathered at the Southern Baptist Convention in the year 2000 decided that inerrancy matters and adopted a revised version of the *Baptist Faith and Message* that attempted to close the gaps and clarify the importance of inerrancy. The very next year, Jimmy Draper and Ken Keathley saw a danger already on the horizon and wrote *Biblical Authority: The Critical Issue for the Body of Christ,* warning Baptists that a denial of the Sufficiency of Scripture would gut the victory over the Bible, by a subtle attack on the authority of the Bible.[78] They wrote the book because they believed inerrancy matters.

These concerns are not unique to the Baptist world. Men like R. C. Sproul and Norman Geisler continually warned those involved in the Evangelical Theological Society of the dangers of denying, downplaying, and redefining the inerrancy of Scripture. In 2013, Norman Geisler renewed publication of *Explaining Inerrancy: Official Commentary on the ICBI State-*

---

78. Draper and Keathley, *Biblical Authority.*

ments to remind the Evangelical world that inerrancy matters.[79] With a fore-word written by J. I. Packer, Norman Geisler and William Roach published *Defending Inerrancy: Affirming the Accuracy of Scripture for a New Generation* in 2011 to once again boldly declare, inerrancy matters![80] There is no question that the previous generation of Baptist and Evangelical leaders believed, boldly declared, and fought for the belief that the inerrancy of the Bible is a crucial doctrine that should not be denied, downplayed, or redefined. The question today remains: *DOES INERRANCY STILL MATTER?*

Standing on the shoulders of those who have gone before, this author unashamedly declares, Yes! Inerrancy still matters! Inerrancy must not be denied, downplayed, or redefined. If we jettison the inerrancy of Scripture, we are left with a manmade religion, based on the authority of whatever individual or group declares something to be true. As Josh McDowell appropriately teaches, for something to be absolutely true it must be objective, universal, and constant.[81] There are four ways to attempt to know truth: intellect, emotion, experience, or authority.[82] Obviously, intellect, emotion, and experience all fail the test of being objective, universal, and constant. However, there are also problems with authority.

If the authority is based on a person or group's experience (culture), intellect, or emotion, then once again the authority fails to meet the objective, universal, and constant test. The only way anything can be absolutely true is if it comes from the One who transcends time, and space. For something to be absolutely true, it must not be culturally dependent. Truth

79. Sproul and Geisler, *Biblical Inerrancy*.

80. Norman L. Geisler and William C. Roach, *Defending Inerrancy: Affirming the Accuracy of Scripture for a New Generation* (Grand Rapids: Baker, 2011).

81. Josh McDowell and Bob Hostetler, *Right from Wrong* (Dallas TX: Word Publishing, 1994), 17.

82. I synthesized this four-fold pattern from various resources produced by Josh McDowell that are no longer available. Much of the material that relates to *Right from Wrong*, mentioned in note 83, including audio, video, and age group workbooks summarized these four options.

is found in the Person of God Himself.[83] To have a clear word that is absolutely true, we must have a Word from God.

The internal and external evidence for the Bible reveals that God spoke through individual writers who certainly lived within a specific time and place and were thus culturally bound. God did so in a way that allowed the personalities and cultural realities of the writers to be seen, yet He superintended the writing in such a way that the very words, parts of words, and even the verb tenses were breathed by God Himself.[84] If God is a God of truth and cannot lie, and if He breathed all Scripture, than the autographs of Scripture are inerrant in all matters to which they speak.

The manuscript evidence demonstrates that our modern Greek and Hebrew texts accurately present God's Word without any major deviation from the autographs that would have a bearing on serious doctrinal concerns. Further, a Bible that has been faithfully translated into a language other than the Biblical languages accurately conveys God's Word. The Scriptures can be understood by a natural reading of the text, placing emphasis on the grammatical-historical context of a particular passage under consideration. Once the meaning of a text is understood, it should be applied to the reader's life by putting it into practice.[85] However, if we have no sure Word from God, we are left to our own devices and will wonder around trying to determine what is true with no hope of ever knowing the truth. Yes! Inerrancy still matters!

CONCLUSION

This chapter began by returning to the Pastor's Conference and the Southern Baptist Convention held in Houston in June of 1979. Attention turned to a consideration of the events leading up to the election of Adrian Rogers

83. McDowell and Hostetler, *Right and Wrong*, 82.
84. See 2 Timothy 3:16, Matthew 5:18, and John 8:58.
85. See James 1:22.

to serve as the SBC President. The chapter then briefly reviewed the history of the Southern Baptist Conservative Resurgence, recognizing the emphasis placed on the inerrancy of Scripture. This author then explained a few of the things that caused him to have renewed concerns over the commitment to inerrancy among some in leadership. Having laid this foundational groundwork, the largest section of the chapter examined four contemporary attacks on the inerrancy of Scripture including, downplaying inerrancy, redefining inerrancy, hermeneutical concerns related to inerrancy, and how subtle shifts in one's view of the sufficiency of Scripture becomes an attack on inerrancy.

The chapter asked the question, "Does Inerrancy Still Matter?" I have answered that question with an unapologetic *Yes*. Craig Blomberg is correct in the early pages of his work, when he claims that "we can *still* believe the Bible."[86] However, contrary to Blomberg's position, we cannot afford to simply give lip service to the term *inerrancy*, while gutting the term of its meaning and redefining it. Nor can we downplay the issue. We must not compromise on the grammatical-historical interpretation of the text; otherwise we shift authority from the inerrant Word of God to an individual or group. Furthermore, we must not exchange the sufficiency of Scripture for the philosophies of men.

I have had the privilege of attending Bible believing Baptist congregations since nine months before I was born. One of my favorite childhood memories is singing "The B. I. B. L. E." at Sunday School. We sang the chorus at the top of our lungs, seriously getting into the hand motions. As fun as it was, there is one line in that childhood song that impacts me to this very day. Consider the following words from the song.

> The B. I. B. L. E., Yes That's the Book for me,
> I'll stand alone on the Word of God,
> The B. I. B. L. E, That spells ... BIBLE!

---

86. Blomberg, *Still Believe*, 12.

Following the pattern of Joshua in his final days of leadership on this earth, today I challenge you, the reader. Why do you falter between two opinions? Choose today what you will believe and do, but as for me and my house, "Inerrancy Still Matters."

2

DOES THE GOSPEL STILL MATTER?

JOHNNY HUNT

Yes. Absolutely. "The gospel still matters."

The statement gets an enthusiastic "Amen" in most conservative evangelical settings. It is a tried and true "Amen line" in Southern Baptist churches and State Evangelism Conferences as well. Yet, even though we say, "the gospel still matters," I am not confident we still believe it. Why?

I will only speak for my own denomination—the Southern Baptist Convention (SBC). After serving forty-four years as a Southern Baptist pastor, holding my favorite honorable title, "Former" President of the SBC, and now as Senior Vice President for Evangelism and Leadership at the North American Mission Board of the SBC, I have some firsthand experience. And it is that experience that calls our "amen for the gospel" into question.

VITAL STATISTICS AND THE GOSPEL

A part of my present job is to motivate Southern Baptist churches toward faithful, effective evangelism. Since facts are our friends, I want to know where we are now. I want to know if we are effectively presenting the gospel to lost people. Are we leading them to receive Jesus Christ, and are we baptizing them as a public declaration of their newfound faith? To be honest, my research into our "gospel sharing," in contrast to our "gospel celebrating," was discouraging.

Each year Southern Baptist churches voluntarily report their vital statistics. The statistics include, among many other things:

» The total church membership
» The annual average attendance
» The total giving
» The number of baptisms for the year

Our theology of "personal salvation," "believer's baptism," and a "regenerate church membership" directs our churches to baptize only those who, as best we can discern, are truly saved by grace through faith in our Lord Jesus Christ. Which brings me to the discouraging information I discovered.

Less With More

As of 2019, just before the COVID-19 nationwide lockdown, our statistics indicated that our denomination's steady thirteen-year decline in professions of faith and baptisms had descended to a seventy year low of 235,748. Not since 1950 had Southern Baptist churches baptized so few people. The deadening danger, of course, is that we will see the facts, but then use our highly developed skills to make a slick video to spin it and explain it away, and make it sound like victory and progress.

Facts are our friends. We need to know where we are so we can repent.

Seventy years ago, Southern Baptist churches had nine million fewer members than in 2020. Seventy years ago, our churches received less than one billion dollars a year. Today they are receiving nearly thirteen billion dollars a year.[1]

I now work for a denominational entity, but I still have a pastor's perspective and use a pastor's vocabulary. It is ingrained in my DNA that we should do more with less. But these days we are doing far less with a whole bunch more.

Facts are our friends. Unless we know what we are doing, we will not know what we should do and can do. The facts compel us to wake up. An unresponsive, uninterested culture is not the problem. Our Lord Jesus said, "The harvest truly *is* great, but [here it is] the laborers *are* few." He also told us what to do about it. "Pray the Lord of the harvest to send out laborers into His harvest" (Luke 10:2), and, with Isaiah, volunteer to be part of the answer to your prayer. "Here *am* I! Send me" (Isa 6:8).

Is it possible for us to reverse this downward trend? Could we do it quickly? Yes. It is possible. Consider a simple strategy that any and every church could use.

A Simple Strategy and the Gospel

The average Sunday morning attendance in the 47,530 SBC churches is just over 5,250,000.[2] If just 1 in 10 of those people sincerely prayed, "Lord, lay some soul upon my heart and love that soul through me," and then over the next twelve months continued to pray, "God, help me to be intentional about winning this family member [friend, neighbor, or work associate] to faith in Jesus Christ," we would baptize more people in the next year than we have baptized in any year since we became a denomination in 1845. The difference-maker in this prayer is the word "intentional."

---

1. "Southern Baptists Face Largest Membership Decline in 100 Years," LifeWay Research, last modified June 4, 2020; https://lifewayresearch.com/2020/06/04/southern-baptists-face-largest-membership-decline-in-100-years/.

2. LifeWay, "Membership Decline."

Effective evangelism is seldom accidental; it must be intentional. With that in mind, I helped develop the strategy, "Who's Your One?"[3]. The goal is not to have another program. Most churches are overloaded with programs. The goal is to encourage every church member to pray for and be intentional about leading one person to faith in Jesus Christ and seeing that person obediently follow Jesus Christ in believer's baptism, in the next twelve months.

It is not enough to invite an unsaved person to visit your church "someday." Instead, take concrete action. Be intentional. Pray for the person by name daily. Spend time with the person. Share the gospel. Be a friend. Invite the friend to a specific church service on a specific day at a specific time. Be intentional.

For example, when I wrote this chapter, Percy was my "one." Every morning, on my knees, I prayed for Percy's salvation. I became his friend. I have often said that I have the spiritual gift of "hangin' out," so I exercised my gift with Percy. Along the way I looked for opportunities to share the gospel with Percy.

A few days prior to writing these lines, I sent a text to Percy. "Hey Percy," I wrote, "my last service Sunday morning is at 11:00. Janet and I want to save a seat for you on the front row. We want you to sit with us in the service and afterward we want to take you to Tuscany and feed you an Italian lunch." That is what I call being intentional.

Percy responded, "I don't know why you and Janet are caring for me like you are, but I will be there." And guess what? He was.

Percy did not trust Jesus that day, but he heard the gospel. Seeds of the Word of God were planted in his heart.[4] I'm praying that those seeds will sprout and produce fruit.

---

3. You can learn about the strategy at www.whosyourone.com.
4. Luke 8:11

Statistics show that 85% of the believers who trusted Jesus and were baptized in our churches, first attended because a friend invited them. We know, of course, that attending church does not save anyone. Jesus, and Jesus alone, saves.[5] "Nor is there salvation in any other, for there is no other name under heaven given among men by which we must be saved" (Acts 4:12). But since we are saved by grace through faith,[6] and since "faith comes by hearing, and hearing by the word of God" (Rom 10:17), could attending church play a part in one trusting Jesus? Could God use the atmosphere of joyful worshiping believers combined with Holy Spirit empowered preaching of the Word to draw people to Jesus?

An unsaved person attends an alive, Bible believing and preaching church. He sits with a friend who has been praying for him every day. He hears the congregation's joyful worship. He senses a different atmosphere among those believers. He looks around and spots someone he knows. "I didn't know he ever went to church," he says. "I haven't seen him at the liquor store or the beer joint lately. I wondered what happened to him."

His friend says, "Oh, didn't you know? He got saved. God changed his life."

He sees the believers, senses the atmosphere, and hears the Word. Soon he begins to connect the dots.

Do you think it is possible that in one of your church's worship services the Spirit of God could use the Word of God to draw a lost person to the Son of God? I not only believe that it is possible, I believe it is probable. In fact, I believe it is promised. That's why inviting my "one" to church is one of the things I am doing to try to reach him for Jesus. It is something any born again church member can do.

---

5. Jesus said to him, "I am the way, the truth, and the life. No one comes to the Father except through Me" (John 14:6). All Scripture quotations, unless otherwise noted, are from, *The Holy Bible, New King James Version* (Nashville: Thomas Nelson Publishers, 1982).

6. Ephesians 2:8–9

Impact of the Gospel

I'm a Christian today, in part, because N. W. Pridgen made me his "one." He would not let me alone until I attended church with him. After I started attending church, it was not long until I trusted Jesus. When I did, Jesus turned my world right side up. He made all things new. I got saved and I have never gotten over it.

Fast-forward about forty-seven years to my last Sunday as pastor of the First Baptist Church in Woodstock, GA. Before I preached that morning it was my privilege to baptize three people I had led to Jesus. One was a thirty-year-old young lady who is on a reality TV show. Since then, she has faithfully attended Woodstock every Sunday. The other two were a young mom and her seven-year-old boy.

Someone may ask, "Do you really think a seven-year-old understood enough to be saved?" He understood as much or more than the average forty-year-old who trusts Jesus. I asked him, "Jackson, do you know what sin is?" He said, "You mean when I lie and steal stuff?" I wish many adults I have witnessed to understood sin that well. Jackson understood exactly why he needed to be saved. I shared the gospel with him, and God did the same thing for Jackson that He did for me all those years earlier. The Spirit of God took the Word of God and led each of us to faith in the Son of God.

As I pondered the question, "Does the gospel still matter?" I thought again of what the gospel meant to me when I was lost. I was a twenty-year-old gambler, pool shark, pool hall manager, and drunk. I was from a broken home and dropped out of high school when I was sixteen. No one suspected that I had potential, but the gospel changed everything. I also thought about Jackson and those young ladies and the thousands of others with whom I have shared the gospel across the years. Without a doubt or a moment's hesitation I gladly declare, "The gospel still matters!" Through the gospel, Jesus Christ still redeems; He sets captives free. He still transforms lives.

My Mindset

For me, the gospel is not a subject for academic deliberation and debate. That is neither my mode nor mindset. For me the biblical gospel is a cause for celebration and proclamation. Of course, I recognize that statement raises a question that demands a clear answer: "What is the biblical gospel?" I am tempted to say, "The biblical gospel is the one that redeems and transforms a twenty-year-old drunk and gambler like me and seven-year-old liar and thief like Jackson." However, I know the question demands more than an experiential response; it demands a biblical and theological response.

To answer the question, "Does the Gospel Still Matter?" I will include my definition of the gospel. To do so, I want to lay an Old Testament foundation. Psalm 126 includes historical experience, theological insight, and practical application. The Psalm will guide our discussion.

Psalm 126 celebrates God's redemption from captivity. It is not hyperbole. The Psalm records a believer's Spirit-inspired worship response to actual historical events.

In expounding the Psalm, I want to be theologically faithful. I do not want to be guilty of reading the New Testament back into the Old Testament, imposing a meaning contrary to that of the original author. However, by linking Scripture with Scripture, I believe we will see that, while Psalm 126 is not a statement of the New Testament gospel, it foreshadows the results the New Testament gospel produces today. Saved people in the Old Testament shared many of the joys we experience. They too were saved by faith and lived by faith. Remember Hebrews 11?

We can allow the Psalmist to speak in his historical context, and at the same time, hear an application of truth for our context. We can join the Psalmist in celebrating God's redemption and deliverance. It states:

PSALM 126
A Joyful Return to Zion
A Song of Ascents

¹ When the LORD brought back the captivity of Zion,
We were like those who dream.
² Then our mouth was filled with laughter,
And our tongue with singing.
Then they said among the nations,
"The LORD has done great things for them."
³ The LORD has done great things for us,
And we are glad.
⁴ Bring back our captivity, O LORD,
As the streams in the South.
⁵ Those who sow in tears
Shall reap in joy.
⁶ He who continually goes forth weeping,
Bearing seed for sowing,
Shall doubtless come again with rejoicing,
Bringing his sheaves *with him.*

Several Bible versions translate the opening phrase of verse 1, "When the LORD restored the fortunes of Zion."[7] Using that translation, some, though not all, suggest the Psalm may address God's people after the Assyrian invasion during Hezekiah's reign in Jerusalem. At that time, God punished the Northern Kingdom's idolatry. The Northern Kingdom went into Assyrian captivity, never to return. The Assyrians also threatened Jerusalem,

---

7. *The Holy Bible: English Standard Version* (Wheaton, IL: Crossway Bibles, 2016), Ps 126:1a. See also the NIV, CSB, and NET bibles.

but King Hezekiah and his people humbled themselves and prayed. God miraculously protected the Southern Kingdom.[8] With that background, the Psalm praises God for deliverance from danger and adversity, rather than from captivity.

Others Bible versions translate the opening phrase, "When the LORD brought back the captivity of Zion."[9] Interpreters, following this translation, believe the Psalmist wrote after the captives returned from Babylon. I prefer that interpretation. In fact, the Psalm seems to best fit the days immediately after the first captives returned to Judah with Zerubbabel.[10] Whatever time period it reflects, one thing is certain—God set His people free.

Psalm 126 describes a saved individual's personal, spiritual reality. There is no way around it; this is a Psalm of redemption. I love this Psalm because it describes exactly what Jesus Christ did within me through the gospel. And by the way, it also describes what He does within anyone who receives Jesus Christ by faith.

The three stanzas of Psalm 126 declare an Old Testament saint's praise for God's redemption and deliverance. We will see that they also foreshadow why "The Gospel Still Matters."

Stanza 1: The Blessing of Being Saved Experienced (vv. 1-3)
Stanza 2: The Burden of Being Saved Exhibited (v. 4)
Stanza 3: The Business of Getting People Saved Enjoyed (vv. 5-6)

Today, revelation is completed. The gospel has been given. We affirm that without the biblical gospel we would not have a salvation to experience, exhibit, or enjoy.

---

8. Isaiah 36-37; cf., Jeremiah 26:18-19
9. For example, see the KJV, NKJV, NASB, NLT, and AMP.
10. Ezra 2:1-2

THE BLESSING OF BEING SAVED EXPERIENCED

Real Salvation

The first stanza describes the blessing saved people of every era experience: we receive a *real* salvation. The Psalm begins, "When the LORD brought back the captivity of Zion, we were like those who dream" (v. 1).

Historical Need

There was a historical reason for the Psalmist's obvious excitement. The captive Israelites needed redemption. Unless "the LORD brought back" the captives, or "restored the fortunes of Zion [Jerusalem]," they would have remained captives. But they did not. They were redeemed. And that is why the Psalmist praised their Redeemer.

Israel's redemption was remarkable because the Israelites were not innocent captives. Their captivity was a self-inflicted wound. It was a result of their persistent personal sins. God sent repeated prophetic warnings to the Northern Kingdom prior to the Assyrian invasion and to the Southern Kingdom prior to the Babylonian invasion. Even so, their forefathers did not repent. They were arrogant. They multiplied their idolatries.

After the Northern Kingdom was taken into captivity, never to return, God rebuked the Southern Kingdom. He said, "Samaria [capital of the N. Kingdom] did not commit half of your sins; but you have multiplied your abominations more than they and have justified your sisters by all the abominations which you have done" (Ezek 16:51). "The sin of Samaria, though not specifically stated, was her idolatry. But Jerusalem's sins were so vile that, in comparison, the sins of both ['your sisters'] **Sodom** and **Samaria** seemed almost like **righteous** deeds!"[11]

---

11. Charles H. Dyer, "Ezekiel" in John F. Walvoord & Roy B. Zuck, eds., *The Bible Knowledge Commentary: An Exposition of the Scriptures*, OT (Wheaton: Victor Books, 1985), 1258. [Emphasis in original]

Note: God is faithful to His Word. He does what He says. He fulfills His promises, whether judging rebels or redeeming the repentant.

God acted on His warning; the Babylonian horde invaded Israel. They ransacked the land and besieged the capital city. When starvation forced Jerusalem's surrender, the best of the defeated Israelites were marched away to Babylon. Captivity was Judah's lot for seventy years.[12]

As the seventy years neared completion, few captives remained who had seen the Promised Land. Most had never approached Jerusalem with their fellow pilgrims. They had not seen Solomon's temple or celebrated an annual festival. Yet, the faithful trusted God and His promises. As He had redeemed their forefathers in Egypt,[13] so He would redeem the captives in Babylon.[14] Somehow, He would move mightily. He would free them from bondage. He would open a way for their return to the Promised Land.[15]

Redemption

At this point I need to comment on Old and New Testament redemption. A clear understanding will be important as this chapter unfolds.

---

12. See Jeremiah 25:11; Daniel 9:2

13. "Therefore say to the children of Israel: 'I *am* the LORD; I will bring you out from under the burdens of the Egyptians, ... and I will <u>redeem</u> you with an outstretched arm and with great judgments'" (Ex 6:6). "For I brought you up from the land of Egypt, I <u>redeemed</u> you from the house of bondage; ... (Micah 6:4). [Emphasis added]

14. "Thus says the LORD, your <u>Redeemer</u>, the Holy One of Israel: 'For your sake I will send to Babylon, and bring them all down as fugitives—the Chaldeans, who rejoice in their ships'" (Isa 43:14). "The Lord calls Himself Israel's **Redeemer** ... He would change **the Babylonians** from conquerors to the conquered." John A. Martin, "Isaiah" in John F. Walvoord & Roy B. Zuck, eds., *The Bible Knowledge Commentary: An Exposition of the Scriptures*, OT (Wheaton: Victor Books, 1985), 1097. [Emphasis in original]

"Go forth from Babylon! Flee from the Chaldeans! With a voice of singing, declare, proclaim this, utter it to the end of the earth; say, 'The LORD has <u>redeemed</u> His servant Jacob!'" (Isa 48:20)

15. See 2 Chronicles 36:22-23; Ezra 1:1-8

The question is, are the two equivalent? Is it appropriate to compare Israel's physical rescue from Egyptian slavery and Babylonian captivity with our spiritual redemption from sin? Those are fair questions. Some who came out of Egypt and Babylon were among the faithful but were not faithful. They lived among the saved, but they were not saved. I believe David answered these questions in a prayer.

The prophet Nathan delivered the Davidic Covenant to David.[16] David responded with praise and prayer.[17] He said:

> [22] Therefore You are great, O Lord GOD. For *there is* none like You, nor *is there any* God besides You, according to all that we have heard with our ears. [23] And who *is* like Your people, like Israel, the one nation on the earth whom God went to <u>redeem</u> for Himself as a people, to make for Himself a name—and to do for Yourself great and awesome deeds for Your land—before Your people whom You <u>redeemed</u> for Yourself from Egypt, the nations, and their gods? [24] For You have made Your people Israel Your very own people forever; and You, LORD, have become their God (2 Sam 7:22-24).

In these praise verses, David celebrates four realities about his covenant-giving God. First, *the Lord is the real God* (v. 22). In other words, "Lord God, you are great and incomparable. There is no God like You. All other gods are impostors. You are the real deal. No one has ever heard of a God like You. No one could have dreamed you up if they had tried."

Second, *the Lord redeems captives* (v. 23). Two verb forms of the Hebrew word, *padah*, are used in this verse—translated "redeem" and "redeemed." It means God paid a price to set His people free from bondage.[18] In this case,

---

16. 2 Samuel 7:1-17

17. 2 Samuel 7:18-29

18. James Swanson, *Dictionary of Biblical Languages with Semantic Domains: Hebrew Old Testament*, electronic ed. (Oak Harbor: Logos Research Systems, Inc., 1997), s.v., *pā·ḏāh*. "**Redeem**, ransom, buy" i.e., to cause the freedom or release of a

David referred back to Israel's "awesome" deliverance from slavery to the Egyptians and their false gods.

Notice also, and this is important, He redeemed them "for Himself as a people." Hebrew scholar and expositor, Dale Ralph Davis, notes:

> This one clause contains both poles of redemption: redeemed from and redeemed for (or, to). When Yahweh redeemed Israel, he liberated them from bondage (Egypt) in order that they might belong to a new Master. Biblical redemption always involves both elements: liberation and possession. Yahweh revealed his power in smashing Egypt's chains but revealed his purpose in binding Israel to himself. … Yahweh grants his people freedom but not independence; they are to belong to him. Changing testaments changes nothing, for if we have been ransomed out of our "empty ways of life" by Christ's costly blood (1 Pet. 1:18-19) we are not our own, precisely because we have been bought with a price (1 Cor. 6:19b-20a).[19]

Third, *the Lord's redemption is permanent* (v. 24). "You have made Your people Israel Your very own people forever."

Fourth, *the Lord's redeemed are privileged* (v. 24). "You, LORD, have become their God." Redeemed people have a privileged, personal relationship with their redeemer. Who has ever heard of a God like this!

Would you agree with me that it is fair and biblical for a New Testament preacher to use Old Testament redemption from slavery and bondage as a picture and illustration of our redemption in Christ? I will give the final word on this subject to the Apostle Paul.

---

person from bondage or ownership, often implying a delivering or rescue of a person in distress (Ex 13:13; 2 Sa 4:9), note: in some contexts the redemption has a special focus of salvation and relationship to the LORD as a person now owned by God."

19. Dale Ralph Davis, *2 Samuel: Out of Every Adversity* (Ross-shire, Scotland: Christian Focus Publications, 1999), 85-86.

Paul said, "He has delivered us from the power of darkness and conveyed [transferred] *us* into the kingdom of the Son of His love, in whom we have redemption through His blood, the forgiveness of sins" (Col 1:13-14). I love the truth that when Jesus died on the cross, paying to the Father the redemption price for all sin—His blood—He was not a victim. He was the victor. He was on a rescue mission, and I was the captive. Jesus invaded Satan's domain of darkness and death, overpowered the warden, released my chains, and airlifted me into His kingdom of love and light. On the cross He did all that was necessary for me to repent, believe, and be set free when I was twenty years old. What a Savior!

Contemporary Need

God's promises to us are no less wonderful, no less sure. Before our salvation, like the Jews in ancient Babylon, our need was urgent. We too were in bondage, enslaved, and captives. Our captors and slave masters, though spiritual, were no less real. We were slaves of sin, Satan, and self. Jesus said, "Most assuredly, I say to you, whoever commits sin is a slave of sin" (John 8:34). To the Jews who defamed His Messianic credential, disparaged His heritage, and denied His Deity,[20] Jesus said, "You are of *your* father the devil, and the desires of your father you want to do" (John 8:44). Likewise, all who reject Jesus's person and work today become the devil's captives and do the devil's will.[21] Paul said they step into "the snare of the devil, having been taken captive by him to *do* his will" (2 Tim 2:26).

When we recognized our urgent need and understood the gospel, we turned to Jesus Christ in repentance and faith. True to His Word, He set us free. "Therefore, if the Son makes you free," Jesus said, "you shall be free indeed" (John 8:36). We trusted His substitutionary death, necessary burial

---

20. John 8:21-29, 35-43
21. Ephesians 2:1-2

(because He was really dead), and victorious resurrection to save, redeem, and justify us. When we believed the gospel[22] we received a real salvation.

Historic Surprise

Something wonderful happened to thousands of the captives in Babylon; they responded to God's Word. They rejected the popular gods in the Babylonian culture, and accepted Yahweh's diagnosis—"For My people have committed two evils: they have forsaken Me, the fountain of living waters, *and* hewn themselves cisterns—broken cisterns that can hold no water" (Jer 2:13). Finally, they responded to God's promise, "And you will seek Me and find *Me,* when you search for Me with all your heart" (Jer 29:13). Like Daniel, they repented of their personal and national sins.

> And I prayed to the LORD my God, and made confession, and said, "O Lord, great and awesome God, who keeps His covenant and mercy with those who love Him, ... we have sinned and ... done wickedly and rebelled ... We have not obeyed the voice of the LORD our God, to walk in His laws, which He set before us by His servants the prophets. ... O Lord, hear! O Lord, forgive! O Lord, listen and act! Do not delay for Your own sake, my God, for Your city and Your people are called by Your name" (Dan 9:4-5, 10, 19).

They sought God with all their hearts, and He kept His promise; they found Him. As one commentator noted:

> We may rest assured that the Jews underwent a great spiritual renewal while they were in Babylon. While there, they came to see that their captivity was due to their sins, and they undoubtedly did a thorough job of repenting.

---

22. 1 Corinthians 15:1-4

Then came the good news that they were going to be allowed to return to their homeland. The psalmist describes the torrent of joy that broke out when they received that word. He and his fellow-captives were 'like those who dream' (v. 1).[23]

Why did the Psalmist say, "We were like those who dream" (v. 1)? "Dream" is the translation of the Hebrew root word, *chalam*. It can refer to a visual prophetic dream, or to the ordinary dream one has while asleep.[24] The sentence structure and context best fit an ordinary dream. Even so, it makes a doxological point. When God supernaturally redeemed the children of Israel from captivity, the reality was so good it was almost unbelievable. It was such a surprise it hardly seemed real. It was as if they were dreaming. In other words when they were set free it seemed too good to be true.

Contemporary Surprise

So it is when Jesus Christ saves a sinner. Because of what we were before our salvation, it seems almost too good to be true.

When a person comes under Holy Spirit conviction,[25] he realizes he is not righteous. He also recognizes the consequence: judgment is coming. He knows he cannot undo his past or improve his future, yet he knows he must do something. But what? Someone is always ready with advice. The legalist says, "Keep the rules. Obey the Laws." The religionist says, "Attend the ceremonies." The moralist says, "Do better. Try harder."

The convicted sinner is desperate. She obeys and attends, tries and fails. It is not long before she is in despair; she sees her case is hopeless. And that is exactly where the Holy Spirit wants her to be. The apostle Paul said,

---

23. R. Ellsworth, *Opening up Psalms*, electronic version (Leominster: Day One Publications, 2006), 85–86.

24. James A. Strong, *Enhanced Strong's Lexicon*, electronic version (Seattle: Logos Software, 1995), s.v., *chalam*.

25. John 16:8-11

"For as many as are of the works of the law are under the curse; for it is written, *'Cursed is everyone who does not continue in all things which are written in the book of the law, to do them'*" (Gal 3:10). Paul quoted Deuteronomy 27:26 to prove that no one can be saved by human effort because the law demanded perfect obedience. "Breaking … only one command even once brings a person under the curse; and since everybody fails at some point, all are under the curse."[26] God is the King of the universe. His law is universal. Everyone is obligated to obey it, but everyone is guilty of breaking all of God's law. "For whoever shall keep the whole law, and yet stumble in one *point,* he is guilty of all" (James 2:10).

Once we are clear on the bad news, we are ready for the good news. Even though we are under the law's curse, Jesus will free us from its curse. How? "Christ has <u>redeemed</u> us from the curse of the law, having become a curse for us (for it is written, *'Cursed is everyone who hangs on a tree'*)" (Gal 3:13). Paul made this point with Deuteronomy 21:23. When Jesus Christ suffered and died on the cross, He received the law's curse in our place. He was our sinless substitute. He was punished in our place. He now forgives our sins based on His payment of our sins. "In Him [Jesus Christ] we have <u>redemption</u> through His blood, the forgiveness of sins, according to the riches of His grace" (Eph 1:7). Not only is the curse lifted and our past forgiven, our holy God declared us righteous. "Being justified freely by His grace through the <u>redemption</u> that is in Christ Jesus" (Rom 3:24).

Seems Too Good to Be True

When we awake to this reality, we cannot help but say, "Is this a dream? Did this really happen to me? I know it did, but it seems too good to be true."

---

26. Donald K. Campbell, "Galatians," in *The Bible Knowledge Commentary: An Exposition of the Scriptures,* John F. Walvoord and Roy B. Zuck, eds., (Wheaton: Victor Books, 1985), 598.

The first time I preached a revival meeting, I was twenty-three years old. I had only been saved for three years. A young man, David Philbeck, came to a service. He heard the gospel again, but this time he really heard it. He was convicted of his sin and trusted Jesus as his Savior.

David came back the next night and again responded to the invitation. He said God had called him to preach. Even I wondered if it could happen that fast. I thought, "How can a person understand God's call when he's only known the Holy Ghost for twenty-four hours?"

Every time I go to preach in a church in David's area, he greets me at the door when I walk in. Recently, I asked one of our mutual friends, "How long has David been a pastor?" "Forty-two years," he said. All I can say is, "I think it took!" It seemed too good to be true, but it was.

As far as I know, it has happened only one time in my ministry. A young lady attended our church for the first time in her life. She said she had never been to a church before, but she came with a friend. That day she heard the gospel for the first time, understood it, and received Jesus Christ. She went home excited. She told her mother, "Mama, I went to church for the first time today and Jesus Christ forgave all of my sins. I'm a changed person."

Instead of being glad, that mama was irate. She called me, and with anger in her voice said, "Are you the pastor of that church?"

"Yes ma'am."

Then she dumped her anger on me. She said, "How dare you tell my daughter she could come into your church and be a changed forever in less than two hours."

I said, "No ma'am. That's not exactly what happened. She was changed forever in about a moment."

Think about it. That seems too good to be true. It is like a dream.

Someone comes in off the street. It does not matter how she has lived in the past. She hears the gospel preached with the touch of Jesus on it. The

Spirit of God, working in communion with the Word of God, exposes, convicts, and convinces her of her sin and her need of Jesus Christ. She responds in faith and God changes her forever. It just seems too good to be true. But it is true.

The hymn, "It's Real," is precious me. Though written in 1907, it expresses my present reality.

> Oh, how well do I remember how I doubted day by day,
> For I did not know for certain that my sins were washed away;
> When the Spirit tried to tell me, I would not the truth receive;
> I endeavored to be happy, and to make myself believe....
>
> So I prayed to God in earnest, and not caring what folks said;
> I was hungry for the blessing; my poor soul, it must be fed;
> Then at last by faith I touched Him, and, like sparks from smitten steel,
> Just so quick salvation reached me, oh, bless God, I know it's real!
>
> *Refrain:*
> But it's real, it's real;
> Oh, I know it's real;
> Praise God, the doubts are settled,
> For I know, I know it's real![27]

It is a *real* salvation. We experience the blessing of being saved. It may seem too good to be true, but it is not imaginary.

"Does the gospel still matter?" Yes, it still matters. It is the only way for one to receive a real salvation. But that is not all.

---

27. Homer L. Cox, "It's Real," accessed June 21, 2021, https://library.timelesstruths.org/music/Its_Real/.

Recognizable Salvation

It is also a *recognizable* salvation. Psalm 126 continues.

[1] When the LORD brought back the captivity of Zion,
We were like those who dream.
[2] Then our mouth was filled with laughter,
And our tongue with singing.
Then they said among the nations,
"The LORD has done great things for them."
[3] The LORD has done great things for us,
And we are glad.

A *real* salvation gave the returning captives a *recognizable* salvation. Genuine joy filled their hearts, and the evidence was on their faces and in their mouths. They could not keep it inside. Their joy shinned through for all to see and hear. People commented on their "laughter" and "singing."

"They said among the nations, 'The LORD has done great things for them.'" The Hebrew word *goyim*, is translated "nations." It can mean gentiles, non-Jewish people, peoples, nations, or heathen.[28] The old King James Version translates it, "heathen." Here is the point. Even lost people acknowledged that "great things" had happened and only God could be the source. Warren Wiersbe noted, "The surrounding nations, some of whom hated Israel, were utterly astonished at this event and openly confessed that the God of Israel has done great things for them."[29]

The redeemed were quick to agree; their joy was justified. "The LORD has done great things for us," they said, "*and* we are glad" (v. 3). "The Jews

---

28. James A. Strong, *Enhanced Strong's Lexicon*, electronic version (Seattle: Logos Software, 1995), s.v. *goyim*.

29. Warren W. Wiersbe, gen. ed., *The Wiersbe Study Bible* (Nashville: Thomas Nelson, 2018), 880, n. Ps 126:2b, 3.

replied that indeed He has done great things for them, and they gave God the glory."[30]

We who are redeemed through the blood of Jesus Christ (Eph 1:7) have the very same testimony. "This ought to be the confession of every Christian and of every local church."[31] When "anyone *is* in Christ, *he is* a new creation; old things have passed away; behold, all things have become new" (2 Cor 5:17). When God makes "all things ... new" in your life, other people will notice.

A real salvation is a recognizable salvation. I certainly found that true in my life.

As I said, I dropped out of high school when I was 16. I was too shy to give an assigned oral report in one of my classes. I skipped that day and decided to go to work instead of back to school. I managed a poolroom from ages 16 to 18. I was a gambler and a pool shark, a drunk and a fighter.

I grew up with a single mom and five siblings in a government project. By making bad choices, I often made a difficult situation worse for myself and harder for my mom. I was in and out of trouble. I was arrested for stealing, arrested for fighting, and arrested for drunken driving. One day the Police arrested me off my front porch. A neighbor called in a complaint. I was bored and thought it was a good idea to drink part of a can of beer and throw the rest of it hard enough for it to burst when it hit the street. I did that with can after can. Once again, I called my mom to come to the Police Station and bail me out of jail.

The officer who arrested me was Richard Herring, the Chief of Police. He knew me because I had been in trouble regularly and also because I knew his son.

Not long after that, God sent the Sherriff from heaven to arrest my soul. I repented of my sin and trusted Jesus Christ to save me. Without me trying, He changed my life in ways that I could not have changed if I had

---

30. Wiersbe, *Wiersbe Study Bible, 3.*
31. Wiersbe, *Wiersbe Study Bible, 3.*

tried. He changed me from the inside out and turned my upside-down world right side up.

Word spread across the town, "Something has happened to Johnny Hunt." I quit going to the poolroom to gamble, but I did go back to tell the owner what Jesus had done for me. When I shared the gospel with him, he too trusted Jesus. He sold the Pool Hall, bought a Tom's Peanut truck, and started selling peanuts.

One day I got a call that Richard Herring, the Chief of Police, had a massive heart attack. The caller said, "He's in CCU at the hospital and he's calling for you."

When I went into his room, he said, "I may not make it through this, and I thought you might be able to help me. Son, I've never seen anyone change like you have. Can you tell me what happened to you?"

That day I was able to get the Chief of Police, who used to arrest me, arrested by the Sherriff from heaven. I told him how to plead guilty and throw himself on the mercy of the court. I shared the gospel with him and led him to Jesus; he repented of his sins and received Jesus. Christ redeemed him just like He had redeemed me.

When God saves any man, woman, boy, or girl, that person is a new creation in Christ. Old things start passing away and all things become new.

J. C. Bullard was the Pool Hall owner. His son was my best friend. After I was saved, we did not see one another for a few weeks. One day he dropped by my apartment. "What happened to you?" he said. "You haven't been down at the Pool Hall. You've missed playing in some tournaments. You haven't even been there to hustle anyone. People are looking for you. They want to gamble with you. Where have you been?"

"Ronald, I got saved!"

"O yeah," he said. "I've been saved too."

I was bold back then. I said, "No you haven't. You ain't got what I got. You've never been saved."

Why did I say such a thing? How could I know whether or not Ronald was saved? Was I being judgmental? No. I was calling it like it was. I knew he was not saved because there was no change in his life. He lived just like I had lived all of my life. There was no God factor in Ronald's life.

Not long after that he recognized the truth and he was saved. That time he got a real, recognizable salvation. He is still walking with Jesus today. We are still friends, and not long ago he went to Israel with me. We can laugh about it now. He was not saved, and he is glad he learned the truth.

The Psalmist said, "Then our mouth was filled with laughter, and our tongue with singing. Then they said among the nations, 'The LORD has done great things for them'" (Ps 126:2). Even lost people can tell when a person has a *real* salvation. It is *recognizable*. And the saved declare, "The LORD has done great things for us, *and* we are glad" (v. 3). The redeemed are not ashamed;[32] they rejoice and give all the glory to God.

THE BURDEN OF BEING SAVED EXHIBITED

A noteworthy emotional shift is in the second stanza. The Psalmist leads us from praise to prayer. "Bring back our captivity, O LORD, as the streams in the South" (Ps 126:4).

What?

What does this prayer mean? As you might expect, commentators emphasize various viewpoints. Notice the similar introductory phrases in each stanza. "When the LORD brought back the captivity of Zion," (v. 1) ... "Bring back our captivity, O LORD" (v. 4). Why did the Psalmist ask God to do what He had already done?

---

32. Romans 1:16

Some suggest that several years had passed since the captives returned, possibly several decades. The Psalmist remembered their previous ecstatic joy. They laughed and sang when they were first redeemed from captivity (vv. 1–3). As reflected in the prophecies of Haggai and Malachi, their joy and fervent faithfulness had waned. Now they were not "as close to God as they had been when they were released from captivity. No, they hadn't gone back to the worship of idols (the captivity broke them of that once and for all), but they had somehow or other become complacent about the things of the Lord."[33] The Psalmist, therefore, asked the Lord to revive and renew their joy.

Others note the emotional shift among the redeemed. In verse 2 they are glad; in verse 4 they are sad, but it was not because of a spiritual drift. What happened? It was God's work; He changed the redeemed from glad to sad. He gave them the joy of their salvation from captivity, and He added a burden for those still in captivity.

Our Great Need—A Burden

I am convinced a burden for the lost is one of the greatest needs of Southern Baptists. Somewhere along the way many of us have lost God's burden to win our own family and friends to Jesus. The Psalmist had not. His burden inspired his prayer. "Bring back our captivity, O LORD, as the streams in the South" (Ps 126:4).

Sometimes we sing a song that says Jesus did not want heaven without us. I think we need to change that theology. We need to ask God to so burden our hearts that we do not want heaven without our family members and friends. We used to speak of the family circle not being broken in heaven. That is the burden saved people can exhibit.

---

33. Roger Ellsworth, *Opening up Psalms*, elec. ed. (Leominster: Day One Publications, 2006), 87.

I believe Jeremiah 24-29 records the historical background of Psalm 126. Jeremiah prophesied the Babylonian invasion and captivity. He also prophesied the return from captivity after seventy years. When the seventy years passed, God finally set His people free. They did not all come out at once, but several thousand at a time.

Those who happily resettled Israel began to think about the ones they left behind. "Mama didn't get out. Daddy didn't get out. I'm glad I'm out, but my brothers and sisters are still there. And what about the neighbors? They're all still in bondage."

And so their burden grew. They began to pray and weep, "Bring back our captivity, O LORD, as the streams in the South."

This is a Hebrew prayer. The Psalmist prayed in faith, "O LORD, bring the rest of them back." Calvin observed, "All the Jews, no doubt, had a door opened to them, and perfect liberty granted them, to come out of the land of their captivity, but the number of those who partook of this benefit was small when compared with the vast multitude of the people."[34] So they prayed, "Let those that remain in Babylon have their hearts stirred up, as ours were, to take the benefit of the liberty granted."[35] In other words, "Lord, give them the holy 'want to'."

That prayer is consistent with the generous invitation in the final chapter of the Bible. Jesus gives the invitation[36] in the power of the Holy Spirit through His bride, the church. "And the Spirit and the bride say, 'Come!' And let him who hears say, 'Come!' And let him who thirsts come. Whoever desires, let him take the water of life freely" (Rev 22:17). The "water of life" is "freely" offered to anyone who wants it.

---

34. John Calvin, *Commentary on the Book of Psalms* in *Calvin's Commentaries*, vol. 5, elec. ed., James Anderson and John King, trans. (Bellingham, WA: Logos Bible Software, 2010), 99.

35. Matthew Henry, *Matthew Henry's Commentary On The Whole Bible*, vol. 3 (Old Tappan, NJ: Fleming H. Revell Co., n.d.), 733.

36. Revelation 22:16

Certainly it means that, but I believe it has a further connotation. It also expresses the burden, "God, if you won't send the rest of my family out, send me back. I don't want freedom without them." That is a radical prayer. No doubt the return would be a rescue mission. But is it a valid biblical idea? Do any other Bible passages affirm such a burden?

Consider Exodus 32. Moses had been on Mount Sinai for 40 days.[37] When he came down, stone tablets in hand,[38] he found that Aaron had made a golden calf and a wild calf-god worship dance was under way. God declared that He would destroy the people of Israel and use Moses's descendants to build a new and greater nation. Moses, however, interceded for his rebellious people. "Then Moses returned to the LORD and said, 'Oh, these people have committed a great sin, and have made for themselves a god of gold! Yet now, if You will forgive their sin—but if not, I pray, blot me out of Your book which You have written'" (Ex 32:31-32). Moses acknowledged and confessed their sin.

> It is instructive that Moses did not try to minimize the people's sin in the process of trying to gain forgiveness of it. Biblically, confession of sin (being entirely honest with God in stating its nature and extent) is part of true repentance; the person who understates his sin is not really demonstrating repentance to God.[39]

Moses understood the seriousness of sin and the urgency of forgiveness. Commentators differ on Moses's exact meaning in verse 32. I believe he was saying, "Forgive them Lord. If it costs my life for You to forgive them, then take me." Could it be that Moses was offering his own life if it would make "atonement" (v. 30) for the sins of his people?

---

37. Exodus 24:18

38. Exodus 31:18; 32:15-16

39. Douglas K. Stuart, *Exodus*, in *The New American Commentary*, vol. 2, E. Ray Clendenen and Kenneth A. Matthews, eds. (Nashville: Broadman & Holman Publishers, 2006), 684.

That is an Old Testament testimony. Is a similar concept in the New Testament?

Consider the apostle Paul's burden. He said, "For I could wish that I myself were accursed from Christ for my brethren [my relatives], my countrymen according to the flesh" (Rom 9:3). The word translated "accursed" is *anathema*, meaning "estrangement from Christ and His salvation. The word does not denote punishment intended as discipline [to correct] but being given over or devoted to divine condemnation."[40] A. T. Robinson said it means, "doomed to destruction."[41] I think the best translation is, "I could wish myself damned."

Paul was not speaking flippantly. This was no pious, off the cuff comment. He spoke out of a deep, passionate burden. His deadly serious offer was, "If it will bring my kinfolks and countrymen to faith in Jesus Christ, send me to eternal hell in their place."

There was a day, not so long ago, when men and women cried out to God at the church altar, "Lord, do whatever it takes to win my son. If You need to take me to rattle him, wake him up, and make him think of eternity, take me home early. Lord, my son needs You. Whatever it takes, please save him; don't let him go to hell."

Of course, we know that no prophet, preacher, or parent is an acceptable sacrifice for a soul. People, no matter how good their lives, die because of their own sins.[42] Only the sinless God-man could make a sufficient sacrifice for any person, let alone for the sins of the world.

The apostle Paul certainly understood that. So why was he so dramatic? Why did he say, "I am willing to be damned for my folks?" I think John MacArthur states it well: "Although Paul understood the exchange he was suggesting was impossible (8:38, 39; John 10:28), it was still the sincere

---

40. Spiros Zodhiates, *The Complete Word Study Dictionary: New Testament*, electronic ed. (Chattanooga, TN: AMG Publishers, 2000), s.v., "ἀνάθεμα, *anáthema*."

41. Archibald T. Robertson, *The Epistles of Paul* in *Word Pictures in the New Testament*, vol. 4 (Nashville: Broadman Press, 1931), 167, 380.

42. Genesis 3:17-19

expression of his deep love for his fellow Jews (cf. Ex. 32:32)."[43] He experienced the burden of salvation.

Again, I will only speak for my own denomination. If Southern Baptists would get that kind of burden for our unredeemed family and friends, our professions of faith and baptisms would not continue to decline. They would skyrocket. We would lead more people to genuine faith in Jesus Christ than ever before.

Distractions Destroy a Burden

Unfortunately, we are more distracted than ever before. For example, I often hear Christian leaders talk about so called "gospel issues." These days, nearly every issue is identified as a gospel issue. For the sake of clarity, consider a few examples. I have heard social justice, race relations, bigotry, white supremacy, poverty, hunger, immigration, adoption, women's rights, the church's attitude toward the LGBTQ+ community, and preferred pronouns all identified as "gospel issues." And that is only a sampling. Whether the speaker is pro or con, on the woke, open, and affirming side of the issue, or resistant to a social issue, we are urgently exhorted to get our churches involved in various "gospel issues." In other words, it is a gospel requirement. Your attempt to share the gospel cannot be effective if you are insensitive to their "gospel issue."

Whether intended or not, when Christian leaders continually repeat the "gospel issue" mantra, it is not long until the "issue" is viewed as a "vital element" of the gospel. When that happens, the content of the gospel is changed, and the gospel is confused and corrupted. Soon afterward the "issue" simply replaces the gospel. If you do not believe it, check the scrapheap of history for the mainline denominations that embraced the "social gospel" in the early to mid-1900s. They all claimed they were making Christianity relevant to "modern minds." But that was not the first time it happened.

---

43. John MacArthur, *The MacArthur Study Bible* (Nashville: Word Publishing, 1997), 1709-10, n. Rom 9:3.

Gospel Corruption

The apostle Paul wrote an urgent letter to be circulated among the churches he planted in the Galatia region. It defended the gospel of grace and the believer's liberty in Christ.

After Paul completed his first missionary journey, which included church planting in cities of the South Galatia region, he and Barnabas returned to their home church in Antioch.[44] Soon, some Judaizers arrived in Galatia. They falsely claimed to represent James,[45] the apostles, and the church in Jerusalem. These men defamed Paul's ministry and teaching, charging that Paul was a false apostle with a faulty gospel. "We've come with an urgent warning," they said. "Paul came here preaching an inadequate and incomplete gospel. His anti-Semitic prejudices caused him to delete vital elements from the true gospel. To be a truly saved and fully spiritual Christian," they warned, "one must not only receive Jesus Christ, but also convert to Judaism, faithfully obey the Laws of Moses, including circumcision, and obey the rabbinic regulations." Unfortunately, many of the gentiles were deceived. They believed and began propagating this supplemented, corrupted gospel.

Paul was shocked and amazed when he heard the news. He said:

> [6] I marvel that you are turning away so soon from Him who called you in the grace of Christ, to a different gospel, [7] which is not another [gospel "of the same kind"[46]]; but there are some who trouble you and want to pervert the gospel of Christ. [8] But even if we, or an

---

44. After Rome, Italy, and Alexandria, Egypt, Antioch was the third largest city in the Roman Empire. It was located on the Orontes River, 20 miles inland from the Mediterranean coast in ancient Syria, and approximately 300 miles north of Jerusalem. See, Trent C. Butler, gen. ed., *Holman Bible Dictionary* (Nashville: Holman Bible Publishers, 1991), s.v., "Antioch." Antioch was the first predominately gentile church in the Christian era. See, MacArthur, 1791, n. Gal 2:11.

45. James was Jesus's half brother, and Acts gives the impression that he was the Pastor of the Jerusalem church.

46. Zodhiates, *Word Study Dictionary*, s.v., "ἄλλος, *állos*."

angel from heaven, preach any other gospel to you than what we have preached to you, let him be accursed. [9] As we have said before, so now I say again, if anyone preaches any other gospel to you than what you have received, let him be accursed (Gal 1:6-9).

The door to salvation is not Jesus plus Judaism, or Jesus plus any "gospel issue" one may name. Jesus said, "I am the door. If anyone enters by Me, he will be saved" (John 10:9).

The inspired apostle's rebuke was certain and severe. He said:

[1] O foolish Galatians! Who has bewitched you that you should not obey the truth, before whose eyes Jesus Christ was clearly portrayed among you as crucified? [2] This only I want to learn from you: Did you receive the Spirit by the works of the law, or by the hearing of faith? [3] Are you so foolish? Having begun in the Spirit, are you now being made perfect by the flesh? (Gal 3:1-3)

Any addition to the gospel adds works, cancels grace, and must not be taken lightly. Whether it is conscious or unconscious, those who add to the gospel corrupt and cancel the gospel. In doing so they bring themselves under Paul's scathing rebuke.

Some reader may think, "That feels harsh and offensive. You're splitting hairs. You're overly critical and judgmental. Remember, Jesus said, 'Judge not, that you be not judged.'[47]" If so, consider how Paul responded to Peter, a fellow apostle and close friend, when Peter cozied up to some Judaizers.

It happened while Paul was back in Antioch. Peter visited Paul and Barnabas's home church. The gentiles as well as the Jews welcomed him. He was an honored guest. How thrilling to hear Peter's firsthand, eyewitness accounts of what Jesus did and said throughout His three-year earthly min-

---

47. Matthew 7:1

istry. Peter was one of the three inner circle Apostles. He, along with James and John, saw and heard a few things even the other Apostle did not.[48] Further, as an Apostle, Peter had Holy Spirit-enabled recall and interpretation of the events.[49] Can you imagine how exciting it would be to hear Peter preach at your church?

Peter enjoyed preaching to this largely gentile congregation. He also enjoyed their food and fellowship. God had directly revealed to Peter that He does not favor Jews over gentiles. He accepts both in Christ. God loves the gentile and the Jew. Jesus died for both, equally. In Christ, believers are free from Old Testament separations and dietary restrictions.[50] One can enjoy table fellowship over gentile food with a holy, happy, and thankful heart. Jew and gentile fellowship does not grieve the Spirit; it delights the Spirit.[51]

Peter regularly ate with the gentiles. He learned to appreciate many of their foods. I suspect he was delighted to discover ham and bacon and shrimp and catfish. He probably took seconds. He, and likely his wife as well,[52] enjoyed living and loving and laughing in the homes of these wonderful gentile believers. That is, until some Jewish legalists from the Jerusalem church visited a service.

The Jerusalem Jews socially distanced themselves from the gentiles during the service and refused to partake of the fellowship meal afterward. They joined the congregation in the fellowship hall (whatever the ancient Syrian version was) but refused to mingle with the gentiles.

I can imagine the unfolding events in light of a present-day church dinner where every family brings a favorite dish or two to share. A line of tables filled with tasty, fresh dishes is in the center of the room. People move

---

48. The Transfiguration for example (Matt 17:1-2; cf., 1 Pt 1:17-18)
49. Note our Lord Jesus's promise to the Apostles in John 14:25-26.
50. Acts 10:28, 34-36; 11:2-4; note the broader context (Acts 10:1-11:18)
51. Ephesians 3:4-6
52. 1 Corinthians 9:5

down both sides of the tables, plates in hand, filling their plates and chatting as they go. It is a joyful, friendly, and festive atmosphere as people move from the buffet line to empty spaces at other tables. That day in Antioch there was the Syrian version of a church dinner.

The men from Jerusalem found the non-kosher dishes disgusting. Can you see them claiming a corner table and moving it as far from the gentile believers as possible?

At the same time, Peter, Paul, and Barnabas are oblivious. They proceed as usual, caught up in the ministry and fellowship. Peter and his wife enter the buffet line, plates in hand. They laugh at a gentile deacon's joke and greet those coming to shake their hands and thank Peter for his powerful message. Several times, Peter steps out of the line to pray with a family or an individual. Finally, back in line, Peter begins dipping food onto his plate. The fork from the ham platter is in his hand when his wife whispers, "Someone's staring a hole through you."

Peter was suddenly aware of the Jerusalem guests. They had slipped his mind. He looked over to see them glaring at him in shock. He realized how the situation looked to them and was immediately reverted to his life-long "kosher-conscience."[53] He abandoned his partially filled plate with the gentile food, and joined the Jews.

Peter's actions communicated volumes to the gentiles. Perhaps he suggested they send someone to the Jewish Deli around the corner for kosher food. When he ate with the separated Jews, rejected the gentile food, and convinced other Jews, including Paul's missionary partner, Barnabas, to join them, it indicated he had withdrawn his fellowship from the gentiles. They understood and were justly confused.

---

53. Acts 10:10-16, 28

Gospel Corruption Corrected

Paul recognized the heart of the problem immediately. It was far more than a food and fellowship choice. It was a devastating spiritual choice. Peter made a withering attack on the biblical gospel. Paul explained:

> [11] Now when Peter had come to Antioch, I withstood him to his face, because he was to be blamed; [12] for before certain men came from James, he would eat with the Gentiles; but when they came, he withdrew and separated himself, fearing those who were of the circumcision. [13] And the rest of the Jews also played the hypocrite with him, so that even Barnabas was carried away with their hypocrisy. [14] But when I saw that they were not straightforward about the truth of the gospel, I said to Peter before *them* all, "If you, being a Jew, live in the manner of Gentiles and not as the Jews, why do you compel Gentiles to live as Jews? (Gal 2:11-14)

Paul refused to tolerate favoritism based on race. He publicly rebuked Peter. Notice, however, that social justice was not his concern; "the truth of the gospel" was. Peter was acting as if the Judaizers were correct. He was acting as if Jewish dietary laws were a vital element of the gospel. The problem was not that he was offending the gentiles' feelings. The problem was that Peter was inadvertently adding to the gospel and thereby corrupting the gospel. Such must not be tolerated in the ancient Antioch church or in any present-day Bible believing church.

The Biblical Gospel

So, what is the gospel we must neither add to nor take away from? A few years ago, as Easter Sunday approached, I began to think: "If I were a defense attorney and a judge called me before his court to give a defense of the gospel, what would I say? How would I define the gospel?" In the two weeks leading up to that Easter Sunday, I again studied 1 Corinthians 15. The Apostle Paul opened the chapter with a summary of the gospel message. He said, "I declare to you the gospel which I preached to you." In other words, "Here is what you heard me say when I preached the gospel in your church." That sounds clear to me; it sounds like his definition of the gospel. We will be safe to stick with the definition the Holy Spirit inspired Paul to write, neither adding to nor subtracting from the biblical gospel. He said:

> [1] Moreover, brethren, I declare to you the gospel which I preached to you, which also you received and in which you stand, [2] by which also you are saved, if you hold fast that word which I preached to you—unless you believed in vain.
>
> [3] For I delivered to you first of all that which I also received: that Christ died for our sins according to the Scriptures, [4] and that He was buried, and that He rose again the third day according to the Scriptures (1 Cor 15:1-4).

The gospel was the message Paul preached everywhere he went (v. 1). The gospel is absolute truth. It is cross-cultural. He did not adjust the content from city to city or from year to year. The gospel saved him when he believed and he knew it would save anyone who believes, anywhere at any time.

The gospel alone answers the primary, though often unrecognized, longing in every human soul. "How can I be freed from my sin and made right with God?" Paul did not answer the question with good works and law keeping, but with the gospel. The biblical gospel message has three non-negotiable elements. They are:

1. "Christ died for our sins" (v. 3).
2. "He was buried" (v. 4).
3. "He rose again the third day" (v. 4).

And He did it all "according to the Scriptures" (vv. 3-4). Consider these three vital, non-negotiable elements of the gospel.

First, "Christ died for our sins" (v. 3). Why? "All have sinned" (Rom 3:23) and rebelled against the righteous, sinless, holy God. Because "the wages of sin is death" (Rom 6:23), we earned "death"—eternal separation from God. Jesus, however, died on the cross receiving the punishment for all our sins. He died in our place. "For Christ also suffered once for sins, the just for the unjust, that He might bring us to God, being put to death in the flesh ..." (1 Pt 3:18). He, the sinless One, pleased the Father when He accepted the punishment for the sinful ones.[54] Christ died for our sins.

Second, "He was buried" (v. 4). Why is that important? Only dead people are buried. Jesus was actually dead.

The "Swoon Theory" is one of the naturalistic denials of Jesus Christ's resurrection. H. E. G. Paulus proposed the theory in his 1828 book, *The Life of Jesus*. The theory goes further than denying the literal bodily resurrection; it denies His death on the cross. It claimed that Jesus passed out on the cross and revived in the cool of the tomb.[55]

The fatal flaws in the Swoon Theory are many. It assumes that though Jesus was mortally injured from having been scourged, crucified, and pierced, He unwrapped Himself, carefully placed and arranged the burial clothes back on the slab, pushed the massive stone out of the way, and escaped, unnoticed by the guards. This, of course, is a physical impossibility.

Here are the facts. Experienced Roman soldiers scourged and crucified Jesus. They made sure He was dead. Pilate was surprised to hear that Jesus was already dead. That is why he double-checked with the Roman Centurion to be sure before releasing His body to His friends.[56] They removed Him from the cross, wrapped Him in strips of burial clothes, and placed Him in

---

54. Isaiah 53:10-11

55. Normal L. Geisler, "Swoon Theory," in *Baker Encyclopedia of Christian Apologetics* (Grand Rapids: Baker Books, 1999), 713.

56. Mark 15:42-47; John 19:31-42

the nearby newly hewn tomb. Jesus was buried because He was dead without a doubt. Christ died for our sins and was buried.

Third, "He rose again the third day" (v. 4). "For Christ also suffered … being put to death in the flesh but made alive by the Spirit" (1 Pt 3:18).

The first resurrection denial was hatched the very day Christ Jesus walked out of the tomb. The Jewish leaders bribed the tomb guards to say His disciples stole His body while they slept.[57] But since when do we accept testimonies from people who were asleep when it happened? On the contrary, Paul said Jesus Christ physically rose from the dead and His resurrection proves His Deity—the Son of God was God in the flesh.[58] His sacrifice, therefore, was sufficient to forgive, cleanse, and transform anyone who will believe the gospel and receive Jesus Christ through faith.

The gospel is the death, burial, and resurrection of Jesus Christ. The gospel plus Judaism, the gospel plus baptism, the gospel plus church membership, or the gospel plus your pet "gospel issue," are all corrupted, false gospels.

How?

Return to the prayer in Psalm 126:4. We have noted *what* the Psalmist asked the Lord to do: "Bring back our captivity, O LORD." Further, he expressed *how* he wanted the Lord to do it: "As the streams in the South."

I have had the privilege of visiting Israel on numerous occasions. I am grateful; I love visiting that wonderful, historic land. It rains some in Jerusalem, averaging 21.9 inches per year. In contrast, it seldom rains in the Negev, the southern desert region. It averages only .9 inches per year.[59] How then could there be "streams in the South"? What did the Psalmist mean?

---

57. Matthew 28:11-15

58. Romans 1:3-4

59. See, "Climate - Israel," Climates to Travel, accessed August 17, 2021, https://www.climatestotravel.com/climate/israel.

As you know, one always ascends to Jerusalem. Its elevation, 2,556 feet,[60] is higher than the surrounding region. When a heavy rain falls on Jerusalem, the water flows down the mountain. At times the dry steam beds in the South are filled and over-flowing. Tour buses have been forced off the road by the floodwaters of the southern desert streams.

The Psalmist, therefore, prayed, "Lord we want to see Israel's redeemed captives returning, not in a trickle but like a surging flood. We don't ask for mercy drops. We ask that 'the highways from the east would be full of returning captives.'"[61]

The Psalmist prayer is an illustration of the burden believers can have for lost people. We long for floods of people coming to genuine faith in Jesus Christ. "O Lord, send a surge of convicted sinners flooding to Jesus Christ for salvation."

Does the gospel still matter? Yes. Only through a faith response to the Biblical gospel can a New Testament believer, like the Psalmist, experience the blessing of being saved (vv. 1-3) and exhibit the burden of being saved (v. 4).

THE BUSINESS OF GETTING PEOPLE SAVED ENJOYED

Finally, we turn our focus to enjoying the business of getting people saved. The third stanza of Psalm 126 states:

---

60. See "Elevation of Jerusalem, Israel," Worldwide Elevation Map Finder, accessed August 17, 2021, https://elevation.maplogs.com/poi/jerusalem_israel.14646.html.

61. Allen P. Ross, "*Psalms*," in *The Bible Knowledge Commentary: An Exposition of the Scriptures*, John F. Walvoord and Roy B. Zuck, eds., (Wheaton: Victor Books, 1985), 885.

⁵ Those who sow in tears shall reap in joy.

⁶ He who continually goes forth weeping, bearing seed for sowing,

Shall doubtless come again with rejoicing,

Bringing his sheaves *with him.*

Sowing, Weeping, Reaping

Do you see the promise in the third stanza? It is simply stated in verse 5; it is beautifully and poetically expanded in verse 6. "Those [plural] who sow in tears" (v. 5), and "He [singular] who continually goes forth weeping, bearing seed for sowing" (v. 6), will celebrate the promised harvest—"sheaves"—bundles of harvested grain. Why the change from plural to singular? Spurgeon suggested, "The general assurance is applied to each one in particular."[62] The promised results are certain for you as well as for me. That is encouraging. Sowers "shall reap in joy" (v. 5), and every sower "shall doubtless come again with rejoicing" (v. 6).

Note, however, that the promised results are not automatic. There are two requirements for a successful harvester.

First, one must believe the promise enough to sow the seed. I wrote in my journal, "A seed in the basket will not produce a harvest." Wishful thinking without intentional action will not get results.

Second, one must be burdened enough to "sow in tears … weeping." No reaping without sowing; no triumph without tears. "Winners of souls must first be weepers for souls."[63]

The connection between the three stanzas is clear. The joy, laughter, and singing of the redeemed in Stanza 1, becomes joyful reaping in Stanza 3. How did the redeemed progress from one type of joy to the other? Stanza

---

62. Charles Haddon Spurgeon, *The Treasury of David*, vol. 3, Part 2, Ps. 120-150 (McLean, VA: MacDonald Publishing Co., n.d.), 70.

63. Spurgeon, *Treasury of David.*

2 is the connecting link. Redeemed captives (v. 1) express their God-given burden in prayer (v. 4). The burden inspires tearful sowing and results in joyful reaping.

"The setting in verses 5–6 is agricultural."[64] When the first remnant of returning captives arrived in Israel, the land had lain fallow for seventy years (2 Chron 36:10-21). It "had been neglected for so long, it was almost impossible to work it."[65] Planting was difficult, but persistence paid off. "The sowing with **tears** (i.e., agonizing over the work)"[66] doubtless produced a harvest. Reports sent back to Babylon that the land was becoming productive again encouraged people to "respond to the Lord and return to the land. The joyful harvesting … would then refer to other people who returned to the land in faith. The psalmist was convinced that continued labor, no matter how agonizingly difficult and frustrating, would result in more people returning to the land of Israel."[67]

The Seed

Jesus told a parable to a curious, gathered, "great multitude" (Luke 8:4). His story was about a sower whose seed fell on different kinds of soil and produced different kinds of results. Later, Jesus's disciples asked Him, "What does this parable mean?" (Luke 8:9). To answer their question, the first thing Jesus said was, "The seed is the word of God" (v. 11).

The Sower

A sower began his work with a large leather or cloth pouch filled with seeds. He hung the pouch around his neck and over a shoulder. As he walked back and forth across the plowed field, he repeatedly reached into his

---

64. Ross, "*Psalms*," 885.
65. Ross, "*Psalms*," 885.
66. Ross, "*Psalms*," 885.
67. Ross, "*Psalms*," 885.

bag, scooped up a handful of seeds, and broadcast them over the field. His job was not to walk around the field with a full pouch of seeds. His job was to sow. Without sowing there cannot be a harvest.

Sharing the Word

According to Jesus, sowing is a picture of preaching and sharing the Word. When I or anyone else preaches, we are scattering the seed of God's Word.

In the parable, Jesus also talked about different kinds of soil that produce different kinds of results. Likewise, different people respond in different ways to God's Word. The preacher or witness cannot control the response; that is up to God and the person who hears the Word. Our job is to be seed sowers, not soil assessors. Of course, I am not suggesting we are indifferent about the harvest. We "sow in tears." We care about the response, but we cannot control the response.

Isaiah's reminder encourages me in this context. God said:

> For as the rain comes down, and the snow from heaven, …
> That it may give seed to the sower …
> So shall My word be that goes forth from My mouth;
> It shall not return to Me void,[68]
> But it shall accomplish what I please,
> And it shall prosper *in the thing* for which I sent it (Isa 55:10-11).

The seed sower will be fruitful. It is God's promise.

Sowers are fruitful because we have a *God-given program*. We are to go forth "bearing precious seed" (Ps 126:6 KJV). We go with the gospel. "Go" is an action word. "Forth" implies leaving something behind. God's program requires that we be intentional; when necessary, we are willing to change our schedules. It suggests a set purpose and an active worker.

---

68. NKJV marginal note: "empty, without fruit."

Sowers are fruitful because we have a *God-given passion*. We can go "forth weeping, bearing seed for sowing." The reason for a lack of soul-winners is a lack of passion. The winners of souls are first weepers for souls. A witness's earnest tears nurture a hearer's repentant tears. Our Lord Jesus is our ultimate example.

The shortest verse in the English Bible is "Jesus wept." The Bible records three times that Jesus wept. First, He wept over Lazarus (John 11:35), therefore He wept over an individual. Jesus cares about you and each person who is on your heart. Second, He wept over Jerusalem, the capital city of Israel (Luke 19:41-44), therefore He wept over a city and a nation. Jesus cares about your community, city, and country. Third, on the cross Jesus wept "vehement cries and tears" (Heb 5:7; cf., Ps 22:1-2, 24; Matt 27:46) as He endured God's wrath and paid the penalty for the sins of the world. Therefore, He wept over humanity, He wept over the horror of our sins against the Father, and He did everything necessary to save anyone who will believe. Jesus's tears are a holy reminder of why the gospel is good news and why the gospel still matters.

We can have a God-given passion for sharing the gospel today. A program without a passion will produce dreams but no streams. You will think of what God can do, but you will not see a harvest until you sow the Word and water it with your tears.

Further, sowers are fruitful because we have *God-given power*. The "precious seed" (KJV) produces precious fruit. The seed is precious. The seed is pure. The seed is productive. The seed is powerful; there is life in a seed.

Have you ever had a new concrete sidewalk or driveway at your house? If skilled workers poured it, it is beautiful, bright, and looks impenetrable. Yet, time passes and one day you notice a blade of grass growing up through that concrete. How is that possible?

I am practical. I have taken a piece of concrete in one hand and blade of grass in the other and tried to poke that blade of grass through the concrete. It did not work. It cannot be done. So how does a blade of grass do it?

A seed germinates beneath your sidewalk and sends a blade of grass in search of sunlight. Somehow in the process, it breaks through the concrete. It does what seems impossible, and that is an illustration of the power in God's Word. God said, "*Is* not My word like ... a hammer *that* breaks the rock in pieces?" (Jer 23:29); "Therefore ... receive with meekness the implanted word, which is able to save your souls" (James 1:21). Because of the God-given power in His Word, there is hope for everyone. His Word can break through the hardest, stoniest heart. "I will give you a new heart and put a new spirit within you; I will take the heart of stone out of your flesh and give you a heart of flesh" (Ezek 36:26).

We hear people say, "You don't know my dad. When he's drunk, which is most of the time, he's as mean as a snake. It would take a miracle for my dad to get saved."

It takes a miracle for anyone to be saved. God does the miracle by His Spirit through the power of His Word. The Spirit of God takes the Word of God and leads us to faith in the Son of God. He convicts, converts, and transforms. He redeems and forgives, regenerates and justifies. And He does it all for anyone and everyone who repents and receives Jesus Christ by grace through faith.

Finally, sowers are fruitful because we have a *God-given promise.* "Those who sow in tears shall reap in joy ... [and] shall doubtless come again with rejoicing, bringing his sheaves *with him.*" It is a certain and sure promise. "Sheaves" refers to a bundle of stalks of harvested grain, tied around the middle to hold it together. Do you see the promise? If you continue to sow you will continue to reap, and before long you will gather an abundant harvest.

CONCLUSION

When I became the pastor of First Baptist Church, Woodstock, Georgia, the average Sunday morning attendance was one hundred and eighty. They called me from what was then the fastest growing Southern Baptist church in South Carolina. It was three times larger than Woodstock. I did not want to leave my church. I was happy in my home state, but my wife and I knew God wanted us to go.

In those early days, things did not go well. Woodstock was a divided church. They had been through serious conflict. The church had fired the previous pastor and music director. Some of the people gave me a hard time too. I developed the habit of journaling my thoughts and found that writing them helped me remember them as well as gain perspective on them.

One of the things I noted in my journal in those days was that pastor-friends began calling me on Monday mornings. "How's it going Bro. Johnny? Some of my people work with some of yours. I hear you've been having a tough time at business meetings. Just want you to know I'm praying for you."

It was tough, but I did the thing I knew God had called me to do. I kept on sowing, broadcasting the gospel seeds, because I knew the Gospel mattered. I knew I had a God-given *program*, a God-given *passion*, a God-given *power*, and a God-given *promise*. I trusted God to send the harvest when it was ripe. I sowed and looked forward to the day when I would reap with joy, bringing in the sheaves.

"Hey Bro. Johnny. How'd it go yesterday?"

"Man, pray for us. God's beginning to move." I had learned a little saying:

Keep on praying till light breaks through.

The Lord will answer; He'll answer you.

He'll keep His promise, for His Word is true.

Keep on praying till light breaks through.

"We're seeing some light. We had three saved."

"Well, praise the Lord."

The next week, "How'd it go Bro. Johnny? I'm praying for you."

"Man, I've never seen anything like it! Twenty-seven were saved."

After that, the calls stopped. I wrote in my journal, "It's easier to find people to sympathize with you in your sorrows than to rejoice with you in your victories."

I wish it were not true, but I know it is. If you want to make a pastor jealous, let a friend's church outgrow his. Jealousy is a problem in the ministry, but I have an easy cure. You may feel jealous of a friend's success. If so, pray and sow. Or you may be the successful one wondering why your friend is jealous. If so, pray and sow. Either way the answer is the same. Pray and sow. Pray and sow. Pray and sow. Do what God called you to do, and you will forget about being jealous or feeling forgotten.

Our Lord Jesus said, "Most assuredly, I say to you, unless a grain of wheat falls into the ground and dies, it remains alone; but if it dies, it produces much grain" (John 12:24). Keep on sowing, and someday you will reap with joy.

> Going forth with weeping, sowing for the Master,
> Though the loss sustained our spirit often grieves;
> When our weeping's over, He will bid us welcome,
> We shall come rejoicing, bringing in the sheaves.
> Bringing in the sheaves, bringing in the sheaves,
> We shall come rejoicing, bringing in the sheaves,
> Bringing in the sheaves, bringing in the sheaves,
> We shall come rejoicing, bringing in the sheaves.[69]

THE GOSPEL STILL MATTERS!

---

69. "Bring in the Sheaves," Knowles Shaw, 1874, *The Cyber Hymnal*, accessed August 9, 2021, https://library.timelesstruths.org/music/Bringing_in_the_Sheaves/.

3

DOES BAPTISM
STILL MATTER?

CHUCK KELLEY

At the Southern Baptist Convention meeting in Houston, Texas, in June 1979, an earthquake struck for the first time in the history of the SBC. The earth itself did not move. In fact, hardly anything moved the needle off of "normal" during that Convention. However, in retrospect, the election of Dr. Adrian Rogers as President of the SBC proved to be the beginning of an earthquake that would eventually reshape the Southern Baptist Convention and turn America's largest Protestant church family away from its liberal drift. The earthquake was not the election of Dr. Adrian Rogers. The earthquake was what happened when a grassroots movement among Southern Baptists organized pastors and church leaders, the majority of whom had always been theologically conservative, to get engaged personally in the affairs of the Convention. They were challenged to

> » attend the annual SBC meeting,
> » vote for committed conservative leaders,

» vote on all issues that came before the annual meeting from a conservative perspective, and

» take the time, whenever given the opportunity, to serve on the trustee boards of SBC entities in order to encourage that respective entity to move in a clearly conservative direction.

The combination of the engagement of steadily growing numbers of rank-and-file Southern Baptists and the chain of SBC presidents who used their appointment power to facilitate that engagement and their platform role to set the SBC agenda proved to be an irresistible force. Few people, even among the leadership of what was eventually called the Conservative Resurgence, imagined how complete a change would come to the Southern Baptist Convention as a result of what started in that 1979 Convention.

Forty-two years have passed since the earthquake began. The fortieth anniversary of the Conservative Resurgence came and went with little notice from any current SBC leaders. The culmination of the Resurgence was the adoption of the Baptist Faith and Message 2000 at the Orlando meeting of the SBC in 2000. The confession of faith is in use at all SBC entities and many state conventions, associations, and churches. As with the anniversary of the Resurgence, the twentieth anniversary of the Baptist Faith and Message 2000 passed with few comments by present SBC leaders. Ironically, no SBC entity leader, not many SBC entity employees, and few serving as entity trustees would likely be in their positions if not for the Conservative Resurgence drawing the SBC back from the brink of theological liberalism.

With that in mind, it is fair to ask if the doctrines and issues the Conservative Resurgence fought so hard to recover and promote still matter in Southern Baptist life today. I agreed to participate in this project to "raise an *Ebenezer.*" *Ebenezer* is a Hebrew word referring to the biblical practice (see 1 Sam. 7:12) of setting in place a stone of remembrance, a lasting reminder of a mighty work of God, lest time dull the memory of the people of God and they forget what great things God has done.

This chapter on baptism is intended to be a reminder that Southern Baptists and baptism must always be inseparable. Believer's baptism does still matter.

INTRODUCTION

The four of us left our hotel in Zurich, Switzerland, with an experienced driver and guide, hoping we would be able to find the obscure site. Leaving the beautiful city behind, we were quickly into the foothills of the Alps, following the limited directions available to us. After stopping a couple of times for further directions, we eventually turned into a farmer's field, driving slowly across the grass until a fence stopped us. From there we got out of the car, crossed the fence, and made our way up the hill and through the trees on foot until we finally found the forgotten cave we were seeking. It did not look like much, but that cave was a sacred space to us.

During the days of the Reformation, Christians began to recover their knowledge of the truthfulness and authority of the Bible and the Gospel that Bible proclaimed. All men were sinners in need of a salvation that only God could provide through repentance and faith in Christ. Various groups of Christians with distinctive identities emerged during those tumultuous years. Among them were a people called Anabaptists, considered by many scholars to be an important part of the family tree of today's Baptists. Anabaptists were a diverse group of Christians sharing convictions about the authority of the Bible and the significance of believer's baptism. One group of Anabaptists were called the Swiss Brethren because they emerged from a Bible study in Zurich.

These Swiss Brethren in the Zurich area and others who were interested in their teaching walked for miles to gather on Sundays to worship in that obscure cave outside the city. They made the arduous journey Sunday after Sunday because in the isolated cave in the woods, they could worship, read Scripture, and pray aloud without fear of being heard. If they had been heard in Zurich, arrest and execution surely would have followed. Zurich was an important center of the Protestant Reformation in those days and a very dangerous place for Anabaptists. They were subject to arrest, torture, and execution - often by drowning - by both Catholics and Protestants across nearly all of Europe.

Why were the Anabaptists the focus of such severe persecution? Believer's Baptism. Their insistence upon the baptism of a believer only following his personal profession of faith in Christ was considered to be so controversial and so dangerous that Catholics and all other Protestants agreed that these Anabaptists had to be eliminated to silence their voices and discourage others from following their examples. Baptism certainly mattered then. For those Anabaptists, baptism carried such great significance, that being baptized after conversion was worth the risk of imprisonment, torture, and death. Some scholars estimate the life expectancy for an Anabaptist following baptism as a believer was approximately eighteen months. Death, often a very cruel death, was the reward for being faithful to the teachings of the New Testament about baptism. Although there are no longer such dangerous consequences involved for followers of Christ in the United States, at least for now, believer's baptism still matters today.

BAPTISM:
THE CHOICE OF JESUS

The beginning and the end of the Gospel of Matthew introduce the meaning of baptism. In Matthew 3, John the Baptist exploded onto the scene in Israel. He was called John the Baptist because baptism was the focal point of his ministry. He preached near the Jordan River, calling people to repent and be baptized. Those who responded to his message were immediately baptized in the river. Jesus began His ministry by going to John to be baptized in the Jordan (Matt. 3:13). The New Testament was originally written in Greek, but when scholars began translating the Greek text of Scripture into English, they did not translate the Greek word for baptism. Instead, they transliterated it. Rather than using an English word with the same or similar meaning of the Greek word, they merely spelled the Greek word with English letters, leaving the word itself untranslated. The English meaning of the Greek word "baptize" is "immerse." When John baptized those who responded to his message with repentance, he immersed them. He dipped them in the river, letting the waters of the Jordan flow over them before bringing them back to the surface. Each time the word "baptism" is used in reference to water in the New Testament, it means to immerse. John the Baptist could be called John the Immerser.

Matthew ends his Gospel with what is often called the Great Commission, in which Jesus commands His disciples to baptize, to immerse all who become disciples in the future.

> And Jesus came up and spoke to them, saying, "All authority has been given to Me in heaven and on earth. Go therefore and make disciples of all the nations, baptizing them in the name of the Father and the Son and the Holy Spirit, teaching them to observe all that I commanded you; and lo, I am with always, even to the end of the age" (Matt 28:18-20, NASB).

Clearly, Jesus intended for baptism to be for those who became His disciples. Jesus began His ministry by being immersed in the Jordan. He concluded His ministry by commanding His disciples to baptize those who would believe on Him in the future.

Most scholars trace the beginning of the church to Acts 2. Jesus had promised the Holy Spirit would come upon His disciples after He returned to the Father. In Acts 2:1-4, the Bible reveals this happened on the day of the Pentecost when, with tongues of fire and the sound of a mighty rushing wind, the Holy Spirit came upon the disciples and inaugurated His ministry in the lives of all who followed Christ. A great crowd gathered to see what was happening, and Peter stood to preach. After he explained who Jesus was and what Jesus had done to bring salvation to those facing the judgment of God, Peter called upon his hearers to repent and be baptized. What Jesus commanded, Peter practiced, beginning with the first sermon preached after the return of Christ to heaven.

As the book of Acts describes the spread of the Gospel from Jerusalem to Rome and beyond, this pattern is implemented from the beginning of the church. People were called to repent and believe in Christ for salvation. Those who responded were baptized, immersed in water, soon after they turned to Jesus. Baptism, then, is an immersion in water that follows soon after repentance from sin and faith in Jesus Christ.

Christians need to know what baptism is. They also need to know what baptism is not. Baptism is not a part of the salvation process. The Bible teaches that baptism should follow soon after one professes faith in Christ. It does not teach that baptism is a requirement for conversion. Salvation comes first as a gracious act of God, providing for us what we cannot do for ourselves. Baptism is an acknowledgement of what God has done for us, but it does not complete the conversion process or facilitate salvation in any way. Being baptized does not make one a child of God. Not being baptized does not prevent one from becoming a child of God. Baptism is a public expression of an inward faith.

Here is the bottom line: Baptism marks the formal beginning of a Christian's new life in Christ. It is the public inauguration moment for a disciple. When I was elected President of New Orleans Baptist Theological Seminary in 1996, my leadership responsibilities and authority began on the date chosen by the trustees. However, my presidential inauguration took place at a time of my choosing, after I was already on the job. The presentation of the presidential medallion, the dedicatory prayer, and my introduction as President in the presence of trustees, donors, faculty, and academic representatives from various colleges, seminaries, and universities from around the country, was the formal, public announcement of what had already happened six months earlier: Dr. Charles S. Kelley, Jr., was indeed the eighth President of New Orleans Baptist Theological Seminary.

In the same way, baptism is the inauguration of a new disciple's life in Christ. It is the official notice of what has already happened in the believer's soul. Thus, it becomes clear why Jesus insisted that John the Baptist baptize Him in the Jordan. As He came out of the water, the Holy Spirit descended upon Him to anoint Him as the author of our salvation. The Father spoke from Heaven, affirming Jesus as His Son, on mission from Him. The work of Christ to accomplish our salvation was officially underway. The process to accomplish the forgiveness of sin and the redemption of broken humanity was initiated. Baptism did not change who Jesus was, but it did publicly declare that His work had begun. In the same way, our baptism is a matter of extreme importance, not because of its effect on us but because it makes who we are in Christ a matter of public record. All who see us baptized know we have already been saved. We are now disciples of Christ, and we will follow Him for the rest of our lives.

BAPTISM:
A SOUTHERN BAPTIST DISTINCTIVE

Baptists of all varieties, including Southern Baptists, define themselves by a commitment to the practice of baptism as taught and illustrated in the New Testament. The practice of baptism is at the center, the core of the identity for all who call themselves Baptists. One cannot be a Baptist, a member of a Baptist church without confessing faith in Christ and being publicly baptized. Southern Baptists explain their convictions about baptism in a particular kind of document called a confession of faith.

Only the Bible is inspired by God and therefore inerrant and author-itative. To make known what they have learned from the Bible, Baptists through the years have used confessions of faith to summarize their key doctrinal convictions in order to teach them to those inside the church, to explain them to those outside the church, and to establish generally accept-ed theological boundaries when such are needed for those who teach and serve Southern Baptists, such as seminary professors. The Southern Baptist Convention adopted a confession of faith for the first time in 1925 in a document entitled *The Baptist Faith and Message*. After nearly forty years, the SBC reviewed and updated *The Baptist Faith and Message* in 1963 to address questions that were not concerns when the original document was approved. Once again, thirty-seven years later, the 1963 statement was re-viewed and updated in light of the issues and questions facing contempo-rary Southern Baptists. That revision was overwhelmingly approved at the annual meeting of the Southern Baptist Convention in 2000. The present edition of the confession of faith in use today is therefore called the Baptist Faith and Message 2000. The entire confession of faith can be found at the official website of the SBC (www.sbc.net), in the Annual of the Southern Baptist Convention published each year, and in a wide variety of websites, books, publications, and brochures from the Convention, its entities, and nearly all related state conventions. The Southern Baptist understanding of what the Bible teaches regarding baptism was included in all three editions of the confession of faith.

Ordinance or Sacrament?

All Christian bodies and families of churches understand that Jesus com-manded His followers to engage in two practices connected with His death, burial, and resurrection. Those two practices are baptism and the Lord's Supper. Most use one of two words to describe the two practices: either ordinance or sacrament.

Roman Catholics and others use the term "sacrament" to indicate their belief that grace is conveyed to the practitioner by means of participation in the ritual. Baptists and other evangelicals use the term "ordinance" to describe baptism and the Lord's Supper because they believe Christ commanded participation in them to memorialize, to bring to mind, His work for us. Grace is not conveyed to the participant through the act. Rather the act symbolizes what Jesus did in order to remind participants of grace already received through faith at the point of conversion.[1] To call baptism a sacrament is to indicate that it is a means of grace given at each participation. To call baptism an ordinance is to affirm that it is a memorial, a symbol reminding participants of grace already received.

To summarize, Southern Baptists understand the New Testament to teach that Jesus Christ commanded His church to observe two ordinances to symbolize and remember His death and resurrection for our salvation. Those two ordinances are believer's baptism and the Lord's Supper.

Keeping in mind this distinction between ordinance and sacrament, here is the formal description of what Southern Baptists believe about baptism, as found in Article Seven of the Baptist Faith and Message 2000:

> Christian baptism is the immersion of a believer in water in the name of the Father, the Son, and the Holy Spirit. It is an act of obedience symbolizing the believer's faith in a crucified, buried, and risen Savior, the believer's death to sin, the burial of the old life, and the resurrection to walk in newness of life in Christ Jesus. It is a testimony to his faith in the final resurrection of the dead. Being a church ordinance, it is prerequisite to the privileges of church membership and to the Lord's Supper.

---

1. T. C. Smith, "Baptism" in *Encyclopedia of Southern Baptists*, vol. 1, ed. Clifton Judson Allen (Nashville: Broadman Press, 1958), 106-109.

This concise statement of Southern Baptist convictions about baptism experienced little change in the review and updating of the confession of faith through the years, and it does reflect the wide convictions and practices about baptism found in the churches of the SBC.

Regenerate Church Membership

One factor setting Baptists apart is their requirement of believer's baptism by immersion for church membership. Southern Baptists practice what theologians call regenerate church membership.[2] You must be born again to become a member of an SBC church. There is no connection between one's family of origin and church membership. You can be born into a Baptist family, but you cannot be born into church membership.

The Baptist Faith and Message statement on baptism notes that baptism is a prerequisite for church membership and participation in the Lord's Supper. Because Baptists practice baptism only for those who believe in Christ and have been born again, baptism is accepted as the confirmation that the regeneration of the soul has taken place and one is truly born again. With one's baptism being a matter of public record, one is therefore eligible for church membership.

Jesus shared the Lord's Supper with His disciples on the night before He died on the cross to make the forgiveness of our sin possible. He Himself commanded His disciples to commemorate His death for our salvation through the observance of the Lord's Supper until His return.

> For I received from the Lord that which I also delivered to you, that the Lord Jesus in the night in which He was betrayed took bread; and when He had given thanks, He broke it and said, "This is My body, which is for you; do this in remembrance of me." In the same way He took the cup also after supper, saying, "This cup is the

2. *Baptist Faith and Message 2000, Article 7.*

new covenant in My blood; do this, as often as you drink it, in remembrance of Me." For as often as you eat this bread and drink this cup, you proclaim the Lord's death until He comes (1 Cor 11:23-26, NASB).

Because the Lord's Supper was to be observed by those who have been redeemed by the sacrifice of Christ, baptism was a prerequisite. The public identification with Christ in believer's baptism was the indication that the requirement of being a follower of Christ was fulfilled.

It Still Matters

Baptism does still matter today because it is an ordinance Jesus commanded His church to observe. Baptism should always be conducted in the name of the Father, Son, and Holy Spirit because that is what Jesus clearly commanded in Matthew 28:19. This verse clearly identifies the ultimate source of the salvation, which baptism celebrates. Salvation came entirely at God's initiative - not ours. Therefore, baptism is a symbol of how God's grace was provided; it is not a means of securing that grace.

As we shall see in the remainder of the chapter, baptism still matters because it conveys a message Jesus wanted His church and all who observed its practice to see over and over again. Baptism must be by immersion because being covered over with water was an essential component of that message Jesus wanted baptism to communicate. As being born again by the grace of God is the necessary qualification for Heaven, the believer's baptism, which portrays that transformation of the soul, is the necessary qualification of membership in an SBC church and for participation in the Lord's Supper.

Baptism is a matter of primary importance for any and all Southern Baptists. In effect, baptism is the door through which one enters into life as a Southern Baptist church member.

BAPTISM:
THE BEGINNING OF OBEDIENCE

One never knows what will happen on any given day in the life of a semi-nary president and his wife. One day, we were quite surprised when Rhon-da received a call from the U.S. State Department, asking if a group of Islamic theologians from universities all over the Muslim world could visit our campus to have a conversation with her about the role of women in Baptist churches. An unpublicized cultural exchange program sponsored visits of groups of Islamic scholars to the United States, and New Orleans was one of the stops on their tour. We were told the professors of Islam had asked for an opportunity to explore the role of women in conservative Christian churches while they were in the United States. We were quite surprised by the request, but willing to host such a meeting. A date was set and all arrangements were made. Rhonda and I, along with members of our faculty, received the group in our home. I offered a brief welcome and description of our school. Rhonda made a brief statement about women in SBC churches and Convention life. We then let their questions guide the conversation for the next hour. Their questions took us to an unexpected place. Two more times the State Department brought international groups of Islamic scholars from across the world, before Hurricane Katrina appar-ently ended the program. Each time we followed the same format. Each time the conversation went to the same unexpected place. The issue that deeply perplexed three different groups of Islamic theologians was: Why would a Christian obey the laws of God and live a moral life if God will forgive any sin you commit?

Fear-Obedience vs Love-Obedience

If the essence of sin is rebellion against God, then the essence of being a born-again child of God must be the practice of obedience to His will.

Self-preservation, self-interest, and self-will are deeply woven into the fabric of human nature. The Islamic scholars assumed that only the fear of God's wrath would keep one on the road to righteousness.

For most Muslims, the knowledge of whether or not ones righteousness is adequate cannot be known until one actually faces the judgment of his or her soul. Therefore, one must seek to live as righteously as possible every day until he dies.

In the Muslim professor's minds, teaching those who come to faith in Christ that they can be certain that God has forgiven all their sin (past, present, and future) would remove the powerful motivation of fear to continually seek holiness in living. We sought to explain to them that the grace of God given to us through the unspeakable sacrifice that Jesus made for the atonement of our sin, inspires a profound love for God. The love of God provides the deep motivation for all of us who are forgiven to pursue a life of faithful obedience to our dear Savior. Having a similar conversation with all three groups of Islamic scholars was a vivid reminder of how important it is to help new believers understand the foundational significance of the issue of obedience to God and the role holy living should play in their new lives. Clearly, an important component of the disciple's life is the cultivation of the habit of obedience to God.

BELIEVER'S BAPTISM: AN IMPORTANT ACT OF OBEDIENCE

The New Testament emphasizes the importance of baptism for believers over and over again. Here are some of the biblical references:

> Then Jesus came down from Galilee to John at the Jordan to be baptized by him. And John tried to prevent Him, saying, "I need to be baptized by You, and are You coming to me?" But Jesus answered

and said to him, "Permit it to be so now, for thus it is fitting for us to fulfill all righteousness." Then he allowed Him (Matt. 3:13-15, NKJV).

Then Peter said to them, "Repent, and let every one of you be baptized in the name of Jesus Christ for the remission of sins; and you shall receive the gift of the Holy Spirit" (Acts 2:38, NKJV).

Then those who gladly received his word were baptized; and that day about three thousand souls were added to them (Acts 2:41, NKJV).

Then Philip opened his mouth, and beginning at this Scripture, preached Jesus to him [the eunuch]. Now as they went down the road, they came to some water. And the eunuch said, "See, here is water. What hinders me from being baptized?" Then Philip said, "If you believe with all your heart, you may." And he answered and said, "I believe that Jesus Christ is the Son of God." So he commanded the chariot to stand still. And both Philip and the eunuch went down into the water, and he baptized him (Acts 8:35-38, NKJV).

So they said, "Believe on the Lord Jesus Christ, and you will be saved, you and your household." Then they spoke the word of the Lord to him and to all who were in his house. And he took them the same hour of the night and washed their stripes. And immediately he and all his family were baptized (Acts 16:31-33, NKJV).

These selected references show the importance placed upon baptism from the earliest days of the church. Faith in Christ saved, but after salvation came, baptism quickly followed. Clearly God had a purpose of great significance in mind for baptism.

God Knows Us

The God who created us knows us more thoroughly and deeply than we can conceive. In Psalm 139, David expressed this with unsurpassed beauty and eloquence:

> O Lord, You have searched me and known me.
> You know my sitting down and my rising up;
> You understand my thought afar off.
> You comprehend my path and my lying down,
> And are acquainted with all my ways.
> For there is not a word on my tongue,
> But behold, O Lord, You know it altogether.
> You have hedged me behind and before,
> And laid Your hand upon me.
> Such knowledge is too wonderful for me;
> It is high, I cannot attain it.
> Where can I go from Your Spirit?
> Or where can I flee from Your presence?
> If I ascend into heaven, You are there;
> If I make my bed in hell, behold, You are there.
> If I take the wings of the morning,
> And dwell in the uttermost parts of the sea,
> Even there Your hand shall lead me,
> And Your right hand shall hold me.
> If I say, "Surely the darkness shall fall on me,"
> Even the night shall be light about me;
> Indeed, the darkness shall not hide from You,
> But the night shines as bright as the day;
> The darkness and the light are both alike to You.
> For You formed my inward parts;

You covered me in my mother's womb.
I will praise You, for I am fearfully and wonderfully made;
Marvelous are Your works,
And that my soul knows very well (Ps 139:1-14, NKJV).

God's intimate knowledge of us forms the backdrop for all of His expectations and requirements for us, including baptism. He knows that the yearning we have for our own desires to be the supreme influence over our choices will have to be replaced with a yearning for Jesus to be the supreme influence over our choices. He knows that this shift to the consistent acknowledgment that He is now our Master and King goes against the grain of both our hearts and our culture and will be one of the biggest challenges to becoming a disciple. The development of this new habit of obedience is so crucial to life in Christ that we must begin working on it immediately after conversion.

God Transforms Us

Our salvation and transformation into a child of God is entirely God's work. He does for us what we cannot do for ourselves. Knowing how deeply rooted self-interest is in the human soul, God intends His divine act of salvation to be followed quickly by baptism, a human act of obedience to a sovereign God. The rebellion of our old self is to be replaced as soon as possible with the obedience of our new self, expressed in a public inauguration ceremony. Baptism is a celebration of both the formal beginning of His work in our souls and the beginning of our submission to His divine will.

We launch the process of discipleship with a practical act of public obedience to His command. This fresh start for living in light of who God is and what God requires is intended to be shared by all of God's children. We were sinners rebelling against God, but we have become children living in obedience to our heavenly Father. God wants us to start the habit of obedience to Him early in our spiritual lives. Baptism is a first act of obedience for the new Christian, but baptism is also a vivid reminder to all believers who observe the ceremony that their own obedience to the Lord is a matter of great importance for their spiritual health.

For some, the command to be baptized is a bigger issue than it is for others. Baptism as an act of obedience is not the only issue of concern that can affect new believers. Being immersed in water in front of a crowd is sometimes an issue for those who avoid public displays of any sort because of the fear of embarrassment. Some new believers find themselves to be the only one in their circle of family and friends who has come to Christ. They feel being baptized publicly would heighten that sense of isolation and loneliness. Some have a serious fear of water or think the infant baptism they have already experienced should be enough. Some have physical limitations that make entering and leaving a baptistry difficult. Some face severe pressure not to be baptized from family members who view believer's baptism as a rejection of family and heritage. For Anabaptists during the Reformation, the very real possibilities of arrest, torture, and death were greater discouragements than many barriers Christians can imagine having to face today. Yet such barriers still exist. The physical persecution of those who follow the Lord's command to be baptized remains a grim reality in some nations of today's world.

Whatever reasons there may be to avoid or defer baptism, again and again through the centuries, God's children have chosen to obey His command and be publicly baptized, not because the decision was simple, but because obedience to His commands was the preeminent concern for those who call Him Savior and Lord. Those who were martyred over believer's baptism were not choosing martyrdom. They chose obedience to the Lord even though martyrdom was the consequence. Those who alienate family members or friends by being baptized today are not choosing to distance themselves from people they love. They are choosing to obey and draw near to their Savior even if it means becoming more distance from people they love.

BAPTISM:
THE HABIT OF DISCIPLESHIP

Baptism still matters today because it remains the first opportunity for a new Christian to make a life decision based upon the will of God rather than his own preferences. Habits are formed by repeated actions. Before conversion can transform a soul, it is in the grip of sin and the selfish desires that sin creates. Contemporary culture programs people to follow the path of personal desires and dreams. Parents can unintentionally add to this self-oriented programming habit by telling children, "You can do anything you want to do or become anything you want to become if you are willing to work hard and make it happen." The problem that arises for believers is that God's call may lead in a different direction than personal dreams. The culture surrounds everyone with a continuous message that says over and over again, "You are in charge of your life."

Christians should not embrace any philosophy that gives God a secondary role. A more appropriate statement for believers to affirm is that we can become anything that God wants us to be or do anything that God wants us to do. When godly parents build that affirmation of God's sovereign role in how a life unfolds, they prepare a child for the habit of discipleship. The children of Christian parents should be encouraged to ask and to seek to know: What then does God want to do with me? In the same way the newly born-again believer needs to begin to ask: What does God want to do with, in, and through my life? Saying yes to baptism is the first step toward the development of the habit of obedience. Ever more opportunities to say yes to the will and purposes of God will follow. The big decisions of life for a believer should be made in light of understanding what God expects you to do. What college will you attend? What career will you pursue? Will you marry? If so, whom will you marry? These are all components of our discipleship as we follow Jesus. The habit of obedience will define who you become as a disciple of Christ, but it will also define who you become as a person.

Obedience and Evangelism

An adult Sunday School teacher in Boston had a young man in his class who knew absolutely nothing about the Bible or Christianity. He only came to church because he promised his mother he would do so after leaving the family farm to find work in the city. That Sunday School teacher felt compelled to go the young man's place of employment and share the Gospel with him. He was very reluctant to do so; but one day, he finally obeyed God's prompting and went to witness to the young man. He was so nervous he walked back and forth in front of the shop, too intimidated to go in and share the Gospel. God continued to push him to do so. Again, he finally chose obedience over apprehension and personal discomfort. The Sunday School teacher walked in, found the young man alone in the shop, and began to share. It is unlikely you ever heard of Mr. Edward Kimball, who was the Sunday School teacher. But the young man who did accept Christ that day was D. L. Moody. Moody went on to become one of the greatest evangelists in the history of the United States. The habit of obedience mattered that day. Hundreds of thousands were saved on both sides of the Atlantic because the habit of obedience overcame the reluctance of a Sunday School teacher to witness.

Obedience and Life Impact

A young school teacher lived and taught in a small North Carolina community. He moved with his family to Whitewright, Texas, and hoped to practice law. He was shocked one Sunday when his church voted to ordain him to the Gospel ministry without bothering to ask if he was interested. The idea never occurred to him. He told them that he could not do it, but they ignored him and proceeded to ordain him. Finally realizing how unusual this was and that God must be calling him in spite of his reluctance, he agreed to be ordained. The young man chose obedience to the manifested will of God over personal preference. His name was George W. Truett. He went on to become the pastor of First Baptist Church, Dallas, and one of the most famous and influential pastors in the history of the Southern Baptist Convention. On May 16, 1920, in connection with the annual meeting of the Southern Baptist Convention, Truett preached a sermon on religious liberty from the steps of the Capitol in Washington, D. C. It captivated the attention of the whole nation and became the most famous sermon ever preached by a Southern Baptist pastor. The habit of obedience overcame a reluctant heart, and the world was different as a result.

Obedience and Life Direction

My wife and I were less than a month away from beginning seminary in a place with a terrific faculty in my area of interest and where my wife had already secured her dream job. All of our married friends were going to this seminary. I had already become known in the region and was preaching revivals and enjoying many opportunities for service. During a day set aside for prayer about this decision, I expected confirmation for my choice of seminary. Instead, God began making it clear He wanted us to go to seminary in New Orleans, where neither one of us had work, where no one knew me and I would not be called on to lead in silent prayer, and where the seminary did not offer the course of study I wanted to pursue. It was one of the toughest decisions Rhonda and I ever faced, and it made no sense to us. But we had been cultivating the habit of obedience. We changed our plans and went into the great unknown of New Orleans. I had no idea that decision would one day result in my becoming President of that seminary. The habit of obedience changed the course of our lives and ministry.

On, and on, and on the stories go. The habit of obedience will shape the life of a believer. Habits always begin with a first action. Baptism matters because for many believers it starts the spiritual habit of choosing obedience to God in spite of personal reluctance. Following the Lord in believer's baptism is a decision that creates ripples affecting the fabric of your spiritual life and relationship with God. How you start the journey of following Christ is often an indicator of how you will finish.

Baptism is not necessary for your salvation but it is essential for your discipleship. It is the transition into what comes next in your new relationship with Christ. He transformed your soul and removed your sin. Once you are saved, the Lord wants to make you more and more like Jesus. Baptism is the foundation on which your emerging relationship with God will be built, replacing the habit of rebellion against God with the habit of obedience to God. **For this reason, baptism delayed is discipleship deferred.** After you repent of your sin and rebellion against God and His ways, baptism provides your first opportunity to embrace obedience and affirm that for you, henceforth and forevermore, Jesus is Lord!

BAPTISM:
A GOSPEL PRESENTATION

Millions of fans all over the world know actor Patrick Stewart as Jean Luc Picard, captain of the Starship Enterprise as featured in *Star Trek: The Next Generation*, one of the best known and most beloved TV and movie franchises ever to come out of Hollywood. However, my favorite role portrayed by Stewart is light years away from the world of sci-fi. Several years ago, the actor played the role of Ebenezer Scrooge and every other character in *A Christmas Carol*, the Christmas classic written by Charles Dickens in 19th century England. Stewart created a one-man show in which he portrays every character in the story as he narrates the work in its entirety on the stage before an audience. It is a brilliant performance, now available in an audio recording my wife and I listen to each and every December.[3] Patrick Stewart demonstrates that a one-man show can be a very powerful means of communication. Not many people know that Dickens himself did something similar, traveling the world in December to read dramatically *A Christmas Carol* in theaters filled with people. Excellent stories have great power, and God intends for baptism to be an important way to tell the story of Jesus. In the next three sections of the chapter, we will look at the importance of baptism as a way to share the Gospel with others.

BAPTISM:
A PUBLIC TESTIMONY

Some Christians are reluctant to engage people in conversations about Jesus. Many reasons why are offered: I don't know enough about the Bible; I am not very good at starting conversations; I am afraid people will reject me —and so on. Whatever the excuse may be, the Bible teaches that every follower of Christ is responsible for bearing witness to what Jesus has done for them, regardless of how comfortable or uncomfortable one may feel. Here is a sample of biblical teachings on the responsibility to tell others about Jesus:

> And He said to them, "Follow Me, and I will make you fishers of men" (Matt 4:19, NASB).

> And He said to them, "Go into all the world and preach the gospel to all creation (Mark 16:15, NASB).

---

3. Patrick Stewart, *A Christmas Carol,* Audio ed. (Simon & Shuster Audio, 2006).

> But you will receive power when the Holy Spirit has come upon you; and you shall be My witnesses both in Jerusalem, and in all Judea and Samaria, and even to the remotest part of the earth (Acts 1:8, NASB).

> Therefore, we ae ambassadors for Christ, as though God were making an appeal through us; we beg you on behalf of Christ, be reconciled to God (2 Cor 5:20, NASB).

The lost need to hear a witness to the Gospel, and God expects us to provide one. Fortunately, God has provided a way for the newest believers to share their conversion stories without speaking a word.

Salvation requires the transformation of a human soul. One's family of origin, religious background, or church experience may be helpful, even influential, but they cannot regenerate the soul. Only the Holy Spirit of God has the power to actually make a sinful heart into a godly heart. The resulting changes are so profound, Jesus described being made ready to enter the kingdom of God as being "born again" (John 3:3). Paul likened being in Christ to becoming a "new creation" (2 Cor. 5:17, NKJV).

As dramatic as the outcome of conversion is on the soul, it is an internal transformation, one that cannot be observed as it unfolds. How can a new Christian explain this miraculous change to others? This brings us to another reason why baptism matters today.

Internal Transformation, Visual Explanation

The New Testament teaches that baptism is a public ceremony for believers and by immersion for particular reasons. One of those reasons is that baptism enables new believers to explain visually what happened in their souls when they repented of their sin and trusted in Christ alone for their salvation. Persecution after conversion quickly became a challenge faced by the early church. For baptism to become a secret ceremony to be observed only by believers, lest outsiders become aware that someone had become a follower of Christ and subject them to attacks would not have been a surprise. There may very well have been such private baptisms, but on the whole evidence indicates that baptisms were conducted in more or less public settings. In the early years, baptisms often occurred in rivers or lakes, as did the baptism of Jesus in the Jordan River by John (Matt. 3:13-15).

As the church outgrew its persecutors and began to build places of worship, immersionist baptistries were included in their designs and put in prominent places as church buildings took shape. North Africa became a center for the expansion of Christianity. On an academic tour of ancient Christian sites across North Africa, we visited nearly two dozen ancient churches, all with baptistries for the immersion of new converts. When the baptism ceremony moved inside, it did not become less public. God wants baptism to be as public as possible because it is a visible testimony to the inward work of God in a human soul. One who was not a Christian has now become a follower of Christ, publicly identifying with Him through the waters of baptism. This physical act is also a public confession of an inward faith that has transformed a life into a child of God. As a public confession, baptism is also a first step in accepting accountability to live life as a disciple of Christ.

Pastor/Narrator

Most pastors take on a role like that of the narrator of a story as they conduct the baptismal service. They explain the symbolic meaning of baptism during the immersion to enable all who are present to understand the story baptism tells. As the baptismal candidates enter the water, the pastor/narrator announces that the new believers are portraying their life before Christ entered their souls. The explanation continues with the lowering of baptismal candidates completely under the water to represent the burial of the old, sinful self. Christ embraced death on the cross for them, and in response candidates are identifying with Christ and embracing the death of their sinful selves in order to be born again. As this happens, the pastor/narrator announces the baptism is in the name of the Father, the Son, and the Holy Spirit, indicating that God Himself is responsible for the spiritual transformation that has taken place. The sinners under the judgment of God are now gone forever. Life without God and His grace is over. As new Christians emerge from the baptismal pool, the pastor/narrator explains that it symbolizes that they have indeed been born again, raised from spiritual death to walk in the newness of life in Christ. All sin is forgiven, replaced by the righteousness of Christ.

The person now emerging from the waters of baptism is a child of God and can be expected to live differently because they serve a different master. Baptism, therefore, not only shares the personal testimony of the new believer. It also begins to establish accountability for obedience to Christ from both other believers and from non-Christians who were there to observe. You gave your life completely to Christ, and you are expected to live with the evidence of this changed life from this time forward. Baptism is both a first step in your responsibility to share your faith and a first step in your responsibility to live out your faith.

Baptism still matters today. The combination of a new believer, the water, and the explanations of the pastor/narrator provide a powerful way for new Christians to begin sharing their faith in Christ and taking their first steps in accountability for discipleship. The longer believers walk with Jesus and study the Bible, the better able they will be to articulate their faith to others, but evangelism and discipleship cannot wait for spiritual maturity. A newly born baby is not able to eat a steak, but she must begin to eat in order to live. New Christians are not able to reflect the Christ in them as clearly and thoroughly as they will be able to in the future, but they must start the journey of spiritual growth to get to that future. Sharing Jesus with others and walking with Jesus in obedience should begin when new life begins. Baptism is a way God provides for believers to start new life with new actions. New believers play the starring role in this visual portrayal of their salvation stories. Assisted by the water and the pastor/narrator, the ceremony explains to all who are there to observe the event what Christ did to transform their lives.

BAPTISM:
A LIVING ILLUSTRATION

Participation in a child's birthday party is an interesting experience for a parent. The spotlight is very much on the child. Both the child and everyone present know who is the center of attention and who is being celebrated. However, while all eyes are on the birthday child, Mom and Dad are keenly aware of another story intersecting with the story of the child. Mom and Dad are reliving the day that child was born and remembering what it was like for them. My sister-in-law likes to call each of her four boys on their birthday and reproduce the sounds of her labor to deliver them so that they do not forget her role in their birth. Many a child is well-versed in the details of the day of their birth from the perspective of their parents because they have heard the story so many times through the years. In the same way, baptism is actually two visual stories portrayed in the same ceremony. It is the testimony of new believers telling the story of their personal stories of conversion. At the same time, baptism is the story of Jesus and what He did to make that salvation possible.

Once again, the importance of the mode of baptism, that it is baptism by immersion, is clearly emphasized. The New Testament teaches that God, not the church, chose the mode of baptism to be used for converts, and He did so for specific reasons. The Bible explains how to become a Christian for the mind to understand; baptism portrays visually what happens when a soul is reborn—the eye sees and one better understands.

The Bible explains that Christ did what was necessary for salvation to be possible. Salvation is so important for lost souls that the Lord revealed and explained it for both the mind and the eye. Baptism is a portrayal of the new believer's testimony. It is a living illustration that paints a picture of the Gospel. Baptism matters today because it illustrates what Jesus did to accomplish our salvation.

As we saw earlier in the chapter, Jesus chose to make His baptism the formal beginning of His ministry. His baptism set the stage for what was to come, illustrating what He was going to do in order to accomplish our salvation. First, the Word had to become flesh. Eternal God became finite man so that He could be the substitutionary sacrifice for our sin (John 1:14). There could be no forgiveness for sin without an atoning sacrifice.

Jesus waited in line, surrounded by all those who came to hear John and to be baptized. The fullness of His humanity was on display for all to see. As Jesus was lowered into the water of the Jordan and the waters closed over His head, He illustrated that He had come to die and be buried, taking our sin and its penalty upon Himself. As John lifted Jesus out of the water, the heavens opened and the Holy Spirit descended upon Him in the likeness of a dove, and the Father's voice cried out from heaven, "This is my beloved Son, in whom I am well pleased" (Matt. 3:16-17). Jesus was going to die and be buried, but He would be resurrected in glory.

> Or do you not know that as many of us as were baptized into Jesus Christ were baptized into His death? Therefore, we were buried with him by baptism into death, that just as Christ was raised from the dead by the glory of the Father, even so we also should walk in newness of life (Rom 6:3-4, NKJV).

The three great facts of the Gospel: the miraculous incarnation, the atoning death and burial, and the glorious resurrection are incorporated into the ordinance of baptism. Jesus commanded all who come to Him for salvation to follow Him in baptism so that His mighty work of atonement for sin could be illustrated and explained again, again, and again. Had there been no incarnation of God into flesh, there could have been no acceptable substitute for sinful humanity before the judgment seat of God. Had there been no atoning sacrifice on the cross by that acceptable substitute in our place, there could have been no grounds for the forgiveness of sin. Had there been no resurrection from the dead after the sacrifice was complete, there could have been no eternal life for the forgiven. In effect, baptism is a three-act play performed each time a new believer goes into the baptismal water, illustrating what Jesus did for salvation to be possible. **Every baptism is a personal testimony. Every baptism is a Gospel presentation.**

Death and Resurrection

Does baptism still matter today? Yes! Each time a new believer is baptized a performance of the Gospel takes place involving the water, the convert, and the pastor/narrator. In a tangible, visible way, the new believer bears witness to all who are in attendance to the spiritual transformation that has taken place in the depths of his soul, while at the same time providing a physical illustration of what Jesus did to make that transformation possible. The water embodies the biblical teaching on the essential role of death in the salvation process. The sinner must die so that a saint can be reborn. Jesus had to make the sacrifice of His death, to satisfy the righteousness of God and make complete forgiveness of sin possible. The believer has become a new, different person in Christ; and the completion of this transformation process will come in the resurrection that Christ will bring to all of His children. The pastor/narrator is more than the one who performs the baptism. He is the one who also explains the testimony of the new believer being portrayed, and the illustration of the Gospel being performed. In His profound wisdom, God made baptism an ordinance of the church to be undertaken by every follower of Christ so that this testimony of salvation and this witness to the cost of salvation could be publicly observed, bringing encouragement to those who already know Jesus and a visual witness and Gospel presentation to those who are still in the grip of sin.

BAPTISM:
A MAGNET FOR THE LOST

Like most men, I am not looking for opportunities to attend a bridal shower. Having grown up in a household with four sisters and a mother, I learned a great deal about bridal showers along the way. A group of women connected to the bride or the groom get together to plan a party to celebrate the engagement or the approaching wedding of a couple. They are the hostesses. The ladies determine who will use her home for the event, and they divide up the responsibilities and the costs. The guest list will include all the females in the families of both the bride and the groom. There must be a theme for the party, and sometimes for the gifts as well. There must be plenty of finger foods, and often a game or two, to be sure the bride has an opportunity to connect all the names and faces. Some she will know, and some she will not. The focal point of most showers comes when all gather around the bride to watch her open her gifts. The groom shows up at the end of the shower to be shown off to all the ladies and to load the gifts into the car. Hostesses always stay to help clean up the house and divide the leftovers. The bride brings a small gift for each hostess and always sends handwritten "Thank You" notes to the hostesses as well as to those who gave gifts. If the bride and groom happen to be from different cities, the process must be repeated at least once in each city to allow the locals a chance to get to know the outsider becoming part of the family.

I know all this because my Mom often hosted such showers in our home, and I was often "volunteered" to help behind the scenes. Of course, all four of my sisters and my wife had to have wedding showers. After

Rhonda and I were married, she often volunteered our home as the place for a shower for brides in our church or the seminary I served. You can see how I became far more of an expert on bridal showers than I ever wanted to be.

I share this body of specialized knowledge as a prelude to a warning. I need to warn all husbands-to-be and their friends that the world has changed. Today, having a couples shower is all the rage. The women are invited to bring their husbands or boyfriends along to give them the joy of participation in this process. If invited, be further warned that there are very high expectations for the men to attend. No manly features have been added to format. There will not be a room with a TV playing a sports channel. Whatever games are played involving the couples who attend are unlikely to be very competitive. The nature of the event has not changed, but the pool of participants has been enlarged. A couple's bridal shower is not a different kind of event from a traditional shower, but it is a shower intended to appeal to a wider circle of those who have a personal connection with the bride or the groom or with the woman who asks them to attend.

Today, many churches recognize that an untapped opportunity for evangelism could come from enlarging the pool of participants in baptismal services and adjusting the way baptism is presented. A baptismal service can be an opportunity to draw people to your congregation who would not normally come. While there, the Gospel can be shared. Also, the foundation for building relationships with people completely outside the influence of the church can be put into place.

For Southern Baptists, the baptism of a new Christian has always been a public event. Most SBC churches are designed with the Lord's Supper table, the pulpit, and the baptistry in alignment at the center of the sanctuary. They can be seen clearly from every seat. Baptisms typically take place at the beginning of a worship service. Baptisms have always been recognized as a significant event for the congregation, the convert, and the immediate family of the convert. What is emerging in Baptist life is a recognition of what can happen when one's baptism is recognized and presented as a significant life event to the extended family and network of friends of the baptismal candidate, much like a wedding or graduation. So many unbelievers today have such little religious background, religious events fall into a narrow category of private affairs to which an outsider might not even be welcome to attend, rather than a life event in which all family and friends are invited and encouraged to participate. As noted above, men rarely attend bridal showers because they thrive on that kind of event, but they will go to support and affirm someone in their circle of family and friends. Most of us care about supporting the people in our lives, especially in the uncertain times in which we live. Baptism is a way for the church to take advantage of this dynamic in a very healthy and positive way.

Baptism is a celebration of an evangelistic success story. It can also be a launching pad for future evangelistic success. Most people join a church because they have family members or friends who are already members of the church. New converts often have more and closer relationships with unbelievers at the time of their conversion than they will five years later. Those family members and friends of a new believer should be considered as the "A List" prospects for evangelism when the evangelistic witness can be incorporated into the celebration of a significant event in the life of someone who is significant to them. Some of the practices emerging from efforts to make baptisms an evangelistic event, include the following:

1. Send invitations to all those whom you would like to attend.
2. Offer to meet those who are unfamiliar with church and ride to the service together.
3. Seat family and friends together and recognize them as their family/friend is being baptized.
4. Show a video of the candidate briefly explaining how he came to Christ before the baptism.
5. Take group pictures after the service.

6. Plan a reception, pot luck meal, etc. after the baptismal service.

7. Invite the pastor to the reception/meal after the service to meet everyone.

8. Have the pastor or a spiritual mentor lead a prayer of dedication for the newly baptized believer at the reception/meal.

9. Present the baptismal candidate with a Bible and invite everyone to sign it or mark a favorite verse.

10. Give all who come a New Testament w/ a brief note of thanks inscribed as a remembrance of the event.

These are examples. The two critical keys are to build traditions that emphasize baptism as a major event in someone's life and to have the pastor explain why baptism matters as he conducts the baptism. The most difficult visit for an unbeliever to make to a church is the first visit. On a first visit, one does not know who will be there or what to expect. A special event centered on someone who matters in their lives can provide the necessary motivation to break the ice and make that first visit to an unfamiliar setting. The more situations like that a church can create, the more likely it is that the church will reach those who need Jesus the most.

Fan the Flame

Baptism does still matter today. When faced with the need to build an evangelistic culture in a congregation, baptism offers an opportunity to fan the flame. Every conversion should be celebrated. Baptism provides a way to celebrate the fruit of evangelism, reminding the congregation that people do need the Lord and will come to the Lord. Adding something new to a practice already in place is often less stressful for people reluctant to change than creating something completely new. Preparing people to make baptism a memorable event is also preparing people to make evangelism a bigger priority. Churches that have had few or no baptisms in recent years can start by getting the baptistry cleaned out and ready for new converts. Gathering as many as possible in and around the baptistry for a prayer of dedication for it to become active afresh is a way to build expectations. Magnifying the act and significance of baptism is a gentle way to magnify the need and significance for evangelism in the community. Baptism is necessary for the new follower of Christ to be faithful to his Lord. Baptism is also necessary for the church to be faithful to the Lord's Great Commission.

BAPTISM:
A UNIFYING CONNECTION

At my university, they called it "Hell Week." When you pledged (joined) a fraternity, the last week of the pledge period was called "Hell Week" because it was an extremely difficult week. There was never any physical hazing on our campus. The schedule was simply made very intense, with little time for ordinary things like sleeping, eating, or studying. You had to schedule a meeting with every member of the fraternity at his convenience. During that meeting you would be given menial tasks of all sorts to do for the member. For one, you might do grocery shopping. For another, you might clean his apartment or wash and fold his clothes or read aloud from a textbook. The tasks were not impossible, dangerous, or controversial, but they were tedious and consuming, taking time when you could have been sleeping or studying. In addition, each pledge had to make a wooden shield, painted in fraternity colors, and carry it absolutely everywhere you went. Classes, meals, church—everywhere. When anyone asked you why you were carrying a shield, you answered, "Because I am protecting the campus from dragons." The absence of dragons was the evidence that you were doing a great job! As the icing on the cake, you did all of this in a coat and tie, all the time, every day of that week. By the end of the week, when every pledge was completely exhausted, they told you the pledge period was over. You were now an official member of the fraternity. Looking back, the process seems rather silly, but that experience was shared by everyone who had ever joined the fraternity. That shared experience, exhaustive and silly though it was, formed the glue cementing fraternal relationships within the group.

Ties that bind people to other people have taken many different forms. Some common experience, expression, or ethnic identity has formed the basis of human relationships throughout the history of humanity. Sports fans wear the same colors. Employees wear the same uniforms or shirts with the corporate logo. Tribal members might have the same markings on their faces or bodies. As evangelist Bob Harrington loved to say: "You can tell who the non-conformists are. They all look alike." Men and women, students, boys and girls throughout history have always tended toward a physical indication of their connection with others who share their identity. The ordinance of baptism still matters today because it connects us with faithful believers throughout the ages of the church. Some faced intense persecution and danger but chose faithfulness to the command of Jesus. Some faced real personal fears or powerful family opposition but chose faithfulness anyway.

As President of New Orleans Baptist Theological Seminary, I hosted many meals for pastors in our dining room. One of my favorite topics of conversation was to ask the pastors who were present to share a story about a memorable baptism during their ministries. Every pastor had stories. Some were hilarious, like the one about the young boy who jumped back in the baptistry after the pastor left to swim a bit while the congregation watched. Some were very emotional, like the pastor who baptized a new believer who had significant physical limitations but insisted on being baptized anyway. The process was very difficult due to the physical limitations, but the pastor said all the effort was forgotten with the expression on the face of that new child of God as he emerged from under the baptismal water. I will never forget a video shown to a meeting of pastors by David Jeremiah. You may recognize his name as one of the great expository preachers of this age of the church. His custom is to have those being baptized in his church share their stories from the baptistry of how they met Jesus. There was not a dry eye in the room as we listened to what Jesus meant to people of all ages and stages of life who were born again, and then watched as they followed Jesus in baptism at the beginning of their spiritual journey. Every pastor around my dining room table had stories, because every believer has a story. Consider how you can encourage more of your people to share the stories of all that was involved in their baptisms.

Each follower of Christ has a personal connection with Him as their Savior and Lord, but that is not all that they have. Followers of Christ today also share a connection with all the followers of Christ though the ages. On every continent and in every age of the church, those who follow the Lord in baptism have a bond with all others who were faithful to the call of Christ. You share that bond with every other member of your church because believer's baptism is the necessary requirement for church membership. You also share that bond with those five young men in Zurich who were studying Greek with their pastor so many years ago. When they realized the New Testament taught baptism was to be by immersion and for believers only, they confronted that beloved and very prominent teacher with the biblical text. That teacher rejected them and ultimately persecuted them severely. And yet, they obeyed what the Bible taught because they knew baptism mattered. All who follow the Lord in believer's baptism have a connection with the story of those early Anabaptists, as they have a connection with faithful believers today. Together in baptism, none of us follow Jesus alone. All of us are part of the great tapestry that is the family God's grace has created.

CONCLUSION

Baptism does still matter today. Jesus chose to put baptism at the beginning of a new believer's life after conversion. He chose to use baptism to launch a life of discipleship for those who follow Him. He chose baptism by immersion so that a watching world might both see and hear a testimony to the Gospel. Believer's baptism is a Southern Baptist distinctive, but it is a distinctive selected by Jesus and not the churches of the Southern Baptist Convention. It is a connecting point for the faithful, giving evidence to the world around us and to ourselves that we are members of a family. By our faithful obedience, we enrich the faith of others who follow Jesus, as their faithfulness enriches us. The health of the churches of the SBC will continue to be measured by the activity of their baptistries. If obeying Christ, encouraging spiritual growth and discipleship, bearing witness to the Gospel, and being connected to believers in every age of the church matter to you, believers baptism still matters.

4

DOES THE TERM BAPTIST STILL MATTER?

MICHAEL W. MCDILL

The term 'Baptist' may not mean much to the general population in today's postmodern, post-colonial, post-gender, posthuman and—it would seem—for our purposes, post-denominational society. This is not overly disturbing as one examines history, however. Many important events and figures of great consequence have come upon the scene and scarcely been noticed at first. Key historical figures have been scoffed at or ignored early on only to be lauded for extraordinary foresight belatedly. Winston Churchill comes to mind. One man asked if anything good could come out of the little village of Nazareth. Likewise, simply gauging the current popularity of an idea may not tell us much in the end. Martin Luther apparently 'rediscovered' a truth which had been staring at anyone with access to the New Testament for a millennium or more when he was confronted with the history-changing phrase, "the just shall live by faith." Living, as we do, in a 'post-truth' culture does not banish truth from existence. To casually encounter it on the streets of Boston, Los Angeles, or New York city, however, is probably unlikely in our current cultural climate.

Not only did Luther reintroduce the theological concept *faith alone* to the world, he also, in effect, wedged open a channel for the flood of denominations that became the norm for the modern western world in the centuries to come. Despite (or perhaps because of) the deluge of new church groups which poured upon the scene of history after the Reformation, the question of how to define the church still hovers in the atmosphere of our times and causes confusion and discomfort for those who claim the name Christian. Throughout the middle ages the church was seen as the gate-keeper of salvation. Since Cyprian famously declared, "Outside the church there is no salvation" in the third century, the accepted idea was that *one had to be **in the church** to be saved.*[1] Although Protestants seized upon a new theology of salvation founded upon faith, it could be argued that they failed to clarify or debunk the idea that salvation is received *through the church*. 'Exhibit A' in this argument would be infant baptism. A baby who is baptized is a member of the church and thus, being inside the church so to speak, is granted salvation. The Roman Catholic church is the model for this notion, but the Protestant reformers also embraced paedobaptism. Inseparable from the practice of infant baptism is the idea that entry into the church is, in some sense, entry into salvation. The great reformers not only retained infant baptism, bequeathed to them by the Roman Catholic church, but also embraced the medieval devotion to the state supported church. To be born and baptized in Lutheran or any other Protestant territory was to receive salvation and also to be registered as a citizen. The question arises: are these biblical ideas?

Baptists, on the other hand, have always believed that *one must be saved to be in the church.* This is directly contrary to the medieval ecclesiology

---

1. The Latin phrase *extra Ecclesiam nulla salus* is translated "outside the Church there is no salvation." This statement comes from a private letter (LXXII.21) of Cyprian, bishop of Carthage, in the 3rd century. The letter was written regarding a controversy over whether it was necessary to baptize subjects who had previously been baptized by heretics.

(*one must be in the church to be saved*) borrowed by many of the Protestants of the sixteenth century. Believer's baptism is the baptizing of those who have made a conscious decision to follow Christ and according to His word have received salvation. Baptism is thus the public and symbolic expression of having already accepted redemption, reconciliation, and rebirth by faith in the promise of God accomplished by Christ's death, burial and resurrection. The result is that to be in the church one must be saved by faith. The church, then, is simply composed of those who are saved through Christ and publicly demonstrate this relationship through baptism. Baptists name this arrangement, which they claim is derived from Scripture, a *believers' church* or a *regenerate church*.

Clearly, this is the biblical definition of church communicated in the New Testament. Without a commitment to believer's baptism the scriptural concept of a church of believers is not possible. Any mixture of infant baptism into the formula introduces unscriptural ecclesiology and with it the questionable notion that salvation is through the church instead of through faith in Christ alone. The human religious inclination is to trust in the institution and its rites rather than in Christ. The New Testament idea of church is that it is made up of those who have already trusted Him and are His disciples. Faith in Christ, therefore, is the groundwork for the establishment of the organic edifice He founded called the church (as Peter likened the church to a building made up of living stones). The temporal institution or organization, which is only the outward human structure, should never be the object of faith. To take the institutional approach is to veer badly from scriptural truth and introduce considerable confusion into people's minds as to the way of salvation.

So, why does the term 'Baptist' and, more importantly, the key concepts associated with the name (believer's baptism and a believers' church) still matter? The chief reason is that ecclesiology (the doctrine of the church) and soteriology (the doctrine of salvation) are interconnected. One of the principal reasons that Baptists insist on their views is that one's understanding of salvation is affected by his or her view of the church. Who's in the church? How do we *know* who's in and who's out? These questions necessarily affect one's conception of salvation. How can we be confident and assured of salvation? How do I know that I am delivered from sin and death and the tyranny of the self, and can look forward to a final and conclusive deliverance ushering into eternal life? These are important queries that call for clear answers. Unfortunately, if a denomination baptizes babies a confounding question is introduced which must be answered when it comes to the biblical truth about salvation. How and when does the baby have faith? The New Testament is full of assertions which emphasize the necessity of faith (on the part of the person who is delivered from sin and death by God through Christ). He or she receives this salvation by simply believing. This is a conscious and personal decision. It is a 'changing of the mind' of which infants and very small children do not appear capable. The potential for someone to think that he or she is right with God because of a baptism in infancy, and yet never to have personally believed and professed Christ, leads the Baptist to take a firm stand on a biblical view of baptism. A true understanding of salvation is at stake. But not every Christian group sees it this way.[2]

So, we have unpleasant contention on this subject of Baptism and seem not to be able to get along. This is distressing to many Christians. Can we all get along? This was the question posed by Rodney King, the unmanageably intoxicated man who was beaten by policemen after a high-speed car chase and ensuing struggle in California in 1991. In response to the race riots in Los Angeles after the officers were acquitted, King uttered his plaintiff call for unity as he emerged from the hospital in a wheelchair: "Can we all get along?" This has become the cry of our times. As an example, you've probably seen the "Coexist" bumper stickers, telling all of those of us who are 'religious' to get along. The premise seems to be that religions

---

2. See note on page 184.

are causing most of the rancor and violence in the world. If we would just be like the peace-loving secularist everything would be smooth sailing for the 'world community.' In America we now have red states and blue states representing differing political ideologies. The map is divided and so we feel that genuine unity is elusive. We can't seem to get along in any area of life.

The same type of question is sometimes heard in Christian circles. Why can't Christians get along? What is the big deal about things like baptism, and how and whom we should baptize? It seems so petty. Can't like-minded believers coexist? Can't we primarily emphasize what we agree on? One answer to that, in part, is that we do actually get along fairly well and celebrate what we share as Christians.[3] But the other part of an answer is that there are principles of biblical truth at stake which cannot be swept under an ecumenical rug. The viewpoint from within the Christian sheepfold put forth here will obviously be that of the Baptist. You might be thinking: "Oh here we go with some guy thinking he and his group are the 'only ones who know the truth.'" Well, can we talk about the truth? Are we to surrender truth for the sake of a shallow unity? Perhaps an appeal to something sure and plain could even be refreshing. Before you come to a conclusion let me ask you to set aside a quick judgment. Baptists have never claimed to have a corner on the market of truth, instead consistently pointing inquirers to Scripture. The request here is for a hearing. This seems fair. Determine for yourself whether the case made is based on solid biblical thinking.

BELIEVER'S BAPTISM AND *SOLA FIDE*

Baptists have consistently made an appeal to the New Testament when it comes to the ordinance of baptism and, based on the authority of scripture, have clung to the idea that baptism is for believers. When tested by the great

---

3. See C. S. Lewis, *Mere Christianity*.

salvation doctrine of faith alone in Christ alone (also firmly attested in the New Testament), believer's baptism is thoroughly confirmed as consistent and true. Salvation precedes baptism and church membership and is preceded by faith. This order establishes the distinction between salvation and the church. It dispels the fog of confusion emanating from the conflation of salvation and church membership which occurs when infant baptism and/or salvation via institutional rites are embraced. Thus, believer's baptism and the necessary companion notion of a believers' church safeguards *sola fide* and *sola gratia* and even *sola scriptura*. No baptism or church is necessary for salvation in the Baptist view. Baptism and church spring from and are founded upon salvation, never the reverse.

If the Bible calls for each individual to respond to God by accepting the truth of the gospel for himself, then infant baptism can mislead those involved in it, whether Catholic or Protestant.[4] Salvation is not because of baptism but because of faith. Faith is by necessity a personal decision, corresponding to the call for repentance in Scripture. Baptist theologian H. Wheeler Robinson wrote that believer's baptism "emphasizes, as no other interpretation of the rite can ever do, the significance, the necessity, and the

---

4. Baptist biblical theologian Augustus Strong made the following unequivocal charges against paedobaptism: "The evil effects of infant baptism are a strong argument against it: First,—in forestalling the voluntary act of the child baptized, and thus practically preventing his personal obedience to Christ's commands. Secondly,—in inducing superstitious confidence in an outward rite as possessed of regenerating efficacy. Thirdly,—in obscuring and corrupting Christian truth with regard to the sufficiency of Scripture, the connection of the ordinances, and the inconsistency of an impenitent life with church-membership. Fourthly,—in destroying the church as a spiritual body, by merging it in the nation and the world. Fifthly,— in putting into the place of Christ's command a commandment of men, and so admitting the essential principle of all heresy, schism, and false religion" (Augustus Hopkins Strong, *Outlines of Systematic Theology*, [Philadelphia: Griffith & Rowland Press, 1908], 251).

individuality of conversion."[5] The choice to trust Christ for salvation cannot be made by someone else on one's behalf. It must be made personally. The nature of the theological case outlined in the Bible is such that each person is estranged from God because of conscious decisions to sin. Therefore, each person is given a way to restore a relationship with God through the sacrifice of Christ. He died for the sins of the whole world so that each individual can now be called to repentance, to turn from self and sin to the grace of God in Christ. This personal response is essential to faith. Faith is saying no to my way and saying yes to Him who said, "I am the way." It is a personal matter between the individual and God. It cannot be decided by a community or a godparent or any other intermediary.

Trusting God personally by trusting Christ individually is the key to biblical salvation. The individual relates to God personally through Christ. The New Testament never recommends trusting any other mediator, representative, or even parent, no matter what institutionally sanctioned claims are made. Christ, our High Priest, shed His own blood for us. He is the mediator of that once-and-for-all sacrifice which is of the highest value, the life of the Son of God Himself. He is also a mediator who continues his role eternally as "our great High Priest who has passed through the heavens," and, because of the resurrection, offers life in exchange for sin and death, which he took upon Himself on the cross.[6] Because of all this He is unassailably trustworthy and thus the Bible calls us to trust Him and no one else. "For there is one God, and one mediator between God and men, the man Christ Jesus; Who gave himself a ransom for all, to be testified in due time."[7]

---

5. H. Wheeler Robinson, *Baptist Principles* (4th ed.; London: Carey Kingsgate Press, 1960; 1st publ. 1938), 17, emphasis added.

6. See the book of Hebrews.

7. 1 Timothy 2:5-6, *KJV*.

So, we see one of the chief failings of infant baptism: the practice necessarily inserts a proxy for the baby, another mediator whose faith or office represents the baby. This is not biblical and is the reason Baptists stand so staunchly upon the principle of *believer's* baptism. A personal decision for faith in Christ must take place or there is no salvation. Baptism symbolizes this faith and all that it represents in view of what God has accomplished for the individual. It is a command of Christ which the believer gladly obeys since it identifies him with his Lord and Savior, to say to the church and the world: this Jesus is *my* Lord and *my* Savior and I am His follower and servant. All the riches of this new relationship and new life are received by faith and are because of God's grace. These riches may all be missed if a person is taught the false doctrine that he or she has salvation conferred because of the mediation of the Roman church or a Protestant clergyman, a parent, godparent, priest, or any other official, in the rite of baptism.

An important Baptist thinker, E. Y. Mullins, wrote in this same vein, stressing "how intensely personal and individual is Christian faith. The element of proxy, or substitutionary faith, is alien to the gospel. Hence the baptism of infants upon the alleged faith of parents or sponsors is foreign to New Testament teaching. Personal faith is the only kind of faith recognized in the New Testament."[8] Baptist historian Henry Vedder concisely expressed the Baptist view:

---

8. Edgar Young Mullins, *The Christian Religion in Its Doctrinal Expression* (Philadelphia: Roger Williams Press, 1917), 375-376. The idea of faith being personal and individual has sometimes been called *soul-competency* by Baptists, although this term may include other aspects of Baptist belief such as religious liberty. It is explained (in this personal faith sense) further by professor Mullins: "Observe then that the idea of the competency of the soul in religion excludes at once all human interference, such as episcopacy and infant baptism, and every form of religion by proxy. Religion is a personal matter between the soul and God" (*The Axioms of*

Religion thus becomes, according to Christ's teaching, a matter between each human soul and God. There is no need of priestly mediation, there is no possibility of regeneration by a magical "sacrament." To baptize one who has not believed is, in the eye of a Baptist, an empty form, but as the act of one who sees in it more than that, it is something worse: it is an impertinent interference with the personal rights of another soul, it is to nullify the fundamental principle of the gospel of Christ.[9]

Salvation is accomplished only by God. This is the clear message of the New Testament: Christ and him crucified. This is God's plan and we must not add to it. These enormously important salvation truths are ob-

---

Religion [Philadelphia: American Baptist Publication Society, 1908], 54).

This Baptist idea of soul-competency is in stark contrast with what the Catechism of the Catholic Church says concerning faith and baptism: "For all the baptized, children or adults, faith must grow after Baptism. For this reason the Church celebrates each year at the Easter Vigil the renewal of baptismal promises. Preparation for Baptism leads only to the threshold of new life. Baptism is the source of that new life in Christ from which the entire Christian life springs forth. For the grace of Baptism to unfold, the parents' help is important. So too is the role of the godfather and godmother, who must be firm believers, able and ready to help the newly baptized - child or adult on the road of Christian life. Their task is a truly ecclesial function (officium). The whole ecclesial community bears some responsibility for the development and safeguarding of the grace given at Baptism" (*Catechism of the Catholic Church*, www.vatican.va/archive/ENG0015/__P3K.HTM, art. 1254-1255). Contrast this nebulous idea of faith and baptism from Catholicism with a simple statement from a Baptist scholar: "We Baptists love our children, and rather than finding false security in the deceptive practice of paedobaptism, we instruct our children about who Jesus Christ is and what He has done for us" (Malcolm Yarnell, *Calvinism: A Cause for Rejoicing, A Cause for Concern*, paper from "Building Bridges: Southern Baptists and Calvinism" 27 November 2008, Ridgecrest Conference Center, North Carolina).

9. Henry C. Vedder, *The Baptists* (New York: Baker & Taylor, 1903), 12.

scured when we introduce any other baptism than for believers alone. This is why Baptists embrace their name and refuse to blanch when others mock and fuss at a perceived hidebound narrowness. Despite this perception, great numbers of Baptists are determined to continue to exercise a simple, fixed tenacity, holding on to what they deem to be biblical truth. The potential for dilution of the simple truth of salvation by faith *alone* is what is at stake.

Thus, for Baptists, baptism is only for those who have made a conscious decision to follow Christ. In the last chapter, and in the last words, of the gospel of Matthew, Jesus instructed his disciples to baptize other new disciples. They were to make disciples, those who followed the teachings of Jesus. These fresh disciples were to identify themselves as Jesus' followers through baptism. The unique claims of Jesus are here demonstrated in the naming of the Trinity in the baptismal ordinance: the Father, the Son, and the Holy Spirit.[10] Jesus is identified not as simply another teacher but as the Son of God. One who trusts that this is true and decides to identify himself with Jesus and His teaching, in an ongoing commitment to follow Him, is a disciple. All of this is evident and straightforward as we look at what is known as 'the great commission' of Matthew twenty-eight. There is, then, a definite and logical biblical order here assigned to baptism from

---

10. Baptist theologian J. L. Dagg emphasized the importance of the trinity in baptism, pointing to Jesus' divinity: "In the formula of Christian baptism it is clearly exhibited. We are baptized into one name, because God is one; but that is the name of the Father, and of the Son, and of the Holy Ghost, because it belongs alike to each of these divine persons. Here, this doctrine meets us, at our very entrance on the profession of the Christian religion. If Christ was not God, he was justly condemned to death, and his religion is false; and the Holy Spirit, the Comforter whom he promised, is as little entitled to regard as he was. If Christ and the Holy Spirit are not God, the form of baptism should be rejected, as of a piece with the false religion into which it introduces us. No man can consistently receive Christian baptism, without believing the doctrine of the Trinity" (John Leadley Dagg, *Manual of Theology* [Charleston: Southern Baptist Publication Society, 1859], 247-48).

the mouth of Christ Himself. Furthermore, baptism is not to signify citizenship in Christendom, as baby baptism often has (which is reflected in the idea of 'christening'),[11] but is a sign of discipleship, joining others (i.e. a church) who have made the same deliberate faith confession, identifying as a follower of Jesus Christ. A venerable Baptist professor put it this way:

> In the New Testament we have no account of any being members of churches except such as were considered to be truly regenerated believers and had actually submitted to the rite of baptism. Now the Baptist churches insist as one of their fundamental principles that only truly regenerated believers in Christ, after having been properly baptized on profession of their faith in the Lord, should be received as members of the church.[12]

If one is to have anything at all to do with Christianity, there seems to be no good reason to add to or take away from this simple order.[13] Deciding to follow Christ, believing that he truly is the Son of God, and therefore has the power, and has already accomplished, what is needed in order for me to be forgiven of sin and reconciled to God, I publicly confess this and witness

---

11. James Leo Garrett writes concerning what I have called 'Christendom' above (the idea of a Christian state-church), as it is associated with infant baptism: "infant baptism, it has often been alleged, has led to the primarily European phenomenon of the *Volkskirche* or *Staatskirche* (state church) with its great masses of non-worshiping, non-practicing church members who in effect have repudiated their baptism" (James Leo Garrett, Jr., *Systematic Theology: Biblical, Historical, and Evangelical*, Vol. 2, 2nd ed. [North Richland Hills, TX: Bibal Press, 2001], ch.73, V, A2). In other words, Garrett is suggesting that infant baptism leads to nominal Christianity, as is seen throughout Europe today.

12. Edwin Charles Dargan, *Ecclesiology: A Study of the Churches*, 2nd ed. (Louisville: Charles T. Dearing, 1905), 167.

13. See note on page 186.

to my sincerity through baptism in His name.[14] Any other formula for salvation or baptism or church is misleading and therefore rejected by Baptists.

BELIEVERS' CHURCH: UNITY AND THE ORDINANCES

There is also a connection for Baptists between a believers' church and the church ordinance of the Lord's Supper. The idea of the church as a spiritual community, based on faith in Christ alone, excludes any hint of sacramentalism (the belief that the 'sacraments' are inherently efficacious and necessary for salvation). Believers meet together to worship, for mutual encouragement and admonition, and to hear a word from Scripture, but there is no sacrament in Baptist life. The idea that physically ingesting wafers of bread somehow imparts salvation is foreign to the New Testament and therefore rejected by Baptist churches. No priest and no special incantation to make the Lord's supper officially efficacious are needed in any way for Baptists. What makes salvation effective is what Christ has already accomplished, once and for all, outside of Jerusalem on a cross, executed by Roman authorities in the first century.

The bread and cup taken in the ordinance are a memorial of those historical events and are significant for modern believers because Jesus of Nazareth is the Son of God. The power of the supper is in reminding believers of God's love for them demonstrated in His Son, not in a priest or in the elements of the 'sacrament.' Nor does it represent faith in any self-authorized institutionalized church which may claim to officiously dispense 'sal-

---

14. Concerning confession (or profession) of faith and baptism George Eldon Ladd, a Baptist New Testament scholar, wrote: "In the early church profession of faith in Christ and baptism were practically simultaneous events. Baptism in water, along with confession of Christ, was the outward sign of faith" (George Eldon Ladd, *A Theology of the New Testament*, rev. ed. [Grand Rapids: Eerdmans, 1993], 326 n. 16).

vation' through the elements as, for instance, the Roman Catholic Church and Anglican Church claim. Thus, the Lord's supper is a sign to remind us of Christ. It is a picture, in essence a metaphor, of the historical realities of suffering and death endured by Christ on the cross. These realities are commemorated in the simple supper of remembrance in order to confirm and recall Christ's work on behalf of the recipient *by faith*. In this same way, Baptism is also a sign, for the believer and for the church, that signifies faith in Christ, as we have already discussed. These two simple ordinances, then, channel the believer's faith toward the person of Christ, not to any priest, institution, or sacrament. Salvation, then, is not assured by being a part of the 'covenant community' or any official church institution, but only by the finished work of Christ.

To summarize concerning the two expressions of union with Christ (and therefore with other disciples) in the believers' church: Baptism and the Lord's Supper are *ordinances*;[15] they are not sacraments, which are represented by Catholic, Orthodox and some Protestant groups as having an actual salvific effect on the participant. Salvation comes through no act or religious rite or priestly ministrations, but through the finished work of Christ, and faith that He accomplished salvation once and for all on behalf of any who choose to believe in Him. The Lord's Supper, therefore, is viewed by Baptists as a *memorial*, with the bread and the cup being symbolic of the body and blood of Christ. These symbols represent the finished work of God in the cross for believers' salvation, to which nothing is to be added. When we commemorate Christ's sacrifice in the Lord's Supper we remember His words: "It is finished," and so our faith is directed to our Savior's work and not our own.

---

15. A helpful definition of *ordinance* is: "A ceremony which the Lord commanded that His church should observe and one in which the gospel is portrayed. An ordinance is practiced as a memorial act of obedience rather than as a sacrament. There are two such ordinances: baptism and the Lord's Supper" (*The Believer's Study Bible*, eds. W. A. Criswell, Paige Patterson, glossary).

BAPTISTS' HISTORICALLY HIGH
VIEW OF SCRIPTURE

"By what authority do you do these things?" Jesus was asked this question by those who were skeptical of him. He employed an effective strategy: He answered a question with a question. He asked his skeptics by what authority John the Baptist baptized, heaven's or men's. They could not return an answer.[16] The question of authority is crucial in all times in all circumstances, whether we are aware of it or not. By what authority? We all constantly make decisions and come to conclusions based on some kind of authority. Many claim authority, but what person, institution, or entity can impose genuine moral accountability upon us? It is rather like the following scenario when my children were still at home: my daughter might instruct her older brother to take out the trash. My son will inevitably reply, "who says?" If the response is "Dad," then he will say, "oh." That little 'oh' is very telling. He respects the authority of his Dad. He considers his sister to have no authority at all which would require acknowledgment. But the trash gets taken out because of Dad's authority.

As we have discussed the importance of a biblical definition of the church and salvation, and see how integral each is to the other, we are led to an even more fundamental question: what authority is the final word on these matters? As has already been claimed, Baptists rely heavily and, one could even say, singularly, on the Bible. Christians, broadly speaking, have a great respect for the Bible. It represents an authentic authority as sacred scripture. Baptists see the scriptures as the only authority for Christians. They have generally not added any institution, creed, pontiff, power structure, judicial body, or any additional ancient writing to the list of authorities by which the Christian life and church are informed. In fact, there is only one authority on the list: the Bible, consisting of the Old and New

---

16. See Luke 20.

Testaments. It's like telling my wife she's my favorite wife. She's my only wife, and that's actually a more exclusive claim than merely a favorite. My wife doesn't mind being the only one on my list, so there seems to be a place for this sort of exclusivity. Baptists have even been accused of placing the Bible on too high a pedestal. This does not bother them much because the standard Baptist view has been to see the Bible as the very words of God Himself.

The conventional wisdom in our world today is that any claim to truth is questionable, on par with my daughter commanding her brother by her own authority. The approved slogan of the times is that truth is relative. The world family has many dissonant voices claiming to be speaking with authority, but no one really has any. "Take out the trash." "Who says?" "I do!" "*Whatever.*" Everything is relative and all statements are a matter of opinion only.[17] According to this postmodern view, there is no father figure to whom we may appeal. Or is there? That is just what the Bible claims: that there *is* a Father-Creator who holds ultimate authority by His very nature, so that whatever He says is true. The Bible claims to be those very words of the Father inscripturated and preserved so that we might know, directly from our Creator, what He has to say to us. This is the historic Baptist view. It is *not* a popular view. Modern people see this view as comparable to one of the many children in the 'world family' claiming to be a parent when there *are* no parents. To say that you have the truth is seen as utter arrogance in our time. But Baptists correct this misunderstanding by saying that Christians who believe the Bible is God's very word to us are *not* claiming to *be* God, they are simply claiming to believe that God has spoken. And if God has really spoken, then by virtue of his nature and authority as God, the creator and author of all, people really need to listen closely to what He says.

Since the turn of the seventeenth century Baptists have held a very high view of Scripture. Of course, not all modern Baptists honor this heri-

---

17. Notice that this argument, which would be supported by many in our current culture, is a statement affirming relativism absolutely and is thus self-refuting.

tage, some tending to rely more on the current science or culture as author-ities, but many still affirm Scripture as a sure word from God. This legacy goes back to some of the very first English Baptists, Thomas Helwys and John Smyth. These two were instrumental in Baptist beginnings in England from 1609, and were the leaders of the earliest Baptists, called General Baptists because of a belief in a general atonement. In a book entitled, *Baptists and the Bible*, L. Russ Bush and Tom Nettles trace the legacy of Baptists as they have trusted the Bible as the one authority which is infallible and with-out error, believing it to be God's very words. A review gives the substance of Bush and Nettles' research:

> Beginning with John Smyth and Thomas Helwys, Bush and Nettles demonstrate that the inerrancy of Scripture was a foundational doc-trine of the earliest Baptists . . . . Additionally, General and Particular Baptists, although differing in their understanding of soteriology, both held to a high view of Scripture. This theological framework pervaded their confessions and sparked the modern mission move-ment through Andrew Fuller, William Carey, and Adoniram Jud-son. . . . Bush and Nettles provide strong support to their arguments that Baptists have a long legacy of believing that Scripture is inspired by God, infallible in its original presentation, and sufficient for all matters of life and doctrine.[18]

Helwys himself said: "The scriptures of the Old and New Testament are written for our instruction (2 Timothy 3:16) and . . . we should search them for they testify of CHRIST (John 5:39). Therefore they are to be used with all reverence, as containing the Holy Word of GOD, which only is our direction in all things whatsoever."[19]

---

18. "Baptists and the Bible," Keith Collier, Baptist Theology, http://www.baptisttheology.org/BaptistsandtheBible.cfm.

19. Thomas Helwys, *A Declaration of Faith of English People Remaining at*

To illustrate that this legacy continued among Baptists we might consult a statement of faith from a little over 200 years after the first English Baptists. One of the most widely used confessions of faith among Baptists in America was the *New Hampshire Confession*. It was issued in 1833 by the Baptist convention of, you guessed it, New Hampshire. Concerning the Bible it says:

> We believe that the Holy Bible was written by men divinely inspired, and is a perfect treasure of heavenly instruction for it has God for its author, salvation for its end and truth without any mixture of error for its matter; that it reveals the principles by which God will judge us; and therefore is and shall remain to the end of the world, the true center of Christian Union and the supreme standard by which all human conduct, creeds and opinions should be tried.[20]

Notice the idea here is that biblical authority trumps all other sources as far as truth is concerned. This statement equates the Bible with the

---

Amsterdam in Holland, (1611), article 23.

20. W. J. McGlothlin, *Baptist Confessions of Faith* (Philadelphia: American Baptist Publication Society, 1911), 301-302. The *New Hampshire Confession of Faith* can be found in various primary resource volumes and is available, as are most published documents one hundred years old or more (being in the public domain), on the internet. A profound idea found in this statement, that could easily be skimmed over and missed, is that unity is founded on scripture truth, so that scripture is "the true center of Christian Union." Unity must be based on truth in the end or it will not last and in retrospect will be seen to have been shallow and perhaps even cynical. Unity for unity's sake may sometimes appear effective if fighting a common enemy, but even then, the unity is based on a shared truth: the enemy is evil or the enemy must be defeated. Baptists have generally built unity around shared principles of truth rather than a hierarchical organization or a desire to be unified in and of itself. The New Hampshire Confession's influence can be seen even today in that it served as the basis for the *Baptist Faith and Message* of the Southern Baptist Convention (1925, 1963, and 2000).

words of God and therefore as eternal and inerrant.[21] These ideas are largely consistent in Baptist history from Smyth and Helwys to New Hampshire Baptists to many Baptists today. Baptists have traditionally maintained an extraordinarily high view of Scripture and its authority.

A Contrast: Early Protestant Zwingli

It may help further to highlight the strength of this Baptist belief in Scriptural authority by way of a contrast. We may be able to show a marked difference between the original English Baptists and the early Protestants who came before them when it comes to biblical authority. Thus, it will be instructive to take a look at one of the original Protestant Reformers, Ulrich Zwingli of Zurich, Switzerland. Early in the sixteenth century, Zwingli led a Bible study composed of some younger students, his protégés.[22] They were all Christian *humanists*, in other words they were interested in ancient sources of truth and wisdom, rather than simply relying upon the traditional

---

21. L. Russ Bush, who was Professor of Philosophy of Religion at Southwestern Baptist Theological Seminary and Southeastern Baptist Theological Seminary, offers the following helpful definition of inerrancy: "Evangelical scholars today are using the term 'inerrancy' to affirm that the Bible, properly understood in light of its ancient cultural form and content, is absolutely truthful in all of its affirmations about God's will and God's way. Furthermore, the affirmation is that, due to inspiration, the bible does not teach or affirm error about any area of reality. Rather, what Scripture says is what God says, and thus Scripture will speak only the truth about reality. The biblical affirmation itself may be figuratively expressed, or it may be straightforward affirmation of historical fact or of a theological doctrine or an ethical norm. In every case, however, to affirm inerrancy is to affirm the truthfulness, and thus the inherent, veracious authority, of the Scriptural passage on its own terms" (L. Russ Bush, *Understanding Biblical Inerrancy* [Formatted for eBook publication by Joshua Bush for LRBush.com, 2013], 13).

22. This account is of events which occurred in the 1520's, around eighty years *before* the early English Baptists, Smyth and Helwys, initiated believer's baptism and inaugurated the first General Baptist church in Holland in 1609. This 1609 date is generally viewed as the beginning of the Baptist denomination by historians.

medieval cultural and intellectual constructs of their age. Thus, this Bible study in Zurich was intent on exploring the original Greek New Testament rather than the conventional Latin translation of the Roman Catholic church, called the Vulgate. This new edition of the Greek New Testament had recently been published by another Christian humanist named Desiderius Erasmus of Rotterdam.

Zwingli led his students to look at the New Testament with fresh eyes, not constrained by officially sanctioned Catholic dogma. When the issue of baptism arose, Zwingli admitted that the New Testament asserted believer's baptism and never prescribed or described any infants being baptized. His pupils took this biblical view of baptism very seriously and eventually became known as *Anabaptists*. This was an evangelical group during the time of the Reformation which held many of the same convictions which Baptists have held through the centuries. They called themselves "brethren" and thus are known to historians as the Swiss Brethren. These 'brethren' sought to follow scripture and, in accordance with their recent New Testament studies, began to advocate adult baptism for believers only, and to claim that infant baptism was illegitimate.[23] In response, there were official debates on the subject in Zurich called disputations, and eventually these former students of Zwingli were outlawed.

Zwingli had decided the best way to advance his reform was by working with the city council of Zurich. His reform, therefore, was a total cultural and governmental program, bearing upon every aspect of the lives of the citizens of this Swiss canton. Despite his earlier position during the Bible study days, which had demonstrated believer's baptism to be properly derived from the New Testament, Zwingli became a champion of infant

---

23. Historian Kenneth Scott Latourette, a Baptist, wrote: "They were called Anabaptists because they insisted that the baptism of infants was not true baptism, that only believers should be baptized, and that if an individual had been baptized in infancy, after he had the experience of being justified by faith he should be re-baptized" (Kenneth Scott Latourette, *Christianity Through the Ages* [New York: Harper & Row, 1965], 102).

baptism due partly to his magisterial (state-supported) approach to reform.[24] Zwingli's reform went forward, then, with the power of the state behind it, and thus the power to punish those with contrary reforming ideas. One of the 'brethren' was put to death for advocating 'rebaptism,' as the leaders of the city called it (thus the name Anabaptist, meaning "one who baptizes again"). On January 5, 1527, Felix Manz was tied down with weights and thrown into the river Limmat which flows through Zurich, drowned for nothing other than his baptismal theology. "Just two days before his drowning, Zwingli wrote to a fellow Reformer: 'The Anabaptist, who should already have been sent to the devil, disturbs the peace of the pious people. But I believe, the axe [execution] will settle it.'"[25] Manz's execution by drowning

---

24. Baptist theologian E. Y. Mullins wrote: "Zwingli's clear mind perceived distinctly that the Reformers' principle of faith necessarily excluded infant baptism and so taught in his earlier career. Under pressure of ancient custom, however, and for expediency's sake he finally decided to retain it, and sought to find Scripture warrant for it" (Edgar Young Mullins, *The Axioms of Religion*, 108).

25. Ruth A. Tucker, *Parade of Faith: A Biographical History of the Christian Church* (Grand Rapids: Zondervan, 2011), 267. The following is Tucker's description of the martyrdom of Manz in full: "In March of 1526 . . . the Zurich city council had enacted a law making believers' baptism (re-baptism) a capital offence punishable by drowning. Manz would become the first Anabaptist martyred for this offence. Insisting that he was not seeking to prevent Reformers from baptizing infants, he argued that his only motive was 'to bring together those who were willing to accept Christ, obey the Word, and follow in His footsteps, to unite with these by baptism, and to leave the rest in their present conviction.' But Zwingli and the city council were determined to make Manz's death a deterrent. Just two days before his drowning, Zwingli wrote to a fellow Reformer: 'The Anabaptist, who should already have been sent to the devil, disturbs the peace of the pious people. But I believe, the axe will settle it.' But Manz would not be axed to death. Rather, officials execute him by his own baptismal prescription—immersion of an adult believer. His death is ridiculed as the third baptism: infant, believers, and drowning—'He who dips shall be dipped!' The story is chilling. Bullinger describes the scene: On a bitterly cold Saturday afternoon in January of 1527, 'Manz was taken out of the Wellenberg prison and led to the fish market there by the Limmat [River]. There his death sentence was read. He was taken to the butcher shop, and then forced into

was derisively named the 'third baptism' by Protestant leaders in Zurich.[26]

This seems an inauspicious beginning for what came to be known as the Reformed tradition in the Protestant Reformation. The Bible does not sanction either infant baptism or execution for those who deny it. Thus, we must look to other sources to find the authority to which Zwingli turned in order to act in this manner in Zurich. An editor of Zwingli's *Selected Works* in English, Samuel Macauley Jackson, comments on Zwingli's change of heart concerning baptism:

> It is doubtless true that in his earlier addresses from the pulpit he exposed the unbiblical character of the church doctrine upon the general subject of baptism, and probable that he inclined towards ruling out infant baptism, as lacking biblical support. . . . Zwingli found himself criticised severely in Zurich when his remarks upon infant baptism were repeated. To those who were brought up to regard baptism as necessary to salvation it was a great shock to be told that the ceremony had no validity. To those who believed that the rite of baptism was the Christian obligation in lieu of circumcision, and just as binding, to hear that there was grave doubt whether it should be so considered was to knock the underpinning from their faith. When Zwingli found that opposition to the popular belief and practice upon this point meant that he would be exposed not only to clerical and lay adverse criticism, but probably would lose him his influence with the city magistrates, who were all friends of the Old faith on this doctrine, he devoted a great deal of attention to it, with

---

a boat, in which the executioner and a pastor were standing.' A crowd of onlookers, including his mother and brother, had accompanied him. Offered an opportunity to recant, he publicly proclaims his faith, encouraged by his family and other supporters. He is then rowed some distance from shore, where he is pushed into the icy water, declaring his faith in Christ until the water engulfs him."

26. See William R. Estep, *The Anabaptist Story,* for the full narrative pertaining to the Swiss Brethren.

the result that he convinced himself that as to the subjects of baptism he had been wrong, and henceforth he took the orthodox [infant baptism] side.[27]

---

27. Samuel Macauley Jackson, ed., *Seclected Works of Huldriech Zwingli, (1484-1531) The Reformer of German Switzerland*, (Philadelphia: University of Philadelphia, 1901), 123-24. Jackson, who was a Presbyterian minister, goes on to describe Zwingli's treatment of his former students who became Anabaptists, whom Jackson calls 'Baptists': "The Confession of the . . . Baptists is in very simple language, showing a very honest and God-fearing mind, and is in itself a triumphant refutation of the charges of fanaticism and immorality which Zwingli brings against them. In fact in this paper Zwingli shows himself up in a very bad light. This is no place in which to describe the *outrageous* treatment which the Baptist party received in Zurich and elsewhere through Switzerland. The writer feels the freer to use such a term because he is not himself a Baptist, but he comes to the subject merely as a historical student. He considers that the part which Zwingli played in this wretched business is a serious blot upon his reputation, and reveals a defect in his character. The Baptists were pursued relentlessly; drowning, beheading, burning at the stake, confiscation of property, exile, fines and other forms of social obloquy were employed to suppress them and prevent their increase. The fact shows plainly that the persecuting spirit in the times of the Reformation was just as rife among Protestants as among Roman Catholics, and that the devil was abroad in the hearts of those who considered themselves on both sides as the true servants of the Lord Jesus Christ, whose tenderness and love must have been greatly tried by these wicked doings of his friends. Peace came at last to Switzerland – the peace of the grave-yard and of the sea which gives not up its dead. The orthodox party congratulated themselves upon having got rid of the pestilential heresy of adult baptism, yet the student of history as he looks upon the large, flourishing and world-wide Baptist church of today asks himself which side really won the battle for the right of private judgment and liberty of action, the side of the persecutor or the side of the persecuted?" (Samuel Macauley Jackson, ed., *Selected Works of Huldriech Zwingli*, 125, emphasis added).

As Jackson points out, Zwingli was not the only one to oppress the Anabaptists (and others who disagreed with the official Protestant-state position). Calvin secured the execution by burning of Miguel Servetus in Geneva (among others who were punished in various ways there) and even Luther the great spark of the Reformation was also guilty of quashing opposition to his own state-supported reform: "'Here I stand, so help me God, I can no other,' cried Lu-

The fact that Zwingli's reform was tied to the city council, and that church and state were not separated in Zurich, would seem to shed light on Zwingli's motivation for supporting infant baptism. Whereas when early on he had floated the idea that infant baptism was improper he had appealed to biblical authority, now as a staunch supporter of infant baptism his reasons appear to be more political. In contrast to the persecuting career of Zwingli, the early Baptist leader Thomas Helwys was thrown into prison for his beliefs in 1612. He had the audacity to challenge the King of England's authority over church and faith and sent King James a personal note to that effect written on a copy of his recent essay on religious liberty. [28] James reacted negatively, seeing religious liberty as a threat to his authority, and locked Helwys away where he languished and died as an outlaw because he was willing to stand for his beliefs no matter what political pressure he faced.

Baptists, like the Anabaptists before them, have desired to uphold the Scripture as the final authority, especially for the Christian life and the life of the church. This view of the Bible eliminates baptism for anyone except for believers only. It also eliminates any definition of church which includes government interference or coercion. This touches on a related issue, Reli-

---

ther, though he refused to allow Anabaptists, whom he regarded as anti-social heretics, to appeal to their consciences against Lutheranism" (Christopher Hill, *The Century of Revolution* [New York: Norton, 1961], 93).

28. The book Helwys wrote on religious liberty was entitled *A Short Description of the Mistery of Iniquity*: "Thomas Helwys wrote the book at a time when men bent the knee and spoke of the 'divine right of kings.' To question the power of church or rule of king was to risk prison and death; but *Helwys had the backing of the scriptures* and a courage from God, and the rights that he proclaimed were the rights of the common man. He denied that kings had divine authority over the souls of men or could in any way shape their worship. Helwys, the founder of the first Baptist church in England, ignored all threat to his personal liberty, and even risk of his life, so that he might proclaim the freedom of his soul and the same freedom for every man" (James Saxon Childers, ed., *A Way Home: The Baptists Tell Their Story* [Atlanta: Tupper and Love, 1964], 4).

gious Liberty,[29] and highlights the distinction between the Baptist view of Scripture and the early Protestant outworking of reform in Zurich (in spite of a claim to hold Scripture as the highest authority)[30] illustrating the exceptional nature of the Baptist (and Anabaptist) perspective. This perspective designates Scripture as the lone authority for the Christian, excluding all others as constructs of men and thus not fully trustworthy.

One of the themes of the Reformation was *Sola Scriptura*, which in Latin means "scripture alone." What were those in the Reformation excluding with this statement? Primarily they were thinking of the Pope, a man-made authority. How can the claim to *sola scriptura* be viewed as distinctively Baptist since so many other groups inherited this approach to religious authority from the Reformers? Baptists would argue that although many denominations claim to give Scripture alone authority for belief and practice, Baptists have followed this great Reformation watchword more closely by faithfully abiding by the New Testament with affirmations of believer's baptism and a believers' church. In other words, not only is there the

---

29. It might be said that biblical authority and religious liberty are connected in a more crucial way than it may seem at first glance. Christians who believe that the Bible is the only authority will be vigilant to exclude all other authorities when it comes to truth about God and therefore about eternity *and* temporality. This exclusion would apply especially to any governmental or any other traditional or man-made authority. To watch any authority other than Scripture dominating or assisting churches is to forfeit Christian liberty. To ensure liberty for the Christian, as he or she acknowledges God's word as the ultimate authority, the Baptist has traditionally urged states to ensure liberty of conscience for all. This is not simply enlightened self-interest but has been considered by Baptists as a biblical principle since Jesus and the apostles never forced people to believe but always invited them to repent.

30. Baptist historian Robert A. Baker comments on Zwingli's commitment to Scripture and his change concerning baptism: "Zwingli claimed that the Scriptures were his only authority. However, because it would have played havoc with his state support to deny the efficacy of infant baptism, he specifically repudiated the Anabaptists and clung to infant baptism; otherwise he would have 'unchurched' all of his political supporters" (Robert A. Baker, *The Baptist March in History* [Nashville: Convention Press, 1958], 35-36).

claim that Scripture is the only authority, there is also actual follow-through in the matters of baptism and church. Somebody who claims 'Sola Scriptura! That's what we're all about!' and then is found baptizing babies appears to demonstrate inconsistency in appealing to biblical authority. Many traditional protestant groups continue to plod along under the weight of this inconsistency. So that's why Baptists count Scriptural authority as one of our distinctive beliefs. After looking at a Protestant example in contrast with Baptist belief, let's look at Catholicism next. The Roman Catholic Church regards its own traditions as on par with Scripture and just as authoritative.

Another Contrast: Catholicism

The Roman Catholic Church represents another contrast by which to distinguish the Baptist stance on Biblical authority alone. The modern Catholic church continues the customs and beliefs of the church which have been added over the centuries like barnacles on the hull of the great institutional ship. If the ship is listing it is because it has added the authority of human words and tradition through the years and ultimately has proclaimed these to be equal with the Bible.[31] In fact the Roman church claims that the Scriptures' authority comes from the church itself. The *Catholic Encyclopedia* has this to say concerning Scriptural authority in an entry under the word 'tradition' (sorry for the long quote but please read as it is very instructive):

> The word tradition in the ecclesiastical sense . . . refers sometimes to the thing (doctrine, account, or custom) transmitted from one generation to another; sometimes to the organ or mode of the transmission . . . . At first there was question only of traditions claiming a Divine origin, but subsequently there arose questions of oral as distinct from written tradition, in the sense that a given doctrine or

---

31. Listing is a nautical term meaning leaning to one side and in danger of capsizing.

institution is not directly dependent on Holy Scripture as its source but only on the oral teaching of Christ or the Apostles. Finally with regard to the organ of tradition it must be an official organ, a magisterium, or teaching authority. Now in this respect there are several points of controversy between Catholics and every body of Protestants. Is all revealed truth consigned to Holy Scripture? or can it, must it, be admitted that Christ gave to His Apostles to be transmitted to His Church, that the Apostles received either from the very lips of Jesus or from inspiration or Revelation, Divine instructions which they transmitted to the Church and which were not committed to the inspired writings? Must it be admitted that Christ instituted His Church as the official and authentic organ to transmit and explain in virtue of Divine authority the Revelation made to men? The Protestant principle is: The Bible and nothing but the Bible; the Bible, according to them, is the sole theological source; there are no revealed truths save the truths contained in the Bible; according to them the Bible is the sole rule of faith: by it and by it alone should all dogmatic questions be solved; it is the only binding authority. Catholics, on the other hand, hold that there may be, that there is in fact, and that there must of necessity be certain revealed truths apart from those contained in the Bible; they hold furthermore that Jesus Christ has established in fact, and that to adapt the means to the end He should have established, a living organ as much to transmit Scripture and written Revelation as to place revealed truth within reach of everyone always and everywhere. Such are in this respect the two main points of controversy between Catholics and so-called orthodox Protestants (as distinguished from liberal Protestants, who admit neither supernatural Revelation nor the authority of the Bible). The other differences are connected with these or follow from them, as also the differences between different Protestant sects–according as they are more or less faithful to the Protestant principle, they recede from or approach the Catholic position.[32]

Baptists through the centuries, for the most part, have seen themselves as representatives of a 'protestant sect' of the 'more faithful' variety regarding the orthodox Protestant view of Scripture, so much so that some Baptists have claimed no connection with Protestantism.[33] As we have seen already, Baptists have often taken the Protestant 'sola Scriptura' (Scripture alone) motto to the extreme, even in the estimation of many Protestants, especially in the matter of believer's baptism (thus the name: Baptist).[34]

Since Catholics claim that Christ handed down other truths to the apostles, apart from the New Testament, who then handed them down to others and so somehow they are with us today, it makes sense that an institutional authority must preside over what may be legitimate and what is not regarding these supposedly surplus apostolic traditions. The problem is that a modern group of men, representing the church, decide these issues. Based on what? What then is the authority to end all arguments to which this modern Catholic magisterium turns? By definition, the church itself serves as this ultimate authority. This appears to be a tautology. In contrast, Jesus appealed constantly to the Scriptures. He was actually the enemy of the Jewish 'magisterium' of His day, the Sanhedrin.[35] Regarding church tradition

---

32. "Catholic Encyclopedia online," www.newadvent.org/cathen/15006b.htm.

33. This question of Protestant origins when it comes to Baptist history is not the subject of this essay and is a complicated and debated issue. Suffice it to say that the author sees both Protestant *and* other forms of influence (namely Anabaptist) as decisive in shaping Baptist origins.

34. Presbyterians, Lutherans, Anglicans, Methodists, Congregationalists, Reformed, and other Protestant groups all have been baptizing infants from the beginning. As has been noted, this introduces a confusion into their theology when it comes to salvation since an adherent of one of these groups can easily conclude that he is right with God as a 'Christian' through baptism and miss the simple biblical necessity of faith.

35. The comparison between magisterium and Sanhedrin is also made by

as authoritative, as is the Roman Catholic approach, makes Catholic dogma depend on human beings, who are faulty at best.[36] Thus the claim that the Roman Catholic institution is the final authority strikes Baptists as dicey at best, and clearly unbiblical compared with the affirmation of the authority of the Scriptures by Jesus Himself, whom the Bible says is the head of the church (and whose followers Peter and John also defied the Sanhedrin).

The Roman institutional approach to religious authority can also be observed in a more formal and official statement of the Church: "Thus it comes about that the Church does not draw her certainty about all revealed truths from the holy Scriptures alone. Hence both Scripture and tradition must be accepted and honored with equal feelings of devotion and reverence."[37] If the Church itself, its tradition, is on a par with Scripture, and the

---

a Catholic television website in a news article: "25-May-2011 -- Catholic World News Brief – *US Jewish-Catholic Dialogue Examines Religious Authority*: Representatives of the United States Conference of Catholic Bishops' Committee for Ecumenical and Interreligious Affairs and the National Council of Synagogues met on May 17 to discuss 'Sources of Authority in Catholicism and Judaism.' 'One of the obvious differences between our two faith communities is that while no one rabbi or religious body can speak for all Jews, the Church has a "Magisterium" made of bishops in communion with the pope, whose interpretation and application of the word of God can be binding on all Catholic believers,' said USCCB official Father James Massa. Rabbi Avram Reisner, professor of ethics at the University of Maryland, noted that only between 200 B.C. and A.D. 70 did Judaism have a body analogous to the Magisterium: the Sanhedrin. He asked, 'Is it any coincidence that the Christian community emerges from Judaism precisely at the time when such a body of authoritative teachers is in place for the parent religion?'" EWTN Global Catholic Network online, (www.ewtn.com/vnews/getstory.asp?number=113507).

36. See note on page 187.

37. *Dei Verbum*, II, 9, in Austin P. Flannery. *Documents of Vatican II* (1975), 755. It is obvious to the outsider that Catholic tradition and Scripture do not always agree. But the tension here between Scripture and tradition is not lost on certain Catholic theologians either. Raymond Brown saw this tension as something of a crisis even in 1975, especially in light of biblical higher criticism: "I do not mean that the voice of Scripture, critically studied, is the only voice that the Church has

church is seen as the source of Scripture, then it follows that salvation is also from the church. This is exactly what the Roman Church claimed for itself in the twentieth century church council known as Vatican II:

> This holy council first of all turns its attention to the Catholic faithful. Basing itself on Scripture *and* Tradition, it teaches that the Church, a pilgrim now on earth, is *necessary for salvation*: the one Christ is the Mediator and the way of salvation; He is present to us in His Body which is the Church. He Himself explicitly asserted the necessity of faith and Baptism (cf. Mk. 16:16; Jn. 3:5), and thereby affirmed at the same time the necessity of the Church which men enter through Baptism as through a door. Hence they *could not be saved* who, knowing that the Catholic Church was founded as necessary by God through Christ, would refuse to enter it or remain in it.[38]

It is clear from this statement that the Catholic Church claims to be the only way of salvation. Although the attempt is made to base this as-

---

to live with and respond to. The voice of Tradition (i.e., church experience and thought in the centuries after the first) has also to have its say. But I do not think that the voice of subsequent Tradition should drown out the voice of Scripture, the tradition of the first century. Nor do I think we should be allowed to gloss over the tensions between the two on the dubious principle that the Spirit always says the same thing. Only when each has had its say, resonant with all the sharpness of the tensions between them, can the Church of our times face its crises with the fullness of Christian experience brought to bear. Scripture is not the master of the Church; but when it is allowed to speak freely, it can serve as the nagging conscience of the Church" (Raymond E. Brown, *Biblical Reflections on Crises Facing the Church* [New York: Paulist Press, 1975], vii-viii). To relegate the Scripture to a 'nagging conscience' status is another example of the troubling nature of the Catholic approach to biblical authority from a Baptist point of view.

38. *Lumen Gentium,* 2,14, in Austin P. Flannery. *Documents of Vatican II* (1975), 365-366, emphasis added.

sertion on the teaching of Christ in Scripture, it is a tortured logic which includes the necessity of baptism in the Roman church for salvation. This conclusion can only be reached via a syllogism which includes the premise that the Roman church is the 'true' church by reason of apostolic succession. This specific claim is not accepted by all Christians (especially the ancient Eastern Orthodox) and is certainly not contained in Scripture. The Bible states that Christ is the *head* of the church, not the church itself, which is His body. This confusion and the direct identification of Christ, who said *He* was the only way (John 14:6), with the Roman Church through the centuries, with all its inquisitions and corruptions, is quite a pill to swallow. Baptists claim no authority other than Scripture in seeking the answers to two great human questions: how may I be delivered from evil and death (salvation in Christ alone) and where do I belong while on this earth (with the people of God, the church). The Bible's answers are much simpler, and yet deeper and more profound, since they are all focused on Christ Himself and His finished work.

The Catholic approach amounts to institutional magic. If only someone is in the church, as Noah was in the ark, then that person is saved. The church offers its seven sacraments as dispensers of the medicine of salvation, which only the church can confer, by special ceremonial incantations of the proper word formulas.[39] Babies are baptized into the church so that the catholic is *safe* as soon as possible after birth. All of these additions to the Scriptural text have the effect of substituting the Roman rites for what Christ offers: Himself. The Bible speaks clearly of a genuine and direct rela-

---

39. Only in the 20th century did the Church officially sanction the saying of the mass in the vernacular (common language) rather than in Latin. For centuries folks knew that unless the proper Latin words were spoken (*Hoc est corpus meum* etc.) in the mass, then the salvific effects were void for the communicant. These words must be said by the proper person, an ordained clergyman of the Roman Church. It was also believed that the bread and wine became the literal body and blood of Jesus Christ. This is known as transubstantiation, which is Catholic dogma to this day.

tionship with God Himself as a result of the atoning work of His Son, enliv-ened through the actual presence of the Holy Spirit in the here and now, so that, as Jesus said, one is born again. This wonderful reality is appropriated by faith, not by the brewing in Rome of a mystical-institutional ceremonial potion. The simple direct approach to God, by faith in Christ, Baptists be-lieve to be the Scriptural truth. No mediator intercedes between God and man except Christ, our High Priest and the Lamb of God who promises the Spirit to those who believe. Thus no pope, priest, cardinal, magisterium, bishop, deacon or any other modern man can stand in the gap and offer sal-vation to a soul.[40] That's why the New Testament called Jesus of Nazareth *the* Messiah, the anointed *one*.

So why is all of this talk about religious authority so important? Well the question comes to this: Who will tell me the truth about deliverance from evil and death? There are differing claims of authority as to the way of salvation. The book that claims to be the word of God is at odds with the Roman Catholic institution which claims to speak for God. A definite choice must be made here, and Baptists have chosen the Bible. In addition, no government or state coercion or influence may alter such a stance for the Baptist, remembering what the apostles said to the Sanhedrin after having been imprisoned: "We must obey God rather than men."[41] The temptation with religion (human approaches to God) is for the institution or religious way to offer a sense of control to the initiate. Just pull the authorized spir-

---

40. The theological issue of mediation is at the heart of another key Baptist principle: the priesthood of the believer. Every believer is a priest with immediate access to God Himself through Christ. Christ is the great High Priest and mediator having given Himself as the sacrifice to open the way back to fellowship with God, doing away with sin and death. No merely human mediator is needed or allowed according to the New Testament (see especially the book of Hebrews). When a priest is required for delivery of salvation benefits doled out by the church, as in Roman Catholicism, this is sometimes called sacerdotalism. Baptists believe this to be dangerously unbiblical.

41. See Acts 5.

itual levers and you will receive divine benefits. This is a man-made way to God. From Roman Catholicism to Islam to Buddhism to Voodoo to the New Age, the allure is that of power to command personal supernatural benefit (salvation), but in the end it is the adherent who is controlled (by rules, institutions, or spirits). The biblical way of *faith* represents a sharp contrast. It is simple childlike trust in God, a *surrendering* of control to a heavenly Father who offers grace and forgiveness, reconciliation and love. This way is the way of God Himself who by His own authority made salvation possible through His own Son.

BAPTIST BY CONVICTION NOT TRADITION: BELIEVERS' BAPTISM AND AMERICAN MISSIONS

Some have embraced this Baptist vision of uncomplicated, non-institutional faith to their own hurt, as we saw with Felix Manz, the first Anabaptist martyr, put to death by his former mentor and fellow Christian, Ulrich Zwingli. Acknowledging believer's baptism can be troublesome for those who come from other Christian traditions, even without paying the ultimate price as Manz did. One example of embracing Baptist beliefs, and thus breaking painfully from a personally dear tradition, is the fascinating story of Adoniram and Ann Judson and the beginning of Baptist missions in America. The seeds of this story were sown in western Massachusetts in the early nineteenth century. The exact location is only thirteen miles from where I sit writing in Bennington, Vermont. This is perhaps the most amazing and unexpected story in the history of Baptist missions because it actually starts with the Congregationalists of New England.

In the early years of the colonization of New England, the Congregational church was the established religion of Puritan Boston and Massachusetts and therefore of New England (with the notable exception of Rhode

Island).[42] For a little background: The Congregationalists were the New England Christians who experienced the Great Awakening led by Jonathan Edwards and others in the early and mid-eighteenth century. There was actually no unanimity concerning the revivals among these Puritans, however. Indeed, the revivals caused a split among the Congregationalists, with those called the Old Lights being suspicious and negative toward the revivals, in opposition to the New Lights, who were in favor of the revivals.[43] Even though the revivals which started among the Congregationalists had a positive impact on the emerging nation as a whole, another side to the story of these New England Christians must be told.

The other side of the story is that the Congregationalists were the official state-sponsored church of Massachusetts. Even after the Bill of Rights was ratified in 1791, the Puritans in Massachusetts did not allow complete religious freedom, and disestablish the Congregational church, until 1833.[44] Up until that time those who did not conform with the Congregational church were fined and at times persecuted by the government, including

---

42. Rhode Island was founded in the seventeenth century by a Baptist named Roger Williams who was expelled from the Massachusetts Bay colony for what were considered revolutionary ideas, among them, religious liberty and acknowledging the land rights of the natives.

43. Many of these 'new light' Congregationalists became Baptists during the revivals.

44. See McBeth, 266. Arnold Olson gives a summary of the early colonies, which became states in the newly formed nation, as they moved toward religious liberty, stating that in Massachusetts "the Congregational Church enjoyed full or partial establishment, as it did in New Hampshire and Connecticut. The influence and power of religion in government was further evidenced by the fact that Anglicanism was the established religion in Virginia, North Carolina, South Carolina, Maryland, and in New York City, and the three counties surrounding the city. Rhode Island led the way in Separation of Church and State and in guaranteeing the free exercise of religion. Pennsylvania and Maryland practiced religious toleration. Disestablishment of the Anglican Church in the South and Congregationalism in the North was not fully achieved until 1833" (Arnold T. Olson, *Believers Only* [Minneapolis: Free Church Publications, 1964], 310).

Baptists, many of whom were actually former Congregationalists. Congregationalists followed a Calvinistic or Reformed theological system which included baptism of infants. And yet out of this group we find the first Baptist missionaries from America (to lands across the Atlantic) emerging. This is their unexpected story: There is a college in a little town in western Massachusetts called Williams College. There, in 1806, a group of young men began to discuss seriously the theological implications of world missions. One day in August this group of students met near the Hoosic River in a grove of trees to continue the discussion when a thunderstorm blew up. Besieged by rain and lightning, they sought shelter underneath a nearby haystack in a farmer's field until the storm passed. The discussion turned into a prayer meeting in which the students began to commit themselves to God to act upon the impulse for missionary work instead of just talking about it.[45]

One of the young men who was a member of this group, but was not there the day they ducked under the haystack, expressed his desire to act upon this new found commitment to reach foreign lands for Christ in a letter: "I have deliberately made up my mind to preach the gospel to the heathen. I do not know, but it may be Asia."[46] This student's name was Luther

45. See McBeth, *The Baptist Heritage*, 344.

46. William A. Carleton, *The Dreamer Cometh: The Luther Rice Story* (Home Mission Board, SBC, 1960), 21. Carleton describes Rice's call to missions: "Even before his college days Luther was concerned with the condition of the heathen. In letters and in conversation he often expressed an anxious regard for their salvation. Soon after entering Williams he became closely associated with a number of young men who shared his views, and led by Samuel J. Mills, they organized a 'Society of Inquiry on the Subject of Missions.' He had come to feel a personal obligation to go himself as a missionary. One day during a period of prayer, alone in the woods near the college, he became very burdened for God's leadership in finding his proper place of service. He had considered foreign mission work before but had about decided to abandon the idea. As he prayed that day the words of Christ, 'Go ye into all the world and preach the gospel to every creature,' came into his mind with such clearness and power that he resolved to spend his life in mission service, whatever it

Rice. The other key name to know at this point in the story is Adoniram Judson. He and Rice eventually became partners in the first attempt to do foreign missions by Baptists from America. As young men, both Rice and Judson ended up attending Andover Seminary in Massachusetts, along with Samuel Mills and James Richards from the 'Haystack' group out of Williams College. "These young men were attracted to each other at Andover by a common dedication to the cause of missions."[47] Propelled by Judson's leadership, they all expressed an abiding commitment to missions and soon were pushing Congregationalist leaders to form a sending agency to support them, and transport them, to foreign fields.[48] Because of the fervor of these young men, a society was soon formed among Congregationalists called the American Board of Commissioners for Foreign Missions.

Adoniram Judson and his new wife Ann were sent by the Board to India. They departed on the ship *Caravan* in 1812. Along the way Adoniram began anew a study of the New Testament on the issue of baptism. He had already been indirectly influenced by Baptists on his journey to surrender to a call to missions.[49] He had also pondered the question of baptism during

---

might cost" (Carleton, *The Dreamer Cometh*, 20-21).

47. Robert G. Torbet, *Venture of Faith* (Philadelphia: Judson Press, 1955), 17.

48. According to Baptist historian Robert Torbet, Judson, from Brown University, was the key leader of the missions group at Andover Seminary. Along with Rice, Mills, and Richards of the Williams College 'Haystack' group, there were three others who joined the missions group at Andover: Samuel Newell, from Harvard, Samuel Nott, Jr., from Union, and another seminarian named Edward Warren. Torbet characterizes Judson's leadership of this group: "From the first, Judson was determined to devote his life to foreign missions. The Williams men were drawn in part, at least, to work among the American Indians. It was largely the vision of Judson that directed the others of the group to a concern for peoples in lands beyond the sea. He was the man of action who took decisive steps to develop an organization which might send him and his colleagues to the mission field" (Torbet, *Venture of Faith*, 17).

49. Torbet tells the story of Judson's surrender to missions: "One day in September, 1809, Adoniram Judson read a sermon by Claudius Buchanan, a chaplain for the British East India Company. It was instrumental in setting the direction of

his earlier studies, looking at the Greek biblical term *baptizo*[50] as he examined the New Testament. One of the motivations for his study aboard ship was that he anticipated meeting the renowned English Baptist missionary William Carey, who was already in Serampore, India. Adoniram wanted to be able to defend his Congregationalist view of baptism, which included baptizing whole households, even unbelievers and infants, in the mode of aspersion (sprinkling). He also did not want to cause confusion for those whom he would be attempting to reach with the gospel since his view differed from the Baptists already there in India.[51]

---

his whole life. The sermon appeared in *The Massachusetts Baptist Missionary Magazine*. It had been preached at St. James Parish Church, Bristol, England, for the benefit of a 'Society for Missions to Africa and the East.' Entitled 'The Star in the East,' the sermon presented a new and compelling idea to Judson. Its appeal for missions in India gripped his imagination as nothing had ever done before. For five months he did not come to a decision. Then, one cold day in February, 1810, he was walking alone in the woods behind the seminary building when suddenly the Great Commission came into his mind. Now it held a personal meaning for his own life. That was the decisive moment. Kneeling in the snow, he resolved to become a missionary to peoples beyond the sea. As in the case of his conversion, there were several factors which influenced Judson's decision to become a foreign missionary. The immediate one seems to have been Buchanan's sermon. Certainly this was reinforced by other reading in *The Massachusetts Baptist Missionary Magazine*, which regularly carried reports of the English Baptists' [William Carey's] work at Serampore" (Torbet, *Venture of Faith*, 16).

50. Speaking of Judson's interest in the biblical view of baptism, Torbet writes: "It was not the first time that the young missionary had been confronted with this subject. As a student in Andover Seminary, Judson's interest in the word *baptizo* had been aroused, while engaged in a private translation of the New Testament from Greek. In his search for the exact meaning of the Greek word, he found to his consternation that it was at variance with his understanding of it" (Torbet, *Venture of Faith*, 20).

51. Judson's anticipation of the baptism issue as perhaps being problematic upon commencing their missionary endeavor in India is summarized by one of Judson's biographers: "The Baptists and orthodox Congregationalists of New England had always been on friendly terms. In fact, Adoniram had met Dr. Lucius Bolles,

So he tackled the subject once again in order to be able to clearly present the doctrine to those to whom he would be ministering. In addition, he wished to be able to uphold his denominational practice since Congregationalists were footing the bill for his mission. Looking at the New Testament in its original Greek, Judson came to the conclusion that baptism literally meant to plunge or dunk under water. The Congregationalist practice of sprinkling was never mentioned in the New Testament. This was disconcerting and somewhat alarming to Adoniram. As has been mentioned, part of the Congregationalist Board's express mission for Judson was to baptize whole households rather than just individual believers. This too was something he did not find commanded in the New Testament.[52]

---

pastor of the First Baptist Church of Salem, before departure of the *Caravan*, and had urged that American Baptists follow the example of British Baptists in forming a missionary organization. But Adoniram was not so sure about his relation with the Serampore Baptists. If they attacked the Congregational position on baptism, how could he defend it? He feared much more, however, the dilemma in which he would find himself if natives asked him to explain the difference! They might even conclude there were two competing religions, each calling itself Christian—and thus find it easier to resist conversion" (Courtney Anderson, *To the Golden Shore: The Life of Adoniram Judson* [Garden City, NY: Doubleday, 1961], 132).

52. Torbet explains Judson's dilemma over baptism as a newly minted Congregationalist missionary: "But now that he was on his way to India, with instructions from the American Board to baptize 'credible believers *with their households,*' the problem took on a more urgent importance. He began to wonder how he ought to treat the unconverted children and servants of the converted when he reached his destination. He also realized that he would be obliged to defend his position before the English Baptists in Calcutta" (Torbet, *Venture of Faith*, 20, emphasis added).

The Congregationalist mandate to baptize whole households primarily cites the story of the Philippian jailor in the book of Acts for scriptural authority. Baptist scholar George R. Beasley-Murray dismisses this passage as a legitimate support for household baptism: "Above all, we should return to the text of Acts and look again at the narrative of the Philippian Jailor. Here it should be admitted in candour that the statement, 'Believe on the Lord Jesus, and you will be saved, you and your household' (16.31) has been abused. It is not intended to teach that the faith of the householder suffices for his wife, children and slaves. Alford rightly commented:

Thus, Judson slowly but surely came to believe that the Baptists were right about baptism. This was a genuine quandary for him, and as he discussed these things with his wife, Ann, she advised him to stay the course as a Congregationalist. There is no better way to convey the anguish and seriousness of the process of making this decision than to hear it in Ann Judson's own words in a letter home to her family from 1813, the year after the events described:

> I will now, my dear parents and sisters, give you some account of our change of sentiment, relative to the subject of baptism. Mr. Judson's doubts commenced on our passage from America. While translating the New Testament, in which he was engaged, he used frequently to say that the Baptists were right in their mode of administering the ordinance. Knowing he should meet the Baptists at Serampore, he felt it important to attend to it more closely, to be able to defend his sentiments. After our arrival at Serampore, his mind for two or three weeks was so much taken up with missionary inquiries and our difficulties with government, as to prevent his attending to the subject of baptism. But as we were waiting the arrival of our brethren, and having nothing in particular to attend to, he again took up the subject. I tried to have him give it up, and rest satisfied in his old sentiments, and frequently told him, if he became a Baptist, *I would not*. He, however, said he felt it his duty to examine closely

---

ʻκαὶ ὁ οἶκός σου does not meant that *his* faith would save his household, but that *the same way was open to them as to him*: "Believe, and thou shalt be saved; and the same of thy household.'" That is why the word of the Lord was spoken to 'all who were in the house' (v. 32), namely that all might hear and all might believe along with him. The process is the same as that which happened to Crispus and his family: 'Crispus believed on the Lord *with his whole house*'; he did not believe *for* them, but they shared his faith *with* him. Such is the common pattern in Acts: the Gospel calls for faith, and both come to expression in baptism" (G. R. Beasley-Murray, *Baptism in the New Testament* [Grand Rapids: Eerdmans, 1962], 319-320).

a subject on which he had so many doubts. After we removed to Calcutta, he found in the library in our chamber many books on both sides, which he determined to read candidly and prayerfully, and to hold fast, or embrace the truth, however mortifying, however great the sacrifice. I now commenced reading on the subject, with all my prejudices on the Pedobaptist [infant baptism] side. . . . But after closely examining the subject for several weeks, we were constrained to acknowledge that the truth appeared to lie on the Baptists' side. It was extremely trying to reflect on the consequences of our becoming Baptists. We knew it would wound and grieve our dear Christian friends in America–that we should lose their approbation and esteem. We thought it probable the commissioners would refuse to support us; and, what was more distressing than any thing, we knew we must be separated from our missionary associates, and go alone to some heathen land. These things were very trying to us, and caused our hearts to bleed for anguish. We felt we had no home in this world, and no friend but each other. Our friends at Serampore were *extremely surprised* when we wrote them a letter requesting baptism, as they had known nothing of our having had any doubts on the subject. We were baptized on the 6th of September, in the Baptist chapel in Calcutta.[53]

Clearly, the Judsons made genuine personal sacrifices to follow what they viewed as the biblical truth concerning baptism. But they were committed to finding the truth and sticking with it. In the midst of their discussions while still trying to come to a conclusion, "Ann continued to hold out against becoming a Baptist. Her husband's reply was steadfast: 'But it is my duty to examine the subject; and even if I have to pay dearly for it, I

---

53. Cited in Robert A. Baker, ed., *A Baptist Source Book: With Particular Reference to Southern Baptists* (Nashville: Broadman Press, 1966), 53-54, emphasis added.

hope I shall not be afraid to embrace the truth.'"[54] So entirely did Adoniram embrace what he considered to be the New Testament truth about baptism, that he was confident to preach on the subject (soon after being baptized himself) to a group of Baptists. William Carey claimed it was the best sermon on baptism he had ever heard.[55]

Before his baptism Judson had written a letter to Carey and the other Baptist missionaries in Serampore (August 27, 1812), in which he explained his change of mind (and requested baptism): "My inquiries commenced during my passage from America, and after much laborious research and painful trial, which I shall not now detail, have issued in entire conviction, that *the immersion of a professing believer is the only Christian baptism.*"[56] In this request for baptism Judson made clear that Ann had also come to the same strong belief. They concluded, based on the conviction stated above, that they had never been baptized according to New Testament instruction: "Feeling, therefore, that we are in an unbaptized state, we wish to profess our faith in Christ by being baptized in obedience to his sacred commands."[57] It was a great encouragement when, shortly after his arrival to India, Luther Rice, their friend and partner in the mission venture, also came to Baptist beliefs. Ann wrote: "Brother Rice was baptized several weeks after we were. It was a very great relief to our minds to have him join us, as we expected to be entirely alone in a mission."[58] Using other terms to express his thoughts, Luther Rice came to the same conclusion as he embraced the Baptist view, after his own careful study: "I am now satisfactorily convinced that those only who give evidence of piety [Judson's words were 'professing believer'], are proper subjects, and that immersion is the proper mode of baptism."[59]

---

54. Torbet, *Venture of Faith*, 21.

55. See Anderson, *To the Golden Shore*, 151.

56. Cited in Baker, ed., *A Baptist Source Book*, 54, emphasis added.

57. Baker, ed., *A Baptist Source Book*, 54.

58. Baker, ed., *A Baptist Source Book*, 54.

59. Cited in Baker, ed., *A Baptist Source Book*, 56. In his diary, Rice described the process of his own deliberation about the issue of baptism, considering

Rice was baptized on November 11, 1812. His diary entry for the day reads: "Was this day baptized in the name of the Holy Trinity. The Lord grant that I may ever find his name to be a strong tower, to which I may continually resort and find safety."[60] In a letter written describing the event the day after his baptism Rice commented: "It was a comfortable day for my soul."[61] Rice's baptism was not only an immediate boost to the Judsons, it proved to be an auspicious moment in Baptist history. The Judsons would end up in Burma, and Rice would go back to America to try to raise funds for Baptist missions, especially for Adoniram and Ann, who became religious celebrities back home as folks heard of their perseverance amidst tribulations on the missions field. Rice never went back to the mission field. He began to organize Baptists for mission support and, in doing so, helped unite Baptists in America as never before. Adoniram himself was

---

that his friends, the Judsons, had already become Baptists: "I have just mentioned that Brother Judson has become a Baptist. As I have here with him considerable means for this purpose, I am endeavoring to investigate thoroughly the subject of the sacred ordinance of baptism. What may be the result of this inquiry, I am not able at present to say; but from the progress already made I conceive it to be possible that a revolution in my own mind, similar to that which my dear brother and sister have experienced, may take place. Should this be the case, I shall in all probability, go with them to Java. It would be peculiarly pleasing to me to be associated with them in the mission, but my affection for them can by no means determine me to become a Baptist without conviction that Baptists are in the right; nor can I on the other hand, be deterred from my conscientiously examining the subject, nor from following what really appears to be the truth; not withstanding my unpleasant considerations attending such a change of sentiment in my situation. And it is a principle with me, that truth can be no loser by the most rigorous examination, provided that examination be conducted in the fear of God with a desire to know the truth, and a disposition to do his will. May the Lord himself lead me in the way in which he would have me go" (Cited in Carleton, *The Dreamer Cometh: The Luther Rice Story*, 25).

60. Carleton, *The Dreamer Cometh: The Luther Rice Story*, 26.
61. Carleton, *The Dreamer Cometh: The Luther Rice Story*, 26.

instrumental in calling on Baptists to unite behind the foreign mission effort.[62] Between the Judsons' riveting ongoing story of stern determination amidst bitter sacrifices (including prison and torture) in Burma and Luther Rice's unrelenting promotion of the mission work, Baptists were galvanized to come together to form a national Baptist union. The Baptist groups which emerged over time out of this union carry on the work of missions all around the world to this day.

One of the telling statements in Ann's letter (quoted above) to her family is that the English Baptist missionaries were 'surprised' by the Judsons' request for baptism, proving that the strength of their new conviction was not in any way a result of influence by the Baptists in India, but simply a personal decision brought about by study of Scripture, as the narrative of

---

62. Adoniram "wrote to Dr. Baldwin [pastor, Second Baptist Church in Boston] and to Dr. Bolles, pastor of Salem's First Baptist Church, whom he had met before sailing. Now he reminded him that, at that time, 'I suggested the formation of a society among the Baptists in America for the support of foreign missions. . . . Little did I then expect to be personally concerned in such an attempt'" (Courtney Anderson, *To the Golden Shore: The Life of Adoniram Judson*, 149).

Even before his actual baptism, Judson's letter to Lucius Bolles explains his call for support among Baptists: "Within a few months, I have experienced an entire change of sentiments on the subject of baptism. My doubts concerning the correctness of my former system of belief commenced during my passage from America to this country; and after many painful trials, which none can know but those who are taught to relinquish a system in which they had been educated, I settled down in the full persuasion that the immersion of a professing believer in Christ is the only Christian baptism. Mrs. Judson is united with me in this persuasion. We have signified our views and wishes to the Baptist missionaries at Serampore, and expect to be baptized in this city next Lord's day. A separation from my missionary brethren, and a dissolution of my connection with the [Congregationalist] Board of Commissioners, seem to be necessary consequences. The missionaries at Serampore are exerted to the utmost of their ability in managing and supporting their extensive and complicated mission. Under these circumstances I look to you. Alone, in this foreign heathen land, I make my appeal to those whom, with their permission, I will call *my Baptist brethren* in the United States" (Cited in Baker, ed., *A Baptist Source Book*, 55).

events demonstrates. Making use of Judson's own words, Baptist historian Robert Torbet confirms that "this decision had not been influenced by consultation with the English Baptist missionaries. That Judson's decision had been reached privately and independently is evident from a lengthy letter which he wrote to the Third Church in Plymouth, Massachusetts, where he held his membership. In setting forth his reasons for becoming a Baptist he explained:

> 'I could not find a single intimation in the New Testament that the children and domestics of believers were members of the church or entitled to any church ordinance, in consequence of the profession of the head of their family. Everything discountenanced this idea. When baptism was spoken of, it was always in connection with believing. None but believers were commanded to be baptized; and it did not appear to my mind that any others were baptized.'"[63]

Judson described his and Ann's new identity as Baptists, and their change of mind concerning baptism, in this way: "we are confirmed Baptists, not because we wish to be, but because truth compels us to be."[64]

Conclusion

Why does the term Baptist still matter? Because salvation truth and biblical authority still matter. These issues have eternal significance. They always matter. Even, or especially, in our confused and conflicted world, they

---

63. Torbet, *Venture of Faith*, 22.

64. Anderson, *To the Golden Shore*, 129. Adoniram Judson carried his steadfast Baptist beliefs through all his mission work in Burma. As he translated the New Testament he rendered the Greek word for baptize into Burmese as 'immerse' (instead of a transliteration).

certainly matter. What difference does it make today? If you are a Baptist or tend to be baptistic in your approach to ecclesiology, perhaps these arguments will help firm up your confidence in your Baptist beliefs. For all Christians, demystifying the relationship between church and salvation by embracing the simple biblical concept of believer's baptism, and therefore freeing ourselves from the woods, weeds, and vines of institutional Christianity (as in infant baptism), may direct us toward a clear pathway where we are able to focus intently on the Lord Jesus Himself, and boldly declare with Paul, "For I resolved to know nothing while I was with you except Jesus Christ and him crucified."[65] According to the New Testament, the only proper response to Christ and him crucified is faith. As the thief on the cross said to Jesus, 'Remember me,' so we trust in Christ's suffering and death on the cross (validated by His resurrection) and nothing else, no matter how venerable or reasonable the institutional addition may appear.

Notes

2. As an example of the confusion which comes from a glossing of Scripture with traditional theology concerning these matters, consider the Tenth Presbyterian Church in Philadelphia. The following is an explanation of infant baptism from their website:

> "Infant baptism is based upon the continuity between New Covenant baptism and the Old Covenant rite of circumcision. A considerable amount of Scripture upholds this continuity. In Romans 4:11, the apostle Paul notes that circumcision was the seal of 'the righteousness of faith.' In Colossians 2:11, 12, Paul points to the same spiritual reality (separation from the sinful nature) by means of both circumcision and baptism. Furthermore, the privileges of the New Covenant are hardly less than those of the Old Covenant. The inclusion of children in the covenant is not rescinded under the New Covenant, but is directly af-

---

65. 1 Corinthians 2:2 (NIV).

firmed in Jeremiah 31:33 and in Acts 2:38-39. Finally, Gal. 3:27-29, one of the key texts on baptism, relates baptism to circumcision by rejoicing that not only men but women may receive the covenant sign, not merely Jews but Greeks, etc. By baptizing infant children of believers, we take seriously the promise at the core of God's covenant: 'I will be your God and the God of your children after you' (Genesis 17:7; Exodus 19:5, 6; Deuteronomy 7:6, 14:2; Jeremiah 31:33). We take seriously Jesus' words regarding the little children, as found in Matthew 19:13, 14: 'Then little children were brought to Jesus for him to place his hands on them and pray for them. But the disciples rebuked those who brought them. Jesus said, "Let the little children come to me, and do not hinder them, for the kingdom of heaven belongs to such as these." When he had placed his hands on them, he went on from there.' This is not just a story about how Jesus was nice to little children. These are the covenant, circumcised children of Israel (at least the boys were circumcised). And here is the Messiah, the Lord of the Covenant, laying His hands on them for blessing and praying for them to the Father. What an encouragement this is for us to bring our children to receive the blessing of the covenant sign of our Lord. Along similar lines, we note that children of believers are accountable as members of the covenant. In Ephesians 6:1, 4 and Colossians 3:20, 21, the apostle Paul commands children to obey their parents 'in the Lord'. Parents, he says, are to bring their children up 'in the training and instruction of the Lord'. Here we find that the children of believers are treated as Christians, to receive the benefits and obligations thereof. Furthermore, in 1 Corinthians 7;14, in a passage discussing marriage and divorce, Paul remarks that children of a believing parent are 'holy'. Paul is not saying that these children are automatically saved or that they automatically come to faith in Christ; however, he is saying that such children are set apart in God's sight. Finally, we take note of the household baptisms seen in the New Testament (Acts 16:15, 33, 34; 1 Corinthians 1:16). Of only twelve actual baptisms recorded in the New Testament, three of them are household baptisms. Scripture does not tell us that infants were baptized in these occasions, nor does it say that all who were baptized believed. Indeed, the clear inference from these household baptisms is that those under the headship of the head of the house received a benefit from his/her belief. That benefit was baptism, and a public identification with the church. It is because of this biblical data that our church, along with the whole of the Reformed tradition, baptizes infants of believing adults." (Christian Baptism," Tenth Presbyterian Church, last modified October 27, 2008, https://www.tenth.org/resource-library/articles/christian-baptism).

From a Baptist point of view, it is telling that in the conclusion of the full explanation of Christian Baptism it is noted that someone joining the Tenth Presbyterian church is "required simply to affirm your faith in the Lord Jesus Christ and your willingness to accept the authority of this church. You are not required to assent to the Westminster Standards nor to the above teachings regarding baptism." Contrast this non-committal stance regarding baptism for those joining this Presbyterian church with the argument put forth here that what a Christian believes about baptism emphatically affects beliefs about the church and, more crucially, potentially fuddles the clarity of the biblical message of personal salvation by faith alone. The idea that children of believers, in some vague fashion, based on conflating the old and new covenants, are in some way part of the church, and therefore ambiguously saved, surely muddies the waters of *sola fide*.

13. John Calvin (who represents, of course, the Protestant Reformed tradition) is a good example of a theologian who is able to exegete clearly the Scripture with regard to believer's baptism, as here in Matthew 28, and *still* go on to support infant baptism. See if you are convinced by his arguments in support of paedobaptism: "Christ enjoins that those who have submitted to the gospel, and professed to be his disciples, shall be *baptized*; partly that their *baptism* may be a pledge of eternal life before God:, and partly that it may be an outward sign of faith before men. For we know that God testifies to us the grace of adoption by this sign, because he engrafts us into the body of his Son, so as to reckon us among his flock; and, therefore, not only our spiritual washing, by which he reconciles us to himself, but likewise our new righteousness, are represented by it. But as God, by this seal confirms to us his grace, so all who present themselves for *baptism* do, as it were, by their own signature, ratify their faith. . . . But as Christ enjoins them to *teach* before *baptizing*, and desires that none but *believers* shall be admitted to *baptism*, it would appear that *baptism* is not properly administered unless when it is preceded by faith. On this pretense, the *Anabaptists* have stormed greatly against infant baptism. But the reply is not difficult, if we attend to the reason of the command. Christ orders them to convey *to all nations* the message of eternal salvation, and confirms it by adding the seal of baptism. Now it was proper that *faith* in the word should be placed before *baptism*, since the Gentiles were altogether alienated from God, and had nothing in common with the chosen people; for otherwise it would have been a false figure, which offered forgiveness and the gift of the Spirit to unbelievers, who were not yet

members of Christ. But we know that by *faith* those who were formerly despised are united to the people of God. It is now asked, on what condition does God adopt as children those who formerly were aliens? It cannot, indeed, be denied that, when he has once received them into his favor, he continues to bestow it on their children and their children's children. By the coming of Christ God manifested himself as a Father equally to the Gentiles and to the Jews; and, therefore, that promise, which was formerly given to the Jews, must now be in force towards the Gentiles, I will be thy God, and the God of thy seed after thee, (Gen.17:7) Thus we see that they who entered by faith into the Church of God are reckoned, along with their posterity, among the members of Christ, and, at the same time, called to the inheritance of salvation. And yet this does not involve the separation of *baptism* from faith and doctrine; because, though infants are not yet of such an age as to be capable of receiving the grace of God by faith, still God, when addressing their parents, includes them also. I maintain, therefore, that it is not rash to administer baptism to infants, to which God invites them, when he promises that *he will be their God*" (John Calvin, *Calvin's Commentaries*, Matthew, 324).

Historian Henry Vedder summarizes well the Baptist view in contradiction to Calvin: "Baptists hold that the baptism of any but believers is contrary to the whole spirit of Christianity, and that it totally subverts the principle on which the Church of Christ was founded. Judaism had been based upon natural descent, upon the law of the flesh, but Jesus came to teach and establish the utterly new law of the spirit. 'Except a man be born from above, he cannot see the kingdom of God. . . . That which is born of the flesh is flesh, that which is born of the Spirit is spirit.' To be a Christian is to enter into a new and spiritual relation to God, through faith in his Son" (Henry C. Vedder, *The Baptists* [New York: Baker & Taylor, 1903], 11).

36. For example, Augustine's belief in needing baptismal regeneration for guilty infants: The argument runs something like this in summary: " . . . a sinner begets a sinner, so that the guilt of original sin has to be removed in infancy by the reception of baptism . . ." Cited in Henry Bettenson, ed., *The Later Christian Fathers: A Selection from the writings of the Fathers from St. Cyril of Jerusalem to St. Leo the Great* (New York: Oxford University Press, 1972), 198. Augustine based this questionable teaching (infant baptismal regeneration) partly upon the fact that infant baptism was already being practiced in the church during his time: "Hence also that other statement: The Father loves the Son, and has given all things into His hand. He that believes in the Son has everlasting life; while he that believes not the Son shall not see life, but the wrath of God abides on him. John 3:35-36 Now in which of these classes must we place infants — among those who believe in the Son, or among those who believe not the Son? In neither, say some, because, as they are not yet able to believe,

so must they not be deemed unbelievers. This, however, *the rule of the Church does not indicate, for it joins baptized infants to the number of the faithful.* Now if they who are baptized are, by virtue of the excellence and administration of so great a sacrament, nevertheless reckoned in the number of the faithful, although by their own heart and mouth they do not literally perform what appertains to the action of faith and confession; surely they who have lacked the sacrament must be classed among those who do not believe in the Son, and therefore, if they shall depart this life without this grace, they will have to encounter what is written concerning such — they shall not have life, but the wrath of God abides on them" (Augustine, *On Merits and Remission of Sin, and Infant Baptism,* translated by Peter Holmes and Robert Ernest Wallis, in *The Collected Words of Augustine of Hippo* [Hastings, East Sussex, UK: Delphi Classics, 2016], ch. 28, emphasis added).

In addition, Augustine's doctrine of infant baptismal regeneration was founded on his belief that every person born is not only affected by, or infected with, original sin inherited from Adam (or Eve as in the case below), but also *guilty* of that original sin. Augustine expressed these notions in the following: "As a consequence, then, of this disobedience of the flesh and this law of sin and death, whoever is born of the flesh has need of spiritual regeneration — not only that he may reach the kingdom of God, but also that he may be freed from the damnation of sin. Hence men are on the one hand born in the flesh liable to sin and death from the first Adam, and on the other hand born again in baptism associated with the righteousness and eternal life of the second Adam; even as it is written in the book of Ecclesiasticus: Of the woman came the beginning of sin, and through her we all die" (Augustine, *On Merits and Remission of Sin, and Infant Baptism,* ch. 21).

The key New Testament passage is Romans 5, which compares Adam as the first man and Christ as the new man. The problem arose, partly, according to James Leo Garrett, because Augustine used an inaccurately translated Latin New Testament: "Augustine of Hippo, who utilized the Old Latin versions of the New Testament that prevailed prior to Jerome's Vulgate, mistakenly read the Greek *eph' hō,* 'because,' as equivalent to the Latin *in quo,* 'in whom,' and thus misinterpreted the phrase to mean 'in whom all have sinned.' This mistranslation served as biblical 'support' for Augustine's doctrine of *peccatum originale,* or 'original sin'" (James Leo Garrett, Jr., *Systematic Theology: Biblical, Historical, and Evangelical,* Vol. 1, ch.36, III, A). We find Augustine using this mistaken rendering from the Old Latin version in speaking about the 'seminal identity' of everyone born from Adam's line, in that we all sinned 'in him,' which is the basis for the idea that infants are born guilty of this 'original sin.': "The apostle cries, 'Sin entered the world through one man, and through sin came death, and thus it passed on to all men, for *in him* all sinned'. Hence it cannot reasonably be asserted that Adam's sin harmed those who did not sin; for the Scripture says, 'All Sinned in him'. And those sins are not spoken of as belonging to someone else, as if they did not affect little children: seeing that in Adam all sinned at that time, since all were already united with him by that power to beget them with which his nature was endowed. But those sins are said to be another's in that Adam's descendants were not at that time leading their own lives; however, the life of one man embraces all that was to be in his posterity" (Cited in Bettenson, ed., *The Later Christian Fathers*, 198).

Just to be clear, Augustine makes a statement about infants and free will: "Although infants do not possess free will, there is no illogicality in calling their original sin voluntary, since it derives from the misused will of the first man, and is theirs as it were by heredity" (cited in Bettenson, ed., *The Later Christian Fathers*, 199). Unfortunately, this troubling misapprehension survived for centuries and is still with us in the form of infant baptism, hardened Calvinistic theology, and Catholic sacerdotalism. As Norman Geisler states: "Augustine (354-430) has been given the dubious honor of being the first to teach the damnation of all *unbaptized* infants—essentially, the wrath of God abides on them. He did allow, however, that unbaptized infants who die do not suffer as severely as those who live to adulthood and commit actual sins" (Norman Geisler, *Systematic Theology*, vol. 3 [Grand Rapids: Bethany House, 2004], 436).

The Southern Baptist New Testament scholar, Walter Conner, unequivocally rejected the idea that infants, or anyone else, is condemned based on Adam's earlier guilt. Commenting on the first chapter of Romans, he wrote: "Paul does not teach here or anywhere else that any man will be condemned purely on the account of Adam's sin." Conner argues that Romans 5 (specifically v. 12) must be interpreted in light of Romans 1, and does so in the following manner: "Paul concluded, then, that all men are under the judgment of God (Rom. 3:19), not on the ground that they have failed to meet the requirements of an ideal and abstract law, of whose requirements they had no specific knowledge, *nor on the ground that they were seminally present in Adam and were responsible for Adam's sin,* nor on the ground that they were held responsible for Adam's sin because Adam represented them in a covenant that God made with Adam. Paul based their condemnation on the facts of experience and history; namely, that they had knowledge of right and wrong–the will of God–revealed through nature and their own inner consciousness, in the case of the Gentiles, and through the Old Testament law, in the case of the Jew, and that in spite of this knowledge they did that which they knew to be wrong. Paul asked men to face the facts of their own experience–facts which they recognized and could not deny–and he pointed out to them that on the basis of these facts they were under the judgment of God" (Walter Thomas Conner, *The Cross in the New Testament* [Nashville: Broadman Press, 1954), 77-78], emphasis added).

The influence of Augustine's wrongheaded interpretation of Romans 5:12, based on a faulty Latin translation, can be seen to this day. An example is in Leland Ryken's *Literary Study Bible* (ESV). In the note for this verse he states: "In the same way that God once justly imputed Adam's sin to the entire human race (resulting in condemnation and death), so now God freely and graciously imputes the righteousness of Christ to everyone who has faith in him (bringing justification and life)." However, the verse in the ESV itself says nothing about imputing Adam's sin to the human race. It says: "Therefore, just as sin came into the world through one man, and death through sin, and so death spread to all men *because all sinned*," which clearly indicates that sin *spread* through the individual sinning of all men and death spread because all sinned. *Because* all sinned, not *in whom* (Adam) all sinned. The guilt and resulting death is due to (*because*) of the sin of each and every person who sinned. No imputation of the guilt and condemnation of Adam's sin is found in a plain and candid reading of this verse.

5

DOES THE LOCAL CHURCH STILL MATTER?

RONNIE W. ROGERS

The Bible speaks of the church as both universal and local. The place of the local church in Christ's plan often either is misunderstood or simply marginalized by what some believe to be a superior plan, particularly in our present individualistic technological milieu. Many Christians seem enthusiastic and eager to talk about the work of the kingdom by primarily using the word church in its universal sense. But any strategy that minimizes the local church conflicts with the plan of our Lord Jesus Christ. A failure to maintain the centrality of the local church in our kingdom work results in three things. One, we lose a critical component for interpreting the New Testament since the New Testament was written to or for local churches. Two, we lose rewards at the judgment seat of Christ (1 Cor 3; 2 Cor 5:10). Three, we fail to honor Christ.

Let me begin by defining the church as she exists both universally and locally. I will describe the local church grammatically, historically, and Baptistically. After establishing a clear understanding of what the church is, we will explore the New Testament teaching of the centrality of the local church in Christ's plan to build his universal church.

THE CHURCH DEFINED UNIVERSALLY

By universal church, I mean the church, regardless of denomination or association, that is composed of all people who have personally trusted Christ as their Savior and are thereby his followers (Rom 10:9–10; 1 Cor 15:1–4). The universal church spans the globe, time, geography, even to heaven itself at any given moment (Matt 16:18). The universal church is an organism that includes all believers of all generations in the present church age. Each member of the universal church is saved and perfected forever in Christ (Eph 5:25–27). As I will elaborate on, a local church is made up of those who are followers of Christ gathered together with others in specific locations all over the world and are organized according to the New Testament to build the universal church. In contrast to the universal church, the local church is an organism and an organization. The local church is at the heart of Christ's plan to build the universal church.

THE LOCAL CHURCH DEFINED GRAMATICALLY

Our English word church is "derived probably from the Greek *kuriakon* (i.e., 'the Lord's house'), which was used by ancient authors for the place of worship."[1] Church is the most common translation of the Greek word *ekklēsía*. Generally, dictionaries define *ekklēsía* as "assembly" and "church." Lexicons distinguish between the church as the whole body and the local

---

1. M.G. Easton, *Easton's Bible Dictionary* (Oak Harbor: Logos Research Systems, Inc., 1996, c1897), Logos electronic ed.

congregation or house church.[2] *Ekklesia* was used in secular Greek to refer to an assembly of citizens to carry out the business of the city. In the Old Testament, it regularly relates, although not exclusively, to the nation of Israel as the people of God, especially as they gathered for worship.

The word *ekklesia*, church, is made up of the preposition *ek* meaning 'out of' or 'from' and *kaleo* meaning 'to call.' The common understanding of the church being "the called out ones" comes from *ekklesia*. Many verses speak of Christians being called. For example, "For the promise is for you and your children and for all who are far off, as many as the Lord our God will call to Himself" (Acts 2:39).[3]

However, while the word includes "called out ones," both historically and grammatically, it involves more than that. One lexicon states:

> Though some persons have tried to see in the term ἐκκλησία a more or less literal meaning of "called-out ones," this type of etymologizing is not warranted either by the meaning of ἐκκλησία in NT times or even by its earlier usage. The term ἐκκλησία was in common usage for several hundred years before the Christian era and was used to refer *to an assembly of persons constituted by well-defined membership*. In general Greek usage it was normally a socio-political entity based upon citizenship in a city-state...and in this sense is parallel to δῆμος. . . . For the NT, however, it is important to understand the meaning of ἐκκλησίαᵃ as "an assembly of God's people"[4] (italics added).

---

2. Gerhard Kittel, Gerhard Friedrich, and Geoffrey William Bromiley, *Theological Dictionary of the New Testament*, translation of *Theologisches Worterbuch Zum Neuen Testament* (Grand Rapids: Eerdmans, 1995, c1985), Logos electronic ed., 397.

3. See also Acts 15:14; Rom 8:30; 1 Thess 2:12; 2 Thess 2:14.

4. Johannes P. Louw and Eugene Albert Nida, *Greek-English Lexicon of the New Testament: Based on Semantic Domains*, Vol. 1, 2nd ed. (New York: United Bible Societies, 1996, c1989), Logos electronic ed., 125.

Accordingly, while *ekklesia* includes the idea of being "called out," it is vital to note that the word referred to *"an assembly of persons constituted by well-defined membership."* It spoke of an assembly where those who were a part and those who were not were clearly discernible. Consequently, it did not include the passerby or visitor. Each assembly was clearly defined by who its members were.[5]

The New Testament Church is divine in its origin, nature, growth, power, and purpose; it is universal in scope and organized locally in its expression. Every local church is to reflect the essence of the universal church. The church is made up of newly created people who have been transformed by the saving power of Jesus Christ (2 Cor 5:17). A person's new spiritual reality transcends their natural heritage of Jew or Gentile. Consequently, any mere sociological, psychological, historical, functional, or pragmatic definition of the church is woefully inadequate and quite disparaging to the nature of the church because the church is supernatural, everlasting, and theological. Moreover, it is disparaging to Christ, the head and source of the church (Eph 4:15–16).

THE LOCAL CHURCH DEFINED HISTORICALLY

The Day of Pentecost marked the beginning of the church with the Holy Spirit coming in a new way to indwell *all* believers (John 14:17). The Holy Spirit baptizes *all* believers into one body (1 Cor 12:13), where Jew and Gentile, male and female, slave and free stand on equal footing to come into and be a part of the church (Gal 3:23–29). The Holy Spirit positioned

---

5.The expression of this is manifested through local churches, concerning which Strong's Concordance says, "an assembly of Christians gathered for worship in a religious meeting." James Strong, *The Exhaustive Concordance of the Bible: Showing Every Word of the Text of the Common English Version of the Canonical Books, and Every Occurrence of Each Word in Regular Order* (Ontario: Woodside Bible Fellowship, 1996), Logos electronic ed., G1577.

every Christian in Christ (Eph 1:1), and Christ in us (Col 1:27). The day of Pentecost was a new phase in God's redemptive plan. The new ministry of Christ, baptizing by the Holy Spirit all believers into the same body, was predicted in the gospels (Matt 3:10) and the early history of the church (Acts 1:5). Peter referred to the fulfillment of this in Acts 11:15–17.[6] Lewis Sperry Chafer says of this new age:

> Things cannot be the same in this age as they were in the past age, after the death of Christ has taken place, His resurrection, His ascension, and the advent of the Spirit on Pentecost. . . Those who see no force in this declaration have hardly considered the measureless meaning of the age-transforming occurrences. In the light of these determining issues, it may be seen (a) that there could be no Church in the world—constituted as she is and distinctive in all her features— until Christ's death; for her relation to that death is not a mere anticipation, but is based wholly on His finished work and she must be purified by His precious blood. (b) There could be no Church until Christ arose from the dead to provide her with resurrection life. (c) There could be no Church until He had ascended up on high to become her Head; for she is a New Creation with a new federal headship in the resurrected Christ. He is, likewise, to her as the head is to the body. Nor could the church survive for a moment were it not for His intercession and advocacy in heaven. (d) There could be no church on earth until the advent of the Holy Spirit; for the most basic and fundamental reality respecting the church is that she is a temple for the habitation of God through the Spirit. She is regen-

---

6. Erickson notes, "The fact that Luke never uses ekklesiain in his Gospel but employs it twenty-four times in Acts is also significant. It would seem that he did not regard the church as present until the period covered in Acts. . . We conclude that the church originated at Pentecost" (Millard J. Erickson, Christian Theology, vol. 3, 3rd ed. [Grand Rapids: Baker Academic, 2013], 1048).

erated, baptized, and sealed by the Spirit. . . A church without the finished work on which to stand . . . is only a figment of theological fancy and wholly extraneous to the New Testament.[7]

THE LOCAL CHURCH DEFINED BAPTISTICALLY

The local church is a body of immersion-baptized believers freely assembled and organized according to the complete New Testament to fulfill the mandate of Matthew 28:18–20 by following the model for local church ministry described in Ephesians 4:11–16.[8] A local church operates under the leadership of one or more pastors (Eph 4:11; 1 Thes 5:12–13; Heb 13:17). All of the pastors are charged with the responsibility to teach and equip the saints and, therefore, must be able to teach (1 Tim 3:2; 2 Tim 2:24, 5:17), but at least one gives himself primarily to preaching and teaching (1 Tim 5:17).[9]

The pastors' teaching, spiritual lives, and leadership protect the body from spiritual untruths and errors such as heresies, cults, aberrant theology, dangers of isolation and anonymity, spiritual predators, spiritual malnutrition, living at the lowest common denominator on milk with little or no

---

7. Lewis Sperry Chafer, *Systematic Theology,* Vol. 4, *Ecclesiology, Eschatology* (Dallas: Dallas Seminary Press, 1976) 45–46.

8. A local church may be considered a New Testament church without fulfilling perfectly all of the New Testament criteria for the church in the same way one may be a Christian without following everything perfectly; however, to the degree that one fails to incorporate all aspects or intentionally neglects the corpus of New Testament teaching concerning the church, it is to that degree failing to be a thorough New Testament church.

9. To preach and teach God's Word is the primary task of elders (1 Tim 4:6, 11, 13, 16; 5:17; 2 Tim 2:15, 24; Titus 2:1). They were given to the church for that purpose (Eph 4:11–14). While all believers are responsible to pass on the truths they have learned from God's Word, not all have gifts for preaching and teaching (1 Cor 12:29, 2 Tim 2:14; Titus 1:9; 2:1). Those who aspire to pastoral duty, however, must be so gifted.

meat, and superficiality (1 Cor 3:1–3). Their teaching also prepares the body for present and future ministry, more significant challenges, more dangerous spiritual combat, and holy living while providing the members with ever-increasing opportunities to minister and contribute to the body and the advancement of the kingdom (Eph 4:12–15).

The regenerate church body encourages and holds one another accountable to live lives reflective of regeneration. The local church does this through the various facets and levels of church discipline as prescribed in the New Testament, which elevates membership commensurate with the nature of the church (Matt 18:15–20; Rom 16:17–18; 1 Cor 5:1–13; 2 Thes 3:6–15;).[10] The local church is the domain of the two ordinances of the church, baptism and the Lord's Supper (Acts 2:41–47; Rom 6:3–4; 1 Cor 11:20, 23–32). In the beginning, some individuals conducted baptism rather than local churches. But as we will see, the development of local churches was a historical process where individuals baptized others because no local church existed.[11] As the local church developed, it became the place of baptism and the Lord's Supper.

Discipleship is the equipping of Christians to serve in and through the local church. The primary place for equipping Christians is the local church (Eph 4:11-16). Equipping endeavors outside the local church must be in concert with a local church. Some people may primarily train and equip others in the local church while others' primary place of equipping people is outside the local church; although, each person may, and probably should have, areas of helping to equip people to serve Christ in advancing his kingdom in both spheres. However, if ministries beyond the local

---

10. Church discipline is not merely the removing of people from the church who do not desire to follow Christ, but, rather, it encompasses ministry to the body at all levels to encourage holiness and maintain a holy fellowship. See my book, *Undermining the Gospel: The Case and Guide for Church Discipline*.

11. "Why Every Healthy Church Practices the Ordinances," International Mission Board, accessed December 17, 2019, https://www.imb.org/2016/12/07/why-every-healthy-church-practices-the-ordinances/.

church seek their own identity apart from the local church, they do so without New Testament authority.

The local church sends people into prisons, schools, and military installations, sends people to work with the impoverished, and does a galaxy of other outreaches to specific groups. These ministries flow from the local church. They do not operate as a ministry apart from building up the local church. They do not exist to build up the universal church and advance the kingdom, all while separated from the strategic and essential place of the local church in Christ's plan. If they do seek to build the universal church apart from the local church, they do so without New Testament authority.

Growing in faith, discipleship, is a life characterized by devotion to learning the Scripture, living what you learn, loving God more worthily (Matt 22:37–39), and engaging people by ministering and speaking the truth in love (Eph 4:15). The primary tool for equipping is the Scripture, which is capable of equipping everyone, as seen in the promise to equip pastors for "every good work" (1 Tim 3:15–17). Other things play a part in maturing the saints, such as training, mentoring, and opportunity, but teaching and learning the Scripture is nonpareil (Eph 4:11–12). All Christians are to desire being matured by the Scripture (1 Pet 2:2).

I would practically define the full range of disciple-making in this way: Disciple-making is the direct and indirect intentional activity of enabling Christians to mature in the faith to follow Christ more faithfully. As Colin Marshal says, "Disciple-making, then, refers to a massive range of relationships and conversations and activities."[12] Consequently, we should see disciple-making as including our family, corporate worship, classes, small groups, and one-on-one as concentric circles, each adding to the process. Those who use select Scriptures to insist true discipleship must be one-on-one or consisting of only small groups are in conflict with the full New Testament teaching on discipleship and equipping (Eph 4:11–16). The New

---

12. Colin Marshall and Tony Payne, *The Trellis and The Vine: The Ministry Mind-Shift That Changes Everything* (Kingsford: Australia: Matthias Media, 2009), 154.

Testament seamlessly incorporates large gatherings, small groups, and one-on-one discipling.

THE IMPORTANCE OF THE LOCAL CHURCH IN KINGDOM GROWTH

The importance of the local church is seen seminally in Christ's plan in the gospels. The word church appears three times in the gospels. Christ's first promise to build his church refers to the universal church (Matt 16:18). He speaks of it as a future event. The other two references are in Matt 18:15–20, where he speaks about the local church and particularly the issue of church discipline. It is noteworthy that his reference to the local church presumes that his followers will actively belong and be involved in a local church in much the same manner as when he assumes his followers will do such things as give to the poor (Matt 6:2), pray (Matt 6:5), and fast (Matt 6:17).[13] These two references give us a glimpse into the work of Christ in this age. He will build his church universal, which will include all who become his followers. He will build it through establishing local churches made up of believers in each specific locality, from which people will take the gospel to the world.

In Acts, we see his mission spread from its origin in Jerusalem unto even the remotest part of the earth through sending his apostles directly and ultimately future followers to evangelize and 'congregationalize' the world (Acts 1:8). The term *ekklesia* appears 20 times in Acts speaking about the church.[14] In the progress of the New Testament, the local church becomes the dominant means of carrying out the Great Commission. This commis-

---

13. I use the word active before words such as joining, belonging, and membership to signify the New Testament is clear that joining and belonging to a local church is not optional nor fulfilled by merely having one's name on a church roll.

14. This includes both the universal and local church. It appears three other times in reference to non-church assemblies.

sion is accomplished through equipping the saints for ministry, evangelism, missions, and 'congregationalizing' the world. Christ carries his plan out by following his mandate through his established model. When considering the full New Testament, we can say that Christ's mandate is the Great Commission (Matt 28:18–20), and the model for carrying out his mandate is Ephesians 4:11–16. This Ephesians passage is comprehensive enough to incorporate the warp and woof of all the details of the New Testament mandate.[15]

The term *ekklēsia* appears one hundred and fourteen times in the NT.[16] Four times the term is used for non-church gatherings (the congregation of Israel in Acts 7:38 and assembly in Acts 19:32, 39, 41). Of the remaining one hundred and ten appearances, only eighteen refer to the universal church, which leaves ninety-two times, 84%, referring to the local assembly of believers.[17] This scriptural focus on the local church is in contrast to the current overemphasis on the universal body of Christ. We see this in such activities as prioritizing personal ministries and parachurch organizations so that they become more and more disconnected from the local church. The overemphasis on the universal church today often skews the meaning of what it means to be a faithful Christian. The New Testament knows of no at-large ministry that is not rooted in and dedicated to strengthening the local church by its gifts and presence.

The history and development of the universal church came about by a continued and systematic effort to further establish the local church as the nucleus of carrying out the Great Commission given by Christ, the head

---

15. See my book *The Equipping Church: Somewhere Between Fundamentalism & Fluff*, chapter 10.

16. *ekklēsia* is translated assembly (3), church (74), churches (35), and congregation (2) for a total of 114 times; Robert L. Thomas, *New American Standard Hebrew-Aramaic and Greek Dictionaries*: updated edition, H8674 (Anaheim: Foundation Publications, Inc., 1998, 1981), Logos electronic edition.

17. This number could vary by 1 or 2 depending on whether one interprets a couple of usages as referring to the universal or local.

of the church (Eph 1:22). We find the term for church, *ekklasia*, used three times in the gospels and twenty times in reference to the universal or local church in Acts. In the beginning, there was one church in Jerusalem to which those who were saved were added (Acts 2:42–47; 8:1). Peter and the apostles served as both apostles and elders of the early church (Acts 6:1–7; 1 Pet 5:1). In the beginning, the local and the universal church were in the same geographical location; consequently, they were the same. But even then, the universal was expressed in and through local meetings of believers. The organization was primitive, as was the church (Acts 2:42–47).

The discipline of Ananias and his wife Sapphira suggest a primitive local gathering of the church. We see the localness in that they were gathered in one place (Acts 5:6) and that church discipline was established by Christ as a local church function (Matt 18:15–20). This understanding becomes even more apparent as the New Testament developed (Rom 16:17–18; 1 Cor 5:1–13; 2 Thess 3:6–15). Word of the divine discipline spread to the whole church in Jerusalem and even to unbelievers. Luke says, "And great fear came over the whole church, and over all who heard of these things" (Acts 5:11). He also says of the Apostles, "But none of the rest dared to associate with them; however, the people held them in high esteem (Acts 5:13). The Greek word associate, *kollao,* indicates joining together in a significantly powerful way.[18] It seems because of the discipline that took place and the

---

18. The word associate in Acts 5:13 signifies a strong connection. For example, Horst Robert Balz comments, "Matt 19:5: join oneself to a woman; 1 Cor 6:16: to a harlot; 1 Cor 6:17: to the Lord; similarly, with the meaning seek intimate contact (Acts 5:13; 9:26; 10:28); Acts 17:34: become someone's disciple; Luke 15:15: press oneself on someone; Rom 12:9 . . . 'attached to what is good.'" K. L. Schmidt, TDNT III, 822f.; TWNT X, 1146 (bibliography), (Horst Robert Balz and Gerhard Schneider, *Exegetical Dictionary of the New Testament* [Grand Rapids.: Eerdmans, 1990–], 306, Logos electronic edition).

Kittel says, "In the NT kolláō, meaning 'to glue or join together,'" Kittel, Friedrich, and Bromiley, *Theological Dictionary of the New Testament*, 452. According to a Logos word study of *kollao* translated *associate* in Acts 5:13, it appears twelve times in the New Testament and once as *proskolláō* in Eph 5:31 in reference

signs done by the apostles (vs. 12), hypocrites, the curious, and superficial seekers would not join with the apostles and what God was doing through them in building his church. Then, as it is today, to not join with the apostles is not to join the universal and the local visible church.

The establishment of local congregations continued through the spreading of the gospel. We see the Antioch church (Acts 11:26), then the appointing of "elders in every church" (Acts 14:23). We observe the gathering of "the church together" (Acts 14:27) and the charge to the elders in the church at Ephesus to "Be on guard for yourselves and for all the flock, among which the Holy Spirit has made you overseers, to shepherd the church of God which He purchased with His own blood" (Acts 20:28).

Henry Clarence Theissen summarizes the development of the local church, saying, "The local church sprang up in a most simple way. At first there was no organization, but merely a simple bond of love, fellowship, doctrine, and cooperation. Gradually, however, the earlier loose arrangement under the apostles was superseded by a close organization. Because members were already members of the true church, they felt impelled to organize local churches in which the invisible realities in Christ might be worked out for the common good and the salvation of the unsaved."[19] Acts 2:42 gives a glimpse into the early developing church and the importance of the local church. Acts continues the advancement of the gospel through primarily preaching and congregationalizing the world. The rest of the New Testament provides us with a complete portrait of the essential and dominant role the local church plays in Christ building his church (Matt 16:18).

---

to marriage. The word study provides various usages such as join, clings, associate, piled up, and hired himself out. Logos word study of *association, kollao,* from Acts 5:13.

19. Henry Clarence Theissen, *Lectures in Systematic Theology* (Grand Rapids: Eerdmans, 1983), 317.

THE IMPORTANCE OF THE CHURCH
IN CHRIST'S LETTERS TO HIS PEOPLE

There are twenty-one Epistles in the New Testament. The weight of the evidence indicates they were all written to local churches or for use in local churches. The first nine, Romans through 2 Thessalonians, were written to specific local churches, with many believing Ephesians was "a circular letter to be distributed to several undesignated local churches in the province of Asia or some other area."[20] 1 & 2 Timothy and Titus were addressed to individual leaders, shepherds, to instruct them in pastoral guidance for local churches;[21] consequently, they are known as the Pastoral Epistles.[22] While Philemon was addressed to Philemon and other individuals, it was also ad-

---

20. Harold W. Hoehner, "Ephesians," in *The Bible Knowledge Commentary: An Exposition of the Scriptures* vol 2, edited by J. F. Walvoord and R. B. Zuck (Wheaton: Victor Books, 1985), 613. Logos electronic edition.

21. Duane Litfin comments, "They are ostensibly addressed not to a congregation but to two young men who were functioning in pastoral roles. This does not mean, of course, that the letters were not read before congregations. The epistles show clear signs that their author intended them to be used widely" (A. Duane Litfin, "1 Timothy," *The Bible Knowledge Commentary: An Exposition of the Scriptures* vol 2, edited by J. F. Walvoord and R. B. Zuck, [Wheaton: Victor Books, 1985], 726–27. Logos electronic edition).

22. Thomas D. Lea comments, "Paul had likely left Titus in Crete to finish the task of organizing and instructing the churches there. He proceeded with Timothy to Ephesus and found a church in spiritual shambles . . . As he wrote 1 Timothy, he probably also reflected on the needs of Titus in Crete. He penned this Epistle at approximately the same time with a view to clarifying and adding to earlier oral instructions . . . The occasion for writing Titus appears in 1:5. Paul had left Titus behind in order to appoint elders in a church younger and less organized than the Ephesian church. . . Paul's purpose in writing was to instruct Titus to appoint and train the newly appointed elders of the Cretan church" (Thomas D. Lea and Hayne P. Griffin, *1, 2 Timothy, Titus*, The New American Commentary, vol. 34, [Nashville: Broadman & Holman Publishers, 1992], 42–44. Logos electronic edition).

dressed to "the church in your house" (Phlm 1:1–2); clearly indicating it was to be used in and for the local church. Hebrews was addressed to a local congregation, a portion of a local congregation, or possibly a group of re- deemed priests, but distinctly written for a local church as indicated in verses such as Hebrews 13:17, which is similar to language used in local congre- gations (1 Thess 5:12; 1 Tim 5:17).[23] Additionally, Leon Morris notes, "The readers were certainly members of the Christian community (e.g., 3:1; 6:9; 10:23). . . .The *hegoumenos* ('leader') applied to church leaders (13:7, 17, 24) occurs in a similar way in 1 Clement and Hermas."[24] James has references that reflect a local body of believers (2:1–4), as does 1 Peter (5:1–5)[25] and 2 Peter (3:1).[26] 1 John seems best understood to have been sent to and for a

23. See David Allen's discussion on the recipients, in David L. Allen, *Hebrews*, The New American Commentary vol. 35 (Nashville: B & H Publishing Group, 2010), 61–70. Logos electronic edition.

24. Leon Morris, "Hebrews" in *The Expositor's Bible Commentary* vol 12, edited by Frank Gaebelein, (Grand Rapids: Zondervan Publishing House, 1981), 4–5.

25. "First Peter is addressed to Christians scattered throughout five Roman provinces of the peninsula of Asia Minor. That area today is northern Turkey. The churches in those provinces were made up of both Jews and Gentiles" (Roger M. Raymer, "1 Peter," in *The Bible Knowledge Commentary: An Exposition of the Scriptures*, edited by J. F. Walvoord and R. B. Zuck, vol. 2 [Wheaton: Victor Books, 1985], 838. Logos electronic edition).

26. "If one understands the first letter to refer to 1 Peter (2 Pet 3:1), as I do, then the letter was sent to churches in Asia Minor, churches that were mainly Gentile. . . there are clues that Peter wrote to a church facing syncretism and that he used the language of their culture to address the church (or churches)" (Thomas R. Schreiner, *1, 2 Peter, Jude*, The New American Commentary, vol. 37 [Nashville: Broadman & Holman Publishers, 2003], 276–77. Logos electronic edition).

"Peter was writing to Christians (1:1) to whom he had written before (3:1). If 2 Peter 3:1 refers to 1 Peter, then he was writing to the mixed Jewish and Gentile churches of 'Pontus, Galatia, Cappadocia, Asia, and Bithynia' (1 Pet 1:1). If, however, he referred to a letter no longer extant, then the destination of 2 Peter cannot be determined" (Kenneth O. Gangel, "2 Peter," in *The Bible Knowledge Commentary: An Exposition of the Scriptures* vol 2, edited by J. F. Walvoord and R. B. Zuck [Wheaton: Victor Books, 1985], 862. Logos electronic edition). Given what we

local church. Danny Akin comments, "First John was written to a church or group of churches in crisis—churches who were being attacked by false teaching (cf. 2:18–28; 4:1–6; 5:6–7).[27]

Regarding the chosen lady referring to a local church in 2nd John, Akin notes, "The majority of scholars, especially recent ones, have favored the first option, believing the phrase to be a metaphorical or symbolic means of identifying a local church and its members. This probably is the wisest option."[28] 3rd John speaks specifically of the local church. For example,

---

know, it seems most probable he wrote to local churches.

27. "First John was written to a church or group of churches in crisis—churches who were being attacked by false teaching (cf. 2:18–28; 4:1–6; 5:6–7)" (Daniel L. Akin, *1, 2, 3 John*, The New American Commentary vol. 38, [Nashville: Broadman & Holman Publishers, 2001], 29. Logos electronic edition).

28. Akin provides this summary of the discussion. "This is a unique designation for the recipient of a New Testament letter, and it has engendered significant discussion. Interpreters are divided over exactly who eklektē kuria kai tois teknois autēs is, and the following views have been offered:

1. It is a figurative reference to a local church and its members. Verse 13 would likewise refer to another local church.
2. It is a reference to the church universal (a view favored by Jerome).
3. The recipient is an individual lady and her children.

The majority of scholars, especially recent ones, have favored the first option, believing the phrase to be a metaphorical or symbolic means of identifying a local church and its members. This probably is the wisest option. Regardless of how one interprets these words, however, the basic application of the epistle remains unchanged. What the author would expect in belief and behavior of a lady and her children he would also expect of a local church and its members" (Akin, *1, 2, 3 John*, 219–20).

"What John tells the members of the congregation is plain enough . . . John looks after this one church in which there is trouble and also promises to come to it in person" (R. C. H. Lenski, *The Interpretation of the Epistles of St. Peter, St. John and St. Jude* [Minneapolis: Augsburg Publishing House, 1966], 550, 555. Logos electronic edition).

Glenn W. Barker notes that we cannot be dogmatic about the recipients, and there are varied opinions of whether it was written to a "designee" or a local

verse 6 says of Gaius that strangers had "testified to your love before the church," which may have been the church where John was, Jerusalem.[29] Verse 9 references the local church, which may have been the one to which Gaius belonged.[30] Verse 10 tells us that Diotrephes was putting people out of the church, which speaks of a local church.

Consequently, even Philemon and 3rd John, which often are noted as being addressed to individuals, were addressing local churches and the issues

church. But he says, "The statement 'whom I love in the truth—and not I only, but also all who know the truth' seems more appropriate as a reference to a church than an individual'" (Glenn W. Barker, "2 John" in *The Expositor's Bible Commentary* vol 12, edited by Frank Gaebelein [Grand Rapids: Zondervan Publishing House, 1981], 361–62).

29. "This may well have been the church at Jerusalem if the epistle was written before A.D. 66 . . . Undoubtedly, if this is so, Gaius would have been pleased to know that the highly respected Jerusalem congregation had heard of his service to the servants of God" (Zane C. Hodges, "3 John," in *The Bible Knowledge Commentary: An Exposition of the Scriptures* vol 2, edited by J. F. Walvoord and R. B. Zuck, vol. 2 [Wheaton: Victor Books, 1985], 913. Logos electronic edition).

30. "The simple reference to 'the church' suggests strongly that this was the church to which Gaius belonged. It sounds as if Gaius may not have known about John's letter to the church. It may well be that Diotrephes had suppressed it and kept it from the church's attention." Hodges, "3 John." See also, "'Church' (ekklēsia) occurs three times in this letter (vv. 6, 9, 10) and only in 3 John in the Johannine material, excluding Revelation. Here it refers to a local body of believers, most likely the church in which the elder himself was a member (Akin, *1, 2, 3 John*, 243. Logos). Even though Akin takes a different perspective on whether Diotrephes and Gaius belonged to the same local church, he is clear that the local church is still the recipient. Akin says, "John begins this section of the letter by informing Gaius that he had written a previous letter to a church, but he had encountered trouble from a man named Diotrephes . . . He had a position of leadership in a local church in the city or area where Gaius lived. Whether they were members of the same church is not stated, but given the information we have in 3 John it would seem unlikely. The elder had written an earlier letter to "the church" (not Diotrephes) . . . It would seem to have contained recommendations for traveling teachers sent from John that would encourage the church of Diotrephes to extend to them hospitality" (Akin, *1, 2, 3, John*, 245–46).

of a local church. Although the precise recipients of Jude are unknown, we can see that it speaks of things that are characteristic of a local church like the "love feasts" (vs. 12; 1 Cor 11:20–22). It is far more likely it was written to or for local congregations rather than individuals or at large Christians just doing kingdom work apart from local churches, which would minimally be in contrast to the rest of the New Testament. Schreiner indicates it was written to the local church when discussing that we do not know the precise destination of "whether Jude wrote to one church or churches."[31] The evidence we have strongly suggests the recipients were one or more local churches, as is the case with the rest of the New Testament. Revelation is addressed to the seven local churches of Asia Minor (Rev 2 & 3). Accordingly, the evidence indicates that all the Epistles and Revelation were written for teaching, governance of the community, and maturing the saints in local

---

31. "We must admit that we really have no way of knowing the letter's destination. Nothing in the interpretation of the letter is based on its destination, nor do we know whether Jude wrote to one church or churches. In the commentary I will refer to Jude's "church," but I do not mean to imply thereby that only one church is addressed . . . He addressed specific circumstances to assist the church in its response to intruders who had invaded the church" (Schreiner, *1, 2 Peter, Jude,* 410–11. Logos).

"The tone of the letter demonstrates that the original recipients may have been Christian Jews of Palestine who were gathered into local fellowships" (Edward C. Pentecost, "Jude," in *The Bible Knowledge Commentary: An Exposition of the Scriptures* vol 2, edited by J. F. Walvoord and R. B. Zuck [Wheaton: Victor Books, 1985], 918. Logos electronic edition). See also J. N. D. Kelly, *The Epistles of Peter and of Jude,* Black's New Testament Commentary (London: Continuum, 1969), 243, Logos electronic edition, and Lenski, *The Epistles of St. Peter, St. John and St. Jude,* 609. Logos.

"Since the address is so general. . . it is quite possible that the author intended the letter to be circulated to a number of churches. Against this are the internal indications that the author knows the conditions within the church or churches to whom he writes" (Edwin A. Blum, "Jude" in *The Expositor's Bible Commentary* vol 12, edited by Frank Gaebelein, [Grand Rapids: Zondervan Publishing House, 1981], 383–84).

churches. The Christians would then take the gospel to the world in word and by a demonstration of its power through their transformed lives (Titus 2:7–10; 1 Pet 2:12, 15; 3:16).

Therefore, all of the twenty-one Epistles and the book of Revelation provide sufficient evidence that we should accept they were written to various local churches. In contrast, there does not seem to be any contravening evidence against such being the case or that they were written so as to find their fulfillment in an abstract universal kingdom, Christian's at-large ministries, and lives lived apart from the local church. It seems we are safe to say this is further evidence that the New Testament does not entertain the idea of a Christian living faithfully to Christ apart from active involvement and commitment to a local church. And that a person cannot be considered to be living faithfully for Christ nor contributing to building his church according to his plan apart from a bond between their life, ministry, and a local church.

The Importance of the Local Church in Understanding Scripture

Understanding the New Testament is dependent upon both a knowledge and esteem of the local church in Christ's plan that is commensurate with Christ's esteem of the local church. As we have seen, Christ made the local church central to his plan. Deemphasizing the local church can be quite overt, but often, it is rather subtle. Here are three ways the local church can be devalued and thereby place the person or ministry in conflict with the heart of Christ's plan to build his universal church.

First, let me mention parachurch ministries. I have worked around several parachurch ministries and have varying degrees of familiarity with others. Many exist as an arm of the local church, such as some colleges, seminaries, and collegiate ministries. However, often the parachurch ministry sends a message that may or may not be subtle, that real ministry happens in their parachurch ministry, and the practical reality of the local church is defective. To wit, they believe their ministry reflects Christian reality more purely than the local church. Many times, people involved in ministries separated from a local body of believers attend a local church, but they only offer a minimal contribution to the health and mission of the church. Unfortunately, some go even further and see their ministry as their church, which is not only unfortunate but is unbiblical.[32]

I remember meeting with a regional director of a national parachurch organization. He showed me their organizational and ministry plan for advancing the kingdom and the gospel. The one thing missing from all the components was the local church. When I queried him about the absence of the local church in their plan, he assured me that they thought it was necessary. All I could think is that it was not important enough to be in the plan you show everyone. That being said, let me say that it is not true of all who are involved in parachurch ministries. Some of them make significant contributions to their ministry as well as the local church. We have members like this, and we thank God for them. Christians who desire to be faithful to the plan of Christ must make sure our emphasis is accordant with the New Testament emphasis, which means we must accentuate the local church.

---

32. Thoralf Gilbrant mentions another view of the church that receives unwarranted affection from which comes the idea of the invisible church. However, "the idea of an 'invisible' church would not have been Paul's view. This concept, albeit 'valid' in the sense that the 'Lord knows who belongs to Him,' was introduced first by Augustine (City of God), and perpetuated by John Wycliff (De ecclesia), [Martin] Luther (Preface to Revelation) and [John] Calvin (Institutes 4.1.7)" (Thoralf Gilbrant, ed., *The Complete Biblical Library: International and Interdenominational Bible Study System*, vol. 12, [Springfield, MO: The Complete Biblical Library, 1990, printed by R.R. Donnelley and Sons Company, Chicago], 337, and Colin Brown, ed., *The New International Dictionary of New Testament Theology*, vol. 1 [Grand Rapids: Zondervan Publishing House, 1975], 299, under "church").

Second, I would mention pietism. This view is at the other end of the spectrum. It is extreme, excessive individualism or excessive pietism.[33] These marginalize the significance of the local church by over-emphasizing one's personal relationship with Christ. While this personal relationship is a vital reality, extreme pietism is out of balance. These do not see a need for fellowship within a local church structured according to the New Testament. Instead, they develop a small group to meet with, which is based upon the select teaching of a portion of the New Testament rather than the full corpus. While they refer to this as their church, it is more rightly a Bible study than a local church. They may have a subtle or not so subtle aversion to anything that resembles an "organized church," such as membership, schedules, meetings, giving, or pastors. The universal body of Christ is all they need. Of course, with modern media, they may find all of the local church they want on television or the internet. But as long as they remain distant to a local church organized according to the New Testament, they fail to build according to the plan of Christ.

Third, I would mention the over-personalization of Scripture. These types of perspectives can wittingly or unwittingly undermine the place of the local church in Christ's plan. They approach and read the Scripture as if it was said to an individual or group apart from the local church when it is clear, in context, that it is speaking to or for the local church. There is the application of Scripture to other contexts. But as an interpretive matter, we are seeking to understand what the author (with Scripture that is God) intended by what he said to the specific people to whom he wrote. That is known as authorial intent. Then we seek to understand how the recipients understood his words.

---

33. Excessive pietism as used here involves an overemphasis on personal religious experience with the concomitant de-emphasizing of living out one's faith in community with other believers in a local church as defined according to the complete New Testament.

2 Timothy 2:2 is an example of a verse that is often personalized in application with little regard for its actual context and meaning, which results in unbiblically marginalizing the local church. One example of this misreading of Scripture happens when someone makes it all about people discipling other people in and outside of the church. People in various Christian ministries like the Navigators frequently cite this verse. This verse can have an application to teachers in the church and those ministering outside the church, but that does not seem to be the correct interpretation of the verse.

Paul is charging Timothy to teach and train faithful men in the local church so they can become church leaders like pastors and evangelists. To wit, it is about correctly teaching and training future elders of the local church whose principal responsibility is teaching and preaching. As the primary congregational teachers in the church, being able to teach is the elder's one functional qualification (1 Tim 3:2; Titus 1:9). Thomas D. Lea says, "The specific people Paul had in mind probably were the elders of 1 Tim 3:1–7 and 5:17–22."[34]

George W. Knight comments similarly, "Since the task committed to these faithful ones is that of teaching others also, it is certain that they are the same group of whom Paul wrote in 1 Timothy, the presbyters who 'work hard in word and teaching' (5:17), and also in Titus, the presbyters/overseers who are' holding fast the faithful word that is in accordance with the teaching' so that they are 'able both to exhort in sound doctrine and refute those who contradict' (1:9). These 'faithful' ones were men. Their task was 'to teach' an audience that included the entire church."[35]

John MacArthur recognizes application to other teachers in the church and, ultimately, all believers but stresses this is speaking first about training

---

34. Lea and Griffin, *1, 2 Timothy, Titus*, 201. Logos.

35. George W. Knight, *The Pastoral Epistles: A Commentary on the Greek Text*, New International Greek Testament Commentary (Grand Rapids; Carlisle, England: W.B. Eerdmans; Paternoster Press, 1992), 391.

leaders in the local church. He comments, "The truth Paul is talking about here is beyond the basic gospel message of salvation. . . . He is rather talking about the careful, systematic training of church leaders who will teach and disciple other believers in the fullness of God's Word . . . This particular ministry is to be selective. It is reserved for faithful men who will be able to teach others also. He is directing Timothy to invest in the lives of spiritually devout men who are gifted to teach potential pastors and evangelists."[36] This responsibility applies especially to the elders, sometimes called teaching pastors, "who work hard at preaching and teaching" (1 Tim. 5:17). When verses like this are merely applied to someone's personal life or ministry outside of the local church, the local church is unjustifiably minimized in God's plan for building his church.

THE IMPORTANCE OF THE LOCAL CHURCH TO OUR REWARDS

(1 Corinthians 3:10–23)

1 Corinthians chapter three provides another example of the importance of the local church in Christ's plan of building his kingdom. Unfortunately, it also provides another example of a passage that is frequently over personalized, thereby subtly minimizing the local church in Christ's plan because they make it about the individual or their particular parachurch ministry. They do so in spite of the unambiguous teaching that it is about building the local church.

This means that while many are familiar with this passage, you may have ordinarily read it and heard it taught as though Paul was speaking

---

36. John F. MacArthur Jr., *2 Timothy*, MacArthur New Testament Commentary (Chicago: Moody Press, 1995), 42.

about building your own spiritual life or living your daily life and receiving rewards. This emphasis is communicated in phrases like **Christ is the foundation; gold, silver, precious stones, or wood, hay, stubble,** and **you are the temple of God** (verses 11, 22, and 16, respectively) being applied to a believer's personal Christian walk. Now it is true that Christ is the foundation of your spiritual life, your works will be tested by fire, and you are the temple of God, but the context of each of these statements in this chapter is the local church. The focus of this chapter is not how you build your personal life, although there is application. But the issue Paul is addressing is how the Corinthians are building their local church, and by application, how we build the local church today. It is essential to understand what God was saying to the Corinthians and us by application. Do not read it as a passage of promises and warnings concerning your isolated Christian life, but rather focus on your life in and as a part of a local church. In other words, at Trinity, where I pastor, we would read it as, be careful how you build Trinity.

The Lord Jesus is building one thing, and that is the church. "I also say to you that you are Peter, and upon this rock I will build My church; and the gates of Hades will not overpower it" (Matt 16:18). He builds his universal church primarily in and through building local churches. As stated previously, in the inceptive stage of the church, the universal and the local were the same. From that, one can see Christ chose to build the universal church by planting and building local churches. Moreover, his plan is not to build the universal church from lone Christians living in isolation from the local church.[37]

Key to understanding the problem that Paul is addressing and the basis for whether a person will receive rewards for his contribution to building a

---

37. This is not to discount the lonely missionary who, because of following Christ into the wilderness, may be isolated. Rather the emphasis is that Christ is not building his church through individuals who resist being an active part of a local church.

local church is found in the contrast between God's wisdom and the world's wisdom in chapters 1–3. In these three chapters, Paul uses the Greek word *sophia* 26 times in the Greek text, and it is translated "wise" or "wisdom." *Sophia* appears only 19 other times in all of Paul's Epistles.[38] In addition, the Greek words *gnosko (6), oída (5), and gnosis (1) are translated in various forms of know a total of twelve times, and moria is translated* in various forms of *foolish* nine times in these same three chapters.

Accordingly, the conflict that Paul is addressing is between the wisdom and knowledge of the world (foolishness), which is the wisdom and knowledge of the man. The Corinthian church was employing the wisdom of the world instead of following God's wisdom from Scripture. In verses 18–23 of this chapter, Paul concludes his challenge to reject human wisdom and embrace God's wisdom with a succinctly cogent juxtaposition of worldly wisdom versus spiritual wisdom, which elucidates the unacceptability of human wisdom for the divine work of building the church.[39]

Consequently, the question is, when a believer stands before the judgment seat of Christ (2 Cor 5:10), will his works in building the local church be rewarded or not—provided that there are any works to test? This chapter lays down the determinative criterion for deciding that. Did the believer build the church by his contribution, evaluation, membership, participation, service, support, and strength based on human wisdom or God's wisdom as revealed in the Scripture? If his contributions were based upon human wisdom (what he or others think is best), they will burn, but if

---

38. Gordon D. Fee and Douglas Stuart, *How to Read the Bible for All Its Worth* (Grand Rapids.: Zondervan, 2003), 63. Fee and Stuart note that one of the key words is wisdom or wise, and that Paul uses it 26 times in chapters 1–3, and it is used only 18 more times in all of Paul's letters. My search of the word resulted in 26 and 19 uses respectively, *Nestlé-Aland 27th Edition Greek New Testament*, Kurt Aland ed. (West Germany, United Bible Societies, 1993), Logos electronic edition.

39. To see the damaging effects of employing human wisdom called progressivism in the church, see my book *The Vulgarization of Christ's Church: Combatting Progressivism's Damning Influence Upon Christian Thinking and Preaching.*

he built according to God's wisdom revealed in the Scripture, they will be magnanimously rewarded.

Much of the evaluation of churches, where to attend or whether a church is considered good or bad, is based more upon human wisdom—preference, friends, convenience, style, tradition, personality, size, location, and other extra-biblical criteria. While these things can be quite compelling and impressive here and now, they will be burned up because they are rooted in human wisdom and therefore dishonor the temple of God. Consequently, one of the most significant issues a Christian must settle is whether he is going to seek to build the local church according to the wisdom of man or God, because this decision affects not only one's life today but his eternity as well.

"God is out to set aside the wisdom of this world (1:18–22, 27–28; 3:18–20). He has done this by the cross (1:18–25), by his choice of the Corinthian believers (1:26–31), and by the weakness of Paul's preaching (2:1–5). Christ, through the cross, has 'become for us wisdom from God' (1:30), and *this* wisdom is revealed *by* the Spirit to those who *have* the Spirit (2:10–16)."[40] As you will see, the Corinthians were seeking to build according to man's wisdom, which is wood, hay, and stubble, rather than God's wisdom, which is foolishness according to men's wisdom but according to God's wisdom, it is gold, silver, and precious stones.

Also, they were arguing that their leaders, emphases, or methods were based upon what was "wise" as well. Gordon Fee writes, "At the least, we can suspect that they are carrying on their division over leaders and their opposition to Paul in the name of wisdom."[41] We hear the wisdom of man in many statements regarding the church today. For example, "You know, you can't teach the deep things of God, the reality of hell, practice biblical church discipline, call people to 'take up their cross' or 'die to self' because times and sensibilities have changed, and we must be wise." Many so-called

---

40. Fee and Stuart, *How to Read the Bible*, 63.
41. Fee and Stuart, *How to Read the Bible*, 64.

church experts use select Scriptures that ostensibly support their plan for building the church, but actually, they are at best, naive approaches that seek to garner the blessings of God upon human wisdom. Regardless of how impressive to the human eye, their methods misrepresent Scripture and corrupt the local church. We have seen that the local church is at the strategic center of his plan for advancing his kingdom in this age. To do so requires his local churches to be built upon his Word and wisdom. Another indicator of the premier place of the local church in Christ's plan is seen in that he has tied many rewards to how we contribute to the local church.

I. The Contributions of the Builder
1 Cor 3:10–15

[10]According to the grace of God which was given to me, like a wise master builder I laid a foundation, and another is building on it. But each man must be careful how he builds on it. [11]For no man can lay a foundation other than the one which is laid, which is Jesus Christ. [12]Now if any man builds on the foundation with gold, silver, precious stones, wood, hay, straw, [13]each man's work will become evident; for the day will show it because it is to be revealed with fire, and the fire itself will test the quality of each man's work. [14]If any man's work which he has built on it remains, he will receive a reward. [15]If any man's work is burned up, he will suffer loss; but he himself will be saved, yet so as through fire.

In verses 10–15, God continues, as he did in verses 1–9, to speak about his temple, the local church. If the Corinthians build his local church according to God's instructions, wisdom, they will be rewarded, and he will be glorified. Through his chastising and correction of the Corinthian confusion, God teaches all of us how to build his church so that we receive rewards, and he is glorified. The fundamental problem the Corinthians had was that they sought to build the church according to human wisdom. Their plans probably included the trends of the day, Greek traditions, their preferences, what was familiar, and the best practices based on human wisdom. But this was a course doomed to degrade into pragmatism. Their dependence upon human wisdom led to and was evidenced and perpetuated by their prolonged infancy, satisfaction with the milk of the Word (vs. 1–2), and extolling purely fleshly allegiances above Scripture (vs. 3–4). Then he delineated the cure for their carnality, which is spiritual wisdom, resulting in a view of all God's people as servants, all ministries as equal, as was the case with Paul and Apollos.[42] And all rewards are based on faithfulness, not results (vs. 5–9).

The local church is God's temple, and therefore Paul warns that each person must be careful how he contributes to building the local church. Paul is not referring to the brick and mortar of the church building, but rather to the spiritual lives of God's people. Therefore, we must be ever so careful about how we build, for we are a holy temple of God.

Foundation Must Be Christ: vs. 10–11

[10]According to the grace of God which was given to me, like a wise master builder I laid a foundation, and another is building on it. But each man must be careful how he builds on it. [11]For no man can lay a foundation other than the one which is laid, which is Jesus Christ.

According to the grace of God which was given to me, like a wise master builder I laid a foundation, and another is building on it. But each man must be careful how he builds on it. For no man can lay a foundation other than the one which is laid, which is Jesus Christ.

---

42. Not all ministries have the same level of influence, but all ministries are equal in the sense that there is no more important ministry for a person to do than the one God desires for him to do.

Paul changes metaphors from **field** v. 9 to **building** v. 10. "Paul repeatedly uses the image of the building trade in his epistles. He presents Christians as God's building (v. 9, 16) and notes that Christ is their one foundation (v. 10–14; Eph 2:20). He describes the spiritual life of believers as a building process (Eph 4:29; 1 Thess 5:11). And he reveals that Christians are being built together in Christ (Eph 2:22; Col 2:7)."[43] Notice that Paul prefaces his ministry description with **according to the grace of God.** That is why Paul was an apostle. That is why Paul came and labored at Corinth. The wisdom with which he builds is not from him but God.

The term **master builder** is the Greek word *architektōn,* from which we get the word architect. But the Greek word includes the idea of a contractor. Consequently, the imagery here seems to be that of Paul being the general contractor who lays the foundation and provides the plans—via inspired revelation—by which others are to build upon the divinely inspired foundation. Similarly, those who come after Paul and build upon the foundation he laid are like subcontractors who must still follow the divine blueprints for every stage of development. Paul, as well as each following worker, is a spiritual artisan. It is essential to observe again that Paul is emphasizing the *local church* at Corinth because Paul did not lay the foundation for all local churches. But he did lay the foundation for the Corinthian church. Then Paul recognized that after he laid the foundation, others like Apollos and Peter, as well as additional leaders and people ministering their spiritual gifts, would contribute to the building of the local church at Corinth. But they must build upon the foundation which Paul built upon, and that is Christ and not human wisdom.

The foundation that Paul laid is the gospel (1 Cor 2:12–13) and the New Covenant (Eph 3:1–9). The word **building** in the phrase **another**

---

43. Simon J. Kistemaker and William Hendriksen, *Exposition of the First Epistle to the Corinthians,* New Testament Commentary, vol. 18, (Grand Rapids: Baker Book House, 1953–2001), 109.

is building on it is in the present tense, thereby signifying a continuous building of the body or Corinthian temple. The local church needs constant building up of the body regardless of how long the church has existed. Neither churches nor Christians arrive at perfection in this world. We are exhorted to submit to God's ordained process and mature. While Christians should become mature, maturing is an ongoing process to continue maturing and remain mature. Similarly, a person is to grow up to be a mature adult and then to live out his adult life as a mature and maturing adult.

Further, believers' involvement in serving, disciple-making, evangelism, and speaking truth does not wait on being *complete* in knowledge or wisdom, but instead, believers serve at their present level of maturity while continually growing and maturing. The process is one of simultaneously building, maturing, growing, edifying, and equipping. The local temple is continuously being built, and although this building does not exclude numerical growth and should include it if it can be done in obedience to the gospel, the focus of the concept of building is increasing in spiritual maturity. True spiritual maturity always results in both an inward focus to building up the body of Christ and an outward focus upon engaging and evangelizing those outside the church.

Paul warns that each person **must be careful how he builds on** the foundation of Christ and Paul's contribution, ensuring that it is consistent with Christ. This command refers to shepherds and leaders but also applies to the Corinthians because they were contributing, for better or worse, to the local church at Corinth. By application, the command applies to all serving in local churches. **Be careful** translates the word *blepō*, which means "see to it," "take care," or "be on guard." It is a present-tense imperative—a command. Consequently, the idea is, the Corinthians are commanded to continually be careful to build the local church according to the wisdom of God, Scripture, and thereby avoid seeking to build the temple of God according to the wisdom of man.

Every local church builds upon the foundation of Christ, and it is actually Christ building his church (Matt 16:18) through his people. Therefore, if a person claims to be building the church in ways that are not the ways of Christ, he is damaging the church by human wisdom. Accordingly, everyone needs to be careful about what they contribute, support, demand, say, and look for in seeking to build the local church. The quality of what each gives to the church is to be of a quality befitting the temple of God. Every thought, word, and deed need to be thoroughly biblical lest one finds himself in the Corinthian predicament of seeking to build the holy with the profane.

A further emphasis of this passage, as well as the New Testament, is that the primary focus of the New Testament is the local church rather than the universal church. That is how Christ is building the universal church. The universal church is a beautiful New Testament reality, but belonging to or seeking to build the universal church apart from building the local church is to put oneself in opposition to the plan of Christ, and therefore to Christ himself. Today, it is somewhat fashionable to emphasize love for the universal church and dissatisfaction with the local church, but that simply does not honor God. Belonging to an intangible universal church or contributing merely to a parachurch organization or substituting a parachurch for the local church is not enough to be considered genuinely building up the body of Christ.

Remember that Christ utterly rejected the religious system built by the Jews (Matt 7:24–28; 23:1–39), and he will reject every work on his church that is not according to God's wisdom; therefore, let every person be careful how he builds the church. The church must not be built according to tradition, personal preferences, trends, or what works, but instead according to the Scripture and, in particular, the New Testament. It is true that even the most devoted followers of Christ, at one time or another, contribute out of immaturity or naiveté. However, *willfully* seeking to build by rejecting part of the New Testament counsel is an entirely different issue, for that is intentionally setting the wisdom of man against the wisdom of God, thereby declaring that man is wiser than God.

Consequently, it is paramount for the church to have mature leaders who can guide the church to build according to the wisdom of God. Avoidance of human wisdom is why so much of the New Testament is about the responsibility of pastors and other God-called leaders (Eph 4:11–16; 1 & 2 Tim; Titus; 1 Pet 5:1–5). It is the reason Paul commanded Timothy to train up new leaders of the local church when he said, "The things which you have heard from me in the presence of many witnesses, entrust these to faithful men who will be able to teach others also" (2 Tim 2:2). Failing to use God's gifting and opportunities to contribute to building the church is human wisdom, as is using them in a way that is not in line with God's plan and manner.

Construction Must Be Quality: vs. 12

> [12] "Now if any man builds on the foundation with gold, silver, precious stones, wood, hay, straw,

Every believer is involved in building the church, but whether his contributions will be rewarded will be decided at the judgment seat of Christ. In other words, that all believers are building a church is certain, but they can choose the materials with which they build, and that determines whether their labors are rewarded. The choice of materials is the wisdom of man (wood, hay, straw) or the wisdom of God (gold, silver, precious stones). The Epistles and Revelation 2–3 reflect different kinds of churches, whereby those building them have either contributed material that is wood, hay, and straw or gold, silver, and precious stones. These different substances represent our works in building and advancing the church (Eph 2:10).

Those who contributed gold, silver, and precious stones will be rewarded, and those who sought to contribute wood, hay, and straw will not be rewarded, regardless of how hard they worked or how sincere their efforts. Therefore, it is of monumental importance for each follower of Christ to be able to differentiate between unrewardable and rewardable labor. Although building for the glory of God is the ultimate test, it still leaves the question of how does a person know whether his contributions glorify God and are, therefore, going to be rewarded?

Some define gold, silver, and precious stones as representing our best for God; however, the best human contribution to building God's spiritual temple is nothing more than wood, hay, and straw. Some seem to make things like numerical growth, size, innovation, perpetuating tradition, or the closeness of their fellowship as the test of whether their works are glorifying God; although, most would deny such. While none of these are bad or evil in and of themselves, and can even be good and holy, all of them fail to differentiate sufficiently between whether one is building the church with rewardable or unrewardable material.

The criterion for what is rewarded when building the church is whether it is based upon, derived from, and motivated by human wisdom or divine wisdom. Paul argued in the first three chapters of Corinthians against the value of human wisdom in accomplishing spiritual good and in favor of divine wisdom as the only path to spiritual good. The Corinthians were building their church according to man's wisdom, the wisdom of the age. This is not to say there were not any spiritual components, but rather it is that their process of determining what the church should or should not do, be or not be, was decided either in part or wholly by human wisdom.

I believe that gold, silver, and precious stones represent building material that is based upon the wisdom of God, as revealed in the Word of God. In contrast, wood, hay, and straw represent that which is based on the wisdom of man, culture, tradition, and preference. When we give our best as given to us by God, according to his Word, wisdom, and plan, that is good. But to depend upon our wisdom, which is evidenced by intentionally neglecting or minimizing knowing and following Scripture, that is sin.

Therefore, the material quality is determined by whether it is based on God's wisdom or man's wisdom. Determining what is based on God's wisdom may sound easy to determine, but it is not. Because some of God's wisdom, God's gold, is the world's rubbish—stumbling blocks. Church discipline, sanctification, sacrifice, living this life for happiness in the next, dependence on providence and sovereignty, humility, contentment, dying to self, and daily taking up your cross are a few such stumbling blocks. The Puritan Prayer entitled "Valley of Vision" sets forth the paradox of the Christian life of gold, silver, and precious stones.

> Lord, high and holy, meek and lowly, Thou hast brought me to the valley of vision, where I live in the depths but see Thee in the heights; hemmed in by mountains of sin I behold Thy glory. Let me learn by paradox that the way down is the way up, that to be low is to be high, that the broken heart is the healed heart, that the contrite spirit is the rejoicing spirit, that the repenting soul is the victorious soul, that to have nothing is to possess all, that to bear the cross is to wear the crown, that to give is to receive, that the valley is the place of vision. Lord, in the daytime, stars can be seen from deepest wells, and the deeper the wells, the brighter Thy stars shine; let me find Thy light in my darkness, Thy life in my death, Thy joy in my sorrow, Thy grace in my sin, Thy riches in my poverty, Thy glory in my valley.[44]

Beloved, my confession to you is that I find that I have a persistent tendency to forget God's clear teaching, to replace it with my own thoughts, to be distracted by the "successful." Only by consistently staying immersed in the Scripture, contemplating the thoughts of God, baptizing my thoughts

---

44. Arthur Bennett, ed., *The Valley of Vision: A Collection of Puritan Prayers & Devotions,* reformatted by Eternal Life Ministries, accessed April 28, 2020, http://www.eternallifeministries.org/prayers.htm#The%20Valley%20of%20Vision.

in the counsel of Scripture can I recognize the subtleties of the flesh, and distinguish between pure gold, silver, and precious stones, and wood, hay, and straw. In addition, such distinctions are made even more difficult because Satan and his world have inlaid the wood, hay, and straw with fool's gold, fake silver, and imitation stones. Therefore, I have to run continuously to the Scripture for my personal walk with God. Then, as a shepherd, I dwell in the Scripture for the church as well for fear that my flock has the same propensity as I.

The Inspection Will Be Thorough: vs. 13–15

> [13]each man's work will become evident; for the day will show it because it is to be revealed with fire, and the fire itself will test the quality of each man's work. [14]If any man's work which he has built on it remains, he will receive a reward. [15]If any man's work is burned up, he will suffer loss; but he himself will be saved, yet so as through fire.

These verses are not speaking about judging our sin because Christ bore our sins (Rom 8:10). Rather it is about granting or losing rewards for service in building the local church. (Rom 8:1; 14:10; 2 Cor 5:10). Consequently, an unfaithful Christian will be saved but lose rewards, which is the idea in verse 15, **he himself will be saved, yet so as through fire**. Fire speaks of refining or purifying (Job 23:10; Ps 66:10; 1 Pet 1:7).

Rewards come to us when we make ourselves vessels for Christ to use in his exclusive endeavor of building his church. While these rewards are directly connected to a Christian's contribution to building a local church, I believe the work can be done both directly by serving in a local church and indirectly by serving in areas that help local churches such as seminaries, campus ministries, and support ministries. However, parachurch ministries that exist to build themselves or the universal church while bypassing the local church are not contributing to building the local church; consequently, the rewards mentioned here do not seem to apply. Therefore, parachurch organizations, beware not to build unto yourselves. Christians, beware not to build unto your own life, and pastors, beware not to build unto your own ministry. Merely building to our own personal lives, ministries, or passions is to lose rewards and find ourselves in conflict with Christ, who is building the church.

Paul lived for the reward of faithfulness at the second coming (Matt 25:21, 23; Phil 3:13–14). His desire to earn rewards was motivated by the fact that he knew that would be the most pleasing to Christ (1 Cor 9:24–27; Rev 22:12). While man can judge and expose sin, which can be known because it is contrary to God's Word, God alone knows thoroughly and judges motives. The nature of gold, silver, and precious stones is that they are better and more valuable after the testing by fire, whereas wood, hay, and straw are consumed.

Rewards in the New Testament are most often referred to as crowns (1 Cor 9:25). There is a crown of righteousness for those who remain faithful until the end (2 Tim 4:7–8). There is a crown of exaltation for those who faithfully proclaim the truth (1 Thess 2:19–20). The crown of life awaits those who love the Lord (Jas 1:12). For those who serve, there is 'the unfading crown of glory' (1 Pet 5:4). MacArthur says, "Each of these is best understood as a Greek genitive of apposition, i.e., the crown which is righteousness, the crown which is exultation, the crown which is glory, and the crown which is life. All refer to the fullness of the believer's promised reward."[45]

Gold, silver, and precious stones are materials for building Christ's church his way, which are derived from God's wisdom as recorded in the Scripture. Wood, hay, and straw are building materials that are derived from human wisdom regardless of how sincere the motives, lofty the goals, or elegant the rationale; they are still the products of human wisdom. Humans

---

45. John F. MacArthur Jr., *1 Corinthians,* MacArthur New Testament Commentary (Chicago: Moody Press, 1984), 85. Logos electronic edition.

seem quite adept at overlaying wood, hay, and straw with gold, making them appear to be pure gold, but the fire of the scrutiny of the Holy One will expose it as mere spiritual cosmetics. For example, if one uses size as the evidence that he is building with gold, he might want to change his church sign to read, *Caution This Place Is Highly Flammable!* Man's spiritual tool chest is full of straw when he looks to human wisdom to determine what the church needs, should be, and should look like, or what parts of Scripture best fit. One church may grow, and one may not; one may be large, and one may be small. But those criteria alone do not tell us the quality of their building materials.

Following are a *few* examples of flammable human wisdom: devaluing preaching the Scripture, intentionally eliding certain biblical teachings, designing the church for the lost or the seeker, and invoking empty traditions. Flammable human wisdom is eschewing the command to exercise church discipline because it is difficult, might result in people leaving, or is ostensibly antithetical to numerical growth. If a body of believers follows the Scripture, even if the church does not grow like the one down the street with its trendy emphases, only the one that follows Scripture will be rewarded. Therefore, we should not come to Scripture to find a verse that seems to support an idea drawn from the wisdom of the world, but labor in the Word of God to build by the wisdom of God. At times, someone will quip that he is only interested in going to heaven and not rewards. However, it will be a tragically sad day for a Christian to stand before his Lord Jesus with no rewards for faithfully obeying Christ's Word, using the gifts he has been given or sacrificing in even the smallest of ways to help build the church for which Christ gave his life. (Acts 20:28; Eph 5:25).

II. The Caution to All Builders
1 Cor 3:16–17

[16]Do you not know that you are a temple of God and that the Spirit of God dwells in you? [17]If any man destroys the temple of God, God will

destroy him, for the temple of God is holy, and that is what you are.

We are listening to God speak to us about his temple, the local church. He is teaching the Corinthians and us how to build the church, specifically the local church, through which Christ will build his kingdom. He is doing this through his chastisement and correction of the Corinthian confusion. The general problem is they were seeking to build the church according to human wisdom, the trends of their day, and the traditions of Greek culture, preferences, or what was familiar, which quickly degrades into pragmatism.

To correct their thinking and the problem of division and strife, Paul taught them from the counsel of God. Then, they must choose to embrace the wisdom of God, which is the gold, silver, and precious stones of biblical fidelity, unity, and spiritual healing, and reject the wisdom of man that is the divisive wood, hay, and straw. Verses 1–9 list three indicators of carnality (fleshly wisdom), which are prolonged infancy (vs.1), satisfied with milk (vs. 2), and fleshly allegiances to family, friends, or leaders over Scripture (vs. 3–9).

Spiritual wisdom from Scripture is the cure for carnality, and a spiritually wise person builds the local church by viewing each choice through the grid of Scripture. The foundation must be Christ, and the construction must be quality—gold—God's wisdom. The construction quality includes our model, motive, and method. This inspection and evaluation of the quality of our contributions, unlike much of today's assessments, will indeed reveal whether we trusted God or man in building his church. This caution applies to all who seek to build Christ's church. These words powerfully remind us that *we must be ever so careful how we build.* Our caution is not only based upon the potential for rewards but also because of what the church *is*

The Church Is the Sanctuary of God: vs. 16

[16]Do you not know that you are a temple of God and that the Spirit of God dwells in you?

The church in the New Testament has replaced the sacred Old Testament temple. The New Testament says that Christ's body is a temple (John 2:19–21), the universal church is a temple, (Eph 2:20–21), the individual Christian's body is a temple, (1 Cor 6:19), and here the local church is **a temple of God** (vs. 16). In contrast to 1 Corinthians 6:19, which speaks of each individual Christian's body, **you** in this verse is plural, signifying the local corporate body of believers. Consequently, every local New Testament church is a temple of God. Paul uses the word **temple**, *naós,* without the article, signifying the quality, the essence of the meaning of temple as opposed to a particular location.[46] Greek scholar Ray Summers says, "When the article is used . . . the thing emphasized is identity; when the article is not used, the thing emphasized is quality or character."[47] The question **Do you not know** implies that they should know and understand. The word **temple,** *naós,* refers to the temple proper, where God dwelt, rather than just the temple complex. It was the sacred, holy sanctuary of the Shekinah glory where only the high priest could enter once a year.

Now, what makes the church sacred? Is it the people, building, or location? No, it is because it is the dwelling place of the Holy Spirit in the New Covenant, like the Holy of Holies in the Old Testament. Why must we be so careful about how we build the church? Because it is the Holy of Holies, the dwelling place of God, the sanctuary of God. The local church is holy because the Holy Spirit dwells in them as a body of believers. Therefore, *any* local *body* of believers constituted as a New Testament local church is a temple of the Holy Spirit and is to be treated as such.

A concomitant aspect of this truth is that each individual believer's body is a temple of the Holy Spirit and should be treated accordingly. Paul says, "Or do you not know that your body is a temple of the Holy Spirit who is in you, whom you have from God, and that you are not your own?

---

46. This is called the anarthrous construction.
47. Ray Summers, *Essentials of New Testament Greek* (Nashville: Broadman Press, 1950), 129.

For you have been bought with a price: therefore glorify God in your body" (1 Cor 6:19–20). Here it is speaking of the individual believer's body. Accordingly, each believer is a sanctuary of the Holy Spirit. The word *naós,* translated **temple** here, is the same as used in 1 Corinthians 3:16.

The emphasis of purity and holiness encompasses both the corporate body of Christ in worship and service as well as in each member's personal life. It does seem incoherent to think that one can exist without the other. If the holiness of both the corporate body and individuals are not emphasized in the corporate gatherings, it is unlikely, with few exceptions, that holiness will be a priority of individuals in the daily living out of our lives. Conversely, if individuals are not seeking to walk in purity and holiness before God daily, truly holy gatherings of the body of Christ for worship and serving will prove to be of little interest.

Personal and corporate holiness means to be set apart unto God in every way and everything. Not uncommonly, when spiritual disciplines of godliness are emphasized, they are pejoratively and summarily dismissed as legalism. Such scorning of them trivializes legalism's virtually impenetrable spiritual lethality as well as all the biblical teaching about spiritual discipline and comprehensive holiness.

Both personal and church disciplines are to drive a wedge between the temple (our redeemed lives) and the vulgar, which is our flesh and the world of Satan (Matt 18:15–20; Rom 16:17–18; 1 Cor 5:1–13; 1 Tim 1:18–20; 2 Thess 3:6–15; 1 Cor 9:27; 1 Tim 4:7–8; Phil 4:8; 2 Tim 2:18). The holiness we are called to is tangibly practical. It is commanded and not optional, and it is to permeate and radiate from our entire being (1 Pet 1:15–16). Ephesians 5 begins, "Therefore be imitators of God, as beloved children" (Eph 5:1). Then it explicitly addresses vital areas of thought and behavior with warnings to exemplify only Christ's love and avoid all thinking, behavior, or speech that is immoral, impure, or deceptive (verses 2–9). It is difficult to imagine a more serious call to godliness than the one issued here, "be imitators of God."

The Church Is Safeguarded by God: vs. 17a

[17]If any man destroys the temple of God, God will destroy him,

"Under the Old Testament, any person other than the high priest on the Day of Atonement who dared to enter the Holy of Holies would drop dead on the spot. He would not need to be put to death by the people. God would strike him dead. Even less does God look kindly upon those who threaten or defile His holy people (Matt 18:6–10)."[48] The things that destroy the temple of God were present in Corinth: pride, jealousy, the unjustifiable elevation of human relationships, prolonged infancy, human wisdom, and milkoholism, all of which are the products of imposing human wisdom upon the temple of God. By supplanting divine wisdom with human wisdom, they place themselves under the patient but the sure judgment of God. Remember, using human wisdom to build the brick and mortar building is fine, but building the church—the spiritual temple of God—with human wisdom is sin.

I use the term "milkoholism" as a designation for Christians who remain on the spiritual bottle far beyond what is a part of normal spiritual growth. It is a sure mark of carnality, choosing to walk in human wisdom. Paul chastised the Corinthians for this in vs. 2, **"I gave you milk to drink, not solid food; for you were not yet able to receive it. *Indeed, even now you are not yet able.*"** (italics added) Paul did not scold them for starting as babes in Christ on milk, but for remaining on milk when they should have been feeding on the meat of the Word and maturing in the faith. Starting as a babe in Christ and feeding on the milk of the Word is part of the maturation process, but choosing to learn only milk and resist feeding on the meat of the Scripture is evidence of carnality and the fuel that perpetuates carnality.

---

48 MacArthur, *1 Corinthians*, 86.

230

Here is a brief summary of some of the characteristics of and differences between the milk and the meat of the Word. The milk of the Word is required for every Christian, and meat is required for every Christian to mature.

Milk's strengths:
1. It is true.
2. It is the simple truths of the gospel and Scripture.
3. It is necessary and good.
4. It is loved even by the mature.
5. It pervades and permeates all doctrines and passages.

Milk's limitations:
1. It is not meat.
2. All meat contains some milk, but milk does not contain meat.
3. It raises questions answered only by meat.
4. It provides essential but limited growth.
5. It requires little thinking or labor in Scripture.
6. It does not provide in-depth or detailed understanding of Scripture, God, or his work, will, and ways.
7. It does not result in maturity regardless of how many times it is heard, said, quoted, or prayed.

Milk is the basic truths of Scripture, whereas meat contains milk, but it also adds depth, breadth, and detail to the basic truths—milk. Meat is required for a better comprehension and coherence of all the truths and details of Scripture. In other words, without meat, it is impossible to blend the truths of Scripture into one complete, accurate, and coherent message from God. Without the meat of Scripture, a person will remain a baby Christian.

If the eschewing of meat is a choice, as was the case with the Corinthians, it is evidence of carnality. Desiring only the milk of the Word and rejecting being taught and learning the meat of the Word is idolatry of self, which is human wisdom. It is to fill God's temple with idols of human wisdom and defame God's holy temple.

Unlike Gentile temples, the construction of the tabernacle and the temple included instructions that excluded idols; this includes those made by hands and those made by carnality. Only the name of God could be there. In like manner, the church or temple of God has no idols, only the indwelling Holy Spirit of God. God strongly warns of the seriousness of vulgarizing his local church. The warning to **be careful how he builds** refers to not only rewards but also the warning of God judging those who destroy his temple, which is precisely what human wisdom does. God will destroy those who destroy his temple through persecution, corruption, carnal divisions, or anything derived from human wisdom.

A local church is more important than people's ministries, ideas, reputations, opinions, feelings, cliques, personal needs, fancies, or hurts because it is the holy temple of God. Christians must treat the church as holy and be willing to sacrifice for her to be the grand temple of God she is designed to be. Sadly, sometimes when people get their feelings hurt, or things do not go the way they think they should, or even when they have genuinely been wronged, they will sacrifice the church in order to promote their vendetta, personal vindication, or agenda. They will idolize themselves by seeking to correct a supposed or actual wrong done against them even if it splits or hurts the church. Placing oneself above the good of the church is human wisdom, which sacrifices the church. God will not forget nor let that human wisdom go unpunished. This love affair with human wisdom resulted in the Corinthians' perpetual carnality, numerous church problems, and some being sick and even dead (1 Cor 11:30).

To hurt a local church in order to vindicate one's reputation, to get one's way, or because of various dissatisfactions is undeniable evidence of carnality. The Corinthians were guilty of this kind of behavior, even treating the holy temple of God as a pagan temple. It is true that the universal church will prevail against the gates of Hades (Matt 16:18) and all attacks by the lost, worldly wisdom, and the fierce powers of Satan; however, the same cannot be said of any particular local church. It may follow the path of the church at Ephesus "who left her first love" (Rev 2:4), Pergamum's acceptance of false teaching (Rev 2:14), or Thyatira's acceptance of immorality and false prophets (Rev 2:20). Or it may succumb to the ravages of earthly wisdom like Sardis, of whom Christ said, "You have a name that you are alive, but you are dead" (Rev 3:1b). The head of the church may reject the once-accepted church as he did at Laodicea, whose lukewarmness nauseated Christ to the point of total rejection (Rev 3:15–16).

The Epistles are full of evidence that human wisdom destroys a local church, whether it is the carnal Corinthians or legalistic Galatians. Moreover, history is riddled with destroyed local churches. Even the church I pastor, Trinity Baptist Church, has been ravaged more than once by the wisdom of men and the cunning attacks of Satan. Our vigilance and humility must be constant because Satan, like a lion, stalks the weak of our churches—those that think like mere men—and will devour them and use them to harm the temple of God (1 Pet 5:8). The words of this verse stand as an eternal warning that God will have the last word for anyone who destroys a local temple of God. Some confuse the patience of God with God's lack of follow-through, but his patience is to give space for repentance as he did with Jezebel, where through the prophet Elijah, he predicted how she would die, but then gave her twenty years to repent (Rev 2:21).

To equate God's patience with procrastination or unwillingness is to make a most severe miscalculation. "Never take your own revenge, beloved, but leave room for the wrath of God, for it is written, 'VENGEANCE IS MINE, I WILL REPAY,' says the Lord" (Rom 12:19) and "It is a terrifying thing to fall into the hands of the living God" (Heb 10:31). The local church is by Christ's design the strategic center of his Kingdom's work in this age, and it is the place where God dwells among his people, the Holy of Holies; therefore, one dare not vulgarize the local church with human wisdom for God will not turn a blind eye (Rom 2:4–8).

The Church Is Set Apart for God vs. 17b

[17b]for the temple of God is holy, and that is what you are.

This temple is anything but common; it is holy. The church is set apart by God as a holy temple. Therefore, to desacralize what God has made sacred will ultimately bring God's destruction to that individual. **Be careful how you build.** Why? Because the building project you are involved in is holy—set apart for God by God. The local church can only honor God and be the holy temple he established her to be when she is built according to divine wisdom, as revealed in the Scripture. She is holy, and if we truly love God, we will love the local church, for she is his temple, his holy dwelling. Our love will be measured by whether we seek his wisdom and build accordingly, which includes what we make the church to be, how she is organized, what she does, and what we are willing to sacrifice for her.

Most assuredly, those who seek to impose their will upon the church always aver that it is because they love the church. But their love of the church is based upon the human wisdom of using select Scriptures that are not directly related to the issue at hand while trampling underfoot the undeniably relevant Scriptures. They make their interpretation the *only* interpretation to which the leaders must bow. They hear everyone but listen to no one, which is carnal pride. Their arrogance is easily seen by anyone who observes them through the full panoply of Scripture, but they are oblivious to their arrogance. Carnality, human wisdom, is the genesis and fuel for destroyers of the temple.

III. The Counsel to All Builders
1 Cor 3:18–23

[18]Let no man deceive himself. If any man among you thinks that he is wise in this age, he must become foolish, so that he may become wise. [19]For the wisdom of this world is foolishness before God. For it is written, "He is THE ONE WHO CATCHES THE WISE IN THEIR CRAFTINESS"; [20]and again, "THE LORD KNOWS THE REASONINGS of the wise, THAT THEY ARE USELESS." [21]So then let no one boast in men. For all things belong to you, [22] whether Paul or Apollos or Cephas or the world or life or death or things present or things to come; all things belong to you, [23]and you belong to Christ; and Christ belongs to God.

These are the concluding verses of this essential subject of building the local church, which God says is his temple. They, as well as everything in the preceding verses of 1 Corinthians and as the entirety of this chapter on *Does the Local Church Still Matter?*, reflect the local church's irreplaceable significance in Christ's plan of building his universal church. Remember verse 10, **But each man must be careful how he builds**, then those solemn words of verse 17, **If any man destroys the temple of God, God will destroy him.**

Reject the Wisdom of Men
in Building the Church: vs. 18–20

[18]Let no man deceive himself. If any man among you thinks that he is wise in this age, he must become foolish, so that he may become wise. [19]For the wisdom of this world is foolishness before God. For it

is written, "He is THE ONE WHO CATCHES THE WISE IN THEIR CRAFT-
INESS;" [20]and again, "THE LORD KNOWS THE REASONINGS of the wise,
THAT THEY ARE USELESS."

Man's wisdom is deceptive. The Corinthians' reliance upon their human wisdom made them feel good and godly, but in reality, it was the
source of their divisions, jealousy, prolonged infancy, and carnality; ultimately, it was destroying the temple of God. That is what human wisdom
brings to the church. Human wisdom placed ahead of God's wisdom is
based upon the sinfully faulty (unspoken) premise that man is wiser than
God. God is never honored, nor is spiritual maturity and true unity ever
realized by human wisdom even though human agreement is frequently
mistaken for divine unity.

Human wisdom has a place in human endeavors like science, hunting,
communication, and building and repairing physical structures. These endeavors can be characterized as valuable knowledge, even without the enlightenment of the Holy Spirit. A person can learn to cook, drive, perform
surgery, or fly without the ministry of the Holy Spirit; lost people do these
all of the time, and many do them quite well. All of this is human knowledge and wisdom, attainable by mere human ability, which God created
in humankind. However, in spiritual endeavors, as in building the church,
human knowledge is disastrous. Human wisdom does not build the temple
of God; it destroys it. John MacArthur notes,

> Even Christians, therefore, do not have a right to their own opin-
> ions about the things God has revealed. When Christians start ex-
> pressing and following their own ideas about the gospel, the church,
> and Christian living, the saints cannot help but become divided.
> Christians are no wiser in their flesh than are unbelievers. The first
> step in a Christian's becoming truly wise is to recognize that his

own human wisdom is **foolishness**, a reflection of **the wisdom of this world**, which **is foolishness before God**. It is the product of intellectual pride and is the enemy of God's revelation. The church must create an atmosphere in which the Word of God is honored and submitted to, in which human opinion is never used to judge or qualify revelation. As far as the things of God are concerned, Christians must be totally under the teaching of Scripture and the illumination of the Holy Spirit. Only then can we be open to God's wisdom and truly **become wise**. Common commitment to the Word of God is the basic unifier.

Where the Word of God is not set up as the supreme authority, division is inevitable because human and divine wisdom will inevitably and repeatedly clash. Such happens even in evangelical churches, when pastors and other leaders begin substituting their own ideas for the truths of Scripture. The substitution is seldom intentional, but it will always happen when the Bible is neglected either in study or teaching. A Bible that is not studied and taught carefully cannot be followed carefully. And where it is not followed there will be division, because there will be no common ground for beliefs and practices.[49]

Man's wisdom is foolishness (vs. 18–19) when it comes to the spiritual realm because it is based upon his rejection of the Word of the Lord (Jer 8:9). Operating the church by human wisdom results in familiar scenes where a man who is successful in the world is made a leader in the church merely because of that success. A banker is placed on the finance committee simply because he is a banker. A man is made an elder because he is successful in business, or a woman is made a Sunday School teacher because she has taught in public education for years.

---

49. MacArthur, *1 Corinthians*, 88.

Some fields of study, like science, have made the world better. I think of medical advances and advances in farming, but to conclude that man's wisdom is suitable for building the church, or that scientific or vocational progress is spiritual progress, is indeed foolishness and pride. Unfortunately, accepting man's wisdom in building God's spiritual temple is precisely where many local churches find themselves today. Christian leaders study the world's ideas for improving or building, and then apply those to building the temple of God, which may seem to work based upon empirical evidence. But it actually is human wisdom—foolishness—and destroys the church. In circles where human wisdom reigns, one will find such things as excessive traditionalism or growth focus, the undue value placed on studies, polls, and the study of secular managerial models, or just the opinions of some above the clear teaching of Scripture.

In portions of the emergent church, human wisdom arises from the thoughtless embracing of postmodernism, and emotionally appealing but intellectually absurd and spiritually bankrupt concepts like "Christianity is a relationship with a person, not affirming a set of propositions."[50] As though you can have a relationship with Christ without affirming the propositions of Scripture or as though everyone outside of the emergent network *merely* affirms propositions without emphasizing a relationship with God. Concomitant to such thoughtless preoccupations are such corollaries as the superficial study of God's word, failing to mature baby Christians with a diet of milk and meat so they can relate to God at a deeper level, failing to recognize human wisdom masquerading as spiritual wisdom, failing to represent God to the world more righteously, and failing to learn how to view the world through biblical lenses. Any criticism of shallowness or doctrinal aberrancy is summarily dismissed by equating the genesis of those criticisms with modernism or with some voguish banality.

---

50. Kevin DeYoung and Ted Kluck, *Why We're Not Emergent: By Two Guys Who Should Be* (Chicago: Moody Publishers, 2008), 73.

Liberals have been notorious for making human reason the test of truth, and the determiner of what Christians can and should accept from God's Word (even what is God's Word in the Bible), so that reason or science easily trumps the Scripture. Wall Street and the CEO model are used to teach shepherds how to be efficient, effective leaders, and shepherds as though the Scripture is insufficient for this task (1 Tim 3:16–17). Such human reasoning results in downplaying biblical mandates like the need to mature the saints and the church being a body of followers of Christ, with the worship service geared toward that end. Human wisdom is applied to biblical teachings such as church discipline, and the conclusion is that it is too harsh or the timing is wrong even though it is commanded in the New Testament (Matt 18:15–20; Rom 16:17–18; 1 Cor 5:1–13; 2 Thess 3:6–15).

Some of the premier leaders in Christianity have unfortunately become more like cultural gurus who can tell us more about the nuances of society than they can about the nature of God and how knowing his nature is indispensably important to everyday life. Far too many who have been called and gifted as pastor/teachers do not attempt to teach the whole and in-depth counsel of God because they say that people will not listen or understand, or it is not relevant in people's lives. The poison in their eschewing the deeper teachings of Scripture is not merely that people do not see the relevance of them to their everyday life, but that shepherds do not. As a result, they are unable to help people to see the relevance of those truths that may not be immediately or superficially relevant.

Seeking to be socially relevant to a fault, they determine their biblical fidelity by the level of seeker friendliness they portray. Seekers, rather than Scripture, end up determining what they can and cannot preach in the church. As a result, the temple of God becomes a place designed for the lost rather than a place for God to be biblically praised by his people and proclaimed to his people in order that they may be equipped to honor him. While always including the call of salvation in our messages as pastors, evangelism, our messages are not to be merely that.

It is good to seek to make everyone—saved and lost—feel welcome, but to make each one feel spiritually comfortable is human wisdom. The church is to mature the saints, and the matured church goes into the world to reach the lost through living and speaking the truth in love (Eph 4:11–16). If the church fails to equip and mature God's people because of tradition, trendiness, seeker fixation, an undue trust of anything from modernity or postmodernity, or any other such reasonings, it is human wisdom. It is not that someone cannot get saved in a church service, or that an appeal and sensitivity to the lost is not present, but the primary focus when the church gathers together is for *the worship of God by his people and the equipping of his people.* And the primary focus outside the church is *evangelizing the lost.* In the end, failing to equip the saints will eventually result in a decrease of true evangelism.[51]

The decline in evangelism and missions is not shockingly precipitous, but rather it is concomitant with the gradual decline in maturity and doctrinal stability of the local body of believers. Such decline may take years or even decades; making it all the more deceptive. This delayed decrease in evangelism and maturity of the saints is one reason the church is so vulnerable to being seduced into shunning the hard work of the pastor laboring in the deep things of God and equipping the saints. Because when the shift is made from a diet of meat to milk, evangelism and outreach continue unabated, and tangible results may even increase. The increase is because you have mature Christians and the pastor devoting more time, as well as church services, to reaching the lost. This upsurge in reaching people, which is deduced to be a direct result of this new emphasis, causes the shepherds and flock to think they have found a better way—which is the allure of human wisdom.

---

51. To see the shortcomings of various church models used today and why they fail to encompass the full corpus of New Testament teaching like the equipping model does, see my book *The Equipping Church: Somewhere Between Fundamentalism and Fluff.*

This new way requires less work and lonely study by the pastor and less effort and patience by the members, but the result is a more shallow knowledge of God. Truthfully, maturing the saints is similar at times to maturing one's child; it is not always enjoyable, and at various times it is just an unpleasant and daunting responsibility. By the time the decline in evangelism is noticeable, and the engaging of culture diminishes, the church is so immature and shallow that rather than realize what has happened, they simply look for the latest and most innovative milk dispenser.[52] Milkoholizing a church is always easier than maturing a church. Regardless of what form, fashion, name, or emphasis is extolled, when a church substitutes anything for the Ephesians equipping model of the church (Eph 4:11–16), she is sauntering along the path of human wisdom (1 Cor 3:1–2).

We can see the cooperation between human wisdom and divine wisdom in the need to build and maintain the physical church building with primarily human wisdom and the spiritual church building with exclusively divine wisdom. The blurring of this distinction is to be in opposition to God. We build the temple according to God's blueprint alone, which is both lucid and sufficient. When man's wisdom is in play, elevated, sought, and depended on, teaching the Scripture will be marginalized. Regardless of those who say otherwise, the place for biblical wisdom in building the church will inevitably diminish. This is true of human wisdom in any form, whether it is liberalism, emergent postmodern litmus test, techniques placed above theology, tradition that strangles the spiritual growth of the church, or following the leader because of his personal giftedness and passion instead of the direction set forth in Scripture. Any form of human knowledge substituted for in-depth and comprehensive knowledge of the Scripture becomes the lens through which people see the Scripture, church, and world.

---

52. Willow Creek's self-study (Hawkins, Parkinson, Arnson, *Reveal*) is an example of this because they saw their failings but answered them with more statistics and human research.

The totality of Scripture, the whole counsel, is quietly disregarded, and only what is consistent with the giftedness or interest of the pastor, be it prophecy, ministry, evangelism, or liberty, is genuinely emphasized.

Still, God catches them in their craftiness, and it will be made evident. True spiritual wisdom is to believe what God says above our human learning, wisdom, and thus pursue his wisdom so that we may indeed be wise. The first thought that should come to our minds when someone brings something up about a topic is, what does the Bible say? We may not know, but we must not let a lack of specific knowledge cause us to fall back on human wisdom and thus foolishness. Moreover, we should be devoted to knowing the deep things God has revealed to us as well as the shallow, lest we implicitly impugn God with having revealed a significant amount of extraneous information. When Christians experience prolonged infancy and satisfaction with milk beyond normal infancy as the Corinthians did (3:1–2), they will have an immature and incomplete Christian worldview, which inevitably results in them advocating ideas that are merely human wisdom. It leaves the church anemic, spiritually obtuse, and impotent, whimpering only for milk because they are milkoholics.

This dismal state of affairs is even more reason to return to an equipping model of the local church. If Christians do not have even a rudimentary understanding of Christianity, how can they communicate Christianity to a lost world, and how can they make biblical decisions in an increasingly secular environment? If the shepherds do not deeply study themselves, they are utterly ill-equipped to handle the task of engaging a hostile world. They also are not capable of training those under their watch-care beyond the most blatantly apparent truths of Scripture, which, when learned in isolation from a balanced knowledge of Scripture, are well suited for being reduced to clichés and the preferred diet of milkoholics. Man's wisdom is not merely ineffective or unhelpful; it is as useless as a ship with no hull (vs. 20). The consideration of what works in building the local church should always be evaluated by asking, is it human or divine wisdom as revealed in Scripture.

If it is human, despite accolades received by the carnal, it is useless in building the temple of God regardless of how fast or large the church grows.

That reality should drive the church and the men who lead her to a devoted life of knowing the Scripture. In building a spiritual temple, human wisdom is devoid of any useful contribution. The word **useless** means powerless, fruitless, worthless, deceptive, ineffectual, and not what it appears to be. "So this I say, and affirm together with the Lord, that you walk no longer just as the Gentiles also walk, in the futility of their mind" (Eph 4:17). Futility is the same word. The Gentiles' wisdom is futile, so do not walk in that wisdom. Everything derived from our human wisdom is from our fallen humanity, and it is exhaustively, categorically, eternally, and spiritually useless. The only thing that makes us think it is useful is our fallen humanity, carnality, or thinking like mere men. In other words, we judge whether something is working in building the church based upon human wisdom—numbers, buildings, likeability, personal proclivities, statistics, research, or whatever is the zeitgeist of the day. We, therefore, conclude that God is doing a great work, and consequently, the means must be spiritual. In addition, we strip the ever-present supporting Scriptures of their proper context to provide some semblance of regard for Scripture, God's wisdom.

A person or ministry can build what Christ is not building, what does not honor Christ, or truly advance his kingdom. When they deemphasize the place of the local church in their personal life or paradigm of ministry, they seek to build contrary to Christ, who made her the very strategic center of his plan. But they also can be working against Christ, even when they emphasize and focus on the local church, if their building of the local church is dependent upon human wisdom to build the spiritual body of Christ.

It is only when we realize that our human wisdom is foolishness in pleasing God, bringing men to Christ, maturing men, and women, living right, and building the church that we come and bow before God. Only then will we truly listen to what he says and gladly and obediently obey regardless of what the immediate impact is or what is the latest fashion in 'doing church.' God looks to those who follow his Word. "'For My hand made all these things, Thus all these things came into being,' declares the LORD. 'But to this one I will look, To him who is humble and contrite of spirit, and who trembles at My word'" (Isa 66:2). We are not to be searching for novelty, new ideas, what the lost deem righteous, or a reinfusion of the divine into the old, but knowledge of our Lord Jesus as revealed in the Scripture. "But grow in the grace and knowledge of our Lord and Savior Jesus Christ. To Him *be* the glory, both now and to the day of eternity. Amen" (2 Pet 3:18).

It is not new knowledge that we reject, for we should always be growing in the knowledge of the Lord. Rejecting new knowledge is the damnation of traditionalism. Neither is it rejecting what has been known for years from what God revealed in his Word because of some superficial changes in culture; that is, the damnation of 'new is better' mantra. Instead, it is continually growing deeper in our understanding of God's person, will, work, and ways so that we can honor him with all of our being. This knowledge comes from learning the Scripture to live the Scripture (John 7:17).

The Scripture often calls the church to remember. Therefore, one of the priorities of biblical preaching is to remind us often of biblical teachings because we tend to forget, and forgetfulness breeds disobedience (2 Tim 1:6, 2:14; Titus 3:1; Heb 13:7; 2 Pet 3:2; Jude 17; Rev 2:5; 3:3). Several biblical concepts are directly connected with remembering; for example, *repentance* is often tied to remembering. "Therefore remember from where you have fallen, and repent and do the deeds you did at first; or else I am coming to you and will remove your lampstand out of its place—unless you repent" (Rev 2:5). "So remember what you have received and heard; and keep *it,* and repent. Therefore if you do not wake up, I will come like a thief, and you will not know at what hour I will come to you" (Rev 3:3). On the dreadful night that our Lord was betrayed, it was only when the Holy Spirit caused Peter to remember what Jesus had said that Peter repented; "'Before a rooster crows, you will deny Me three times.' And he went out and wept bitterly" (Matt 26:75).

Lack of faith is often exposed through being reminded, as with the Apostles when Jesus said to them, "HAVING EYES, DO YOU NOT SEE? AND HAVING EARS, DO YOU NOT HEAR? And do you not remember" (Mark 8:18). *Processing new experiences* in a biblical manner are often dependent upon remembering as when the angels spoke to the women at the tomb of Jesus on that resurrection morning, "He is not here, but He has risen. Remember how He spoke to you while He was still in Galilee . . . And they remembered His words" (Luke 24:6–8).

Understanding righteous anger is, at times, only understood by remembering, like when Jesus cleansed the temple. "His disciples remembered that it was written, 'ZEAL FOR YOUR HOUSE WILL CONSUME ME'" (John 2:17). *Spiritual growth* is tied to remembering, "These things His disciples did not understand at the first; but when Jesus was glorified, then they remembered that these things were written of Him, and that they had done these things to Him" (John 12:16).

Humility and preparing for persecution at times requires remembering, "Remember the word that I said to you, 'A slave is not greater than his master.' If they persecuted Me, they will also persecute you; if they kept My word, they will keep yours also" (John 15:20).

Understanding future experiences need remembering: "But these things I have spoken to you, so that when their hour comes, you may remember that I told you of them. These things I did not say to you at the beginning, because I was with you" (John 16:4). "And I remembered the word of the Lord, how He used to say, 'John baptized with water, but you will be baptized with the Holy Spirit'" (Acts 11:16). "In everything I showed you that by working hard in this manner you must help the weak and remember the words of the Lord Jesus, that He Himself said, 'It is more blessed to give than to receive'" (Acts 20:35).

Thankfulness and gratefulness often require remembering. "Therefore remember that formerly you, the Gentiles in the flesh, who are called 'Uncircumcision' by the so-called 'Circumcision,' *which is* performed in the flesh

by human hands" (Eph 2:11). "*Remember* that you were at that time separate
from Christ, excluded from the commonwealth of Israel, and strangers to
the covenants of promise, having no hope and without God in the world"
(Eph 2:12). "Remember Jesus Christ, risen from the dead, descendant of
David, according to my gospel" (2 Tim 2:8).

Therefore, Christians are to be on an endless quest to learn and be
reminded by the Scripture, which requires knowing the Scripture. "That
you should remember the words spoken beforehand by the holy prophets
and the commandment of the Lord and Savior *spoken* by your apostles" (2
Pet 3:2). "But you, beloved, ought to remember the words that were spoken beforehand by the apostles of our Lord Jesus Christ" (Jude 17). "But I
have written very boldly to you on some points so as to remind you again,
because of the grace that was given me from God" (Rom 15:15). "For this
reason I have sent to you Timothy, who is my beloved and faithful child in
the Lord, and he will remind you of my ways which are in Christ, just as I
teach everywhere in every church" (1 Cor 4:17). "For this reason I remind
you to kindle afresh the gift of God which is in you through the laying
on of my hands" (2 Tim 1:6). "Remind *them* of these things, and solemnly
charge *them* in the presence of God not to wrangle about words, which is
useless *and leads* to the ruin of the hearers" (2 Tim 2:14). "Remind them to
be subject to rulers, to authorities, to be obedient, to be ready for every good
deed" (Titus 3:1).

Faithful ministers know all too well of their own inability to retain
what they have learned or to thwart the corrupting influence of their own
flesh upon what they have learned. True reliance on God requires consistent time in the Word, always allowing the Holy Spirit to remind them of
the great truths of Scripture, as well as essential nuances. Therefore, they
are continually studying the Scripture and seeking God to exhort, teach,
convict, correct, encourage, and remind them of what they do not know,
have forgotten, or expose what they have allowed human reasoning of the
flesh to corrupt.

This kind of pastor will be so keenly aware of the charge of the Scripture upon his life, and his need of daily reminding by it, that no trick of hell will cause him to fail to be devoted to reminding the flock of God continually. This raises the question; how pray tell can a minister be so devoted to reminding the flock if he is unaware of the need in his own life? Quite probably, this is at the root of why some ministers see so little need to teach the deep things of God to the people of God because they personally either rarely or never go there. How can one fulfill the mandates to remember, when one has not heard or has himself forgotten? Shepherds, being reminded and reminding the flock of God, are crucial to building God's holy temple according to his holy Word.

Refuse to Boast in Men vs. 21–23

> [21]So then let no one boast in men. For all things belong to you, [22]whether Paul or Apollos or Cephas or the world or life or death or things present or things to come; all things belong to you, [23]and you belong to Christ; and Christ belongs to God.

Boasting in men is human wisdom, which is useless. Christians follow one man, and that is Jesus Christ. We follow his leaders as far as they lead according to his instructions, and that always leads us to him. While there are certainly a vast host of good teachers, writers, leaders, and speakers, when a person gets so committed to any one of them that he refuses to learn from other biblicist, it is human wisdom rather than divine wisdom. The teacher of human wisdom will often seek to build a following, and the ones being taught via human wisdom become unwilling to learn from others. Moreover, from experience, I can tell you that regardless of how sincere the one is that the person follows, or how committed the follower is, the person that relies on one individual as the depository of all the highest knowledge of God is very difficult to shepherd.

Paul, Apollos, and Cephas should be esteemed as God's leaders (1 Thess 5:12–13) as should all who handle the Word with diligence and care (1 Tim 5:17); however, this esteem is always based on Scripture and not on such things as personality, affinities, or prominence. We should esteem those who reflect God and obedience above lazy shepherds, but not above Christ or Scripture. Those who have blessed us spiritually will have a special place in our hearts, but not above our love for God. Neither the Corinthians nor we should pick sides among those whom God sends to contribute to the building of the church. Instead, we should rejoice (vs. 21–22). If someone is a true disciple and, therefore, allows God to disciple him, he will have many disciplers. I know God has enabled me to be a pastor/teacher, and thus by his grace, I can help people grow in Christ, but I am limited, and so is everyone else. Consequently, I cannot teach anyone everything he needs. We all have something to contribute to building the temple of God, discipling a person, equipping, but none of us has everything that is required to give every one of God's people what they need to be all that God wants them to be.

Everything is from God, and God has granted us everything in this life and the life to come because of Christ. He will even transform that which is evil into good (Rom 8:28). We will possess the earth (Matt 5:5; Rev 21). All life is ours, specifically all spiritual life, but particularly the new life in Christ. Death is overcome, and we can appreciate and understand life, its purpose, origin, and destiny far better than any lost person can understand.

Further, we should be truly thankful for and esteem godly leaders that God has given us (1 Thess 5:12–13), and follow them (Heb 13:17). When we boast, we boast in the cross (1 Cor 2:31) because if not for the cross, no one could enhance our spiritual lives. Be thankful for all contributors and contributions to your spiritual life; then thank God that he saved them and gave them that ability and desire. Boasting in man, friends, or family creates division. Boasting in truth, creates unity.

You belong to Christ (vs. 23). This truth of Scripture is the most excellent reason not to seek man's wisdom in building the local church.

Christ bought us with his own blood, and no man ever loved us with infinite love like that. Do you think that he failed to give us what we need to live for him, to please him? Do you think he deposited that in the life of the ungodly? "He who did not spare His own Son, but delivered Him over for us all, how will He not also with Him freely give us all things?" (Rom 8:32). "Blessed be the God and Father of our Lord Jesus Christ, who according to His great mercy has caused us to be born again to a living hope through the resurrection of Jesus Christ from the dead" (1 Pet 1:3). He gave us the Holy Spirit, his Word, his teachers, his spiritual gifts, and others who are regenerated to share our shared spiritual life in Christ, fellowship. He made us one (1 Cor 6:17; 12:13; Eph 4:3–4). Because we all belong to Christ and are one in him, we have the capacity and motivation to be like him. The pattern for unity and spiritual growth is embodied in the word humility, which is graphically and movingly portrayed in the life of Christ for us to model (Phil 2:1–9).

Therefore, let us not spend our lives seeking to build Christ's kingdom as if it were our own over which we are king. For to do so is to build with human wisdom, wood, hay, and straw, which shall be burned as rubbish on the day in which Christ rewards all his followers who built the church as he instructed with gold, silver, and precious stone. Only they who build according to his Word, placing the local church at the center of his plan to build his church, will be rewarded for building the local church. Consequently, **each man must be careful how he builds.**

CONCLUSION

The following summarizes several reasons why every Christian should be an *active and contributing member* of a local church:

1. The New Testament demonstrates the local church is at the center of God's plan of carrying out his mandate to build the universal church (Matt 16:18; 28:18–20; Eph 4:11–15). The term *ekklēsia* appears one hundred and fourteen times in the NT.[53] Four times the term is used for non-church gatherings.[54] Of the remaining one hundred and ten appearances, only eighteen refer to the universal church, which leaves ninety-two times, 84%, referring to the local assembly of believers.[55]

2. Local church commitment is a prerequisite for properly understanding and applying the New Testament to our Christian lives because all the epistles and Revelation were written to or for the local church. They teach us how to live, first in the community of a local church.

3. Scripture repeatedly commands Christians to submit to their leaders (Heb 13:17; 1 Thess 5:12–13); these verses are in the context of local church leaders.

4. The church is the pillar and support of truth (1 Tim 3:15). While this is clearly true of the universal church, it is no less true of the local church. That Paul has the local church in mind is also evidenced when he says he is writing Timothy for the express purpose, "but in case I am delayed, I write so that you will know how one ought to conduct himself in the household of God, which is the church of the living God, the pillar and support of the truth" (1 Tim 3:15). The context further confirms Paul has the local church primarily in mind, as seen in him addressing the place of men and women in the local church (2:11–15). And

---

53. *ekklēsia* is translated assembly (3), church (74), churches (35), and congregation (2) for a total of 114 times (Thomas, *New American Standard Hebrew-Aramaic and Greek Dictionaries*. Logos).

54. It is used of the congregation of Israel in Acts 7:38 and a non-church assembly in Acts 19:32, 39, 41.

55. This is an approximation, which could vary by 1 or 2 depending on whether one interprets a couple of usages as referring to the universal or local.

in the immediately preceding verses are the qualifications of the officers of the local church (vs. 1–13).[56]

5. The local church is the nucleus for caring for those in need. This can include such needs as widows who meet the qualifications of a "widow indeed" (1 Tim 5: 3, 9), those suffering, sick, or in need of prayer (1 Cor 12:26; Jas 5:13–16).

6. The local church is where Christians are to regularly serve one another with our spiritual gifts (Rom 12:3–21; 1 Cor 12–14; 1 Pet 4:10–11).

7. The local church is where Christians are to be matured in the faith under God's leaders (Eph 4:11–12; 1 and 2 Tim, Titus; Heb 13:17) in order to minister truth and the gospel to the church and world (Eph 4:11–17).

8. The local church is where Christians are to be cared for by God's undershepherds (John 21:15–17; Eph 4:11–12; Heb 13:17; 1 Pet 5:1–3).

9. We are commanded to give weekly to *our* local church (1 Cor 16:1–2).[57]

10. The New Testament uses terms like *whole church* to speak of local churches to which surrounding Christians belong (1 Cor 5:6; 14:23).

---

56. I understand vs. 11 to refer to the wives of deacons rather than deaconesses. The word is women or wife (gynē) and not the word deaconess (diakonon). It is the same word used in verses 2 and 12 in the requirement for overseers and deacons that they "must be the husband of one wife." Additionally, it seems odd that the Holy Spirit would address deacons in verses 8–10, then deaconesses in verse 11, and return to deacons in verses 12–13. It does not seem odd to address the wives of deacons in the context of addressing deacons. My experience of pastoring would strongly indicate that the wives of deacons are vital to the ministry and suitability of a man for the office of deacon.

57. The words *do* vs. 1 and *put aside* vs. 2 are commands, 2nd person plural, aorist, active tense, imperative and 2nd person singular, present tense, imperative respectively.

11. A lack of commitment and active involvement in a local church indicates a spiritual problem. Why would a Christian seeking to obey Christ not commit and actively belong to a local church, as is the New Testament pattern?[58] Christians have no qualms about joining a school, athletic club, sports team, or signing legal contracts to secure material blessings.

12. New Testament metaphors of the church, such as body, flock, and household, are intimate images, which are most poignantly and superbly expressed in the body life of the local church.[59] We see these images used of the local church, body (1 Cor 10:16–17; 12:27; Eph 4:12),[60] flock (Acts 20:28; 1 Pet 5:2), and household (1 Cor 3:9; Gal 6:10;[61] 1 Tim 3:15). These images are all characteristics of local units of relationships that are up-close and personal.

13. The ordinances of the church, baptism and The Lord's Supper, are within the domain of and carried out in the local church (Acts 2:41–47; Rom 6:3–4; 1 Cor 5:11;11:20, 23–32).

14. The context for Christian accountability is the local church (Matt 18:15–20; Rom 16:17–18; 1 Cor 5:1–13; Gal 6:1–2; 2 Thess 3:6–15; 1 John 2:19).

---

58. We see this throughout the entire New Testament.

59. This is not to say these images are not also applied to the universal church, but rather to say they are applied to the local church.

60. 1 Corinthians 12 speaks of spiritual gifts in the universal body and local body of Christ and 1 Corinthians 14 immediately applies the body concept to the local church at Corinth.

61. Timothy George notes, "Luther and Calvin, following Jerome, saw a linkage between this verse and Paul's earlier admonition in v. 6 concerning the liberal support of the ministers of the churches. Others have interpreted the adverb "especially" (malista) as an oblique reference to Paul's collection of funds for the poor saints in Jerusalem. The language Paul used can allow for either of these interpretations, but it is more likely that he was here simply pointing to the special responsibility all Christians have to help alleviate the suffering of their needy brothers and sisters in Christ." Note the local church emphasis. Timothy George, *Galatians*, The New American Commentary, vol. 30 (Nashville: Broadman & Holman Publishers, 1994), 428.

15. The idea of a faithful *at-large Christian* who is not identified by a commitment to and active participation in a local church is not entertained in the New Testament.

16. The local church is like marriage and family, but on a larger scale. It is where we learn to live out the principles of Christianity in real relationships with other believers, up close and personal (1 John 4:20).

17. Living local church life is essential to submitting to God by following his command to be committed to a local body of believers "not forsaking our own assembling together, as is the habit of some, but encouraging one another; and all the more as you see the day drawing near" (Heb 10:25).

18. The regular gathering of local churches for fulfilling the Great Commission by visibly worshiping, equipping, serving, and loving each other in fellowship and going out to advance the gospel is the greatest and most perennial image of the work of Christ building his universal church (Matt 16:18).

19. Every Christian needs to be a part of the temple of the Holy Spirit (1 Cor 3:16).[62]

20. Active membership is required in order to be eligible to receive rewards that will be given at the judgment seat of Christ for our contribution to building a local church (1 Cor 3:10–15).[63] To not be an active member of a local church is to lose those rewards.

---

62. The *you* is plural here referring to the local body of believers, whereas 1 Cor 6:19 refers to each person's physical body.

63. The context of these rewards and losses is the local church. Christians will be rewarded if their contributions to the local church were according to God's plan.

6

DOES THE HISTORICAL-GRAMMATICAL METHOD STILL MATTER?

PAIGE PATTERSON

Like a nova in the eastern sky, the last quarter of the twentieth century was marked by an explosion of radiant splendor in the biblical firmament as the science of hermeneutics engulfed the field of biblical studies. Hermeneutics was certainly not novel. The word itself is utilized by New Testament writers. Luke records that the resurrected Christ ignited the gloomy hearts of the Emmaus disciples by "beginning at Moses and all the prophets, He expounded to them in all the Scriptures the things concerning Himself" (Luke 24:27). "Expounded" (Gk. *diermēneuō*) means "interpret." This word combines the Greek preposition *dia* (through) with *hermēneuō* (Gk. "interpret"), giving the intensified meaning of "explain thoroughly." Jesus demonstrated for His disciples that He is the fulfillment of the Law and the Prophets. As Johannes Behm states the matter, Jesus was "the expounder of the OT prophecies of His passion and exaltation."[1]

---

1. Johannes Behm, "ἑρμηνεύω," in *Theological Dictionary of the New Testament*, Vol. II, edited by Gerhard Kittel (Grand Rapids: Wm. B. Eerdmans Publishing Company, 1964), 665.

The Greek term *hermēneuō* is derived from the name of the Greek god Hermes. Madeleine Jost of the University of Paris attests earliest references to Hermes in the Mycenaean pantheon and especially in Homeric hymns.[2] Taught divination by Apollo, Hermes became "the interpreter of the gods," who were capricious and frequently in need of an ombudsman. Also, Hermes served in a similar capacity between the gods and mere mortals. He is commonly presented as a youth with the caduceus or rod in his hand, wearing a brimmed hat and winged shoes.[3]

Interpretation is a part of life. From my physician, I receive a prescription. Most physicians failed to receive instruction in penmanship; so often I have no idea what the prescription demands. Fortunately, most pharmacists seem to have been taught to decipher medical hieroglyphics, and hopefully their interpretations lead to a healed patient. Attorneys recognize "legalese," and a portion of the money expended with the legal profession is for the favor of the "interpretation" of the title on my house.

In high school, my English teacher had the students read the British bard Shakespeare, assuring us that this was "great literature." But I was lost. This was 16th century English at its best, but a host of Shakespearian analogies would have been lost if not for my English teacher delivering interpretation.

Or what about John Greenleaf Whittier's lovely memory of history called "The Vaudois Teacher"? A portion of it reads:

"O Lady fair, these silks of mine
   are beautiful and rare,—
The richest web of the Indian loom, which beauty's

---

2. Madeleine Jost, "Hermes" in *The Oxford Classical Dictionary*, Third Edition, edited by Simon Hornblower and Antony Spawforth (Oxford: Oxford University Press, 1996), 690-91.

3. "Hermes" in *The Oxford English Dictionary,* Volume VII, Second Edition, prepared by J.A. Simpson and E.S.C. Weiner (Oxford: Clarendon Press, 1989), 169.

queen might wear;
And my pearls are pure as thy own fair neck, with whose
radiant light they vie;
I have brought them with me a weary way, —will my
gentle lady buy?"

The lady smiled on the worn old man through the
dark and clustering curls
Which veiled her brow, as she bent to view his
silks and glittering pearls;
And she placed their price in the old man's hand
and lightly turned away,
But she paused at the wanderer's earnest call, —
"My gentle lady, stay!"

"O lady fair, I have yet a gem which a purer
lustre flings,
Than the diamond flash of the jewelled crown on
the lofty brow of kings;
A wonderful pearl of exceeding price, whose virtue
shall not decay,
Whose light shall be as a spell to thee and a
blessing on thy way!"

The lady glanced at the mirroring steel where her
form of grace was seen,
Where her eye shone clear, and her dark locks
waved their clasping pearls between;
"Bring forth thy pearl of exceeding worth, thou
traveller gray and old,

And name the price of thy precious gem, and my
    page shall count thy gold."

The cloud went off from the pilgrim's brow, as a
    small and meagre book,
Unchased with gold or gem of cost, from his
    folding robe he took!
"Here, lady fair, is the pearl of price, may it prove
    as such to thee
Nay—keep thy gold—I ask it not, for the word of
    God is free!"[4]

What is a Vaudois teacher? Without hermeneutics and a hermeneutician, I will miss one of the great insights into Waldensian history and the spread of the gospel in the late middle ages.

The Bible, also, must have interpretation. Jesus said, "If your right eye causes you to sin, pluck it out and cast it from you…" (Matt 5:29). If this is to be understood literally, the church will become known as the Church of the One-Eyed. Nicodemus is informed that he must be "born again" to gain acceptance with God. Puzzled, the elderly Israelite replied, "Can a man enter into the womb a second time and be born?" (John 3:4). In Acts 2:4, the apostles "spoke with other tongues." What precisely happened here? Is there an interpreter who can assist by explaining the historical circumstances at the Feast of Pentecost?

In the Apocalypse, chapter 12, we are introduced to three characters: a great red dragon, a newborn child who shall rule all, and a radiant woman.

---

4. John Greenleaf Whittier, "The Vaudois Teacher" in *The Poetical Works of John Greenleaf Whittier with Numerous Illustrations* (Boston and New York: Houghton, Mifflin and Company, 1892), 73.

The text proceeds to identify clearly the first two, but who does the radiant woman represent?

Interpretation is part of the task assigned to every biblical preacher and teacher. Interpretation is not the entire task, but it is an essential task. The preacher/teacher has the task of bringing back the words of Christ and the Bible to the memory of the follower of Christ. He also carries the tasks of warning, of inspiration, and of motivation. He must magnify the clear teachings of the Scriptures. But some of the most demanding work of the preacher/teacher is spent in his study seeking to comprehend what exactly the passage means. Then he must discern the most appropriate way to transmit these insights to people who frequently possess miniscule biblical knowledge but almost always hear the preacher/teacher out of supreme need. The preacher must find a way to interpret what may be an esoteric text like "the spirts in prison" in 1 Peter 3 in a way that maintains the interest of the listener and motivates him to address in his own life what the Bible is revealing. This endeavor is the hermeneutical task, and every noble preacher must comprehend its word and devote incalculable labor to its message.

The Bible is a book written hundreds of years ago. About much of its message there is no doubt. "You shall do no murder" is clear any time and any place. "Love your enemy" is a task sufficiently demanding as to stand in little need of explanation. But to grasp fully the engaging story of the Good Samaritan, one needs an interpreter to provide the historical background. Armed with the Bible alone and the guidance of the Holy Spirit (John 16:12-13; 1 John 2:27), the yearning heart of a follower of Christ can follow the broad outlines of the entire Bible and gain what he needs to negotiate life and happiness. But he will hunger for a deeper grasp, and that is precisely what the grammatical-historical approach to the Bible is designed to provide. So what is the grammatical-historical approach to the Bible, and how is it practiced?

A Brief Look at
Contemporary Hermeneutics

The '50s and '60s of the last century recognized the essential nature of hermeneutics. But shorter monographs like *Protestant Biblical Interpretation* by Bernard Ramm were deemed adequate for youthful preachers like me.[5] Spurgeon recognized the preacher's interpretive task and devoted attention to it in *Lectures to my Students*.[6] In his critically important volume *Commenting on Commentaries*, the masterful preacher of Great Britain confessed that he spent far more time attempting to understand a text than he did in actually preparing the message.[7]

Bernard Ramm's essays on interpretation were significant and sufficient for interpreters in the middle of the twentieth century. They reflected the processes that had guided interpreters in the Patristic era and the Reformation period of the church. In the last decade of the twentieth century, scholarly fascination with the subject of interpretation abounded. In 1992 Anthony Thiselton penned *New Horizons in Hermeneutics*.[8] Already Grant Osborne had published *The Hermeneutical Spiral* in 1991.[9] 1998 prepared for the new century with Kevin Vanhoozer's *Is There a Meaning in This Text?*[10]

---

5. Bernard Ramm, *Protestant Biblical Interpretation: A Textbook of Hermeneutics for Conservative Protestants*, Rev. Edition (Boston: W.A. Wilde Company, 1956).

6. C.H. Spurgeon, *Lectures to My Students* (Grand Rapids: Zondervan Publishing House, 1954).

7. C.H. Spurgeon, Lecture II, "On Commenting" in *Commenting and Commentaries* (London: The Banner of Truth Trust, 1969), 21-32.

8. Anthony C. Thiselton, *New Horizons in Hermeneutics: The Theory and Practice of Transforming Biblical Reading* (Grand Rapids: Zondervan Publishing House, 1992).

9. Grant R. Osborne, *The Hermeneutical Spiral: A Comprehensive Introduction to Biblical Interpretation* (Downers Grove: Intervarsity Press, 1991).

10. Kevin J. Vanhoozer, *Is There a Meaning in This Text? The Bible, The Reader, and the Morality of Literary Knowledge* (Grand Rapids: Zondervan Publishing

2011 witnessed *Invitation to Biblical Interpretation* by Andreas Köstenberger and Richard Patterson.[11] These were only a few of the volumes published with intent to enlighten the biblical landscape. Hermeneutics was suddenly the new theological rush of the academy. And with no necessity to endorse every syllable of those books, one must acknowledge remarkable insights arising in those tomes.

> IN HIS CRITICALLY IMPORTANT VOLUME COMMENTING ON COMMENTARIES, THE MASTERFUL PREACHER OF GREAT BRITAIN CONFESSED THAT HE SPENT FAR MORE TIME ATTEMPTING TO UNDERSTAND A TEXT THAN HE DID IN ACTUALLY PREPARING THE MESSAGE.

Henry Virkler, a psychologist, published *Hermeneutics: Principles and Processes of Biblical Interpretation*, in which his argument was that "four blocks" inhibit what he terms "a spontaneous understanding" of Scripture. These four are a historical block, a cultural block, a linguistic block, and a philosophical block.[12] These are blocks that may be dispelled by the science of hermeneutics.

Conservative biblical exegetes, many of whom claim inerrancy or at a minimum infallibility for the biblical text, have been fond of saying that they follow a grammatical-historical approach to biblical interpretation. What exactly is intended by those terms, and are they still useful?

Robert Kolb in discussing the contribution of Matthias Flacius Illyricus (1520-1575) defines "grammatical interpretation" as concerning itself with "the definition of individual words on the basis of the original languages and the understanding of these words in their literacy context."[13]

House, 1998).

11. Andreas J. Köstenberger and Richard D. Patterson, *Invitation to Biblical Interpretation: Exploring the Hermeneutical Triad of History, Literature, and Theology* (Grand Rapids: Kregel, 2011).

12. Henry A. Virkler, *Hermeneutics: Principles and Processes of Biblical Interpretation* (Grand Rapids: Baker Book House, 1981), 19-20.

13. Robert Kolb, "Flacius Illyricus, Matthias" in *Dictionary of Major Bibli-*

No substitute exists for capturing the biblical languages: Greek, He-brew, and Aramaic. Little space is available to pursue this idea; but if I may request a point of personal privilege, I point you to my address given in 1998 at the Evangelical Theological Society and later reprinted in the jour-nal *Faith and Mission*.[14] In this article on rethinking an evangelical semi-nary, I argue vociferously for thoroughness in teaching biblical languages. Among other critical thoughts, the article states,

> Students must be taught that while the languages may be profitably
> employed in the actual delivery of the sermon, such is not their pri-
> mary venue of helpfulness. Biblical languages and exegesis are to ex-
> position what the weight room is to the athlete. While it would be
> highly unusual to see a linebacker in the middle of the third quarter
> dragging a Nautilus machine out to the forty yard line to work a bit,
> it does not require a biogeneticist to figure out that the 235-pound
> linebacker has spent time in the weight room when he easily throws
> aside the 320-pound offensive tackle and knocks the wheels from
> under the speeding 210-pound locomotive who is trying to abscond
> with what is left of the pig. Accordingly, students are urged to do
> four relatively simple exercises so that after graduation they will not
> "sin" as do most busy pastors by promptly forgetting the languages
> they paid so dearly to master. (1) Never preach from a passage that
> you do not first translate. (2) Translate at least one verse from both
> testaments every day, working steadily through a book. (3) Carry
> your Hebrew Bible or Greek Testament to preaching and follow

cal Interpreters, edited by Donald K. McKim (Downers Grove: Intervarsity Press, 2007), 440.

14. Paige Patterson, "What Athens Has to Do with Jerusalem: How to Tighten Greek and Hebrew Requirements and Triple Your M.Div. Enrollment at the Same Time," *Faith and Mission* 17, no. 1 (Fall 1999): 54-68.

the text in the biblical language. (4) Keep your vocabulary cards—in fact, expand them. Build and review vocabulary all your life.[15]

A single example of the importance of the language and the context occurs in Romans 6:2 in answer to the rhetorical question of 6:1, "Shall we continue in sin so that grace may abound?" The King James Version said "God forbid," but the Greek text has no such reading. The text reads, "*mē genoito*" or "let it not be." Some contemporary translations render the text, "Certainly not," which is better. The point here is that as much as I love the KJV, this translation "God forbid" suffers at two points. First, no Jew would ever have thought about employing the word "God" in such a manner. Second, the word "God" does not even appear in the text!

Furthermore, *genoito* is a relatively rare aorist optative in Greek. The optative references an unrealized action of some kind. There are, according to A.T. Robertson, only 67 examples in the New Testament, 31 in Paul and 28 in Luke.[16] Here in Romans 6:2 the optative provides a fervent hope and anticipation that Christians would never even contemplate a return to a life of sin in order that grace might abound. For the purposes of this discussion, one may observe that even a poor English reader can get the gist of the proclamation. But the reader who is armed with the Greek language and syntax has a telescopic perspective. On certain clear evenings, a man can regard the face of the moon and discern the mountains and valleys open to the earth. But looking through a telescopic lens, he can discern much greater detail and color. This is how the languages of Holy Scripture function.

There is no way to overemphasize the importance of biblical languages. The New Testament was written in *koine* Greek, that is, the common parlance of the *agora*. Because of this and aided by the teaching ministry of

---

15. Patterson, "Athens with Jerusalem," 58–59.
16. A.T. Robertson, *A Grammar of the Greek New Testament in the Light of Historical Research* (Nashville: Broadman Press, 1934), 326.

the Holy Spirit (John 16:12-13; 1 John 2:27), a preacher with no opportunity to study biblical languages, nevertheless, can "get it right." He can develop good theology and preach exegetical messages based on the English text. In fact, better to have that pastor than one who reads the biblical languages with a predisposition to disbelief.

But why would anyone interested in lunar observation view the surface of the moon only with naked eye when a powerful telescope was available? Why would an interested interpreter of Scripture with an opportunity to appropriate a biblical language not grasp that opportunity? Why would a preacher determined to comprehend the Word of God and to preach faithfully the whole counsel of God to the sheep of God's flock not want to use the linguistic tools available? If preaching, or explaining to the people the meaning of God's Word, is the most pivotal task of the pastor/teacher, the importance of securing an understanding of the languages in which the Bible was written must be reasserted in the schools.

Certainly, I am familiar with arguments to the contrary. Some insist that they possess no facility in language. Others object that making a living is so time consuming that they have no time to focus on languages. Still others complain that the professors of language are colossally boring. While this criticism is manifestly false, a president or dean of a school makes a monumental contribution whenever he proposes that the professors of biblical language be the finest faculty choices. A colorful, resourceful Hebrew or Greek professor is worth his weight in platinum. By the same token, a boring professor of biblical languages is like a shortstop who cannot catch a ball. Probably, I have heard most of the objections. And I have already stated that through careful study and concerted prayer, a man can become a profound expositor of the Word utilizing only an English text. But why would any preacher not want to gain every detail of the biblical text? Why would he not wish to gain the benefit of this for his preaching? F. F. Bruce and J. J. Scott Jr. sum up the matter saying,

This grammatico-historical exegesis is commonly practiced in the classroom, and is distinguished from exposition, which is more appropriate to the pulpit. Exposition aims to apply the text and its meaning to men and women today, enabling them to answer the question: What message has this for us, or for me, in the present situation? To be valid, exposition must be firmly based on exegesis: the meaning of the text for hearers today must be related to its meaning for the hearers to whom it was first addressed.[17]

The grammatical aspect of the grammatical-historical approach involves the grammar, syntax, style and approach of the biblical languages. The method recognizes that a word normally maintains a range of meanings and that the meaning of a particular word is shaped and occasionally transformed by the context in which it occurs. The preacher/teacher soon learns that Hebrew, Aramaic, Greek are primarily for use in the study. When actually employed in a message, there must be an actual rationale for doing so—something that is educatively accomplished, thus inspiring the use of the term itself.

Recognizing the strategic importance of words, Gerhard Kittel edited the massive, 10-volume philological endeavor, *Theological Dictionary of the New Testament*, translated and edited by Geoffrey W. Bromiley in 1964.[18] This constituted one of the early efforts to focus on the range of meanings

---

17. F. F. Bruce and J. J. Scott Jr., "Interpretation of the Bible" in *Evangelical Dictionary of Theology*, Second Edition, edited by Walter A. Elwell (Grand Rapids: Baker Academic, 2001), 611.

18. Bromiley is the classic instance of an under-appreciated theologian. In addition to his own scholarly books, Bromiley translated Karl Barth's mammoth *Church Dogmatics* and *The Theological Dictionary of the New Testament* from German to English. A fair amount of this translation reportedly was done during faculty meetings, thus transforming an otherwise innocuous meeting into something of universal significance to the church.

that often characterized words in the New Testament. James Barr, professor of Old Testament at the University of Edinburgh, published in 1961 his widely disseminated work on biblical semantics. Noting the cultural and other gaps between Semitic languages and contemporary expressions, Barr observed, "It is doubtful whether any other sphere of life than the theological has common people without special training so continually attempting a sematic transference across such gaps."[19]

Grammar is supplemented by the historical method. Robert Thomas notes:

> Traditionally, the historical dimension in interpretation has referred to the historical setting of the text's origin, as Terry describes: "The interpreter should, therefore, endeavor to take himself from the present and to transport himself into the historical position of an author, look through his eyes, note his surroundings, feel with his heart, and catch his emotion. Here in we note the import of the term grammatical-historical interpretation."[20]

This is sometimes denominated as the diachronic method. "Diachronic" means "between the times" and references the interpreter's ability to connect antiquity with modernity through his teaching.

Consider the pericope of the Good Samaritan in Luke 10:25-37. The average reader with little or no historical awareness gets the point. In the story, Jesus speaks of the two men who should have exercised compassion on the bludgeoned victim but failed to do so. There was a third man who

---

19. James Barr, *The Semantics of Biblical Languages* (Oxford: Oxford University Press, 1961), 4.

20. Robert L. Thomas, *Evangelical Hermeneutics: The New Versus the Old* (Grand Rapids: Kregel, 2002), 357. Thomas is quoting M. S. Terry, *Biblical Hermeneutics: A Treatise on the Interpretation of the Old and New Testaments* (1885; reprint, Grand Rapids: Zondervan, 1947), 231.

put himself at risk to care for a stranger. That man, a man from Samaria, was the real neighbor. The message of Scripture is clear, and most understand it.

But when one places these verses in their historical context, new vistas of understanding emerge. In 722 BC, the Northern Kingdom of Israel fell to the Assyrians with their capital at Nineveh. The Assyrians began the process of what became known as the *diaspora*, the dispersion of the Jewish people, placing the captives in other defeated lands and repopulating Israel with foreigners who eventually intermarried with the remaining Jews, creating the Samaritan race. Hated by the Jews of Judah, the Samaritans become well acquainted with discriminating behavior.

A knowledge of Judaism in the Second Temple Period and the time of Christ amplify the contrast between the Samaritan on the one hand and the Priest and the Levite on the other. The representatives of the Torah and orthodox leaders of the people failed to care about the wounded man or else allowed fear to overcome instincts of faith; but the mixed-race, heretical Samaritan risked both time and possibly life to care for the needs of the helpless. Hence the poignancy of the question floated by the Lord, "Who was the neighbor of the wounded man?"

More apropos, how shall one understand the death of Jesus on the cross? A reader of a gospel account who had little or no familiarity with the Old Testament could understand that the death of Jesus was for us. He might even get something of the idea of a substitutionary sacrifice. The necessity of repentance toward God and faith in Jesus would be obvious. No comprehension of the Old Testament would be necessary for this man to be saved.

When, however, this man reads the account of the exodus and reflects on the Old Testament instruction of the Day of Atonement and the Passover, will not the tones of the anthem of salvation be richer than ever? When he reads Isaiah 53 and Psalm 22, will he rejoice in this amazing plan and purpose of God? Will his comprehension of the incarnation and atonement of Jesus be exponentially broadened? Historical interpretation understands the setting and the culture of Judaism and the Old Testament as the matrix from which exegesis arises.

Biblical texts were transmitted to the human family over a minimum period of 3400 years. Cultural developments, political alliances, and literary developments all contribute to the content and methods embraced by the prophets and apostles. The rise and fall of political empires in Assyria, Babylon, Egypt, and Persia and the invasion of Egypt by the Hittites all affect the understanding of the biblical authors.

Consequently, the Bible is clear for all who wish to honor and follow its message. Thorough interpretation of the biblical text demands grammatical-historical interpretation. There is no substitute for the biblical languages and for engagement with the historical circumstances that generated the writing of the Bible.

THE COMPLICATION
OF HERMENEUTICS

"Grammatical-historical" is not terminology found in Holy Scripture. So why did this become an identifying expression in evangelical theology, and how has the field of hermeneutics developed? In a sense, the use of "grammatical-historical" was an evangelical response to the propagation of the historical-critical method developed in Germany. "Inerrancy" was not a term in common use in the Patristic era or in the Reformation. Christians found it sufficient to speak of the "authority" of the Bible. But when critics began to allege that there were "errors" in Scripture, "inerrancy" became the evangelical response. In much the same way, "grammatical-historical" was an evangelical answer to those teaching the "historical-critical" method.

As for the origin of the historical-critical method, Gerhard Maier writes,

The historical-critical approach to the Bible has its history, of course. Johann Salomo Semler (late 18th century) is usually designated as father of the technique which not only handled the Bible as an object for historical scrutiny and criticism, but also as a book little different from and no more holy than any other, and surely not to be equated with the Word of God.[21]

> BUT WHEN CRITICS BEGAN TO ALLEGE THAT THERE WERE "ERRORS" IN SCRIPTURE, "INERRANCY" BECAME THE EVANGELICAL RESPONSE. IN MUCH THE SAME WAY, "GRAMMATICAL-HISTORICAL" WAS AN EVANGELICAL ANSWER TO THOSE TEACHING THE "HISTORICAL-CRITICAL" METHOD.

Early advocates include figures such as Gotthold Ephraim Lessing (1729-1781), son of a Lutheran pastor who studied theology at Leipzig. Henry Chadwick notes that "he was above all a critic, and his attitude may be described as one of 'passionate detachment.'"[22]

Chadwick's assessment of Lessing continues: "There is more relativism than skepticism in Lessing's view. He did not think that absolute truth is revealed; but even if it were, and even if he were capable of apprehending it, he would not have wished to apprehend it."[23]

Lessing has become known for his famous "ugly ditch." R.V. Pierard presented the existence of such a ditch this way:

---

21. Gerhard Maier, *The End of the Historical-Critical Method*, translated by Edwin W. Leverenz and Rudolph F. Norden (St. Louis: Concordia Publishing House, 1977), 8.

22. Henry Chadwick, "Lessing, Gotthold Ephraim" in *The Encyclopedia of Philosophy*, Volume 4, edited by Paul Edwards (New York: MacMillian, Inc., 1967), 444.

23. Henry Chadwick, "Lessing, Gotthold Ephraim" in *The Encyclopedia of Philosophy*, Volume 4, 445.

But Lessing went further to question whether authentic belief could properly be bound up with particular historical events. No historical truth, he said, could be demonstrated nor could it be used to demonstrate anything. There was a "ditch" between history and eternal truths that could not be crossed. Thus, he rejected the idea of revelation in history, arguing that if religious truth is genuine, it must be so universally and is of a different order from that of historical events. He called upon people to adopt a "natural" or "positive" religion, one that recognizes God, forms noble conceptions of him, and directs their thoughts and deeds.[24]

Historical-critical methodology proceeded to develop along multiple lines. One of the most helpful discussions of "criticism is found in George Eldon Ladd's succinct volume *The New Testament and Criticism*. Ladd optimistically defines criticism in this way:

> Criticism means making intelligent judgments about historical, literary, textual, and philological questions which one must face in dealing with the Bible, in the light of all of the available evidence, when one recognizes that the Word of God has come to men through the words of men in given historical situations.
>
> The Greek word from which "criticism" is derived is *krisis*, which means simply "a judgment."[25]

But Ladd understands the perversion of the purity of this method. He adds:

> Having said this, we must add a further word of clarification. It must be recognized that modern biblical criticism was not the prod-

---

24. R.V. Pierard, "Lessing, Gotthold Ephraim" in *Evangelical Dictionary of Theology*, 681.

25. George Eldon Ladd, *The New Testament and Criticism* (Grand Rapids: Eerdmans, 1967), 37.

uct of a believing scholarship concerned with a better understanding of the Bible as the Word of God in its historical setting, but of scholarship which rejected the Bible's claim to be the supernaturally inspired Word of God. Biblical criticism as a distinct discipline has developed only in the last two centuries.

Unquestionably, it has often undermined confidence in the Bible as the Word of God, and has resulted in violent controversy in the churches. In many circles today, especially in Germany but also in America, the "historical-critical method" *by definition* assumes a theological stance which regards the Bible exclusively as the words of men, in other words, as a purely human, historical product.[26]

Eta Linnemann, star student of Rudolf Bultmann, stated a less charitable perspective. Bultmann, a famous German scholar, was an advocate of "demythologizing." He believed that many pericopes in Scripture are not to be taken as historically accurate. In order to recover the kernel of spiritual truth, one must strip the husk of mythology to get to the truth. This "demythologizing" technique was anticipated by Peter who said, "We have not followed cunningly devised fables [Gk., μῦθος, transliterated into English as "myth"] when we made known to you the power and coming of the Lord..." (2 Pet. 1:16).

Linnemann experienced a conversion to Christ whom she had formerly believed was so shrouded in myth as to be virtually inaccessible. After she provided a repudiation of all her former works and something of a confession she wrote,

That is why I say "No!" to historical-critical theology. I regard everything that I taught and wrote before I entrusted my life to Jesus as refuse. I wish to use this opportunity to mention that I have pitched my two books *Gleichnisse Jesu...* and *Studien zur Passionges-chichte*, along with my contributions to journals, anthologies, and

---

26. George Eldon Ladd, *The New Testament and Criticism*, 38-39.

Festschriften. Whatever of these writings I had in my possession I threw into the trash with my own hands in 1978. I ask you sincerely to do the same thing with any of them you may have on your own bookshelf."[27]

What are these modern approaches that Linnemann later so vociferously abandoned? **Linguistic criticism** as practiced by British New Testament scholar C. H. Dodd was, for example, quite certain that ἱλάσκομαι had the meaning only of "cover" and, therefore, was translated in error as "propitiated." The idea that God was wrathful in His attitude toward sin was foreign to the New Testament. Leon Morris penned a devasting assessment of this perspective in his 1955 study *The Apostolic Preaching of the Cross.*[28] This case demonstrates the appropriate use of linguistics in Morris versus the misuse of linguistic criticism in the work of Dodd.

Other forms of criticism have been suggested. **Source Criticism** seeks to determine the written documents that lay behind the writing of a biblical text. Occasionally, these sources were extant, but some—like the famous "Q" document in synoptic exegesis—were manufactured by the imagination of the scholars. **Form Criticism** recognized the oral nature of the earliest material finally embodied in the text of Scripture and seeks to reconstruct such material. **Redaction Criticism** allows each biblical author to tell his own story, focusing particularly on the author as an artist and complier of material coinciding with his own interests.[29] The redaction critic seeks to

27. Eta Linnemann, *Historical Criticism of the Bible: Methodology or Ideology?*, translated from the German edition by Robert W. Yarbrough (Grand Rapids: Baker Book House, 1990), 20.

28. Leon Morris, *The Apostolic Preaching of the Cross* (Grand Rapids: Eerdmans, 1955). See Ladd's discussion of C.H. Dodd's study as well as Morris' book in *The New Testament and Criticism*, 105.

29. James D. Hernando, *Dictionary of Hermeneutics: A Concise Guide to Terms, Names, Methods, and Expressions* (Springfield: Gospel Publishing House, 2005), 74.

lay bare the theological perspectives of a biblical author by analyzing the editorial techniques involved in the shaping of his own writing.[30]

Eventually, more novel methods of reading biblical texts developed. French philosopher Jacques Derrida introduced **deconstructionism** as an approach to literature in general, suggesting the epistemological inadequacy of language to convey truth about reality. **Reader-response** hermeneutics, according to Hernando, views the reader of the text as the determinative agent in discovery and construction of meaning.[31] What matters is not what a text meant to the author but what it means to the reader.

These approaches gave way to the imposition of certain grids on a text. For example, in **feminist hermeneutics** the effort is to correct the patriarchal interpretation, which had allegedly come to dominate the thinking of the church and adopt a method that would allow for an appreciation of women in the Bible.[32] Feminist hermeneutics as practiced by Rosemary Radford Ruether in church history and Elisabeth Schüssler Fiorenza in biblical studies often sought to enhance the role of women at the cost of the evident meaning of Scripture. **Liberation theology**, with its origins in South America, imposed upon Scripture the plight of the poor in favelas and read most of the Bible as a document advocating the exodus from oppression. **Black liberation theology** developed next but relived many of the same themes.

Hermeneutics became much more complicated and far more extensive than had been the case in the patristic world, the Reformation era, or the contemporary period before the middle of the twentieth century. There are insights that are helpful in most of these approaches, but the level of complication and the difficulty of comprehension

---

30. Richard Soulen, *Handbook of Biblical Criticism* (Atlanta: John Knox Press, 1976), 142-43.

31. Richard Soulen, *Handbook of Biblical Criticism*, 87-88.

32. Richard Soulen, *Handbook of Biblical Criticism*, 83.

for the common man create formidable frustration for the new or relatively untutored believer. The attitude of many who advocate some of these principles that the Bible is not entirely reliable complicate Christianity. In effect, the complication of hermeneutics often risks the creation of a priesthood of the scholars who sport their own priestly jargon to the tragic exclusion of the man in the pew who was the intended recipient of the Bible.

> *IN EFFECT, THE COMPLICATION OF HERMENEUTICS OFTEN RISKS THE CREATION OF A PRIESTHOOD OF THE SCHOLARS WHO SPORT THEIR OWN PRIESTLY JARGON TO THE TRAGIC EXCLUSION OF THE MAN IN THE PEW WHO WAS THE INTENDED RECIPIENT OF THE BIBLE.*

John Woodbridge, in discussing the Reformation, cites Roman Catholic scholar, James Burtchaell as follows:

> Christians early inherited from the Jews the belief that the biblical writers were somehow possessed by God who was thus to be reckoned the Bible's proper author. Since God could not conceivably be the agent of falsehood, the Bible must be guaranteed free from any error. For centuries this doctrine lay dormant, as doctrines will: accepted by all, pondered by few. Not until the 16th century did inspiration and its corollary, inerrancy, come up for sustained review. The Reformers and Counter-Reformers were disputing whether all revealed truth was in Scripture alone, and whether it could be interpreted by private or by official scrutiny. Despite a radical disagreement on these issues both groups persevered in receiving the Bible as a compendium of inerrant oracles dictated by the spirit.[33]

---

33. John Woodbridge, "Some Misconceptions of The Impact of the 'Enlightenment' on The Doctrine of Scripture" in *Hermeneutics, Authority, and Canon*, edited by D.A. Carson and John Woodbridge (Grand Rapids: Zondervan Publishing House, 1986), 242. Woodbridge is citing James T. Burtchaell, *Catholic Theories*

This paragraph from Burtchaell illustrates the extent of the change in approaches to the Scriptures in modernity.

There is one form of endeavor denominated "textual criticism" or sometimes termed "lower criticism" which is both helpful and critically important. Old Testament textual criticism compares and evaluates the readings of the Septuagint and the Masoretic texts. The discovery of the Dead Sea Scrolls added some variant readings, though fewer than anticipated by many. New Testament textual criticism boasts a field of texts numbering more than seven thousand partial and a few full texts. Textual criticism identifies, classifies, and evaluates these variant readings.

As one example, consider John 1:18. The King James Version states that "No one has seen God at any time. The only begotten *Son* who is in the bosom of the Father, He has declared Him." When a pastor or scholar examines the textual apparatus, he discovers that the word translated "son" is actually the word "God" in superb documents such as the Codex Sinaiticus, Codex Vaticanus, papyrus p[66], and other documents, as well as the rending followed by Church Fathers such as Irenaeus, Clement, Origen, and interestingly, even Arius. "Son" also boasts a number of readings, most of which are considered less definite than those supporting "God."

The doctrine of the Deity of Christ is not adversely affected by either reading. As is usually the case, no vital doctrine is overturned by alternative readings. However, if the "only begotten God" is right, then John 1:18 becomes one of the most essential verses for supporting the doctrine of Christ's Deity. A pastor working with a mature congregation may want to use this to teach his people about variant readings in the text. Textual criticism has great potential value and, unlike many other methods, does not assume a contaminated text.

However, even here, man-made rules for evaluating the value of certain textual readings may not always be reliable. This caution simply insists

---

of Inspiration Since 1810: A Review and Critique (Cambridge: Cambridge University Press, 1969), 1-2.

on care in the exercise of textual criticism. Nevertheless, the potential values are great.

UNDERSTANDING THE BIBLE IN THE 21ST CENTURY

The proliferation of hermeneutical concepts and the complication of texts on interpretation provide fertile fields of scholarship with which the academy must appropriately spar. But the greater need is for pastor and congregants in the churches to hone the basis of Bible interpretation so that all can grasp the message of the Bible. William B. Tolar pricelessly stated the matter:

> No element of interpretation is more important to an accurate understanding of the Bible than is the grammatical-historical method. It is the *sine qua non* for any valid understanding of God's Word. Without an honest, careful, intelligent use of grammatical and historical knowledge, there is little or no hope for a correct interpretation of documents written in foreign languages within several different ancient historical contexts. To fail to use proper grammatical rules or to ignore those historical contexts is most certainly to guarantee failure in understanding the writers' intended meanings.[34]

Pastors preparing for the preaching responsibilities in their future congregations must first be instructed that multiple pastoral duties cannot be neglected, but nothing is more important than the preaching/teaching assignment of the pastor. And there can be no substitute for the careful in-

---

34. William B. Tolar, "The Grammatical-Historical Method" in *Biblical Hermeneutics*, second edition, edited by Bruce Corley, Steve W. Lemke, and Grant I. Lovejoy (Nashville: Broadman & Holman Publishers, 2002), 21.

vestigation of the texts from which he will preach. And as part of that, seminaries and Bible schools must expose young pastors to the finest of biblical hermeneutics as provided in works such as *Protestant Biblical Interpretation* by Bernard Ramm.

As the preacher expounds the Scriptures to his people, his fervent prayer must be that the hearts of the people would burn within them as he interprets the Bible (Luke 24:32). But as a secondary purpose, the pastor must also teach his flock the basic principles of hermeneutics so that they may grasp the meanings of the book as they read it devotionally. Whether the vocabulary "grammatical–historical" is employed is not so crucial, but the method itself cannot be replaced. There is still and will always be a need for the grammatical–historical method of interpretation.

7

DOES EXPOSITORY PREACHING STILL MATTER?

DAVID L. ALLEN

The preaching of the Word of God by men who believed it to be inerrant was a crucial factor in the success of the Conservative Resurgence
of the Southern Baptist Convention from 1979–2000. Preaching mattered
then . . . and it still matters today.

PREACHING AND THE
SBC CONSERVATIVE RESURGENCE:
The Influence of W.A. Criswell[1]

When the subject of preaching and the Southern Baptist Convention Conservative Resurgence is on the table, there is no better place to begin than

---

1. For an overview of Criswell's ministry, especially his preaching, see David
L. Allen, "W. A. Criswell: Expositing the Whole Counsel of God—from Genesis
to Revelation," in *A Legacy of Preaching: Enlightenment to the Present Day*, eds. Benjamin K. Forrest, Kevin L. King, Bill Curtis, and Dwayne Milioni, vol. 2 (Grand
Rapids: Zondervan, 2018), 409–27.

the influence of one man: W. A. Criswell, famed pastor of the First Baptist Church in Dallas, Texas for fifty years.

He was the author of fifty-four books. He was a denominational leader who served two terms as president of the Southern Baptist Convention. As the key figure who identified the liberal drift in the convention, he furnished the inspiration for a groundswell of grassroots Southern Baptists to bring the SBC back to her theologically conservative roots.

Criswell's most powerful influence within his own denomination and beyond was his unswerving commitment to the inerrancy and infallibility of the Scriptures. In his preaching and writing, he inveighed against the liberalism which had infected Protestantism as well as his own Southern Baptist Convention. He became the patriarchal champion of biblical inerrancy in the SBC, the stack pole around which others united, resulting in what was probably the single largest shift of a denomination back to her orthodox roots in the history of the Christian church.[2] As O. S. Hawkins put it at Criswell's funeral: "He was our standard bearer. Let those who one day may be prone to rewrite history and temper his influence, let them know that what Spurgeon was to the Downgrade controversy in 19th century England, he was, much more, to 20th century American Christianity."

Under Criswell's preaching, First Baptist Church became the prototype for the mega-church with her membership rolls swelling to over 25,000 by the mid-1980s.[3] He proved you could build a great church on

---

2. For the history of the conservative resurgence within the SBC which began officially in 1979, consult Jim Hefley, *The Truth in Crisis*, 5 volumes, (Hannibal, MO.: Hannibal Books, 1986-1990); Paul Pressler, *A Hill on Which to Die*, (Nashville: Broadman and Holman, 1999); and Jerry Sutton, *The Baptist Reformation: The Conservative Resurgence in the Southern Baptist Convention* (Nashville: Broadman and Holman, 2000).

3. See Paige Patterson, "W. A. Criswell," in *Theologians of the Baptist Tradition*, eds. Timothy George and David Dockery (Nashville: Broadman and Holman, 2001), 236.

the preaching of the Bible as the inerrant Word of God. His view of preaching was informed by his view of the Bible as the infallible, inerrant Word of God. His view of both would influence a generation of preachers who would lead the Conservative Resurgence of the Southern Baptist Convention.

Criswell's influence upon pastors, both within the Baptist world and beyond, is enormous. The "School of the Prophets" was begun in 1971 as an annual seminar for pastors to come to the campus of the First Baptist Church in Dallas and learn about the methods used by Criswell to grow a church. Here also his views on preaching were imbibed by young pastors.

Criswell's lifetime preaching legacy influenced future generations of preachers to employ the expository method of preaching.[4] Perhaps more than any other single preacher in the last half of the twentieth century, W. A. Criswell has fostered the expositional preaching of the Bible. Adrian Rogers, pastor of the great Bellevue Baptist Church in Memphis said to him: "You have been my hero since I have been a young preacher."[5] Carl F. H. Henry, dean of Evangelicals, wrote of Criswell:

> More and more he became for countless pastors the voice of evangelical theology at the pulpit and Bible conference level. His ministry and his influence has extended far beyond Baptist life into the larger Christian community. To the evangelical world he remains the living symbol of proclamation in the expository tradition, and of biblical theology articulated so relevantly that the man in the street and the minister in the pew must alike come to terms with it.[6]

---

4. Paige Patterson, "*The Imponderables of God,*" in *Criswell Theological Review* 1 (Spring 1987): 245.

5. "Letters of Appreciation," *Criswell Theological Review*, vol. 1.2 (1987), 230–31.

6. Carl F. H. Henry, "A Voice for God," *Criswell Theological Review*, 235–36.

Criswell's expository preaching influenced myriads of preachers in the generations to follow.[7] He profoundly influenced a young Adrian Rogers, Jerry Vines, Paige Patterson, Jimmy Draper, and many others who would become leaders during the Conservative Resurgence. Patterson, along with Paul Pressler, would set the strategy for Resurgence; Rogers would become the first president of the Southern Baptist Convention that launched the Resurgence; Draper would play a significant role through his preaching and leadership; and Vines, pastor emeritus of the First Baptist Church of Jacksonville, Florida, would be the preacher whose sermons would have perhaps the greatest impact through his own preaching along with the annual pastor's conference held at First Baptist Church in Jacksonville during his pastorate (1982–2006).

Jerry Vines acknowledges his own debt, as well as that of the Southern Baptist denomination, to Criswell for breaking ground in the area of expository preaching.[8] Vines said Criswell:

> …has gained international recognition as a Bible expositor…His books are veritable storehouses of information and guidance for the preacher who would preach expositorily. His volumes on Revelation are among the finest. His word study is excellent, and his interpretation is clear and concise. Though a clearly discernable outline often does not appear, the preacher will learn much about expository preaching by a careful study of his work.[9]

In an interview by Paige Patterson, Criswell was asked what he con-

---

7. See W. A. Criswell, *Criswell's Guidebook for Pastor's* (Nashville: Broadman Press, 1980), 50–53.

8. Jerry Vines, *A Practical Guide to Sermon Preparation* (Chicago: Moody, 1985), xiv.

9. Jerry Vines and Jim Shaddix, *Power in the Pulpit: How to Prepare and Deliver Expository Sermons* (Chicago: Moody Press, 1999), 41.

sidered his greatest contributions God had enabled him to make to the kingdom of God. His response:

> I would think it is my emphasis on preaching the Bible. Dr. Pat-
> terson, I do not know whether this is correct or not, but I read
> often the observation that it was my ministry here in Dallas that
> turned preachers to preaching the Bible. It is said that preachers just
> preached subject sermons before but that when I started preaching
> here as I did, that became a model and a pattern for countless num-
> bers of other pulpiteers to preach the Word of God. If that is true, I
> say "Praise God that I could do such a thing as that!"[10]

W. A. Criswell was the single greatest influence theologically and homiletically in the lives of the key leaders of the Southern Baptist Convention's Conservative Resurgence.

Preaching still matters.

PREACHING AND THE
SBC CONSERVATIVE RESURGENCE:
Preaching at the SBC Pastor's Conference and SBC

The Conservative Resurgence of the Southern Baptist Convention began officially in 1979 in Houston Texas at the annual convention meeting. Twenty years later, the die was cast, and the convention was firmly in the hands of conservatives. I was a part of it all from the beginning. I remember when as student pastor at Prestonwood Baptist Church in Dallas and a student at SWBTS, an article appeared in the Baptist Standard (the state Baptist

---

10. "Interview with Dr. W. A. Criswell," *The Church at the Dawn of the 21ˢᵗ Century: Essays in Honor of W. A. Criswell*, ed. by Paige Patterson, John Pretlove and Luis Pantoja (Dallas: Criswell Publications, 1989), 15.

paper of Texas) chronicling the accusations of liberalism at Baylor University by then president of the Criswell College, Paige Patterson.

The Monday after the article had appeared, the youth pastors who normally attended the weekly Dallas Baptist Pastor's Conference were seated at our usual table toward the back of the room. Someone brought a copy of the article and the guys began to criticize Patterson's accusations of liberalism at Baylor mercilessly. I was the only one at the table who suggested that since Patterson had merely quoted comments in books and articles written by the Baylor professors he was accusing, the problem seemed real. "No, it is only politics," someone mused.

As time went by, while some politics were no doubt involved, it became clear over the next few years that some Baptists did indeed have a different view of Biblical authority than the majority of laypeople in the pews. Clear denial of inerrancy was a reality, to one degree or another, at all of the Southern Baptist Convention's six seminaries, one of which I attended.

There are many factors that played a role in the Southern Baptist conservative resurgence as it came to be called, but none more significant than preaching. The preaching of conservative pastors in their pulpits drew the attention of the people to the theological problems. The preaching at key pastor's conferences, like the annual conference held at First Baptist Church, Jacksonville, Florida, under the leadership of co-pastors Homer Lindsey and Jerry Vines, had a strong influence on the resurgence. This conference regularly had an attendance in the thousands. The preaching of the annual SBC's own Pastor's Conference, held each Sunday night and Monday before the SBC formally began on Tuesday in June, coupled with the sermons delivered during the actual SBC, played an incalculable part in spearheading the resurgence year by year.

Simply put, as Nancy Ammerman said, the conservatives outpreached the moderates and the conservative resurgence was achieved in no small measure due to the fiery pulpit rhetoric that kept the issue of biblical authority clearly before the mind's eye of the people. Ammerman concluded from her research that the homiletical skill of the conservatives was a factor in their eventual success. She described them as "preachers of remarkable ability, able to stir crowds with their words, able to evoke response in their hearers."[11]

Nine years after Ammerman's book, Carl Kell and Raymond Camp, communications professors and Baptists, published *In the Name of the Father* in 1999. They concluded that moderates failed to match the rhetorical preaching concerning an inerrant Bible of the conservatives during the previous twenty years. "From a rhetorical perspective, the victory of the battle was won on national rostrums in the sermons of the presidents."[12] "For 15 years, the leaders of the Southern Baptist Convention produced the finest defense of pulpit sermons on a single theme that had ever been seen or heard in the 150-year history of the denomination."[13]

There were many sermons preached by conservatives at the SBC Pastors' Conference and Convention between the years 1980 and 2000, but five stand out has having particular influence.[14] The first is Adrian Rogers' sermon "The Decade of Decision and the Doors of Destiny," preached at the 1980 annual meeting of the SBC in St. Louis, Missouri.

---

11. Nancy Tatom Ammerman, *Baptist Battles: Social Change and Religious Conflict in the Southern Baptist Convention* (New Brunswick, NJ: Rutgers University Press, 1990), 178. See also William Stanley Stone, Jr., "The Southern Baptist Convention Reformation: 1979-1990: A Social Drama," (Ph.D. diss., Louisiana State University, 1993); Carl L. Kell, and L. Raymond Camp, *In the Name of the Father: the Rhetoric of the New Southern Baptist Convention* (Carbondale and Edwardsville: Southern Illinois University Press, 1999); Joshua David Bonner, "An Examination of the Role of Preaching in the Conservative Resurgence of the Southern Baptist Convention," (DMin. diss. The Southern Baptist Theological Seminary, 2016), and Matthew Beasley, "A Cohesive Moderate Ideology: An Ideological Critique of the Sermons of Moderate SBC Pastors during the SBC Forum," (PhD diss., SWBTS, 2018).

12. Carl L. Kell and L. Raymond Camp, *In the Name of the Father: the Rhetoric of the New Southern Baptist Convention*, Southern Illinois University Press, 1999, 51.

13. Kell and Camp, *In the Name of the Father*, 61.

14. Kell and Camp, *In the Name of the Father*, 159–63.

Rogers had been the surprising winner of the presidential election in Houston in 1979, the official launch date of the SBC Conservative Resurgence. Roger's won 51% of the first vote against several candidates. His 1980 presidential address on the topic of the inerrancy of the Bible laid the groundwork for the next twenty years of sermons that would be preached often on this topic, as well as the successive conservative victories that followed. When a theological moderate said to him, "Adrian, if you don't compromise, we will never get together," Rogers firmly replied: "I'm willing to compromise about many things, but not the Word of God." Later he would say: "So far as getting together is concerned, we don't have to get together. The Southern Baptist Convention, as it is, does not have to survive. I don't have to be the pastor of Bellevue Baptist Church. I don't have to be loved; I don't even have to live. But I will not compromise the Word of God."[15]

These words were a line in the sand and become something of a watchword for the many Southern Baptists who over the next twenty years would by their votes turn the SBC in a conservative direction.

The second sermon that proved influential was W. A. Criswell's sermon "Whether We Live or Die," preached at the Pastors' Conference on Monday evening prior to the 1985 annual meeting of the SBC in Dallas, Texas. This sermon has been described as a "watershed" in the conservative resurgence and one of the most important and significant sermons in his entire ministry. Criswell surveyed the history of theological drift among Baptists. He referenced the famous "Downgrade Controversy" in England in the last decade of the 19th century and Spurgeon's role in championing Biblical fidelity. Criswell chronicled the loss of Baptist schools in America that had been founded on the principle of an inerrant Bible: Brown University, the University of Chicago, etc. He demonstrated how each of these once great bastions of conservative theology were now solidly in the hands

15. Gene Brooks, "Sunday in the South: Adrian Rogers on the Word," *Sunday in the South*, September 15, 2018, accessed September 25, 2021, https://gene-brooks.blogspot.com/2018/09/adrian-rogers-on-word.html.

of liberals. Criswell opined that the same would occur to the Southern Baptist Convention unless she takes her stand on the inerrant Word of God.

The third sermon with huge impact was Jerry Vines' sermon "A Baptist and His Bible," preached at the 1987 annual meeting of the SBC in St. Louis, Missouri. This message focused on the inspiration and inerrancy of the Bible and was an exposition of 2 Tim 3:14 – 4:13. Vines arranged the sermon around three points: (1) The Intention of the Bible (2 Tim 3:14-15); (2) The Inspiration of the Bible (2 Tim 3:16-17); (3) The Implications of the Bible (2 Tim 4:1-13). Reflecting upon this sermon, Vines wrote, "I did some word study. I included some down-to-earth stories. I used a little humor. And I pulled no punches. Then I titled the message 'A Baptist and His Bible.'"[16]

Vines' belief in the importance of inerrancy for doctrinal integrity and preaching is illustrated in this sermon. "I'm getting ready to shoot where you stand. If you don't believe the Bible, don't take a salary for preaching it. If you don't believe the Bible, do the world a favor and get a milk route. You will do more good."[17]

Vines believes that one's doctrine of Scripture has implications for his homiletical method. His convention sermon of 1987, "A Baptist and His Bible," most clearly articulates this when he says, "What the preacher believes about the Bible is crucial to the task of exposition. A low view of inspiration erodes the very foundation of preaching. Decide the Bible is not totally the Word of God and there will be no responsibility to study its text minutely and to preach its message authoritatively."

Charles Stanley, himself a former president of the SBC, described Vines' sermon "A Baptist and His Bible" as "the greatest sermon I had ever heard on the Word of God."[18]

---

16. To read the entire sermon, see Jerry Vines, "A Baptist and His Bible," in *Preach the Word!: A Collection of Essays on Biblical Preaching in Honor of Jerry Vines*, ed. David L. Allen and Peter Lumpkins (Carrollton, GA: Free Press, 175–92).

17. Vines, "A Baptist and His Bible," 189.

18. Jerry Vines and Charles Stanley, "Jerry Vines and Charles Stanley," accessed July 26, 2015, https://youtu.be/VAL89Bb0mSk.

The fourth sermon that played a crucial role in the first ten years of the conservative resurgence was **W. A.** Criswell's sermon, "The Curse of Liberalism," preached at the 1988 SBC in San Antonio, TX. Criswell's sermon was not an exposition of a text; he didn't even have a text. It was a topical treatment of the rise of liberalism in America and in the mainline denominations.

Criswell opened the sermon with a bit of rhetorical flourish that brought the house down:

"May I speak on The Curse of Liberalism? Because of the opprobrious epithet 'liberal,' today they call themselves 'moderates.' A skunk by any other name still stinks!" From this point forward, Criswell held the audience in his hand.

> To my great sorrow, and yours, we have lost our nation to the liberal, and the secularist, and the humanist, which finally means to the atheist and the infidel. America used to be known as a Christian nation. It is no longer. America is a secular nation. Our forefathers who came on the Mayflower founded here a new republic, a new nation, and it was Christian. Our Baptist forefathers founded a state, and it was Christian. When I was a youth growing up, the name of God and the Christian faith was a part of the civic and national life of our people. It is not anymore.

Criswell continued:

> We have not only lost our nation to the liberal and to the secularist and to the humanist, but in great areas of our Baptist life we have lost our denominations and our Christian institutions, our colleges and our universities. All of the Christian schools called "Baptist" in the north, all of them have been lost – all of them: Brown Universi-

ty, McMaster University, Chicago University. There's not one that remains.

The two sermons Criswell preached at the SBC Pastor's Conference in 1985 and 1988 contributed much to the continued conservative direction of the SBC.

The fifth influential sermon was Jerry Vines' "Glory in the Church," preached at the 1990 SBC in New Orleans, LA. Taking as his text Ephesians 3:20–21, Vines spoke of the church universal, the church local, the church denominational, and the church eternal. Vines pointed out one does not find a full-blown denominational structure in the New Testament. We do find principles of cooperation whereby churches can work together for the gospel. Vines made the point that loyalty to a denomination must never supplant loyalty to Christ and his Word. Denominations have to be constantly on guard against bureaucracy and apostasy. The church must not become "mustard seed trees, sprouting bureaucratic branches inhabited by blasphemous birds."

Vines spoke of a "legitimate denominationalism" which should include "local identity," "doctrinal integrity," and "evangelical intensity." The church denominationally should remain true to the inerrant, inspired, infallible Word of God. If she remains true to these doctrinal distinctions, she has a great future; if not, she is headed for the garbage dump of all other apostate denominations.

Vines' President's sermon at the SBC in 1990 was the culmination of ten years of preaching that all but solidified the conservative resurgence. From this time forward, the moderates of the convention knew they had lost.

Preaching still matters.

PREACHING AND THE CHURCH TODAY

Preaching is absolutely essential for church planting, evangelism, teaching, ministry, and growth. The mission of the Church is the evangelism of the lost and the equipping of the saved.

It is interesting to compare the account of the giving of the Great Commission in Matthew and Mark. Whereas Matthew 28:19 speaks of going into all the world and "making disciples," Mark 16:15 says "Go into all the world and preach the gospel. . . ." Obviously, preaching plays a paramount role in the Church's mandate to fulfill the Great Commission.

There are many reasons why preaching is foundational for the mission of the church.

Biblical Reason:
Scripture Commands that We Teach

This is clearly articulated in Paul's swan song, 2 Timothy. He exhorts Timothy to "Preach the Word" (2Tim 4:2). The New Testament vocabulary for preaching is rich and varied. It includes "heralding," "announcing," "teaching," "reasoning," "exhorting," "encouraging," among others. Luke informs us that Paul "opened the Scriptures" when he preached in Acts 17:2. The Pauline, Petrine, and Johannine letters are essentially written sermons; they contain what Paul, Peter, and John would have preached had he been there in person. Hebrews is a written sermon where the Old Testament becomes the text to alternatively teach, exhort, and encourage Christians to press on to spiritual maturity.

Theological Reason:
The Nature of Scripture

Every preacher should operate on the following four foundational principles:

Preaching has a Divine Source

God is a God who speaks. He has spoken in Christ and he has spoken in Scripture. From Genesis to Revelation, God speaks. "In the beginning was the Word, and the Word was with God and the Word was God" (John 1:1). "God, having spoken of old to the fathers by the prophets, has in these last days spoken to us in his Son" (Hebrews 1:1-2).

God's speech is revelation. In no other way could we know him. Though the universe declares the glory of God and bears witness to his power, it could never tell us of his love. Though history tells us of the sovereignty of God, it can never explain what Christ was doing on the cross. Though our conscience bears witness to the morality of God, it can never teach us how to live and love rightly. Unless God speaks, we would never know him or his love for us. To us, the universe, history, and conscience are all one great undecipherable hieroglyph until we discover God's Rosetta Stone—Jesus!

God's speech is a vehicle of communication. God is the perfect communicator and Jesus is God's perfect communication to us. Jesus is God's ultimate communication because he is God's perfect representation according to Hebrews 1:1-4. Jesus perfectly represents God and Scripture perfectly represents Jesus. Jesus is God spelling himself out in language we can understand. Jesus does not reveal something other than Himself, nor does He reveal something other than God. "The word became flesh and dwelt among us. We behold his glory, even the glory of the only Son from the Father... No one has ever seen God; the only Son, Jesus, has made him known" (John 1:14, 18). Jesus is the speech of eternity translated into the language of time. The inaudible has become audible. The invisible has become visible. The unapproachable has become accessible. God's revelation in Jesus is personal, plenary, and permanent. Jesus is God's final and ultimate communication.

Speech is a vehicle of salvation. God's speech in Christ resulted in his making "purification for sins" (Hebrews 1:3). God's perfect communication has as its goal the salvation of all sinners. God longs for people to know His salvation. God is not willing that any should perish but that all should come to repentance (2 Peter 3:9). Because of these things, Paul admonished Timothy to "preach the word"! The first theological foundation for preaching is the fact—God has spoken!

Preaching has Divine Authority

As the word of God, Scripture is inspired, inerrant, and sufficient according to 2 Timothy 3:16–17, "All Scripture is God-breathed, and is profitable for doctrine, reproof, correction and instruction in righteousness." The authority of Scripture is the very authority of God. Jesus is the living Word and Scripture is God's written word. God is the ultimate author of all Scripture according to 2 Timothy 3:16. It is interesting how New Testament authors quote the Old Testament. Often, God and Scripture are interchangeable terms via metonymy when quoting the Old Testament. For example, God is viewed as the author when he himself is not the speaker, as in Matthew 19:4-5. On the other hand, "Scripture says" is used when God himself is the direct speaker, as in Romans 9:17, Galatians 3:8, 22. I like what J. I. Packer said: "Scripture is God preaching."[19]

Jesus links himself to the Old Testament throughout his ministry. In Luke 4:14–30, when Jesus preached, he spoke from a text. He took a text of Scripture from Isaiah and startled his synagogue hearers by applying it to himself and claiming its fulfillment on that very day. After his resurrection, while walking with the two disciples on the road to Emmaus, he chided them for their unbelief and laid the fault at the feet of their failure to consider the Scriptures. He then referenced the three sections of the Hebrew Bible, the Law, the Prophets, and the Writings, and asserted that each "testified" concerning himself.

---

19. J. I. Packer, *Engaging the Written Word of God* (Peabody, MA: Hendrickson, 2012), 162.

Paul's method of evangelistic preaching according to Acts 17:2–3 is informative: "As was his custom, Paul went into the synagogue, and on three Sabbath days he reasoned with them from the Scriptures, explaining and proving that the Messiah had to suffer and rise from the dead." Paul's New Testament letters to the churches are mostly written sermons. They contain what Paul would have preached to them had he been with them in person. Hebrews is itself a written sermon that develops several Old Testament texts of Scripture, Psalm 110:1, 4 being primary.

Our authority for preaching comes from God himself and from his word, Scripture. As Haddon Robinson reminds us, "Ultimately the authority behind preaching resides not in the preacher but in the biblical text."[20] The preacher is God's mouthpiece. As the 2nd Helvetic Confession stated: "The preaching of the word of God is the word of God."

To preach, *kerrusō*, is an authoritative public proclamation of the Word. Its authority derives from God himself. In 1 Thessalonians 2:12-13 Paul writes: "For this reason we also constantly thank God that when you received the word of God which you heard from us, you accepted it not as the word of men, but for what it really is, the word of God, which also performs its work in you who believe." Here both the source and authority are God.

Preaching is the Delivery of Divine Content

In Paul's swan song, 2 Timothy, he admonished young Timothy to "preach the word" (2 Tim 4:2)! In context, the word is the written Scripture of 2 Timothy 3:16–17. Preaching is the ministry of the word and should be shaped by the nature of the word. The focus here is on preaching to the church, as evidenced by context and the use of "teaching" in the final phrase.

---

20. Haddon Robinson, *Biblical Preaching*, 16.

Jesus critiques the misreading of Scripture on five occasions, in each chiding the Jewish leaders: "Have you not read?" I wonder if Jesus critiques our mis-preaching of Scripture….?

Next to a lack of truth, a sermon's greatest fault is a lack of biblically developed content. Preaching must be "text-driven" and "Christ-centered." It cannot be the latter unless it is first the former.

Luke records Paul's approach in his evangelistic preaching in Acts 17:2–3, "And according to Paul's custom, he went to them, and for three Sabbaths reasoned with them from the Scriptures, explaining and giving evidence that the Christ had to suffer and rise again from the dead. . . ." Perry and Strubhar are correct "The biblical text must be the foundation of every evangelistic sermon."[21]

Since God himself speaks in and through Christ and Scripture, it is incumbent on preachers to expound the meaning of Scripture to their people. In so doing, they are preaching Christ through the very words of God, Christ, and the Holy Spirit in Scripture. To preach the Word (Living and written) is to hear Christ and encounter him.

Therefore, we are not just preaching sermons; we are preaching texts—inspired texts!

The word "text" comes from the Latin word meaning "to weave." The word figuratively expresses thought in continuous speech or writing. The product of weaving is the *textus* in Latin. It is a linguistic composition expressed orally or in writing. A text is a cohesive and structured expression of language that intends a specific effect.

Biblical preaching should be the development of a text of Scripture: its explanation, illustration, and application. Our focus should not be only on what the text says, but as much as is possible, on what the author is trying to *do* with his text—what linguistics call "pragmatic analysis."

---

21. Lloyd M. Perry and John Strubhar, *Evangelistic Preaching*, rev. ed. (Eugene, OR: Wipf & Stock, 2000), 56.

One of the goals of preaching is to communicate the meaning of the text to an audience in terms and contexts they understand. One way to think about preaching is to view it as a form of translation. We are translating the meaning of our text to our audience. The word "translate" comes from the Latin word meaning "to transfer." In a sense, we are "transferring" meaning. And meaning is fragile! Freight can be altered or damaged in shipment. Handle with care!

Many a preacher uses a text of Scripture, but his sermon is not derived from the text. In such a sermon, the text is not the source of the sermon; it is only a resource. For some preachers, the Bible is something of a happy hunting-ground for texts on which to hang what they want to say to the people. G. Campbell Morgan spoke of one preacher whose habit was to write his sermons, and then choose a text as a peg on which to hang them. Morgan went on to say that the study of that preacher's sermons revealed the peril of the method.[22] Preaching is not just playing with the subject of your text as one observer said of Lancelot Andrewes' preaching in the court of King James I. Preach the text!

Unfortunately, some preachers subordinate the text to their sermon. This becomes evident when preachers preach sermons filtered through preconceived doctrinal systems that sometimes are imposed on the text. Other preachers subordinate the text to their application in the sermon. You can't have legitimate application until you first have exposition of textual meaning that grounds the application. Scripture links exegesis and application. You cannot preach the word right until you cut it straight. 2 Timothy 2:15.

Genuine expository preaching is text-driven preaching—where the substance, structure, and spirit of the text guides and informs the sermon's structure and content. The text is king. Any method of preaching, if it conveys biblical truth, is to some extent related to the text of Scripture because everything you preach is found only in Scripture! "Faithful engagement

---

22. G. Campbell Morgan, *Preaching* (Eugene, OR: Wipf and Stock, 2018), 32.

with Scripture is a standard by which preaching should be measured, and the normal week-in, week-out practice of preaching should consist of sermons drawn from specific biblical texts."[23] The text gets the first word. The text gets the last word. There is a bond between Scripture and Sermon. What God has joined together let no man put asunder. The stream of the sermon will never run clear if the source of the sermon is other than a text of Scripture.

Preaching has a Divine Mandate

The centerpiece and climax of the discourse structure of 2 Timothy is 4:2: "Preach the Word." This is the only place in Scripture where "word," (*logos*) occurs as the direct object of the verb "to preach." Preaching is God's method of heralding the Gospel to a lost world. Preaching is God's method of teaching His church doctrinal and ethical truths. We refer to these two aspects as *kerygma* (heralding the gospel) and *didaché* (teaching). Both words occur in 2 Timothy 4:2-5.

Every time we preach, eternity is at stake. We must realize that with every sermon we are not only spiritual surgeons, "rightly dividing the word of truth," but are ourselves under the probing knife of the very Word we preach, as Hebrews 4:12-13 says. Those of us in the pew must hold our pastors accountable to a high standard for preaching God's Word, all the while remembering that we too are being probed by the Word. Preach the Word!

John Stott insightfully commented that the essential secret of preaching is not "mastering certain techniques, but being mastered by certain convictions."[24] All preaching rests upon certain convictions about the nature of God, the Scriptures, and the Gospel. Haddon Robinson's statement is right

---

23. Thomas Long, *The Witness of Preaching*, 2nd ed. (Louisville: Westminster/John Knox Press, 2005), 5.

24. John Stott, *Between Two Worlds* (Grand Rapids: Eerdmans, 1982), 92.

on the money: "Expository preaching, therefore, emerges not merely as a type of sermon – one among many – but as the theological outgrowth of a high view of inspiration. Expository preaching then originates as a philosophy rather than a method."[25]

The theological foundation for preaching is the fact God has spoken in his living Word—Jesus, and his written Word—Scripture. J. I. Packer once said "Scripture is God preaching."[26]

Biblical authority entails inerrancy. But inerrancy alone, though foundational, is not enough. The conservative resurgence won the battle for the inerrancy of Scripture in SBC; now the issue is over its sufficiency.

PASTORAL REASON: THE NATURE OF THE CHURCH

The nature of the church requires that preaching be paramount in the fulfillment of her mission. The Great Commission as recorded in Mark 16:15 indicates how Jesus viewed preaching as the necessary means for the church to fulfill the Great Commission.

The church was birthed in preaching according to Acts 2. In Acts 6:4, Luke records the Apostles placed a high priority on prayer and preaching as their primary focus: "But we will give ourselves continually to prayer and to the ministry of the word." Paul says in Romans 10 that faith comes by hearing and hearing by the word of God." Evangelistic preaching grows the church. Biblical preaching edifies the church. The book of Acts clearly shows this.

25, Haddon Robinson, "Homiletics and Hermeneutics," in *Hermeneutics, Inerrancy, and the Bible*, ed. Earl Radmacher and Robert Preus (Grand Rapids: Zondervan, 1984), 803.

26. J. I. Packer, *Engaging the Written Word of God*, 162.

In his swan song, Paul tells young Timothy to "preach the Word" (2 Timothy 4:2). You cannot have a church without preaching. You cannot have church growth without preaching. You cannot have church revitalization without preaching. Preaching is fundamental to New Testament ecclesiology. The church cannot be the church unless she is the preaching church.

Preaching was viewed as the primary method of pastoral care in the history of the church. The classical definitions of pastoral care throughout church history speak of preaching as the primary method of doing pastoral care. For example, Luther said: "If any man would preach let him suppress his own words. Let him make them count in family matters and secular affairs but here in the church he should speak nothing except the Word of the rich Head of the household otherwise it is not the true church. Therefore, this must be the rule God is speaking that is why a preacher by virtue of this commission and office is administering the household of God and dare say nothing but what God says and commands. And although much talking is done which is outside the Word of God, yet the church is not established by such talk though men were to turn mad in their insistence upon it."[27]

Preaching within the church both equips and challenges the church to fulfill the Great Commission. Are you planting a church? Are you growing a church? Are you revitalizing a church? Preaching must be your top priority. Expository preaching will grow the church, the people, and the preacher.

In summary, expositional preaching begins with God and his truth. God has revealed himself and truths about himself in history (1 Cor 2:6–13). We don't create the message. God did that. We create the sermon. God's revelation has been recorded and preserved in Scripture (2 Tim 3:16; 2 Peter

---

27. Martin Luther, "Sermon in Castle Pleissenburg, Leipzig, 1539," in *Luther's Works, Sermon I,* ed. and trans. John W. Doberstein (Philadelphia: Muhlenberg Press, 1559), 305.

1:19–21). The meaning of Scripture has to be determined by using the tools of hermeneutics and exegesis. Finally, the message must be delivered. Preaching still matters.

EXPOSITORY PREACHING AND THE CHURCH TODAY

Given the nature of Scripture and the needs of the church, all preaching, regardless of the form it takes, should be basically expositional in nature. The word "homiletics" itself etymologically derives from the Greek word *homo* meaning "same," and "*legō*, meaning "to speak." Homiletics is the art and science of sermon construction and delivery that says the same thing the text of Scripture says.

What then is expository preaching? Here are three definitions that answer the question well:

> Expository Preaching is the communication of a biblical concept derived from and transmitted through a historical, grammatical, and literary study of a passage in its context, which the Holy Spirit first applies to the personality and experience of the preacher, then through him to his hearers."
>
> Haddon Robinson

> A discourse that expounds a passage of scripture, organizes it around a central theme and main divisions which come from the text, and then decisively applies its message to the listeners.
>
> Jerry Vines

> Expository preaching is text driven preaching that honors the truth of Scripture as it was given by the Holy Spirit. Discovering the

God-inspired meaning through historical- grammatical-theological investigation and interpretation, the preacher, by means of engaging and compelling proclamation, explains, illustrates and applies the meaning of the biblical text in submission to and in the power of the Holy Spirit, preaching Christ for a verdict of changed lives.

Danny Akin

What is the role of the text in preaching? The word "text" comes from a Latin word meaning "to weave," and refers to the product of weaving, hence "composition." The word is used figuratively to express structured meaning in speech or writing. In expository preaching, sermons should be not only based upon a text of Scripture, but should actually expound the meaning of that text. The biblical text is not merely a *resource* for the sermon; it is the *source* of the sermon. A sermon should not only *use* a text of Scripture, but should be *derived* from a text of Scripture, and should *develop* a text of Scripture.

Having listened to preaching now for more than 55 years (starting at age 9), and having studied it for more than 45 years, I am forced to conclude that many of today's pulpits are filled with their fair share of curiosities, mediocrities, and even some atrocities. I've heard texts eisegeted rather than exegeted. I've seen preachers skirmish cleverly on the outskirts of a text, but never getting to its meaning and thrust. I've witnessed sermonic magic shows where a preacher keeps reaching into an empty hat, and extracting a handful of nothing. I've heard texts bludgeoned and battered; twisted and tortured into submission. I have sometimes felt when the preacher completed his sermonic surgery, he failed to rightly divide the Word of truth, and I half hoped that the text would rise up and sue the negligent preacher for exegetical and theological malpractice. Expository preaching is needed now in our churches more than ever.

I once heard Kent Hughes talk about "disexposition" in a lecture on preaching. He said disexposition occurs when we: 1) take a text and straightway depart there from; 2) preach the same basic sermon outline no matter what the text; 3) engage in "decontexted" preaching—taking the text out of context; 4) engage in "lensed preaching, such that most of our sermons focus on our hobby horses: domestic issues, political issues, eschatology, abortion, etc.); 5) engage in "moralizing," as, for example, when a sermon on Philippians 3:12–16 becomes a sermon on the importance of setting goals for your life. Expository preaching rightly done avoids these errors.

When I teach preaching, I like to explain the meaning of expository preaching as text-driven preaching in a three-fold way: preaching that attempts to stay true to the substance of the text, the structure of the text, and the spirit of the text.[28] The "substance" of the text is what the text is about (theme) and what is it saying about that theme. The "structure" of the text concerns the way in which the author develops the theme via syntax and semantics. A text has not only syntactical structure but also semantic structure, and the latter is what the preacher should be attempting to identify and represent in the sermon. The "spirit" of the text concerns the author-intended "feel" or "emotive tone" of the text which is influenced by the specific textual genre, such as narrative, expository, hortatory, poetic, etc. Given the nature and inspiration of Scripture, and what Scripture itself says about preaching, we are not just preaching sermons, we are preaching texts. Preaching should be "text-driven."

Sermon preparation for expository preaching that is truly text-driven involves two important things: **exegesis** and **exposition**. The term "exegesis" means "to lead out the meaning." Exegetical analysis of a text is the process or procedure we use to determine the meaning of a text. Here we examine the sentences, clauses, phrases, and words of the Scriptural text. We look at the conjunctions to determine how clauses and sentences are related

---

28. See Steven W. Smith, *Recapturing the Voice of God: Shaping Sermons Like Scripture* (Nashville: B&H Academic, 2015), who first used these descriptors several years ago.

to each other. We determine what clauses are independent and which ones are dependent grammatically.

The term "exposition" means "to explain the meaning." Exposition is what the preacher does in preaching the sermon such that he lays open a text in such a way that its original meaning is explained, illustrated, and applied—brought to bear on the lives of contemporary listeners.

Expository preaching also asks the questions: "what is the author's purpose of this text?" and "what does an author desire to accomplish with his text."[29]

The text-driven preacher is always attempting to accomplish something with every sermon. Preachers should always be preaching with three purposes in mind: (1) affect the ideas of people, (2) affect the emotions of people, and (3) affect the behavior of people. We should be attempting to affect the mind with the truth of scripture (doctrine). We should be attempting to affect the emotions of people because emotions are often (some would say always) the gateway to the mind. Finally, we should be attempting to affect the behavior of people by moving their will to obey the Word of God.

Expository preaching is at its best when the preacher preaches through a book of the Bible section by section and paragraph by paragraph. Each of the biblical books has a certain structure that is conveyed in large units composed of sections, paragraphs, and sentences. The expository preacher will analyze the structure of a given book of the Bible and then determine the best way to preach through that book based on its structure.

Let's take a New Testament letter as an example—1 John. When you look at the actual structure of this letter, its five chapters are composed of 20 paragraphs in the Greek text. When I preach through 1 John as a series, I have 20 sermons—one sermon per paragraph. When it comes to preaching

---

29. Abraham Kuruvilla has reminded us of the importance of this aspect of text analysis for preaching in his *Privilege the Text!: A Theological Hermeneutic for Preaching* (Chicago: Moody, 2013).

the New Testament letters, I advocate preaching not less than a single paragraph per sermon. The paragraph is a linguistic unit of meaning. To preach less than a paragraph is to miss all of the dynamics (meaning) that occur in any given paragraph. Sometimes the text will be best preached by covering two or three paragraphs in a single sermon. This is especially true when preaching the narratives of Scripture. Genesis 22:1-19 is a narrative unit that can only be preached as a whole. Otherwise, we truncate the text and miss the meaning. When it comes to meaning in a text, always remember this principle: "the whole is more than the sum of its parts."

Effective speech is not heard as separate sentences. Speech is heard as larger and more complex units of thought. If it cannot be fitted together into larger units, it cannot be fully comprehended. We not only hear in larger units, we speak in larger units when we talk naturally.

This is why it is better in my opinion, when preaching through books of the Bible, to make sure you always preach at least a paragraph unit of text.

Another important principle of expository preaching is to structure the sermon according to the main clauses and subordinate clauses in the text. Main points of the sermon should come from main clauses in the text. Sub-points should come from the subordinate material in the text. Here a careful observance of the participial clauses and conjunctions of a text will greatly aid in sermon preparation.[30]

---

30. Listen to these wise words from John Broadus: "One difficulty is the proper handling of the details in a text. If we simply take the topic and the heads (points) which the passage affords and proceed to discuss them in our own way, that is not an expository sermon....an expository sermon is one where the leading ideas and its details are suitably explained and made to furnish the chief material of the discourse. In order to manage this, we need to study the details thoroughly, so as to master them, instead of being oppressed by them....Then we must select and group. Here the inexperienced preacher often errs. Having minutely studied the details of the passage, he desires to remark upon a greater number of points than the limits of his discourse will allow. Thus it becomes so crowded that the hearer follows with annoying difficulty, and none of the numerous points presented have time to impress themselves upon his mind" (Broadus, *On the Preparation and Delivery*

Expository preaching teaches people how to read and interpret their Bible. It avoids the atomistic treatment of the Bible where one verse from the Old Testament is the text this week, and then a verse or two from the New Testament is the text for next week. Jumping from small text to small text week by week hinders the people from seeing the big picture of God's plan of salvation from Genesis to Revelation.

One reason why some preachers don't do expository preaching is they think it is too difficult to prepare and deliver such messages. I am reminded of what John Broadus, first president of Southern Seminary and author of one of the most famous books on preaching, said: "You will find expository preaching difficult only if you don't learn how to study the Bible."[31] If the preacher determines to preach through books of the Bible, and then outlines the book according to its paragraph structure, he will be able to see how the parts comprise the whole and not miss the forest for the trees.

What, then, does an expository sermon that is truly text-driven look like? The following characteristics are important:

1. The sermon is based on a text of Scripture, is about that text; is derived from the text; and explains the meaning of the text.

2. The sermon focuses on the textual theme as that theme is textually developed.

3. The sermon will only have as many "points" as the text has and those points are *always* drawn from the text.

4. Textual secondary information (all subordinate clauses, etc.) are developed in relation to the main clauses which convey the main point(s) in the text.

---

of Sermons, 149.)

31. John Broadus, *On the Preparation and Delivery of Sermons*, 148.

5. The sermon structure is based on the structure of the text.

6. The sermon application flows directly and exclusively from the text and is derived first from the main point(s) of the text, and then secondarily from the sub-points.

7. Creativity in the sermon is generally guided by the genre and textual clues of the text. Cogent illustrations will be used to com municate textual meaning.

8. The sermon will cover a natural thought unit, pericope, or para graph unit of text.

9. The sermon will surrender to the author's intended meaning and present that meaning in terms the audience understands.

10. Context is vital to the sermon's development.

CONCLUSION

Forty-plus years after the beginning of the SBC Conservative Resurgence in 1979, we have settled the question of the inerrancy of Scripture. However, the question of the sufficiency of Scripture remains up in the air for many as reflected in some of our preaching. Though expository preaching is taught in each of the six Southern Baptist seminaries, not all of our pastors are practicing expositors in their preaching. Danny Akin's warning in 2008 still rings true today:

> Skiing across the surface needs of a fallen, sinful humanity we have turned the pulpit into a pop-psychology side-show and a feel-good pit stop. We have neglected preaching the whole counsel of God's

Word and the theology of God's Word. Too many of our people know neither the content of Scripture nor the doctrines of Scripture. Preaching the cross of Christ and the bloody atonement accomplished by His death is the exception rather than the norm. Some simply want to be cute or edgy. Others choose to focus on politics, the emotions, or relationships, and the list goes on and on. If the Bible is used at all, it is usually as a proof-text out of context with no real connection to what the speaker is saying. Many who claim and perhaps believe they are expositors betray their confession by their practice.[32]

I'm afraid Dr. Akin is correct. And what more can I say, for time would fail me to tell of the many great preachers of the past,

of Paul, Peter and John, of Chrysostom and Augustine, of Wycliffe, Savanarola, Luther, Calvin, Wesley, Whitfield, Knox, Jasper, Moody, Spurgeon and King to name only a few, who through preaching, subdued kingdoms, stopped the mouths of critics, and launched reformations. Some were beheaded, others were crucified upside down, or exiled on a lonely isle in the Aegean Sea. Some were burned at the stake for their preaching, others languished in prisons, though the word of God which they preached was not bound. Some preached in pulpits and others in the fields. Some preached under the banner of Calvinism, others under the banner of a more Arminian persuasion. These all died preaching – either

---

32. Danny Akin, "A Crisis in 21st Century Preaching: a Mandate for Biblical Exposition," (Lecture delivered at SWBTS in 2008). He went on to state: "Unfortunately, in our therapeutic culture, where felt needs and how-to sermons are dominant and deemed essential, even by a number of evangelicals, text-driven preaching is viewed as simply inadequate for the day. On more than one occasion I have had a mega-church pastor or a church planter, who is a friend, tell me you cannot build a church in our context on expository preaching."

with tongue or pen or life. Therefore, seeing we are surrounded by a great cloud of preachers, and laying aside every inadequate view of language and any homiletical approach that does not properly acknowledge Scriptural authority, let us preach the word, having our eyes fixed on Jesus the Logos of God, who is indeed, according to Hebrews 1:1,2, God's final revelation.[33]

A high view of biblical authority creates a solid foundation for expositional preaching. The view of biblical authority advocated here requires that the umbrella term for preaching today should be the expository method. Listen to Haddon Robinson: "So if you ask why is expository preaching more important today, it is that we don't have the authority that preachers had in the past...Therefore in a postmodern age one reason that we work with the biblical text is to have the authority of the text—and behind that the authority of God—behind what we say."[34] Biblical exposition week after week from the pulpit is the logical outcome of a high view of biblical authority and the most effective means of fulfilling Paul's mandate to "Preach the Word!"

Preaching still matters.

---

33. David L. Allen, "A Tale of Two Roads: Homiletics and Biblical Authority," *JETS* 43.3 (2000), 513–14.
34. Michael Duduit, "Expository Preaching in a Narrative World: An Interview with Haddon Robinson," *Preaching*, vol. 17.1 (July/August, 2001), 4–5.

307

8

Does Gender Identity Still Matter?

Candi Finch

Have you seen the Joseph Backholm video that went viral several years ago? Backholm, who at the time was the Director of the Family Policy Institute of Washington, interviewed several college students on the campus of the University of Washington about his identity?[1] Clearly, he is an adult white male, less than 6 feet tall (5'9" to be exact). He asked several college students a series of questions about his identity:

"If I told you I was a woman, what would your response be?"

"If I told you I was Chinese, what would your response be?"

"If I told you that I was a 7-year-old, what would your response be?"

"If I told you I was 6'5", what would you say?"

If you have seen the short 4-minute video, you know it is surreal. The students were not willing to tell him he wasn't a woman or Chinese or a 7-year-old or 6'5" even though he is visibly not any of those things. One

---

1. Joseph Backholm's, "Gender Identity: Can a 5'9, White Guy Be a 6'5, Chinese Woman?" *Family Policy Institute of Washington*, April 13, 2016, video, 4:13, https://www.youtube.com/watch?v=xfO1veFs6Ho.

student was finally willing to tell him he wasn't 6'5" though she appeared very uncomfortable in doing so.

Backholm then asked, "Would you be willing to tell me I'm wrong?" Each student expressed *extreme* discomfort at the thought. One young lady felt it was not her place to tell other people if they were wrong or to draw lines or boundaries for them. Another student felt that as long as a person is not harming society, then it is fine for him to believe or behave any way he wants. The "you do you" and "I'll do me" mentality that has permeated our culture since the advent of postmodernism is clearly alive and well. Too many people have fallen for the lies that truth is relative, biology is meaningless, and gender is self-defined. *How did we get to this place?*

The answer to that question lies in the rise of gender ideology in the last half century. Rooted in the redefinition of the terms gender and sex, this worldview argues that differences between men and women are social constructs and not biologically established. Gender ideologues are found within the feminist, cultural Marxist, and LGBTQ communities.

In the opening chapter of Lewis Carroll's famous work, *Alice's Adventures in Wonderland*, young Alice sees a peculiar white rabbit and watches him plunge into a large hole under a bush. Carroll records: "In another moment down went Alice after it, *never once considering* how in the world she was to get out again."[2] That fateful decision to go down the rabbit hole takes Alice to places she never imagined. In the same way, the redefinition of sex and gender in both secular and religious circles has had a "down the rabbit hole" effect. Many people who have plunged headlong down the rabbit hole regarding sex, gender, and identity have arrived at a place unimaginable fifty years ago.

In this chapter, we will examine several specific battles that have been fought to promulgate gender ideology. Each battleground is critical on its own. However, when taken together, these battles have yielded *significant,*

---

2. Lewis Carroll, *Alice's Adventures in Wonderland* (Edina, MN: ABDO Publishing, 2005), 8, 10, italics added.

even *catastrophic*, results. In a culture where the concept of gender has increasingly lost any significance and meaning, we will explore the question, "Does gender still matter today?"

BATTLEGROUND # 1:
LANGUAGE

Do you remember hearing this nursery rhyme about boys and girls when you were a kid?

> What are little boys made of?
> Snips and snails
> and puppy dogs tails
> That's what little boys
> are made of!
> What are little girls made of?
> Sugar and spice and
> all things nice
> That's what little girls
> are made of!

This whimsical verse was originally written by the English poet Robert Southey sometime prior to his death in 1843 and subtlety reflects the idea that a person's biology (sex) has significance—it means something to be born a boy or a girl. Now, whether that rhyme reveals truth about what it means to be a boy or girl is a discussion for another day!

Unfortunately, during this same century, women and people of color were barred from some educational opportunities because of arguments based on biology. In 1872, the Women's Educational Society of Boston sought to enroll women at Harvard. Dr. Edmund Clarke, a Harvard professor, argued that if young women studied too much, they would divert blood from their uterus to the brain, rendering themselves "irritable and infertile." He concluded that women should not attend college based on his faulty and tragic understanding of biology.[3]

Close to a century later in the 1960s, a pivotal time arose for the discussion of biology, gender, and sex. Secular and religious feminists[4] and psychologists asserted "rights" and advanced gender ideologies that have contributed to the gender bending and gender confused society we find ourselves in today. In 1963 the American journalist Betty Friedan published the book, *The Feminine Mystique,* launching the second wave of secular feminism just in time for the cultural unrest that characterized America in the 1960s. Feminist activists became strategically involved in politics, the publishing industry, and higher education in order to give a voice to women's experience as the locus of truth.[5] A person's subjective experience was placed on the same level as objective truth, and women's experiences moved from being an informative source to being an authoritative norm.[6] Wom-

---

3. Sue Zschoche, "Dr. Clarke Revisited: Science, True Womanhood, and Female Collegiate Education," *History of Education Quarterly* 29, no. 4 (1989): 545-69.

4. For a brief discussion about the predecessors of feminist theology that arose during this time, see Rosemary Radford Ruether, "The Emergence of Christian Feminist Theology" in *The Cambridge Companion to Feminist Theology*, ed. by Susan Frank Parsons (New York: Cambridge University Press, 2002), 4-10; for a more thorough treatment, see Gerda Lerner's book, *The Creation of Feminist Consciousness: From the Middle Ages to Eighteen-Seventy* (New York: Oxford University Press, 1993).

5. Some good resources for studying the movement or "three waves" of secular feminism are Margaret Walters, *Feminism: A Very Short Introduction* (New York: Oxford University Press, 2005); Rory Dicker, *A History of U.S. Feminists* (Berkeley: Seal Press, 2008); and Gail Collins, *When Everything Changed: The Amazing Journey of American Women from 1960 to the Present* (New York: Little Brown and Company, 2009). Mary Kassian gives an excellent assessment of this movement from a Christian perspective in *The Feminist Mistake: The Radical Impact on the Church in Culture* (Wheaton: Crossway, 2005).

6. For a discussion on the inherent danger in this experiential hermeneuti-

en claimed the right to name and define themselves based on their own experiences.

Definitions do matter. Words matter. Dr. Clarke's faulty defining of women's biology impacted women's access to education for a time. Early feminist advocates realized that whoever controlled language had power. Simone de Beauvoir, a French philosopher and forerunner to the second wave of feminism, famously claimed that one is not born, but rather *becomes* a woman. She believed that biological determinism was harming women and that "social discrimination produces in women moral and intellectual effects so profound that they appear to be caused by nature."[7] Feminists began to seek to redefine what it means to be a woman in order to "liberate" women from biological determinism.

Kate Millett in her seminal work, *Sexual Politics*, said that differences between men and women are established in "essentially cultural, rather than biological bases" that result from differential treatment.[8] For her, the term gender meant "the sum total of the parents', the peers', and the culture's notions of what is appropriate to each gender by way of temperament, character, interests, status, worth, gesture, and expression."[9] In order to distinguish biological differences from social and psychological ones and to talk about the latter, feminists misappropriated the term gender and redefined it to reflect cultural norms regarding how one manifested biological sex.

Dale O'Leary in her book, *The Gender Agenda: Redefining Equality*, notes feminism's departure from a traditional understanding of gender.

---

cal approach, see George Lindbeck, *The Nature of Doctrine: Religion and Theology in a Postliberal Age* (Philadelphia: The Westminster Press, 1984), 30-45. Also, for a feminist theologian's perspective on women's experience as a source and norm in feminist theology, see Pamela Dickey Young, *Feminist Theology/Christian Theology: In Search of Method* (Minneapolis: Fortress Press, 1990), 46-69.

7. Simone de Beauvoir, *The Second Sex* (New York: Bantam Books, 1972 [original 1949]), 18.

8. Kate Millett, *Sexual Politics* (Chicago: The University of Illinois Press, 1970), 28-29.

9. Kate Millett, *Sexual Politics*, 31.

Feminists do not talk about the "sex" of a person anymore because the word "gender" has replaced "sex." This may seem like an innocent shift, but it is part of what O'Leary sees as the Gender Agenda.[10] If gender can be culturally constructed, then the gender of a person is not inherent within that person. By "deconstructing" gender, men and women can be "liberated." Kate Bornstein, a man who underwent a sex-change operation wrote, "Women couldn't be oppressed if there was no such thing as 'women.' Doing away with gender is key to doing away with patriarchy."[11]

However, it was psychologists writing on transsexuality who were the first to employ the term gender to refer to something other than masculine and feminine words (as in language studies) or as synonymous with biological sex. There is some disagreement about who first redefined the term. In 1968 psychologist Robert Stoller wanted to explain why some of his clients felt trapped in their own bodies. He used the term "sex" to refer to biological traits and "gender" to refer to how a person expressed femininity or masculinity. A transsexual, according to Stoller, was a person whose biology (sex) did not match the expression of his sex (gender).[12]

Dr. John Money, a psychologist and sexologist and "affectionate pedophilia" advocate, experimented on vulnerable children, causing at least two of his patients (twin boys) to commit suicide. He was one of the early practitioners of gender reassignment surgery and one of the early writers to employ such terms as "gender identity, gender role, and sexual orientation" so that one contemporary writer has dubbed him the man who "invented gender."[13]

---

10. Dale O'Leary, *The Gender Agenda: Redefining Equality* (Lafayette: Vital Issues Press, 1997), 11.

11. Kate Bornstein, *Gender Outlaw: On Men, Women and the Rest of Us* (New York: Rutledge, 1994), 115.

12. Robert Stoller, *Sex and Gender: The Development of Masculinity and Femininity* (New York: H. Karnac Books Ltd., 1968).

13. See Terry Goldie's book *The Man Who Invented Gender: Engaging the Ideas of John Money* (Vancouver: UBC Press, 2014).

Money believed that using a term like "sexual orientation" instead of "sexual preference" expressed the idea that maybe a person's sexual preference was, in fact, not a choice.[14] By introducing new terms and definitions into the cultural lexicon, psychologists like Money and Stoller and feminists like de Beauvoir and Millett were seeking control. They realized the power of words and that whoever controls language controls people.[15]

Consider some examples of shifts in language today: gender inclusive language instead of gender neutral language. Birthing persons instead of pregnant women. Parent 1 and Parent 2 instead of Mother and Father. Sex reassignment surgery to gender reassignment surgery to gender confirmation surgery to now gender affirming surgery. Gender identity disorder to gender dysphoria. Each shift of terms signals a distinct worldview regarding sex and gender. For example, the *Diagnostic and Statistical Manual of Mental Disorders-5* (DSM-5) shifted the term from Gender Identity Disorder to "Gender Dysphoria" in 2013 to remove the stigma associated with the term disorder. Do you catch the irony and sense how politicized gender ideology has become? In a book with "disorder" in the title, the authors chose to rename a mental disorder relating to gender to remove the stigma attached!

Conceptualizations of sex and gender have evolved quite a bit since the 1960s when the terms were divorced from each other. Current definitions by social theorists have expanded so that now gender supposedly represents several distinct things:

---

14. See John Money and Richard Green, *Transsexualism and Sex Reassignment* (Baltimore: John Hopkins University Press, 1969). For an earlier paper where Money started articulating his ideas about gender identity, see John Money, Joan G Hampson, and John Hampson, "An Examination of Some Basic Sexual Concepts: The Evidence of Human Hermaphroditism," Bull Johns Hopkins Hosp. Johns Hopkins University 97, no. 4 (October 1955): 301–19.

15. This concept is popularly attributed to Saul Alinsky and his work, *Rules for Radicals: A Pragmatic Primer for Realistic Radicals* (New York: Random House, 1971). An earlier version of his ideas were published as, *Reveille for Radicals* (Chicago: University of Chicago Press, 1946).

» Our bodies (gender biology)
» How we dress and act (gender expression)
» How we feel inside (gender identity).[16]

Sam Killermann's *A Guide to Gender: The Social Justice Advocates Handbook* expanded some of these terms in 2017 to include the following:

» Gender Identity – who you know yourself to be on the inside
» Gender Expression – what you present on the outside
» Anatomical Sex – the physical make-up of our bodies
» Attraction – the romantic and sexual ways some of us are drawn to others.[17]

Several visual representations of these categories have been produced in order to teach people about these new concepts regarding gender. I think the most grievous is the Gender Unicorn produced by Trans Students Educational Resources [TSER], which is aimed specifically at young children to teach them about gender ideology.[18] Killermann popularized and expanded the "Genderbread Person"[19] illustration, which was originally created by trans people:

---

16. For a discussion of the evolution of terms see https://www.genderspectrum.org/quick-links/understanding-gender/. Sam Killermann popularized the "Genderbread Person" as a way to distinguish the expressions of the term gender (expression, identity, biology) in his book *A Guide to Gender: The Social Justice Advocate's Handbook* (Austin: Impetus Books, 2013), 56-59. However, just a few years later, the terms relating to gender had evolved so rapidly that he needed to issue a second edition that included "spectrums" of the Genderbread Person (Austin: Impetus Books, 2017), 81-88. Another "guide" from a secular perspective on gender identity is Nicholas M. Teich's, *Transgender 101: A Simple Guide to a Complex Issue* (New York: Columbia University Press, 2012).

17. Killermann, *A Guide to Gender*, Second Edition, 71-79.

18. See https://transstudent.org/gender/.

19. Killermann, *A Guide to Gender*, Second Edition, 80.

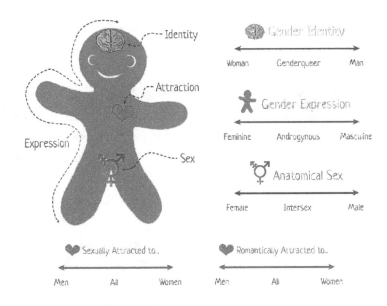

Within each of those four categories, Killermann said there is a spectrum or fluidity[20] because at the heart of gender ideology is a rejection of binaries like male and female so that now we have "non-binary" persons.[21]

---

20. Killermann, *A Guide to Gender*, Second Edition, 81-87.

21. In 2015, Megan DeFranza wrote *Sex Difference in Christian Theology: Male, Female, and Intersex in the Image of God* (Grand Rapids: William B. Eerdmans Publishing Company, 2015) where she critiques a strictly binary understanding of sex as male and female. For a critique of her work see Owen Strachan's response in *Understanding Transgender Identities: Four Views*, edited by James K. Bailey and Paul Rhodes Eddy (Grand Rapids: Baker Publishing Group, 2019), 179-183. As evangelical scholars have entered the discussion regarding gender identity, there has been a variety of academic resources produced in the last decade such as the two books noted above. See also Mark A. Yarhouse, *Understanding Gender Dysphoria: Navigating Transgender Issues in a Changing Culture* (Downers Grove: Intervarsity Press, 2015). For a more lay level treatment, see Vaughan Robert, *Transgender* (Charlotte, NC: The Good Book Company, 2016) or Ryan T. Anderson, *When Harry Became Sally: Responding to the Transgender Moment* (New York: Encounter Books, 2018) or Andrew T. Walker, *God and the Transgender Debate: What Does the Bible Actually Say About Gender Identity?* (Charlotte, NC: The Good Book Company, 2017).

So, within gender identity, Killermann argues that there is a spectrum ranging from female to genderqueer to male:

> How much one identifies with "woman" or "man" (or in-between) will be based on how a person aligns with the social roles, attitudes, dispositions, and/or personality traits that they associate with those identities. If, when pondering "man," and considering oneself, there's a 1:1 match (i.e., every trait that pops into mind for "man" also describes that person), odds are they identify strongly on the right side of the spectrum. It's important to note that many people consider their identity to fall outside of the binary (and limited) woman-to-man spectrum.[22]

Within gender expression, the spectrum ranges from feminine to androgynous to masculine. Yet, even within this spectrum, a person's expression is not static; it is fluid. Killermann explains, "Because gender expression is so fluid, a lot of folks will see themselves as a range of points on this spectrum, or as expressing in many ways depending on the situation."[23] For anatomical sex, the spectrum goes from female to intersex in the middle to male. And for attraction, the spectrum goes from women to "all" in the middle to men.

Super complicated, right? What God made very simple (male and female) has morphed into a giant, convoluted mess. There has been an explosion of terms. How gender identity, gender expression, sexual attraction, romantic attraction, and anatomical sex intersect in an individual person depending on how he chooses to define himself produces a dizzying number of options in the ever-expanding gender lexicon.

On February 13, 2014, Facebook's Diversity page released a post: "We want you to feel comfortable being your true, authentic self. An import-

22. Killermann, *A Guide to Gender*, Second Edition, 82.
23. Killermann, *A Guide to Gender*, Second Edition, 83.

ant part of this is the expression of gender, especially when it extends beyond the definitions of just male or female. So today, we're proud to offer a new custom gender option to help you better express your own identity on Facebook."[24] The "custom" gender options that people could select when setting up their profiles on Facebook included 56 options other than male or female![25] The list is growing, though, and by one count there are now over 100 custom gender options! The "LGBT" acronym (lesbian, gay, bi-sexual, and transgender) also has expanded to include queer, questioning, intersex, pansexual, two spirit, affirming, and allies, giving us LGBTQQIP2SAA as a "short-hand" way of referring to the gender movement. In fact, the rainbow "pride" flag which once represented the movement was updated to be more inclusive of the evolving identities. Now, there are at least 51 different pride flags to represent a person's expression of gender identity.[26]

The implications of claiming the power to name is a slippery slope. If we can define our own gender, does that also mean that we can define our own age, race, or even species? If you think that is a bridge too far or a boogeyman, fear tactic, take into consideration that people are making these very arguments. Rachel Anne Dolezal made headlines in 2015 when she was "outed" by her parents as a white woman. Rachel was president of a NAACP chapter in Washington and a civil rights activist who lived as

---

24. See https://www.facebook.com/facebookdiversity/about/.

25. The options Facebook listed back in 2014 were "Agender, Androgyne, Androgynous, Bigender, Cis, Cis Female, Cis Male, Cis Man, Cis Woman, Cisgender, Cisgender Female, Cisgender Male, Cisgender Man, Cisgender Woman, Female to Male, FTM, Gender Fluid, Gender Nonconforming, Gender Questioning, Gender Variant, Genderqueer, Intersex, Male to Female, MTF, Neither, Neutrois, Non-binary, Other, Pangender, Trans, Trans Female, Trans Male, Trans Man, Trans Person, Trans Woman, Trans*, Trans* Female, Trans* Male, Trans* Man, Trans* Person, Trans* Woman, Transfeminine, Transgender, Transgender Female, Transgender Male, Transgender Man, Transgender Person, Transgender Woman, Transmasculine, Transsexual, Transsexual Female, Transsexual Male, Transsexual Man, Transsexual Person, Transsexual Woman, Two-spirit."

26. See https://www.prideflags.org/.

a black woman and claimed she had been the victim of hate crimes. Borrowing the arguments of gender ideology, Dolezal argued in an interview that her racial identity as a black woman (who she felt she was inside) was not based on biology or ancestry: "I acknowledge that I was biologically born white to white parents, but I identify as black."[27] While some people critiqued Dolezal of cultural appropriation, the truth is that the cultural commentators did not have a leg to stand on because they had accepted the reasoning that human beings can define themselves. If people can define their gender, why not their race?

In 2018, Emile Ratelband of the Netherlands petitioned the courts to legally change his age because he identified as someone 20 years younger, but the courts denied his petition:

> "Mr. Ratelband is at liberty to feel 20 years younger than his real age and to act accordingly," the court said in a press release, NBC News reported. "But amending his date of birth would cause 20 years of records to vanish from the register of births, deaths, marriages and registered partnerships. This would have a variety of undesirable legal and societal implications." Ratelband is 69 years old, but he wanted to be 49 legally, The Associated Press reported. He likened his petition to those who have changed their name or gender.[28]

While the Dutch court correctly noted that allowing a person to legally change his age would have a variety of legal and societal implications,

---

27. Quoted in Sam Frizell's interview, "Rachel Dolezal: I Was Born White," *Time* (November 2, 2015), available at https://time.com/4096959/rachel-dolezal-white/.

28. See "Court Says No to Man Who Legally Wants to Change His Name" in *The Atlanta Journal-Constitution* (December 3, 2018), available at https://www.ajc.com/news/world/court-says-man-who-wanted-legally-change-his-age/JpYiFtUL2E3VLWbTJN29BJ/.

the same is true of allowing a person to change his gender, yet that battle appears to be surrendered. When President Biden assumed office, the contact page for the White House was updated on January 19, 2021, with a place for people to indicate what their preferred personal pronouns were.

Many feminists lauded the "brave" transition of former Olympic athlete Bruce Jenner to Caitlyn Jenner saying that his decision to transition "would have a tremendous impact on popular culture."[29] Just as feminists fought for the right to define what it means to be a woman, the logical outworking of their arguments would be to allow Bruce to define himself. However, when he was named *Glamour* magazine's "Woman of the Year," some feminists said that was going too far. Germaine Greer, a radical second-wave feminist, told the BBC: "I think misogyny plays a really big part in all of this, that a man who goes to these lengths to become a woman will be a better woman than someone who is just born a woman."[30] The problem for Greer and other feminists who objected to Jenner's award and those who objected to Dolezal's self identification as a black woman is that by accepting the idea that human beings can define themselves, they are facing the logical outworking of arguments they have championed.

This slippery slope has gotten even more bizarre in that there are people who identify so strongly with non-human species that they don't consider themselves human. They fall into two main groups:

» Otherkin – people who identify with mythical creatures. "If otherkin don't think of themselves as wholly human, what's the 'other' part?...Essentially the 'other' part of otherkin is exactly that,

---

29. Sarah Lyall and Jacob Bernsteinfeb,"The Transition of Bruce Jenner: A Shock to Some, Visible to All," *The New York Times* (February 6, 2015), see http://www.nytimes.com/2015/02/07/sports/olympics/the-transition-of-bruce-jenner-a-shock-to-some-visible-to-all.html?_r=0.

30. See https://www.lifesitenews.com/news/feminist-icon-germaine-greer-males-who-call-th,mselves-transgender-arent-wo/.

other than human. Some of the more prevalent kinds of otherkin include things such as animals [such as unicorns], fae [fictional supernatural beings], angels, and dragons, but the community includes far more than that, as the identity is anything other."[31]

»   Therian – people who identify with animals like wolves, dogs, cats, etc.[32]

If culture accepts that you can decide your own identity, then otherkins and therians are a logical outcome of that type of reasoning.

Pointing to the "extremes" as setting up a strawman or boogeyman type of argument has no weight in the current discussion because culture has embraced the extremes. Social commentators used to critique opposition to homosexuality that made any link to pedophilia a false link.[33] However, when "sexual attraction" or sexual preference or sexual orientation is a matter of one's own personal choice or makeup, (i.e., "I was born this way" or "I can't help who I love"), then that opens the door for adults to be attracted to children or even in more bizarre cases to inanimate objects like chandeliers.[34] Because culture embraced the idea that who a person loves is just natural or normal, it has lost any foundation for objecting to adults who say they are sexually attracted to children or inanimate objects. What once would have been diagnosed as mental illness is now shamefully embraced as natural.

---

31. See http://otherkin.com/who-and-what-are-otherkin/.

32. See https://therian-guide.com/index.php/2-therianthropy.html.

33. See Joe Kort's article, "Homosexuality and Pedophilia: A False Link," in the *Huffington Post* (October 15, 2012), available at https://www.huffpost.com/entry/homosexuality-and-pedophi_b_1932622.

34. For an example of stories of people who actually married the inanimate objects they were attracted to, see https://www.insideedition.com/gallery/meet-people-who-are-married-inanimate-objects-44311.

BATTLEGROUND # 2: EDUCATIONAL SYSTEMS AND MATERIALS

Just as controlling language and redefining definitions is a strategy for influencing culture, educational institutions from colleges and universities down to elementary schools are seen as breeding grounds for disseminating gender ideology. **"Educational institutions play an important part in most societies as agents of social control, cultural change, and, not least, social selection."**[35] **Nelson Mandela once famously recognized that** "education is the most powerful weapon which you can use to change the world."[36] **Using education is not a new strategy; the movements of cultural Marxism and feminism both have used educational institutions to their advantage. Believers cannot be blind to the battle raging in public educational spaces.**

Cultural Marxism is a branch of western Marxism and is also called critical theory, postmodernism, political correctness, or multiculturism. It is an ideology that says that all history has been determined by those in power because those in power create culture which then can construct and perpetuate inequalities. The inequalities relate to race, culture, religion, gender, and sexual orientation. Cultural Marxists often try to eradicate these inequalities by essentially manipulating and censoring culture, often by means of controlling education and mass media.

This movement began after World War I when two Marxist theorists, Antonio Gramsci in Italy and György Lukács in Hungary, concluded that until both the Christian religion and Western culture could be destroyed,

---

35. A.H. Halsey, "Education and Social Selection," *Power and Ideology in Education* (Oxford: Oxford University Press, 1977), 167.

36. Nelson Mandela made this statement in a speech he gave at the launch of the Mindset Network on July 16, 2003, at the University of the Witwatersrand in Johannesburg, South Africa. You can view a transcript of that speech here: http://db.nelsonmandela.org/speeches/pub_view.asp?pg=item&ItemID=NMS909.

communism would not flourish. That is, they believed economic Marxism could not prevail until cultural Marxism destroyed Western culture and the Christian religion. Where did these ideologues seek to disseminate their teachings? Herbert Marcuse, a leading cultural Marxists, who fled Germany in 1933, set his sights on American college students to convert them to his cultural Marxist ideas. Over his career he taught at Columbia, Harvard, Brandeis, and the University of California and popularized his worldview with his book, *Eros and Civilization*.[37]

In the same vein, when second-wave feminism gained ground in North America in the 1960s and 1970s, many key leaders recognized the strategic role that colleges and universities could play in influencing and indoctrinating the next generation.[38] One of the most fertile spaces for feminists to cultivate their ideologies has been within higher education. Christina Hoff Sommers traced the influence of the feminist agenda within the academy and points out that campuses are virtual breeding grounds for young feminists. "All indicators are that the new crop of young feminist ideologues coming out of our nation's colleges are even angrier, more resentful, and more indifferent to the truth than their mentors."[39]

Gender ideology is no different, yet we are seeing its teaching reach all the way down to the youngest students. Parents have weaponized their own children to push their own gender agendas. A UK based couple, Beck Laxton and Kieran Cooper, made news in 2012 when it was revealed that they had spent five years hiding the gender of their son Sasha. They were forced to "come out" publicly when they enrolled him in school. Sasha had an older sister and brother, but his mother decided to experiment with "gen-

---

37. Herbert Marcuse, *Eros and Civilization: A Philosophical Inquiry into Freud* (Boston: Beacon Press, 1955).

38. Mary Kassian's *The Feminist Mistake* provides an excellent summary of how feminism advanced through the halls of higher education, 141-155.

39. Christina Hoff Sommers, *Who Stole Feminism? How Women Have Betrayed Women* (Carmichael, CA: Touchstone Books, 1995, reprint ed.), 18.

der neutral" parenting with her third child. When Sasha headed to school, Laxton had to "put a label on her son's gender" because questions about which bathroom he would use and which uniform he would wear had to be answered.[40]

In 2013, a Colorado couple sued a school for the right of their first grade child Coy Mathis to use the girls' bathroom since he identified as transgender.[41] The Colorado Rights Division ruled in favor of the Mathis family against the Fountain-Fort Carson School District:

> The Transgender Legal Defense & Education Fund praised the ruling that was filed under Colorado's Anti-Discrimination Act. Michael Silverman, the group's executive director, called the ruling "a high-water mark for transgender rights." This is the first of its kind ruling in the country regarding the rights of transgender students. No court, no tribunal has ever said what the Colorado Division of Civil Rights has said today which is that transgendered students must be treated equally. They specifically referenced the outmoded concept of separate but equal and told us that separate but equal is very rarely equal and it is certainly not equal in Coy's case. Coy's mother, Kathryn Mathis, said she's pleased that Coy can return to school and put this behind her. The first-grader has been home schooled during the proceedings, "We're very thrilled that Coy is able to return to school and have the same rights that all the other girls had, that she should have had and was afforded by law to begin with. We're extremely happy that she's going to be treated equally and we thank the civil rights division for coming to

---

40. See https://www.dailymail.co.uk/news/article-2089474/Beck-Laxton-Kieran-Cooper-reveal-sex-gender-neutral-child-Sasha.html.

41. CNN Staff, "Transgender child barred from girls' restroom prompts complaint," *CNN* (February 27, 2013), https://www.cnn.com/2013/02/27/us/colorado-transgender-girl-complaint/index.html.

this conclusion," Kathryn Mathis said. "We're very grateful to the voters of Colorado for putting its laws into place to begin with."[42]

A decade ago, the stories of Sasha or Coy seemed like outliers. Where once gender activists were arguing for "tolerance," now no less than complete acceptance and adoption of gender ideology will be accepted. Legal battles are being fought with elementary schools as the arenas and children as the players in a high stakes game. School policies regarding transgender students vary in the United States. Some elementary schools are forcing teachers to refer to students by their preferred personal pronouns. An elementary school gym teacher in Virginia was put on leave in May 2021 for refusing to refer to transgender students by their preferred pronouns. Tanner Cross refused to abide by the "rights of transgender and gender-expansive students" policy that was put in effect in his county. At a meeting of the Loudoun County Public Schools, Cross spoke out:

"My name is Tanner Cross and I am speaking out of love for those who are suffering from gender dysphoria," the Leesburg Elementary teacher said, according to video posted online.

He referred to the recent "60 Minutes" special which highlighted teens who were now "de-transitioning" after rushing their decisions.

"It's not my intention to hurt anyone, but there are certain truths that we must face when ready," he told the board, which has already bitterly divided parents and educators by pushing critical race theory.

"I love all of my students, but I will never lie to them regardless of the consequences…I'm a teacher, but I serve God first, and I will not affirm that a biological boy can be a girl and vice versa because it's against my

42. Ed Payne, "Transgender first-grader wins the right to use girls' restroom," *CNN* (June 24, 2013), https://www.cnn.com/2013/06/us/colorado-transgender-girl-school/index.html#:~:text=The%20Transgender%20Legal%20Defense%20%26%20Education%20Fund%20praised,the%20country%20regarding%20the%20rights%20of%20transgender%20students.

religion….It's lying to a child, it's abuse to a child, and it's sinning against our God," he said.[43]

The Virginia Supreme Court upheld a lower court's ruling that Cross be reinstated in August 2021, yet the outcome is still uncertain. The Loudoun School district argued that they based their policies on Virginia's Department of Education's directives for the treatment of transgender students in elementary and secondary school and are simply enforcing state-mandated policies for public education.[44] Cross and two other Loudoun country teachers have sued the school district for their policies, and the outcome of this case could prove to be a landmark for other schools, teachers, and parents facing state-mandated transgender policies.[45]

Cross noted that accepting the policy is harmful for children, yet segments of American society appear dead set on advancing the narrative that transgenderism is a natural choice not a disorder. Books like *Beyond Magenta* aimed at educators and parents have been published to help people understand "the fluidity of gender and sex."[46] The explosion of resources aimed at teens and parents is unbelievable.[47] However, the books aimed at young children are the

---

43. Lee Brown, "Gym teacher put on leave after refusing to use preferred pronouns for transgender students" in *New York Post* (May 28, 2021), https://nypost.com/2021/05/28/gym-teacher-put-on-leave-after-refusing-to-call-transgender-students-by-preferred-pronouns/.

44. You can access the 28 page policy at https://equalityvirginia.org/wp-content/uploads/2021/03/Transgender-Student-Model-Policies-March-2021-final.pdf

45. Douglas Blair, "3 teachers now suing Virginia School System over Transgender Pronouns," *The Daily Signal* (August 31, 2021), https://www.dailysignal.com/2021/08/31/3-teachers-now-suing-virginia-school-system-over-transgender-pronouns/.

46. Susan Kuklin, *Beyond Magenta: Transgender Teens Speak Out* (Somerville, MA: Candlewick Press, 2014), 165.

47. Consider just some of the books published over the last decade: Irwin Krieger, *Helping Your Transgender Teen: A Guide for Parents* (New Haven: Gender-

most alarming. One author wrote *A is for Activist* for his young son to teach him the ABCs with more "inclusive" words and images:

The "L" Page:

L-G-B-T-Q!
Love who you choose,
'cuz Love is true!
Liberate your notions of Limited emotions.
Celebrate with pride, our Links of devotion.

The "T" Page:

T is for Trans.
For Trains, Tiaras,
Tulips, Tractors, and Tigers Too!
Trust in the True,
The he she They That is you![48]

One mother wrote a children's picture book called *My Princess Boy* to encourage children to express their "authentic" self and accept others for who they are and how they wish to look.[49] Toy companies have joined the

---

wise Press, 2011). Arin Andrews, *Some Assembly Required: The Not-So-Secret Life of a Transgender Teen* (New York: Simon and Schuster, 2014); this book is written by a girl who decided to have gender reassignment surgery as a junior in high school. Diane Ehrensaft, *Gender Born, Gender Made: Raising Healthy Gender-Nonconforming Children* (New York: The Experiment, 2011).

48. Innosanto Nagara, *A is for Activist* (New York: Seven Stories Publications, 2013).

49. Cheryl Kilodavis, *My Princess Boy: A Mom's Story About a Young Boy Who Loves to Dress Up* (New York: Aladdin, 2011).

bandwagon as well. In 2019 the toy company Mattel, best known for creating Barbie, launched its first gender neutral doll in the "Creatable World series" with the slogan, "A doll line designed to keep labels out and invite everyone in." In 2021, the Mr. Potato Head toy with the Hasbro toy company went gender neutral by dropping the "Mr." from its name in order to reflect contemporary sensibilities.

Whether on college or elementary school campuses or in children's books or educational literature or in toys used for play, it is clear that contemporary society is more accepting of gender ideology than it was even a decade ago. What took decades for homosexual advocacy to accomplish has been accomplished in a fraction of the time with transgender advocacy. Abigail Shirer's groundbreaking 2020 book, *Irreversible Damage: The Transgender Craze Seducing Our Daughters*, rings out the call for society to consider the damage being done to young women with its wholesale acceptance of transgenderism. Shirer, an Oxford University and Yale Law School educated free lance journalist, noted a sudden spike in the 2010s of teenage girls with transgender identification. She attributes this to a social contagion in a demographic of teen girls who fell prey to disorders like anorexia or bulimia in previous generations.[50] When I was growing up, if a girl liked typical boy activities or styles of dress, she may have been called a "tomboy." However, through the manipulation of language and the advocacy of educational institutions, today a young child may be told she is really a boy and encouraged to live that way, take hormones, and even get surgery to alter her body. What incredibly tragic lunacy!

Dr. Joe McIlhaney, a board-certified obstetrician and gynecologist, observed over his decades long career caring for girls and women that Western culture has stopped protecting its girls. He

---

50. Abigail Shirer, *Irreversible Damage: The Transgender Craze Seducing Our Daughters* (Washington, DC: Regnery Publishing, 2020).

argued that we have abandoned our protective role for young women, especially in regards to guiding them in male-female relations, romance, love, sex, marriage, etc. Young women are made to grow up *much too* quickly—clothing stores advertise push-up bra bathing suits for 7 to 9-year-olds, 12-year-olds can buy shorts with "sexy" written across the backside, and Hollywood in programs geared to teens and young adults often glamorizes the idea of young women who are sexually aggressive and loose.

Like Shirer, McIlhaney rang out the alarm for how culture is damaging its youngest—in his case he examined the impact, both physically and emotionally, that America's sexualized culture is having on young women.[51] The back cover of Dr. McIlhaney's book, *Girls Uncovered*, states, "Our daughters live in a culture that sees sex as both a sacred right to be exercised with anyone, at any time, and also as 'no big deal.' This culture of 'hooking up' among teens and young adults is no longer a secret." And, it is having disastrous and long-term effects on our young women. Since the sexual revolution erupted in America in the 1960s decades before the current transgender revolution, more data is available on what hypersexualization does to young women. However, it is clear that gender ideology is taking our children down "the rabbit hole," and the long-term consequences are yet to be fully realized.

---

51. If you are interested in learning more about this subject, see two books by Joe McIlhaney and Freda McKissic Bush called *Girls Uncovered: New Research on What America's Sexual Culture Does to Young Women* (Chicago: Northfield Publishing, 2011) and *Hooked: New Science on How Casual Sex is Affecting Our Children* (Chicago: Northfield Publishing, 2008).

BATTLEGROUND # 3:
MASS MEDIA AND POP CULTURE

I am firmly convinced that the transgender agenda has infiltrated our society so rapidly in part because of the weaponizing of mass media and the influence of pop culture. When I started high school, it was a big transition in my life. I was moving from the small, private school that I had attended for my entire childhood to a large, public high school. One of my first days of school another student shouted an obscene word loudly in the hallway in between class periods.

Immediately, I stopped in my tracks. I was shocked! At my old school, such behavior would have gotten him sent straight to the principal's office. And the principal, an Episcopalian priest, would have caned him on the hands pretty severely for such an infraction. However, teachers in the hall didn't say a word. Everybody just went on about their day. The shocking thing that day was that I was the only one shocked.

When I was about to graduate high school, I heard two kids cursing in the hallway, and I remembered that incident from my freshman year. After four years, someone cursing at school just seemed commonplace because I had seen it happen over and over and over again. *Continued exposure to something takes away the shock value.* Mass media works in a similar way in influencing public opinion. The media's reach is extensive (think TV, movies, internet, radio, newspapers, books, magazines, social media, advertising, etc.). Maxwell McCombs in *Setting the Agenda: The Mass Media and Public Opinion* notes: "The mass media are teachers whose principal strategy of communication is redundancy."[52] By exposing people to the same idea over

---

52. Maxwell McCombs, *Setting the Agenda: The Mass Media and Public Opinion* (Malden, MA: Blackwell Publishing Inc., 2004), 47.

and over and over again, what once was shocking becomes commonplace. What once skirted the margins becomes mainstream.

Think about sexuality. While different forms of media have unquestionably simply *reflected* already shifting perspectives on sexuality over the last few decades, media has also played a role in *swaying* perspectives. Biblical sexuality—the idea of one man and one woman joining in an exclusive, life-long union of marriage and the idea that marriage is the only appropriate setting for sexual intimacy—is a shocking concept in our culture today. What the Bible calls sin in regards to sexuality (sex outside of marriage, 1 Thess 4:3; adultery, Ex 20:14; lust, Matt 5:27-28; and homosexuality, Rom 1:27) is now often the new normal.

The debut issue of the magazine, *Entertainment Weekly*, in 1990 was considered "boundary-breaking" because it featured K.D. Lang, a gay country singer, on the cover. On its 25th anniversary in 2015, the magazine noted that such a cover "couldn't be any less shocking" today.[53] Again, continued exposure to something takes away the shock value. The fact that media is swaying popular opinion cannot be denied. However, now more and more writers, actors, directors, and producers are openly acknowledging using media to advocate for gender ideology. Consider just some of the "boundary-breaking" forms of entertainment of the last decade.

How to Get Away with Murder (Primetime TV Show) was the highest-rated new show of fall 2014 and was called provocative and groundbreaking in part because of its "depiction of sexuality."[54] Pete Nowalk, the show's creator and a gay man himself, states: "I want to put things on TV that people haven't seen before, so if that makes it progressive, that's great....I'm just writing what my life experience is like. To me, it's just

---

53. Stephanie Schomer, "EW Turns 25," *Entertainment Weekly* (February 13, 2015), 19.

54. Tim Stack, "How to Get Away With the Most Provocative Show on Television," *Entertainment Weekly* (October 31, 2014), 8-9.

contemporary."[55] Tim Stack, a writer for *Entertainment Weekly*, notes, "Part of Nowalk's goal in writing the [promiscuous homosexual] character is to destigmatize gay sex on TV."[56] Nowalk contends: "Visibility leads to acceptance."[57]

In its 2014 "Year in Review" Issue, *Entertainment Weekly* noted that 2014 was the year that TV transformed the way we think:

> It's easy to believe that pop culture has the power to change the world. It's rare to witness that change in real time, but that's what happened. Across the country, our minds were opened to the varied experiences of transgender people by watching television. Laverne Cox—Litchfield's beloved hairdresser, Sophia, on *Orange is the New Black*—endeared herself to both inmates and the Television Academy, becoming the first openly trans actor nominated for an Emmy. Then on Amazon, the new drama *Transparent*, about a transgender woman named Maura (Jeffrey Tambor) and her troubled family, was a hit with viewers and was hailed as one of fall's best TV shows by many critics. On Broadway, Neil Patrick Harris sold out early his entire run in the musical *Hedwig and the Angry Inch* and won a Tony award for starring as the title character, a trans singer in a glam-rock band. These fully formed roles suggested that trans people aren't heroes or villains. They're just human.[58]

---

55. Stack, "How to Get Away With the Most Provocative Show on Television," 9.

56. Stack, "How to Get Away With the Most Provocative Show on Television."

57. Stack, "How to Get Away With the Most Provocative Show on Television."

58. Melissa Maerz, "TV Transformed the Way We Think," *Entertainment Weekly* (December 12, 2014), 24.

Laverne Cox, a male actor who now lives as a woman, made waves for his role as a transgender person in *Orange is the New Black*, but also because he was the first openly transgender actor nominated for an Emmy. *Time* magazine named his TV character the 4th most influential character of 2013 and featured him on the cover in 2014 under the headline "The Transgender Tipping Point."[59] Cox has used his "celebrity to give trans activism a public forum."[60] MTV showed a documentary special in October 2014 that was hosted by Cox that chronicled "the challenge and triumphs of seven transgender youths as they navigate varying stages of transitioning."[61]

In January 2016 many in the world mourned the passing of musical icon and innovator David Bowie from liver cancer. The influence of Bowie's 1970s, androgynous, glam rock alter ego, Ziggy Stardust, lives on in contemporary discussions about gender and gender identity, even if you are not a child of the 70s or if you would rather just forget the era that brought the world lava lamps and bell bottom pants. Within the swirling social discussions on gender in the 1970s, glam rock entered the mix, and David Bowie became one of its most acclaimed practitioners. Glam rock, also called glitter rock, "began in Britain in the early 1970s and celebrated the spectacle of the rock star and concert. Often dappled with glitter, male musicians took the stage in women's makeup and clothing, adopted theatrical personas, and mounted glamorous musical productions frequently characterized by space-age futurism."[62]

This style of music and performance was regularly called "gender bending" or "gender rebellion." The lyrics often touched on taboo topics and pushed the boundaries of sexual norms as seen in Bowie's song "All the

<hr>

59. See Laverne Cox's bio on her webpage: http://www.lavernecox.com/bio-2/. See also "The Transgender Tipping Point," *Time* (May 29, 2014).

60. Maerz, "TV Transformed the Way We Think," 24.

61. "Must List," *Entertainment Weekly* (October 24, 2014), 9.

62. See http://www.britannica.com/art/glam-rock.

Young Dudes" that became a glam rock anthem (he wrote this song for Mott the Hoople):

> *Now Lucy looks sweet*
> *'cause he dresses like a queen*
> *But he can kick like a mule*
> *it's a real mean team…*

Feminist scholar Camille Paglia, author of, *Sexual Personae*, reflected on the impact of Bowie on her own life:

> Bowie's Ziggy Stardust period in the early 1970s had a staggering influence on me. I had been writing about androgyny in literature and art in my term papers in college and grad school, so Bowie's daring experiments seemed like the living embodiment of everything I had been thinking about.[63]

Ziggy Stardust for Paglia was a "bold, knowing, charismatic creature neither male nor female" and viewing one of his costumes for her was "a sacred epiphany, like seeing a splinter from the True Cross."[64] In fact, another columnist noted that David Bowie's Ziggy Stardust "paved the way for future generations of androgynous, gender-bending icons in pop," and Bowie himself will always be remembered as a "barrier-busting hero who acted as an avatar for gender fluidity before that was even a term."[65]

---

63. David Daley, "'A bold, knowing, charismatic creature neither male nor female': Camille Paglia remembers a hero, David Bowie," *Salon.com* (January 12, 2016), http://www.salon.com/2016/01/12/a_bold_knowing_charismatic_creature_neither_male_nor_female_camille_paglia_remembers_a_hero_david_bowie/.

64. David Daley, "'A bold, knowing, charismatic creature neither male nor female.'"

65. Kyle Anderson, "David Bowie," *Entertainment Weekly* (January 22, 2016), 29.

335

Bowie's gender activism continued throughout his career even though he retired his Ziggy Stardust persona after only a few years. In 2014, he appeared in a PSA that proclaimed, "Gender is between your ears, not between your legs."[66] Remembering Bowie, Madonna commented that she "was so inspired by the way he played with gender confusion. [He] was both masculine and feminine."[67] Martin Scorsese, who directed Bowie in *The Last Temptation of Christ*, said that Bowie has "left a deep imprint on the culture."[68]

Unfortunately, the glam rock movement of the 1970s is not very different from the gender rebellion movement we see today through the likes of Bruce Jenner. Glam rock sought to defy sexual stereotypes through sexual and gender ambiguity and androgyny. The leaders essentially desired to thumb their noses at constructed understandings of sex and gender. *They wanted to define themselves.*

Pharrell Williams, a popular singer and songwriter, was featured on the cover of the November 2019 issue of GQ's "The New Masculinity Issue: An Exploration of Identity, Culture, and Style in 2019." As masculinity became increasingly defined as "toxic" in 2018, there was a mainstreaming of pop culture icons expressing "feminine styles" and wearing makeup. Pharrell describes himself as gender fluid in his gender expression.[69] Harry Styles, a British pop singer and actor and former member of the boy band One Direction, made history in 2020 for being the first ever male star to grace cover of the fashion magazine *Vogue* for its December 2020 issue. Styles was wearing a dress on the cover, and the headline read, "Harry Styles

---

66. Kyle Anderson, "David Bowie," 29.

67. Interview with Kyle Anderson, "David Bowie," *Entertainment Weekly* (January 22, 2016), 30.

68. Interview with Kyle Anderson, "David Bowie," 33.

69. Will Welch, "Evolver: Pushing the Masculinity Conversation Forward with One of Pop Culture's Most Influential Futurists, Pharrell Williams" in GQ (November 2019), 70-82, 124.

Makes His Own Rules." Terms like gender expansive, gender fluidity, and genderqueer are just some of the new entries into the current lexicon to describe men like Williams and Styles.

David Bowie's gender rebellion in the 1970s clearly paved the way for the gender fluidity movement of our day. His legacy is found in comments like the 2015 statement by the television network ABC Family when it changed its name to Freeform. Why pick the name Freeform? The elusiveness is what the station found alluring: "The audience's identity and experience are fluid as they explore endless possibilities and their passions take shape," the press release said. "Freeform personifies this fluidity and will deliver ideas, forms of content and ways of interacting with the brand."[70]

Or, consider the Disney starlet Rowan Blanchard, who starred in *Girl Meets World*. This 14-year-old teen and self-proclaimed feminist activist declared herself "queer" in a tweet because she didn't want to be labeled. Blanchard tweeted, "In my life – only ever liked boys…However I personally don't wanna label myself as straight, gay or whateva so I am not gonna give myself labels to stick with – just existing." In a follow-up to that tweet, she said, "Yes open to liking any gender in future is why I identify as queer."[71] *Time* magazine named Blanchard one of the 30 most influential teens of 2015.[72]

Miley Cyrus, a singer and the one-time Disney star of the show *Hannah Montana*, spoke about her sexuality in an issue of *Elle UK*, telling the magazine, "I'm very open about it — I'm pansexual. But I'm not in a rela-

---

70. Josef Adalian, "ABC Family Is Changing Its Name to … Freeform?" *Vulture* (October 6, 2015), https://www.vulture.com/2015/10/abc-family-is-changing-its-name-to-freeform.html.

71. Rebecca Rose, "*Girl Meets World* Star Rowan Blanchard Opens Up to Fans: 'I Identify as Queer,'" *Cosmopolitan* (January 18, 2016), see http://www.cosmopolitan.com/entertainment/news/a52308/rowan-blanchard-identifies-as-queer/.

72. http://time.com/4081618/most-influential-teens-2015/#4081618/most-influential-teens-2015/.

tionship…I'm going on dates, but I change my style every two weeks, let alone who I'm with."[73] Posing nude for the 2015 summer music edition of *Paper* magazine, Cyrus spoke about identifying as gender fluid and her open view of sexuality: "I am literally open to every single thing that is consenting and doesn't involve an animal and everyone is of age," she said. "Everything that's legal, I'm down with. Yo, I'm down with any adult — anyone over the age of 18 who is down to love me. I don't relate to being boy or girl, and I don't have to have my partner relate to boy or girl."[74]

JoJo Siwi, a singer, dancer, and teenage TV personality, came out as gay on TikTok in January 2021 by dancing to Lady Gaga's 2011 hit song *Born this Way*. Siwi will be featured on the reality dancing competition *Dancing with the Stars* as part of the franchise's first same-sex dancing team during the fall 2021 season.

Pansexuality, gender fluid, queer—when pop culture icons use these terms just consider the impact. Today, if you or your children or your grandchildren grow up watching shows like *Hannah Montana* or *Girl Meets World* or *Dancing with the Stars* and like the personalities, you have instant access to them through social media platforms like Instagram, TikTok, Twitter, YouTube, etc. When they espouse worldviews and gender ideology, it has a normalizing effect, taking away the "shock" value.

---

73. Lena de Casparis, "Miley Cyrus Is ELLE's October Cover Star," *Elle UK* (August, 27, 2015), https://www.elle.com/uk/life-and-culture/news/a27013/miley-cyrus-elle-uk-october-2015/.

74. See Caven's Sieczkowski, "Miley Cyrus Talks Fluid Sexuality, Homelessness And Fundamentalism In NSFW Paper Mag Spread," *Huffpost* (June 9, 2015), https://www.huffpost.com/entry/miley-cyrus-sexuality-paper-magazine_n_7543810. I have included the link to the *Huffpost* interview (which does include some vulgarity) instead of the direct link to the *Paper* interview because of the images included in the *Paper* link.

BATTLEGROUND # 4:
CHRISTIANITY

The final battleground we need to discuss, albeit briefly, is Christianity. As language has been redefined, educational institutions have become breeding grounds for disseminating gender ideology, and mass media has become weaponized to mainstream gender ideology, a significant, yet tragic battleground is the measure to which Christians have embraced gender ideology. Some religious feminist writers have charged religion with being an oppressive force in the lives of women. For suffragist and first wave feminist, Elizabeth Cady Stanton, all religions provided a framework that enabled the oppression of women to be proliferated. Until those religions were rehabilitated, no lasting freedom would come for women.[75]

This nineteenth-century social reformer provided Elisabeth Schüssler Fiorenza, a Harvard Divinity School professor and pioneer in the field of feminist theological studies, with the model of a "professed" Christian who was not afraid to address directly the perceived role that Christianity and the Bible played in women's and minorities' (sexual, racial, socio-economic, etc.) oppression and then call for a change. However, the development of Schüssler Fiorenza's own critique of religion, and Christianity in particular, was nothing less than a reimagining of Christianity and God's Word:

> It is therefore time to call publicly to repentance anyone, be it man or women, clergy or lay, who espouses sexism as a Christian value. We have to do this not because women want to be ordained into patriarchal church structures, not because women want a share in the "ecclesiastical pie," but because the credibility of the Christian

---

75. Elizabeth Cady Stanton, *The Woman's Bible: A Classic Feminist Perspective* (New York: Dover Publications, 2002; originally published in two volumes published in 1895 and 1898 respectively), Part I, 12.

gospel and church is at stake. In doing so we have to follow Jesus, who paid for his resistance to the religious and cultural establishment of his day with his life. *We have to follow Jesus, who broke religious law because he cared for the weak, the sick, the outcasts, and women.*[76]

Schüssler Fiorenza's argument is that the witness and credibility of the church was hindered when anything she defined as "sexist" or oppressive was allowed to continue to impact Christianity regardless of what the Bible taught. To borrow popular phraseology, Schüssler Fiorenza saw this as a "gospel issue." For example, she argued that oppression occurs when a person articulates a heterosexual understanding of biblical sexuality, hindering those who identify as homosexual from pursuing their authentic self.[77] Schüssler Fiorenza's feminist ideology fed her gender ideology.

Within progressive Christianity there has been an embrace of this worldview as well. In 2010 the documentary, *Thy Will Be Done: A Transsexual Woman's Journey Through Family and Faith*, was released that followed the journey of Sara Herwig, a man who was a male to female transsexual who sought ordination in the Presbyterian Church USA. The documentary portrayed "the organized Christian Church, with all its political and financial power, as one of the fiercest battlegrounds for LGBT rights and gender recognition."[78] Sara is cast as an empathetic hero who not only seeks "to participate in the ministry as an openly transgendered person, but as an activist who seeks to transform a world—spiritual and otherwise—that operates by conventional notions of sex and gender."[79]

---

76. Elisabeth Schüssler Fiorenza, *Discipleship of Equals: A Critical Feminist Ekklēsia-logy of Liberation* (New York: Crossroads, 1993), 150, italics added.

77. Elisabeth Schüssler Fiorenza, *Transforming Vision: Explorations in Feminist The*logy* (Minneapolis: Fortress Press, 2011), 100.

78. Quote taken from *Thy Will Be Done* the documentary produced by New Day Films, available at https://www.newday.com/film/thy-will-be-done-transsexual-womans-journey-through-family-and-faith.

79. *Thy Will Be Done.*

In 2015, I attended the inaugural "Why Christian?" conference organized by progressive Christians Rachel Held Evans and Nadia Bolz-Weber.[80] Over the course of a couple days, I heard testimony after testimony of people who answered the question of why they were a Christian, when, as Rachel Held Evans said, "Why—with all the atrocities past and present committed in God's name, amidst all the hostile divisions ripping apart Christ's Church, in spite of all our own doubts and frustrations and fears about faith—are we still Christian? Why do we still have skin in the game?"[81]

Daniel Robinson, who goes by the name Allyson Dylan Robinson and who presided over Bruce Jenner's naming ceremony when he transitioned to the name Caitlyn, was the first openly transgender person ordained in a Baptist Church. When it was his turn to present at the conference, he said, "I have some problems with God. God hurt me...It is in God's very nature to allow bad things to happen to people. God has the compassion of a slum-

---

80. Rachel Held Evans died at the age of 37 in May 2019. She was a active critic of evangelical Christianity through social media, blogs, and her books. In August 2021, Rev. Nadia Bolz-Weber was installed as the Evangelical Lutheran's Church first Pastor of Public Witness in part for her work in advocating for gender ideology, see https://um-insight.net/in-the-church/ordained-ministry/nadia-bolz-weber-installed-as-elca-s-first-pastor-of-public-/. An admitted provocateur, Bolz-Weber had a drag queen on staff as a "minister of fabulousness" at the church she founded called the House for All Sinners and Saints, and in 2018 she sent out a call for women to send her their purity rings, which she melted down and formed into a vagina statue to make it a source of healing as opposed to, according to her, the harmful "purity culture" she was raised in within her fundamentalist, Christian church. In 2019 she published *Shameless: A Sexual Reformation* (New York: Convergent Books, 2019). The book argues for alternative interpretations of biblical passages about sexual ethics (sex outside of marriage is no problem for her) and gender in order to allow all people, regardless of gender biology (she believes there is more than just male and female), gender identity, or gender expression to experience sexual flourishing, 1–13.

81. Rachel Held Evans, "On Giving Testimony: Why 'Why Christian?' Worked" (October 6, 2015), https://rachelheldevans.com/blog/why-christian-conference-recap.

lord....Why am I a Christian? I don't know."[82] As the audience cheered for Robinson possibly for his unguarded moment of "authenticity," I felt such grief for this individual who, though dearly loved by God, felt so far from Him.

Author Matthew Vines also spoke at the conference, and Rachel Held Evans lauded Vines as "one of my generation's most important Christian leaders, not only on matters of sexuality but also on what it means to follow Jesus with wisdom, humility, and grace."[83] His book, *God and the Gay Christian*, represents just one in the plethora of books advocating for gender ideology. Like Schüssler Fiorenza, Vines correlates advocacy for gender ideology with gospel faithfulness: "As more believers are coming to realize, affirming our gay brothers and sisters isn't simply one possible path Christians can take. It isn't just a valid option. This kind of love and affirmation—regardless of sexual orientation or gender identity—is, in fact, a requirement of Christian faithfulness."[84]

---

82. Transcribed from my own notes from the conference. You can read about his journey here: https://www.christiantoday.com/article/meet-allyson-robinson-the-first-openly-transgender-baptist-minister/75672.htm.

83. Matthew Vines, *God and the Gay Christian: The Biblical Case in Support of Same-Sex Relationships* (New York: Convergent Books, 2014), frontmatter.

84. Vines, *God and the Gay Christian,* 178. A similar book of a young man who grew up within the evangelical church and then came out as gay is by Justin Lee, *Torn: Rescuing the Gospel from the Gays -Vs.-Christians Debate* (New York: Jericho Books, 2012). For a sampling of gender advocacy works by progressive Christians, see Rachel Murr, *Unnatural: Spiritual Resiliency in Queer Christian Women* (Eugene, OR: Resource Publications, 2014). See also Virginia Ramey Mollenkott and Vanessa Sheridan, *Transgender Journeys* (Cleveland: The Pilgrim Press, 2003). Mollenkott's own journey represents and reflects the changing cultural lexicon. In 1978, she co-authored a book, *Is the Homosexual My Neighbor?* At the time, Mollenkott had not publicly come out as a lesbian, though the work advocated on behalf of homosexuals. When the book was reissued in 1994, Mollenkott identified publicly as a lesbian. However, towards the end of her life, she identified as transgender or bi-gender, saying she "identified as male and female" in and interview with David E. Weekley, "Becoming Grateful Allies: An Interview with Dr. Virginia Ramey Mollenkott" in the *Journal of Feminist Studies in Religion* (34, no. 1, Spring 2018): 25-36.

Within evangelical Christianity, when a person begins to question the Bible's teachings regarding homosexuality, it often serves as a catalyst to question the trustworthiness or inerrancy of God's Word. Well-known "Christian celebrity" Jen Hatmaker, who was once platformed by Lifeway Christian Resources, the publishing arm of the Southern Baptist Convention, caused waves when she expressed an affirming position regarding LGBTQ relationships in 2016. In 2021, Jonathan Merritt, son of pastor and former president of the Southern Baptist Convention James Merritt, came out on Instagram as homosexual so he could live as his authentic self:

> In 2012, just days before my 30th birthday, I was publicly and painfully outed by a person who had earned my trust only to betray it. It took many months and a boatload of therapy to process the trauma of that experience—and to learn to love the delightful human that God made when God made me.
>
> Some of you may not know this part of my story. I have learned to live authentically in my personal life, sharing with friends the fullness of who I am. But the experience of being outed left me bruised and untrusting and dead dog afraid to offer these vulnerable parts of myself for public consumption and critique. So, I haven't really written about my identity online. Recently, however, this disconnect between my private and public life has felt unnecessary and unsustainable. I don't want to live fearful of the opinions of strangers or the venom of bigots.
>
> Today is my 39th birthday, which means I get one more trip around the sun before entering my next decade. I want to enter the second half of life with more authenticity, alignment, and integrity than I exhibited in the first half.
>
> So today, I'm raising a glass to my full and complete self—a gay man, beloved by God, who has endured the worst the world could throw at him and fought his way to health and wholeness.[85]

85. Jonathan Merritt post on Instagram, August 4, 2021, https://www.insta-

Pay attention to what Merritt communicates—he wants to be "whole" and "authentic." In 2019 Merritt tweeted, "Like many, evangelicalism provided me with some wonderful gifts for a season, but I feel like I have grown beyond it in many ways. Its tools and frameworks are no longer sufficient to sustain me in this phase of life. While I honor my heritage, I'm mostly seeking God elsewhere."[86] Merritt's journey, like Jen Hatmaker's and Rachel Held Evans', is part of a larger movement that has come to be known as #exvangelical or #exvangelicalism. As men and women who have grown up in evangelical Christianity start to allow gender ideology to be more authoritative than the Bible, they leave evangelicalism for progressive forms of Christianity or leave Christianity altogether.

Even those within evangelicalism are struggling with how to respond to gender ideology, evidenced by the debate over preferred personal pronouns. Unlike Tanner Cross, the elementary PE teacher who refused to call children in his classes by their preferred pronouns, saying that would be lying, some evangelical Christians advocate for what author Preston Sprinkle has called "pronoun hospitality."[87] JD Greear, pastor and former president of the Southern Baptist Convention from 2018 to 2021, said in a podcast in November 2019 that when it comes to pronoun usage, there is a spectrum that runs from truth telling to generosity of spirit.[88] Citing Sprinkle and also Andrew Walker's book, *God and the Transgender Debate*,[89]

---

gram.com/p/CSJp8JRI4h4/?utm_medium=copy_link.

86. Jonathan Merritt tweet on Twitter, September 6, 2019, https://twitter.com/jonathanmerritt/status/1170009681017933826?lang=en

87. Preston Sprinkle, *Embodied: Transgender Identities, the Church, and What the Bible Has to Say* (Colorado Springs: David C. Cook, 2021), 204. See the entirety of chapter 12 to understand Sprinkle's argument in favor of pronoun hospitality, 199-220. Sprinkle advocated for pronoun hospitality through blogs and social media prior to 2021, but the book *Embodied* presents his most thorough arguments to date.

88. https://jdgreear.com/podcasts/when-talking-with-a-transgender-person-which-pronoun-should-you-use/.

89. Walker, *God and the Transgender Debate*. Walker, a professor of ethics at Southern Baptist Theological Seminary, says, "Christians disagree—hopefully char-

as influential in his thinking, Greear said that if a transgender person came to his church, he would call him by his preferred pronoun, practicing generosity of spirit.

The danger with the concept of "generosity of spirit" set up in opposition to "truth telling" is that these concepts are not set up in opposition in Scripture (Eph 4:15). We are called to speak the truth in love. In addition, while I believe the desire to be "hospitable" or "generous" comes from a place of care for individuals, this comes from a dangerous place when "care for individuals" allows accommodation of sin. Love of neighbor does not mean disobedience to God. If we love God, we are to do what He says and not bear false witness. In addition, one must wonder, to what extent is generosity of spirit and hospitality extended? If a person identifies as a unicorn, a firetruck, or a child, do we accommodate those ideas? Not too long ago, we would rightly say that a person who believed himself to be a unicorn or identified as a child (if he was in fact an adult) or identified as something other than his biological gender, was delusional. But to say that today or to put transgender people in the same category as otherkins or therians is considered intolerant and employing a fear-mongering, "boogeyman" argument, yet I believe it is simply pointing out where that "rabbit hole" could lead.

---

itably—about pronoun usage. Some think that as a personal courtesy, you should refer to a transgender person by their preferred pronoun....Others think that it is wrong to inject further confusion into a person's situation by referring to them with a pronoun that is not aligned with their biological sex. Some Christians argue that referring to a person by their preferred pronoun furthers the deception and delusion within a person's mind. Seen this way, calling a biological male, "she" is to bear false witness. My own position is that if a transgender person comes to your church, it is fine to refer to them by their preferred pronoun....If and when this person desires greater involvement or membership in the church, a church leader will need to meet with them and talk about how they identify....The best solution is to avoid pronouns altogether if possible. Calling a person by their legal name or preferred name is more acceptable because names are not objectively gendered, but change from culture to culture" (156-157).

Is There Any Hope for Our Gender Confused World?

Dr. Martin Luther King, Jr. once proclaimed that the ultimate measure of a person is not where he stands in moments of comfort and convenience, but where he stands at times of challenge and controversy. We are facing a time of great challenge and controversy in our world today when many people (Christians and non-Christians alike) are rejecting God's standards for living. For Christians, when considering how far down the rabbit hole our culture has gone with gender ideology, the only way to regain our footing is to stand upon the firm foundation of the Word of God. What does God say about gender? And who gets to define our identity?

Claiming the right to define ourselves is at its very core rebellion against God. The problem with claiming that right is that we are created beings. We have a Creator God who has already defined us. With great intentionality God created two distinct genders (Gen 2:18-25). This truth is affirmed in the New Testament by Jesus (Matt 19:5). Gender is a gift from God, not something that is socially constructed or self-determined. As the book of Isaiah declares, "But now, O LORD, you are our Father. We are the clay, and you are our potter; we are all the work of your hand" (Is 64:8). In the Old Testament, even the way a person dressed was to reflect an embrace of God's unique design for the genders (Dt 22:5). In the New Testament, this principle was repeated in the discussion of head coverings (1 Cor 11:2-16). Peter commanded husbands to relate to their wives in a protective posture, and acknowledge the distinctions between them (1 Pet 3:7). The timeless principle that runs through all those passages is that we should "express" ourselves in ways that display an embrace of God's unique design for men and women.

You see, God designed us and gave us careful directions on how we are to approach life. When we veer from the directions, we are essentially saying that we think we know better than our Creator. As the Master Designer, He made each one of us and fashioned us as Psalm 119:73 proclaims. For every believer, you have a vital role to play in God's plan. It is ever more important that we embrace our God-created identity, not redefine, reinvent, or reimagine it. Despite what our nation or any particular worldview may say, we must remember three key truths.

Truth # 1: You are the created not the Creator

You are not an accident, nor just some random fluke of some evolutionary process. You have a Creator. He formed you in your mother's womb. That very fact should have significant implications for each believer on a daily basis. God says our identity and worth is not grounded in how we look, our marital status, our socio-economic bracket, or even how many likes we get on Facebook or Instagram. The truth is that we are all sinners (Rom 3:23). I am and so are you. Our "sin lists" may look different, but Christ died for you and for me. Because of that, you and I and any person who accepts Christ can have a restored relationship with God; we are called forgiven, redeemed, holy and dearly loved children of God, saints and citizens of heaven, conquerors and new creations, set free and complete, friends of God (Eph 1:7; Col 3:12; Gal 3:26; 1 Cor 1:2; Phil 3:20; Rom 8:37, 2 Cor 5:17; John 8:38; Col 2:10a; John 15:15). That is a believer's identity.

In C.S. Lewis' classic work, *Mere Christianity*, Lewis remarks, "But the question is not what we intended ourselves to be, but what He intended us to be when He made us. He is the inventor, we are only the machine. He is the painter, we are only the picture."[90] As Isaiah warned, "Woe to those who quarrel with their Maker, those who are nothing but potsherds among the potsherds on the ground. Does the clay say to the potter, 'What are you making?' Does your work say, 'The potter has no hands'?" (Is 45:9).

---

90. C. S. Lewis, *Mere Christianity* (New York: The MacMillian Company, 1960), 203.

Truth # 2: Your sexuality isn't ultimately about you.[91]

We have really made a mess of God's design for the sexes and have made it so complicated! God created men and women as distinct, yet complementary beings (Gen 1:27, 2:18). While both girls and guys are created in the image of God (Gen.1:27), God had a specific purpose in mind when He created Eve—she was to be a "helper" for Adam (Gen 2:18, 20). Being a helper does not mean that Eve was inferior to Adam in any way, but she was distinct from him. Men and women need each other, and this truth about the importance of community was part of God's plan from the beginning of creation (Gen 2:18). Why would God create two distinct sexes anyway? One reason is that the way a husband and wife interact with each other should be a picture of the way God interacts with the church (Eph 5:32). Christian marriages are to be a witness to lost people about the way Christ (pictured through husbands) loves the church (pictured through wives). Our sexuality expressed in marriage was designed to portray/proclaim the very heart and character of God towards His church!

Truth # 3: You are called to be a living witness of the goodness of God's plan.

Probably one of my favorite authors of all time is Jane Austen. In her book, *Mansfield Park*, Austen remarks, "It will, I believe, be everywhere found, that as the clergy are, or are not what they ought to be, so are the rest of the nation." If we could expand that sentiment to include all Christians and not just clergy, I think it is a chilling reminder of our call to be salt and light (Matt 5:13-16). As the analogy goes, we are not meant to be thermometers that reflect the temperature of the culture, but instead to be thermostats that set the temperature of the culture (Rom 12:1-2). I am afraid the reason

---

91. See Dorothy Patterson's chapter, "Do Gender Roles Still Matter?" in this volume for an expanded discussion of this truth.

so many people are embracing gender ideology is that far too many who claim the name of Christ live lives that mock or discount His plan for men and women.

Isaiah 5:20 warns, "Woe to those who call evil good and good evil, who put darkness for light and light for darkness." Don't let this world drag you down to its level of immaturity regarding gender ideology, sexual sin, or any sin, for that matter. Don't let any form of media or educational dogma have more sway on your thoughts than the Word of God. Do you ever feel like we are fighting a losing battle when it comes to the culture and popular opinion? Don't lose heart! Stand for truth, and proclaim truth with gentleness and respect (1 Pet 3:15). We must have courage in the face of opposition and compassion for those who do not yet see the truth of God's plan.

We must pray for changed hearts and remember that God is in charge; regardless of the outcome, our call is to remain faithful. Pray for those who have been deceived by sin. Pray for opportunities to speak the truth in love to them. And pray for and encourage fellow believers so that none of us will be deceived by sin and become hardened to God's way of living (Heb 3:13).

In Westminster Abbey in London, there is a monument to the English abolitionist William Wilberforce that says many great things about his accomplishments. However, my favorite line from the tribute says, "In an age and country fertile in great and good men, *he was among the foremost of those who fixed the character of their times*; because to high and various talents, to warm benevolence, and to universal candor, he added the abiding eloquence of a Christian life." Brothers and sisters, let's be men and women of God who help fix the character of our times. Portray the abiding eloquence of a truly Christian life. As you live day by day, though we may be tempted to wring our hands because of the direction of the culture and the lunacy of gender ideology, we must not lose heart! God is still on His throne. Our mission has not changed. Our call in these times is to "be steadfast, immovable, always abounding in the work of the Lord" (1 Cor 15:58).

CONCLUSION

Do you remember Hans Christian Anderson's story, *The Emperor's New Clothes*? Two weavers fool an emperor into believing that his new clothes, which actually don't exist, are invisible, especially to those who are unfit for their positions, stupid, or incompetent. These underhanded characters prey upon the ruler's pride and insecurity. The Emperor isn't willing to admit he can't see the clothes because he is afraid people will think he is unfit.

When the Emperor parades before his subjects in his "new" clothes, at first no one dares to say that the Emperor is walking around naked; instead they pretend to see the clothing. Finally, a young child cries out, "But he isn't wearing anything at all!" It takes a child to point out the lunacy of the situation.

Christians must be like that child. Contemporary culture has lost its mind. The world is drowning in lies, but each time we shine the light of truth, we help push back the darkness. Unlike the college students that Joseph Backholm interviewed at the University of Washington who were afraid to confront his erroneous statements, followers of Christ must speak the truth. Secular culture popularizes its ideologies through various forms of media and education and persuades people that to disagree is to be unenlightened, backwards, or hateful. Yet, the simple elegance of telling the truth is a courageous and loving act. We must be willing to do so even if it is unpopular.

Paul displayed that kind of courage. He confronted the churches of Galatia when they started succumbing to lies about how a person is saved. Paul lovingly yet boldly confronted the errors. He knew there could be consequences. The church could reject him, speak ill of him, malign his ministry, or worse. In his letter he asked, "Have I become your enemy by telling you the truth?" (Gal 4:16). Yet, he still wrote the letter because he knew that correcting the lies was more important than what the Galatians thought of him.

Jesus also modeled this approach during this earthly ministry. He was willing to confront lies because He knew our enemy is the father of lies (John 8:44). Satan wants to pervert truth and peddle his harmful deceptions like some sleazy snake oil salesman of the old west or those fictitious weavers in *The Emperor's New Clothes*. He wants us to exchange truth for lies. One of the enemy's most successful strategies today is deluding people into believing that truth doesn't matter. Worse yet, he has cultivated fear in those who do see clearly so that they will be scared into silence.

Despite the battles that have raged to perpetuate gender ideology through the redefinition of language, the manipulation of educational institutions, the weaponization of pop culture and mass media, and the compromise of some within Christianity, take heart brothers and sisters. Truth does matter. It is not relative. Truth is a person. His name is Jesus Christ, and over two thousand years ago He proclaimed, "You will know the truth, and the truth will set you free" (John 8:32). Truth matters because it is the key to real freedom. Lies enslave and destroy. Truth liberates and empowers. Go and speak the truth in love so people enslaved by contemporary gender ideologies can be set free by the good news of Jesus Christ!

9

DO GENDER ROLES STILL MATTER?

DOROTHY PATTERSON

Perhaps the better question for this chapter would be, "Do Gender Roles Matter to God?" If the answer is "yes," then that should settle whether or not gender roles "still" matter. What matters to God should matter to every believer in any generation regardless of what the culture, the elites who have the rule, or even other believers may say. In the ensuing chapter the challenges from the present cultural milieu will be considered, but the biblical data on gender roles will also be investigated in answering this timely question.

God has a good, beautiful, and unique plan set forth in what is clearly His creation order. To be created as a woman or as a man according to His design means something. From the beginning God has had a purpose for how men and women are to relate to one another. The fact that this divine plan offends people both inside and outside the church is of no importance. Over the last several decades, aside from the nature of Scripture itself, one of the most vigorously debated issues within Christianity has been the concept of gender roles.

Some women and men have trouble embracing the biblical teaching on gender roles. In a sin-infested world, abuses and injustices do happen and are perpetrated even by people of faith (or those who at least purport to be believers) regarding gender roles in the home and church. Such distortions of biblical truth can make the following of these clear teachings challenging. However, you dare not base personal beliefs on the bad examples and abuses of sinful behavior. Rather you must search the Scriptures for yourself to see what God really says and then set the course of your life by that standard.

Yes, this issue is deeply personal for both women and men because it strikes at the heart of your identity. Does your gender matter? Is there any significance in being created as a woman or a man? Does your personal identity impact how you relate to others? Discussion on the topic of gender roles can bring out the worst in all of us. Someone who holds a different position invokes a challenge. Our humanity often leads to using the worst examples of each belief system and developing stereotypes. Language may become inflammatory and reasoning skewed so that discussion is neither helpful nor Christ-honoring. Whatever your position, engage this topic with gentleness and respect, avoiding anger and bitterness. Most of all, seek to know what God says. The Bible does speak on being a woman and on being a man and on how the woman and man relate to one another.

Coming to Term with Some Terms

Recently my niece came to help me on a busy weekend. We rewarded ourselves with viewing an old movie. The romantic comedy *The Princess Bride* was released in 1987, and actor Mandy Pantikin, who portrayed the swordsman Inigo Montoya, uttered the classic line "You keep using that word, I do not think it means what you think it means." When people discuss gender roles, part of the misunderstanding comes because they are using words that are unclear or when the speaker and the hearer have different meanings for the words. Some important definitions may be helpful.

Gender Roles: In secular culture, the concept of gender roles is understood to be the role or behavior learned by a person as appropriate to his/her gender and as determined by the prevailing cultural norms.[1] In this definition, "prevailing culture" serves as the arbiter of meaning for discussion. However, a believer looking for a biblical perspective, sees a gender role as one appropriate to a specific gender as determined by God and recorded in Scripture regardless of what the culture or any individual says. The idea that God would have some gender-specific ways for women and men to relate despite our gender-neutral and gender-deconstructing society; yet for every believer the task remains—what does God have to say about gender roles? Fortunately, His words are clearly recorded in Holy Scripture!

Complementarianism: This term is new to the world of words—for example, the word is still not found in my online dictionary. As a member of the founding board of the Council for Biblical Manhood and Womanhood, I was part of the team who drafted the Danvers Statement—now the standard adopted by many evangelical institutions. The short definition for this term is "equal yet distinct." This view espouses that the Bible teaches that men and women bear the image of God fully but in different ways (equal in essence and value). God has distinct, yet complementary roles or functions for men and women, especially in the home and church, and their different roles blend together to provide a picture of who God is and how He relates to His people.[2] I personally hold this position. In recent years, intra-complementarian debates have made the discussion about gender roles even more heated within the Southern Baptist Convention. In order to adapt the popular position (because of its tight connection to the biblical

---

1. See https://www.dictionary.com/browse/gender-role.

2. See my definition on complementarity in *The Women's Study Bible* (Nashville: Thomas Nelson, 1995), 1967.

text) and yet adapt to cultural changes and individual desires, some have redefined the distinctly coined word to suggest neo-complementarianism, "soft" complementarianism, or broad complementarianism. Solid exegetical truths are morphed in hermeneutical casuistry with fallacious and misleading applications.

Egalitarianism: The short definition for this term, which has been in the dictionary for many decades, is "the equality of all people" (to some "equal" must mean potential for the same). This position teaches that the Bible affirms that men and women are both created in the image of God (equal in essence and value, just as complementarians believe) and that God has no distinction of roles or functions for men and women in the home or church. On the other hand, in Scripture equality and role distinctions are different but compatible aspects of our humanity put in place by God Himself. There is a difference in who a person is and what she does. A task, especially one assigned by God, does not lessen personal worth![3] Some Bible-believing evangelicals hold this position, yet when the biblical evidence is weighed, this interpretation falls short.

Equality: This word is used extensively, but to understand what people mean when they use the word without context is important. So, for many egalitarians, if men and women are truly equal, they must have access to the same roles or functions. This position often assumes a woman's heavenly reward is based upon her earthly role in the kingdom rather than upon her faithfulness to fulfill the assignment God has given her. Her "feeling" a call to some position in the kingdom trumps biblical guidelines for the tasks God assigns. Nevertheless, the Bible teaches that something or someone can be equal in value and worth yet have distinctions in role or function. For example, each member of the Triunity is equally and fully God, but God the Father has some roles distinct from God the Son and from God the Holy Spirit and vice versa in the ways they relate to each other and accomplish

3. See my definition on egalitarianism in *The Women's Study Bible*, 1880.

respective tasks. Another example is the discussion of spiritual gifts found in 1 Corinthians 12. Every Christian is equally part of the body of Christ, but each has distinct gifts to serve within that body.

Presupposition: This term is important because it describes something that is assumed or taken for granted as being true. When you study the Bible, every interpreter of Scripture starts with certain presuppositions or assumed principles. As a believer, I have formulated these presuppositions for myself. In harmony with the nature of divine revelation, Arthur Holmes has well stated that "all truth is God's truth."[4] Truth is absolute, not relative; therefore, it is unchanging. I believe that God exists and that He is determined to reveal Himself through His written Word and indwelling Holy Spirit. I believe His revelation of Himself is absolutely reliable and trustworthy; I know that His revelation is sufficient for me not only to know Him but also to know what He wants me to do and how He wants me to live.

Having set forth definitions of these terms, consider some cultural shifts that have obfuscated the discussion of gender roles in the modern era. Before the biblical passages are examined, having an understanding of these two cultural shifts, one within secular culture and one within Southern Baptist culture, can enable you to discern some of the challenges to be considered as believers seek answers on how to understand gender roles in modern society not only through a cultural lens but more importantly through an understanding of biblical truth.

---

4. Arthur F. Holmes, *All Truth is God's Truth* (Grand Rapids: Wm. B. Eerdmans Publishing Co, 1977).

EXAMINING THE SHIFTING CULTURAL LANDSCAPE

Secular Culture

God started in Genesis from the beginning of Creation with a family—not a village or a religious institution. Because the Creator Himself defined the family as the foundational building block of society, one is not surprised that the Devil does all he can to subvert the family. In so doing he can destroy the church, the community, and take down every individual God created. One of the family's most ardent opponents has been the movement of secular feminism. In 1963, the publication of Betty Friedan's *The Feminine Mystique* served as the catalyst for the second wave of secular feminism in America. Friedan, a college-educated woman who came to prominence in the *Leave it to Beaver* era, was a suburban housewife who struggled to find happiness as she envisioned it. In trying to voice the discontent she felt and noticed in some other women in her stage of life, Friedan said, "Each suburban wife struggled with it alone . . . . She was afraid to ask even of herself the silent question—'Is this all?'"[5] Her question and emotional response resonated with many women who began to rise up when Friedan challenged, "We can no longer ignore that voice within women that says: 'I want something more than my husband and my children and my home.'"[6]

In the subsequent years, American culture has shifted in significant ways. Carolyn McCulley in her book *Radical Womanhood* observed:

> Feminism is a given. We breathe it, we think it, watch it, read it. Whenever a concept so thoroughly permeates a culture, it's hard to step back and notice it at work. *Feminism has profoundly altered our*

---

5. Betty Friedan, *The Feminine Mystique: 50 Years* (New York: W.W. Norton & Company, 2013), 1.

6. Friedan, *The Feminine Mystique*, 22.

culture's concept of what it means to be a woman. We need to understand
how this movement came about and what its goals have been because these
are now our culture's assumptions.[7]

For women, feminism's message has become the modern culture's de facto default setting. Candi Finch explains:

> At the heart of this movement is a message that shuns God and exalts humanity, specifically women. It is a message that the American culture has embraced, and to some extent, the church has allowed to creep within its doors. The essential problem for any Christian with feminism is that this ideology exalts women and their experience as a source of truth, and in turn women's experience becomes more authoritative than Scripture. For example, if the idea that God may have distinct roles for women in the home or church seems "unfair" to you, then many feminists would say to reject what God teaches and go with what you "feel" is right since you are the barometer of truth. The Bible clearly states that all people—men and women—are sinful (Rom 3:23); and whenever anyone's experience is seen as trumping Scripture, red flags should immediately flash in your mind.[8]

Friedan, based on her own experience with a tumultuous marriage and unhappy home life, believed that the biblical idea of distinct gender roles harmed women, and she unleashed a whole movement casting the home in a negative light. Whereas many women in previous generations

---

7. Carolyn McCulley, *Radical Womanhood: Feminine Faith in a Feminist World* (Chicago: Moody Publishers, 2008), 28; italics added.

8. Candi Finch, "The Impact of Feminism on the Home and Family," in *The Christian Homemaker's Handbook*, edited by Pat Ennis and Dorothy Kelley Patterson (Wheaton: Crossway, 2013), 38.

were probably not ashamed to call themselves homemakers, young women today, when asked what they want to do with their lives, rarely admit that they want to be a wife and mom. The "home" is something that is seen as a prison holding a woman back from achieving all she's meant to be. In 1969 in the early stages of second wave of feminism, a leaflet entitled, "Do you know the facts about marriage?" was produced to hand out at a protest at the New York Marriage License Bureau. It ended with this statement: "We can't destroy the inequities between men and women until we destroy marriage. We must free ourselves. And marriage is the place to begin."[9]

Friedan argued that women could not have their greatest happiness and impact unless they entered the "public" sphere. In the minds of many people (even those who identified themselves as believers), a subtle shift occurred to the position that only paid work could be valuable. Martha Stewart and Joanna Gaines can make millions marketing the pursuit of excellence and creativity in "homemaking," but a woman who chooses to stay at home and devote her primary energies to watching "over the ways of her household" (Prov 31:27) is often belittled by contemporary society. She is praised for pursuing these tasks for a salary but denigrated for doing so because of a loving commitment to her family and obedience to divine mandate.

Friedan's question, "Is this all?" is not a bad question. Every person asks this question about life at some point. That emptiness Friedan experienced in trying to find fulfillment in her marriage and children is the same emptiness that many women today experience in trying to find fulfillment through their jobs, education, or social media platforms. Women (or men) who look for their ultimate contentment in their homes or in their workplaces will eventually realize that their lives are lacking something; they are simply, as the writer of Ecclesiastes states, "striving after the wind" (Ecc

---

9. "Do you know the facts about marriage?" in *We are the People: Voices from the Other Side of American History*, ed. by Nathaniel May, Clint Willis, James W. Loewen (New York: Thunder's Mouth Press, 2003), 185.

1:14). True fulfillment, peace, and satisfaction can only be found in a relationship with Jesus Christ. As C.S. Lewis poignantly wrote,

> The moment you have a self at all, there is a possibility of putting yourself first—wanting to be the centre—wanting to be God, in fact. That was the sin of Satan, and that was the sin he taught the human race...What Satan put into the heads of our remote ancestors was the idea that they could "be like gods"—could set up on their own as if they had created themselves—be their own masters—invent some sort of happiness for themselves outside God, apart from God. And out of that hopeless attempt has come nearly all that we call human history...the long terrible story of man trying to find something other than God which will make him happy. The reason why it can never succeed is this. God made us...**God cannot give us a happiness and peace apart from Himself, because it is not there.** There is no such thing.[10]

Because God never entered Friedan's equation, her proposed solution for women will never achieve what she wanted—failure was guaranteed.

In October, 2009, the cover of *Time Magazine* proclaimed that women are more powerful but less happy. After over 50 years of second-wave feminism, women in many ways are just as unhappy as they were in Friedan's day. Danielle Crittenden admits this in her book *What Our Mothers Didn't Tell Us: Why Happiness Eludes the Modern Woman*,

> For all the ripping down of barriers that has taken place over a generation, we may have inadvertently also smashed the foundations necessary for our happiness...American women have achieved the

---

10. C. S. Lewis, *Mere Christianity* (New York: The MacMillian Company, 1960), 53-54.

most egalitarian marriages in the history of the world. And yet they actually feel more oppressed in their marriages than their grand-mothers did. *How is this possible?*[11]

This reality is possible because no woman or man will ever find en-during happiness apart from a relationship with Jesus Christ. The last de-cades of feminism have proven that Friedan's solution to women's unhappi-ness has not brought lasting satisfaction. Sadly, though, millions of women and men have fallen for the siren song of "empowerment" and "egalitari-anism" strumming throughout modern feminism without realizing that the self-centered outcome is doomed.

Southern Baptist Culture

At the same time that second wave feminism was shifting the cultural land-scape in America (1960s—1990s), Southern Baptists were experiencing their own shifting sands. This period within Southern Baptist life has come to be known as the Conservative Resurgence or Conservative Renaissance. My husband discusses this historical event in his booklet, *Anatomy of a Reforma-tion: The Southern Baptist Convention, 1978-2004.*[12]

To understand why the Conservative Resurgence is pertinent to the discussion of gender roles, you must understand that the 1970s and 1980s proved to be a turning point within our denomination. While inerrancy was the central doctrine under view, gender roles or biblical anthropology became a hotly debated doctrine. And the battle over gender roles was re-vealed predominantly within the seminaries. "As go the schools, especially

---

11. Danielle Crittenden, *What Our Mothers Didn't Tell Us: Why Happiness Eludes the Modern Women* (New York: Simon and Schuster, 1999), 25, 80.

12. Paige Patterson, *Anatomy of a Reformation: The Southern Baptist Conven-tion, 1978-2004* (Fort Worth: Seminary Hill Press, 2004).

the theological seminaries in denominations, so largely go the pastors, and hence the people."[13] This warning by the late L.R. Scarborough has proven to be prophetic.

Southern Baptist Theological Seminary in Louisville, Kentucky, the first of six seminaries to be established by Southern Baptists, began admitting women in 1902, sixty-three years after it first opened its doors. Women could "sit quietly in the classroom and take examinations, but they would not receive course credit at the Seminary. Nor would they have the privilege of reciting or speaking in class."[14] The only class that women were not allowed to sit in was Pastoral Duties.[15] In 1904 the first class offered at SBTS exclusively for women was called Practical Work and focused on methods of evangelism and missionary service for women. Twenty-five women enrolled, and this class was the start of the growth of a curriculum developed to meet the needs of women students.[16] Clearly from the beginning the way women were encouraged to participate in theological education differed from men.[17] Some understanding of gender roles, though not explicitly

---

13. L.R. Scarborough, *A Modern School of the Prophets: A History of Southwestern Baptist Theological Seminary, a Project of Christ, a Product of Prayer and Faith, Its First Thirty Years—1907-1937* (Nashville: Broadman Press, 1937), 153.

14. T. Laine Scales, *All That Fits a Woman: Training Southern Baptist Women for Charity and Mission, 1907-1926* (Macon: Mercer University Press, 2000), 60. For a good overview of seminary education from 1900 to the end of the twentieth century see R. Alan Culpepper, "Reflections on Baptist Theological Education in the Twentieth Century," *Baptist History and Heritage* (2000): 24-50.

15. Scales, *All That Fits a Woman*, 109. Barbara Miller Solomon notes that often women even auditing classes in secular universities at this time were treated as unwelcome, uninvited guests, *In the Company of Educated Women: A History of Women and Higher Education* (New Haven: Yale University Press, 1985), 58. However, in contrast, Scales notes that the men at the seminary were hospitable to the women on campus (110).

16. Scales, *All That Fits a Woman*, 114.

17. T. Laine Scales, "Southern Baptist Colleges," in *Women in Higher Education: An Encyclopedia*, eds. Ana M. Martínez Alemán and Kristen A. Renn (Santa Barbara: ABC-CLIO, Inc., 2002), 52.

stated, governed the way that seminary officials approached women's education. One author noted that "at the turn of the twentieth century, when Southern Baptists opened theological education to women, they did so with a clear understanding that women were preparing for different vocations than male ministers."[18]

In 1908 Southwestern Baptist Theological Seminary was founded in Texas for the primary purpose of training preachers and presenting theological education.[19] In that same year, B. H. Carroll, the founding president, wrote an article for the *Baptist Standard* affirming that while the seminary's primary focus was "to be mainly for the promotion of theological education," it was also for "the instruction of a Woman's Training School."[20] In the first year, twenty-five women were enrolled as students.[21] In 1910, only two years after opening its doors, a department of training for women was added.[22] This program had the same requirements for the bachelor of theology degree with additional courses in "domestic science, kindergarten,

---

18. Scales, *All That Fits a Woman*, 256.

19. L.R. Scarborough in his history of SWBTS recounted a comment Dr. Carroll once made to him, "I want a seminary that will turn out Resurrection preachers—men who can raise the dead and do exploits in the churches—make the valley of dead bones live with flesh and blood, life and power—men who can write commentaries, textbooks on systematic theology, and hold great revivals and construct a kingdom for Christ's truth," *A Modern School of the Prophets*, 184. It is implicit in his statement that men would be the ones serving as preachers and pastors.

20. Robert A. Baker, *Tell the Generations Following: A History of Southwestern Baptist Theological Seminary, 1908-1983* (Nashville: Broadman Press, 1983), 136, quoting B. H. Carroll, "Southwestern Baptist Theological Seminary," *Standard* 26 (March 1908), 1. This wording is also listed in second section of the original charter for the school in 1908, see Baker, 488.

21. Charles Deweese and Pamela Durso, eds., *No Longer Ignored: A Collection of Articles on Baptist Women* (Atlanta: Baptist History and Heritage Society, 2007), 154.

22. Scarborough, *A Modern School of the Prophets*, 188. In fact, this department was added five years before the music and religious education departments were added in 1915.

child problems, nursing, and women-in-mission work."[23] However, women did not have to restrict their studies to a certain department. In 1920, Mrs. E. O. Thompson was the first woman to receive a Doctor of Theology degree from Southwestern.[24]

L. R. Scarborough, the second president of SWBTS, outlined his understanding of the importance of having trained women in his inaugural address:

> Also, we have the Woman's Missionary Training School, a vital part of our Seminary. Our purpose is to do for women in their work what we are doing for men in theirs—give them trained workers, thus reaching the fields opening to Christian womanhood for service. Our aim is not to turn out women preachers, but to give the world trained women in all the teaching, missionary, and soul-winning activities of Christ's coming kingdom.[25]

Clearly, the early leaders of both Southern Seminary and Southwestern Seminary understood that women serving in the pastorate was prohibited by Scripture.

In the late 1970s, just before the Southern Baptist Convention erupted over the controversy between moderates and conservatives regarding the inerrancy of Scripture, Leon McBeth, noted church historian and one-time professor at Southwestern, wrote an important work on the role of women in Baptist life. Minette Drumwright in the foreword to his work wrote:

---

23. Baker, *Tell the Generations Following*, 157.

24. Culpepper, "Reflections on Baptist Theological Education in the Twentieth Century," 29.

25. Scarborough, *A Modern School of the Prophets*, 183. He later reiterates this point in his book when he states, "And then look at the challenging demand for trained women in all lines except the preaching ministry, and our seminaries and training schools must give these women leaders" (201).

Those who agree that the Bible is the authoritative Word of God for our faith and practice do not always agree about its interpretation. Therefore, Southern Baptists have had a history of wide diversity of opinion on "the woman question," as some call it. The debate does not question women's service in the everyday work of the church, for that level of involvement is encouraged and welcomed. The controversy arises at this point: Is it right for women to serve in leadership, policy-making roles?[26]

The answer to Mrs. Drumwright's question was not so easily answered in Southern Baptist life at this time. McBeth observed that this revolution beginning to occur in Southern Baptist life in regards to women came about for several reasons: an abundance of prepared women, a response to spiritual need, a response to the feminist movement in society, a response to other denominations, a reinterpretation of Scripture, and expanded concepts of ministry.[27] McBeth commented that "one Southern Baptist statesman suggested that the presence of prepared women will in the long run do more to determine the church roles of Southern Baptist women than our theology or biblical views."[28] The fact that women were prepared for ministry was seen as greater evidence for them to be allowed access to all avenues of service beyond the guidelines clearly stated regarding this issue in Scripture. Couple this with the rising tide of feminism, and Southern Baptists were headed for a collision. They were faced with a decision of what, if anything, would trump or override Scripture!

At least at this point in history, during the late 1970s and early 1980s in Southern Baptist seminaries, some people were beginning to change their understanding of gender roles from what had been previously believed by

---

26. Leon McBeth, *Women in Baptist Life* (Nashville: Broadman Press, 1979), 6.
27. McBeth, *Women in Baptist Life*, 19-21.
28. McBeth, *Women in Baptist Life*, 19.

Southern Baptists. In the *Southwestern Journal of Theology* in 1977, the theme of the issue was "Baptists Deal with Controversial Issues." One of those issues was tackled by Ralph Langley in his article on the role of women in the church in which he argued for no boundaries for women's participation in ministry.[29] This interpretation was a clear departure from what Carroll and Scarborough had articulated.

The changing theology of some within the seminaries during this time did not accurately reflect the position of the majority of the people within the SBC churches. Though some within the seminaries at that time had drifted, the majority of Southern Baptist churches had not compromised the denomination's long-held beliefs regarding gender roles, which were based upon a natural reading of Scripture. Although partly in response to the drift of some seminaries regarding gender roles and the influence of feminism, my husband and I established the first program in women's studies at Southeastern Seminary in the late 1990s because of our commitment to the theological training of women and the admonition in Titus 2 for women-to-woman teaching. In my article "A Biblically Based Women's Studies Program," I describe the need for such a program in light of so many secular presentations from a feminist point of view; Christian women must be equipped to engage cultural movements like feminism from a biblical worldview.[30] This program was designed to prepare women "for Christian leadership positions other than the pastorate."[31] This approach to women in theological education was a marked

---

29. Ralph H. Langley, "The Role of Women in the Church," *Southwestern Journal of Theology* 19 (1977): 60. In his article he argues strongly for the ordination of women citing as support Galatians 3:28, which is a soteriological passage and not a gender discussion, and the daughters of Philip in Acts 21:9, whom Langley lists as "preachers," though the text identifies them as "four virgin daughters who prophesied" (Gk. *prophēteuousai*). See a more extensive, yet brief, discussion in *The Woman's Study Bible*, 1850.

30. Dorothy Patterson, "A Biblically Based Women's Studies Program," *Faith & Mission* 14 (1996): 76-79.

31. Jason Duesing and Thomas White, "Neanderthals Chasing Bigfoot?

change from the 1970s, 1980s, and early 1990s, yet it was a return to the original positions modeled in the seminaries in their founding years. Effectively, what we wanted to demonstrate was an affirmation of the importance of equipping women to serve God, while at the same time encouraging a complementarian understanding of gender roles.

Southern Baptists as a denomination have honored their women. All our major mission offerings are named for godly women. Baptist women traditionally and to this day have been the custodians of our SBC missionary prayer calendar as well as the architects of our denomination-wide promotion of missions. Women have served as working members on the boards of every denominational agency and institution. Women have served on mission fields from the inception of the SBC missions program. Biographies of Baptist women have continued to surface. Countless female authors have published with our denominational press. I am the product of SBC theological education.

When my husband and I moved to New Orleans, he was determined that I pursue a theological degree alongside him. Because of my extensive illness during college years, I would not have made that choice. I am indebted to my husband's financial sacrifices and to his encouragement for me to pursue these studies resulting in the gift of a thorough theological education. I was the only woman in the NOBTS School of Theology, and there were few women in 1965 pursuing major studies in theology. Yet I cannot resist noting that despite my grades and publications, SBC leaders (women and men) with few exceptions did not ask me to lead in silent prayer. Yet I have never lacked opportunities for kingdom service, even though they have seldom come through my denomination—probably largely because my positions then, as now, were not culturally acceptable. The SBC did have a "renaissance" for biblical womanhood from the mid-1980s to 2015, at which time the slippery slope to egalitarianism and feminism again appeared!

The State of the Gender Debate in the Southern Baptist Convention," *Journal of Biblical Manhood and Womanhood* 12, no. 2 (2007): 11.

All of this does not mean, however, that we are left to abandon biblical directives; rather those directives guide us to the most effective preparation for using our time and energies to extend the kingdom. We do not have to redefine words or re-interpret Scripture. We must dig deeply into Scripture to find answers.

Traditionally, Southern Baptists have taken a complementarian understanding of gender roles aside from that contentious period in the late 1970s, 1980s, and early 1990s. Many Southern Baptists and virtually all their leaders by the turn of the century were supportive of the Council for Biblical Manhood and Womanhood. Seminaries began to use the Danvers Statement as a document to be affirmed by incoming faculty. [32] Possibly sensing the growing popularity of egalitarianism or as a reaction to the controversy that had erupted, in 1998 Southern Baptists added to their statement of faith an article on the family to include a clear articulation of complementarianism for the home and later revised article VI on the Church in 2000 by adding the statement that "While both men and women are gifted for service in the church, the office of pastor is limited to men as qualified by Scripture."[33] The *Baptist Faith and Message 2000* article XVIII on the Family states:

God has ordained the family as the foundational institution of human society. It is composed of persons related to one another by marriage, blood, or adoption.

Marriage is the uniting of one man and one woman in covenant commitment for a lifetime. It is God's unique gift to reveal the union between Christ and His church and to provide for the man and the woman in marriage the framework for intimate companionship, the

---

32. I had the privilege of being on the founding board of CBMW when we penned the Danvers Statement. See https://cbmw.org/about/danvers-statement/.

33. The Southern Baptist Convention, see http://www.sbc.net/BFM/bfm2000.asp.

channel of sexual expression according to biblical standards, and the means for procreation of the human race.

The husband and wife are of equal worth before God, since both are created in God's image. The marriage relationship models the way God relates to His people. A husband is to love his wife as Christ loved the church. He has the God-given responsibility to provide for, to protect, and to lead his family. A wife is to submit herself graciously to the servant leadership of her husband even as the church willingly submits to the headship of Christ. She, being in the image of God as is her husband and thus equal to him, has the God-given responsibility to respect her husband and to serve as his helper in managing the household and nurturing the next generation.

Children, from the moment of conception, are a blessing and heritage from the Lord. Parents are to demonstrate to their children God's pattern for marriage. Parents are to teach their children spiritual and moral values and to lead them, through consistent lifestyle example and loving discipline, to make choices based on biblical truth. Children are to honor and obey their parents.[34]

In 1998, I had the privilege of serving on the SBC committee appointed by President Tom Elliff with the specific task of drafting an article on the family in response to a 1997 motion at the annual meeting.[35] We on the committee believed:

Doctrine and practice, whether in the home or the church, are not to be determined according to modern cultural, sociological, and ecclesiastical

---

34. See https://bfm.sbc.net/bfm2000/#xviii-the-family.

35. The motion made at the SBC in 1997 was as follows: "That the President of the Southern Baptist Convention appoint a committee to review the *Baptist Faith and Message* of May 9, 1963, for the primary purpose of adding an Article on The Family, and to bring the amendment to the next convention for approval." See https://bfm.sbc.net/report-of-committee-on-baptist-faith-and-message/

trends or according to personal emotional whims; rather, Scripture is to be the final authority in all matters of faith and conduct (2 Tim. 3:16-17; Heb. 4:12; 2 Pet. 1:20-21). God chose to reveal Himself to His people through family language: He used the metaphor of the home to describe the heavenly dwelling where believers will join Him for eternity. He selected the analogy of family relationships (husband/wife and parent/child) to illustrate how believers are to relate to Him: God is the Father; Jesus is the Son; the Church is the Bride of Christ; believers are His children. The most basic and consistent spiritual teaching, character development, and discipleship training should occur within the family circle (Deut. 6:4-9). A Christ-centered family has the potential to give a "word about God" to a world indifferent to spiritual truths. Those within the family circle have a unique opportunity to study the Bible and to learn theology through object lessons built into the very structure of the family. Godly families help build the church just as churches ought to help build godly families. Scripture makes frequent connections between the life of the family and the life of the church (1 Tim. 3:5; 5:1-2). Leadership patterns in the family are consistently reflected in the church as well (1 Tim. 2:9-14; 3:1-7; Titus 1:5-9). We heartily affirm and commit ourselves to upholding the concept of the family as God's original and primary means of producing a godly offspring and thus passing on godly values from generation to generation (Deut. 6:4-9; Ps. 78:5-7).[36]

In addition to these revisions to the *Baptist Faith and Message*, SBC seminaries moved to take a stand on gender roles. Eventually most Southern Baptist seminaries adopted the Danvers Statement, a complementarian statement on gender roles developed by the Council for Biblical Manhood and Womanhood, as a guide in hiring and evaluation processes.[37] These

---

36. See full report of the committee: https://bfm.sbc.net/report-of-committee-on-baptist-faith-and-message/. I was honored to be asked by the committee to prepare the draft for a more extensive treatise on this addition to our formal statement of faith to prepare SBC messengers for the vote to adopt the Family article.

37. For the adoption of the Danvers Statement at Southwestern Seminary as one of the guiding documents and statements in the Policy Manual, see Bob

actions combined signaled that Southern Baptists understood the complementarian position to be the biblical position on gender roles.

EXAMINING GOD'S WORD

Some Interpretive Guidelines for Interpreting Gender Passages

Hermeneutics, which is the study of how we interpret the Bible, is an ever-burgeoning field with new guidelines being hatched faster than rabbits. However, in the process of unlocking the Word of God, a few basic hermeneutical principles have stood the test of time and have been useful to this interpreter in unlocking the treasures of Holy Scripture.

> » All verses have to be understood in the light of context—
> that of the immediate passage, of the broad paragraph discussion, of the book itself, of the Old or New Testament
> as a whole, and finally of the Bible in its entirety. The
> passage is to be interpreted *contextually*.
> » Looking at the historical situation out of which the passage comes, weighing the various grammatical structures
> found within the passage, and using lexicons and dictionaries to determine the range of definitions for the words

Allen, "Southwestern Seminary adopts statement asserting male Headship," *Associate Baptist Press* [on-line]; available from http://www.abpnews.com/index.php?option=com_content&task=view&id= 4520&Itemid=53. For the adoption of the statement at Southeastern in 1994 and then at Southern in 1995, see Duesing and White, "Neanderthals Chasing Bigfoot," 11. For the adoption of the Danvers Statement at Midwestern Seminary, see Bob Allen, "Midwestern Seminary Adopts Danvers Statement," *Associate Baptist Press* [on-line]; available from https://baptistnews.com/article/midwestern-seminary-adopts-danvers-statement/#.YHjBASWSk2w.

themselves, are *grammatico-historical* aspects that are important to the interpretation of the text.

» Difficult verses must be interpreted in light of verses that are clear in order to maintain *consistency* in interpretation.

» The verses that describe or make application ought to be set in relationship to the overall teaching of Scripture and be used to elucidate further the message of the teaching text. Verses that are part of a particular *historical* narrative ought not to be interpreted without the truths/principles found in *didactic* passages.

» Pertinent verses must not be discarded simply because they seem irrelevant or out of step with modern culture. One must yield to the principles found in the whole counsel of God as recorded in Scripture under the illumination that comes from the *Holy Spirit*, who ultimately opens the Word to the diligent and faithful interpreter (John 14; 16; 2 Pet. 1:21). The Holy Spirit, as He interprets a passage in the heart of an individual, will not contradict what He has inspired to be written in the biblical record.

Some Foundational Observations for Interpreting Gender Passages

In personally struggling with the challenge of issues regarding gender roles, I have noted four additional guidelines for biblical interpretation that have been helpful to me, especially in considering passages such as 1 Timothy 2.

1. **The spiritual privileges in the body of Christ come equally to men and women.** In Genesis 1:27, the man and the woman are given joint dominion over the world, which in no way precludes each having unique functions and both

fulfilling their respective complementary assignments. In 1 Peter 3:7, both the man and the woman are declared to be "joint heirs" in Christ; and Galatians 3:28 clearly teaches that no distinction exists between men and women with regard to their salvific position "in Christ." At the same time, this does not mean that *equality* with regard to *salvation* equals *sameness* with regard to *role*.

2. **Sharing in the same privilege on the part of the woman and the man does not amount to uniformity of practice nor does it entail the obliteration of all differences between the sexes.** This conclusion is evident in Genesis 2:15–25, where God's creative purposes for the man and the woman are clearly laid out within the context of the man's priority in creation and the woman's clearly designated position as the man's "helper" in the context of this one man/one woman union, which we know as marriage. The man's assignment, coming directly from the Creator, is to tend the garden, to guard it, and especially to exercise leadership in obedience to the important spiritual directive concerning the tree of the knowledge of good and evil in the midst of the garden. Also in these verses, the woman is described as a "helper" to the man, a term carefully chosen by the Creator to unveil His purposes for the woman in her complementarity to the man. In Ephesians 5:21-33, the wife is admonished to submit herself to her husband's leadership even as he submits himself to assuming the responsibility of exercising loving servant leadership in the home, following the example of Christ. First Corinthians 11:1-16 and Colossians 3:18-19, together with 1 Peter 3:1-7, consistently affirm the same teaching as found in

Ephesians 5 concerning how husbands and wives are to relate to one another within the home.

3. **The New Testament contains numerous regulations concerning activities of women "in the church."** An understanding of this important matter does not rest upon narrative passages that are relevant only in an indirect sense, such as the pericope in John 4, where Jesus shares the gospel with the woman at the well. The Samaritan, having been introduced to the Messiah, returned to her village and shared her testimony in the marketplace and neighborhood with anyone who would listen. Nothing in the text indicates that she preached crusades or addressed the synagogue or even delivered her message from the local amphitheater (John 4:5–30). Mary Magdalene was instructed by Jesus Himself to go to His disciples and share her personal testimony about the empty tomb and the living Jesus risen from the dead. This witness Mary was faithful to discharge: "I have seen the Lord" (see John 20:18). Mary of Bethany took advantage of a unique opportunity to sit at Jesus' feet to learn the deep truths of Scripture (Luke 10:38–42). Both clear examples and straightforward directives related to church order are readily available in Scripture for women who earnestly seek a word from God concerning their roles in the kingdom.

4. **Underlying Paul's answers to these difficult questions concerning the roles of men and women in the church is the apostle's own deep concern for the preservation of the Christian home according to the plan God had from the very beginning as to how men and women are to relate to one another.** Although the apostle ascribes

to women a position distinct from that assigned to men, he does not regard a woman's role in the church to be any less important (1 Cor. 14:33–35; 1 Tim. 2:8–15; Titus 2:3–5).

If you want to get a good idea about God's view on the subject of gender roles, there are several key passages within the Bible you must spend time studying. These passages reveal God's mind on the matter.

Genesis 1—3

These three chapters are foundational—you will not fully understand what God is doing in the rest of the Bible if you don't understand His unique plan at creation for man and woman. The theological foundation for manhood and womanhood is found in the Genesis account of creation. As principles for how the man and woman are to relate to one another unfold in Scripture, this unique creative design is a frequent point of reference, including its citation in 1 Timothy 2:13.

God's design is not based on the intellect and giftedness of a man or woman nor on current cultural setting or circumstances. Rather, God designed marriage in the beginning according to His own plan. This design has been woven into the fabric of manhood and womanhood from creation until now and will ever be so—an intricate and colorful tapestry to bring unity and happiness to the man and the woman and to facilitate their usefulness in the kingdom. At the heart of this design is an unchanging principle that *the man and woman are equal in their essential being but different in their role assignments* (Gen, 1:26, 27; 2:15-18). In other words, the divine design calls for the man and woman to be *equal* to each other, but not for one to be the *same* as the other. Each is both *equal to* the other and yet *different than* the other.

God designed the differences between the man and woman so they would complement each other. The man is given a threefold task. First, he is charged with "tending" or working the garden so that it will be fruitful, providing sustenance. He is also to "keep" (protect or preserve) or care for the garden. Finally, God gives to the man alone (before the woman was created) the most important commandment—not to eat from the tree of the knowledge of good and evil. Disobedience to this command would lead to certain death. Being entrusted with these responsibilities is indicative of the leadership role assigned to the man (Gen. 2:15-17).

God created the woman from the man. Both are "in His image" (Gen. 1:27; 2:22). The woman from her creation is inseparably linked to the man. The man was formed from the dust of the ground, and the woman was made from the rib (Heb. *tsela,* meaning "side") of the man—the same flesh and blood and in her being equal to him in every way. Thus, her worth and dignity are affirmed even by the act of creation. There is no hint of inferiority. The woman was not a divine afterthought, for the man was created physically, emotionally, socially, and spiritually with her in mind. Adam expresses this unity in Genesis 2:23 with a unique play on words ("man," Heb. *ish,* and "woman," Heb. *ishshah*).

Being a "helper" (Heb. *'ezer kenegdo,* literally "a help like or corresponding to him") is not demeaning. The word was chosen to describe the woman's function (what she does) rather than her worth (who she is). Because this "helper" was an inspired ideal before her creation, the words used to describe her had to express God's own purpose (Gen. 2:18). Although in the modern day the term *helper* suggests to many a menial position, careful examination of the word's biblical usage does not indicate a servile role. This assignment is a challenging and rewarding responsibility and a role God Himself assumes on occasions (Ps. 40:17, "You *are* my help and my deliverer; / Do not delay, O my God"; Heb. 13:6, "So we may boldly say: 'The LORD *is* my helper'"). This terminology does not suggest that the Lord is an inferior being nor that He should divest Himself of His deity and supernatural powers when called to help but speaks of His desire to respond to the needs of those whom He loves with an everlasting and unconditional love.[38]

---

38. Dorothy Kelley Patterson, "Aspects of a Biblical Theology of Woman-

The woman is also identified as one "comparable to him [the man]" (Heb. *kenegdo*, only used in Gen. 2:18, 20). In other words, the woman is like and equal to the man in her person (both are "in the image of God," Gen. 1:27). However, *identical* is not a synonym for *equal*, and you do not achieve equality by mimicking someone else or by doing the same thing as another. In their respective differences and unique functions, men and women reach their full potential and greatest productivity. Their commonality was just as clear as their distinct role assignments. Both were created in the image of God, and each was to participate in having dominion over the earth and continuing the generations.

Galatians 3:28

This verse is often used to argue that there are no longer distinctions in roles. However, if that were the case, then Paul (who wrote this verse) contradicts himself when he articulates role distinctions in other passages. This verse actually speaks to the fact that each person comes to salvation the same way—through the cross of Christ. Some try to pit Scripture against Scripture and claim that equality must mean without any distinction. For example, they would point to Galatians 3:28 to affirm this equality as meaning "the same." Even aside from the contextual problem in such a position and the fact that the context is discussing salvation cannot be ignored, there is the problem of logic. Would any prisoner say that his state is exactly the same as that of the free man? Would any woman really stand before a mirror and claim that she is made exactly as a man? Would a Jew avow that he is exactly as a Gentile in his ethnic heritage? I do not think so. However, all of these can affirm an equal status *in Christ*; i.e., in coming to Christ the road is the same whatever your status, ethnic heritage, or gender. That is clearly not only the promise of Galatians 3:28 but also the message of all Scripture.

---

hood" (Th.D. diss., The University of South Africa, 1998), 119-30.

Marriage Passages
(Colossians 3:18-19, Ephesians 5:22-33, 1 Peter 3:1-7)

These passages (known also as "household codes") teach that there are some distinctions in how a husband and wife relate to one another in a marriage. In the biblical creation narrative, God's boundaries for marriage are clear. The man and woman are created and then united by God Himself (Gen. 2:24). The New Testament reaffirms these same boundaries (Matt. 19:4-5; Mark 10:6-9; Eph. 5:31). There is complete consistency without any contradiction within God's plan for marriage throughout Scripture. Ephesians 5:22-33 is especially important because it explains why God designed this unique union as He did—marriage communicates the truth about how Christ relates to believers. Each Christian marriage should serve as a witnessing tool! Marriage is not merely a flexible contract; it is a covenant commitment to the permanent union of one man and one woman, and the most important witness to this covenant is the Lord Himself.

Husbands are commanded to love their wives as Christ loved the church (Eph. 5:25). This *agapē* love is protective, nurturing, serving, and edifying. It is accompanied by—but not overshadowed or replaced with—servant headship in which a husband cares lovingly and responsibly for his wife's spiritual, emotional, and physical needs. The husband's headship was established before the Fall and is part of the creation order (Gen. 2:15-17) and is also affirmed in the New Testament (1 Cor. 11:3). The unique understanding of biblical headship parallels the paradox found in biblical submission. To lead, a husband must be humble enough to serve those over whom his authority and guidance extend. As he meets their needs, they look eagerly for his leadership. To submit, a wife must choose to line up under her husband's authority, and in turn this gracious action on her part awakens in him the desire to serve her and meet her needs. There is a balance between leadership and servanthood, which is perfectly modeled in Jesus. Just as He models selfless submission for wives, He is also the perfect example of servant leadership for husbands. The mutuality comes as the husband humbles himself to meet his wife's needs for loving care and as the wife submits herself to her husband's leadership to receive his care and correspondingly to meet his needs.

The apostle Paul clearly lays out the immense responsibility of the husband in the divinely appointed plan for marriage (Eph. 5:25-33). He emphasizes self-sacrifice and service due a wife from her husband. The love (Gk. *agapaō*) described is one in which the husband is willing to give up his own best interest so that his wife's needs are covered. Even the care a husband would bestow on his own body should be equally bestowed on his wife (Eph. 5:29-30). Her well being is indissolubly bound up with his own (Eph. 5:31-33; 1 Tim. 3:2). A husband is to pursue a personalized understanding of his wife—of her needs and even her desires (1 Pet. 3:7). His role modeling is important not only to his children but to others as well. A husband does well to show his respect and esteem for his wife. In fact, if he fails to treat his wife respectfully, he not only damages his relationship to his wife but also hinders his relationship to God (1 Pet. 3:7).

Headship is a responsibility to assume with humility not a right to autocratic rule. Headship is not the right to grasp in order to rule and control; rather it is the responsibility to love like Christ and to execute the same servant leadership characteristic of His life. Human headship must guard against abuses. It is a high and holy calling for a husband to assume the primary responsibility for Christlike servant leadership, protection, and provision in the home. Biblical headship calls for the husband to exercise servant leadership (Eph. 5:23-29). In turn, this godly leadership awakens a response from his wife to honor and affirm that leadership (Eph. 5:21-22,33; 1 Pet. 3:1-4). Headship is not merely a plan of action; rather it is a way to accomplish family goals in an efficient and edifying way.

Mutual submission (Eph. 5:21) does not rule out distinctive roles. The analogy includes Christ and the church, and they certainly do not mutually submit one to the other. Christ did submit to the church with His servant leadership, which cost Him His life on the cross. The church mutually submits to Christ but not in the same way—rather the church affirms and honors His leadership, while Christ submitted Himself to death on the cross for our redemption. Thus mutual submission does not have to mean that each submits in the same way. A husband must put aside his own self-interest in the best interest of his wife, not in the sense of transferring his decision-making to her but in making his decisions based on what is best for her. As a husband leads his wife in a God-glorifying partnership through loving headship, he is humbling himself to meet her needs—loving, nourishing, and cherishing her as a treasure (Eph. 5:25-29; 1 Pet. 3:7).

Any attitude or action suggesting a woman as being insignificant, inferior, or lacking in worth originated in the aftermath of the Fall (Gen. 3:1-19). The stigma of inferiority is no more appropriate for the wife than it would be for Christ. You can be subject to a superior, as Israel was subject to the Lord (Deut. 6:1-5) and as believers are subject to Christ (Phil. 2:9-11) or as Abraham submitted to the priesthood of Melchizedek (Heb. 7:7). Yet subordination is also possible among equals: Christ is equal to God the Father and yet subject to Him (Phil. 2:6-8); believers are equal to one another and yet are admonished to submit "to one another in the fear of God" (Eph. 5:21). In fact, you can be called to subordinate yourself to someone who is inferior, as Christ willingly submitted to the authority of Pontius Pilate, "He answered him not one word." (see Matt. 27:11-14, NKJV). The mere fact that wives are told to be subject to their own husbands tells you nothing about their personal worth (Eph. 5:21-33). The comparison of the relationship between husband and wife to the relationship of God the Father with God the Son settles the matter of worth forever.

Ministry Passages
(1 Timothy 2:8-15, 1 Corinthians 11:2-16, Titus 2:1-5)

These passages show that both men and women should be involved in ministry, though there are some distinct ways in which men and women respectively engage in ministry. The only boundaries given to women are that they should not teach men in the church or have authority over men in the church.

1 Timothy 2:9-15

Following the appeal for a modest appearance and faithful good works (vv. 9-10) is a call for "silence" (*hēsuchia*, v. 11) and "submission" (*hupotagē*, v. 11), which denotes more an attitude of "quietness" than the absence of sound. This idea is perfectly expressed by Charlotte von Kirschbaum, the protégé of Karl Barth, "The silent women represent the listening church—which the teaching church must constantly revert to being."[39] There is no suggestion of a surrender of mind or conscience or private judgments. In fact, many interpreters miss the fact that the apostle is encouraging women to learn in a cultural setting where that was not popular or common. He is also clear that this submissive attitude cannot be forced, as can obedience or compliance, but is rather a willingness on the part of a woman to choose to yield her will to another. Other passages clearly affirm that the silence mandated here distinctively does not exclude women from participating in worship services since they may both pray and prophesy (1 Cor. 11:5).

In addition to the general statement found in 1 Timothy 2:9–11, the apostle continues with very specific boundaries. Paul even used his own personal authority to affirm what the Holy Spirit had inspired him to record as the boundaries to guide women in exercising their gifts and accepting their opportunities for service (1 Tim. 2:12). He also tied these boundaries to theological moorings—namely, the creation order and its concomitant design for the family.

The first prohibition is that women should not teach men (1 Tim. 2:12). No one should be confused by the meaning of this clear directive. These words under the protection of the infallibility of Scripture say pre-

---

39. Charlotte Von Kirschbaum, *The Question Of Woman* (Grand Rapids: Eerdmans, 1996), 112.

cisely what God means, and the Lord does not bring confusion: He means what he says. In the New Testament, the Greek word *didaskein*, with its derivatives, occurs almost 100 times, of which only 3 seem to refer to *individual* instruction, making it clear that the reference here is probably to the teaching of a *group* of men.

The individual instruction of Apollos shared by Priscilla and Aquila does not fall in the category of group instruction. Nor do you find another specific New Testament reference in which a woman instructs a man! It is interesting to note that *didaskein* is used to describe the "teaching" done by Apollo; whereas a different word, *ektithemai* (lit. "to set forth, explain"), is used in the interchange of Priscilla and her husband Aquila with Apollos. The former word—usually both linguistically and theologically—refers to a uniquely faithful proclamation of God's Word, which involves authority beyond the mere sharing of general information.

Perhaps this distinction should not be summarily dismissed. The difference in words could affect the meaning of the passage even if only subtly or indirectly. Even if both words are treated as virtually synonymous, nonetheless the text in question awards no official ecclesiastical status to whatever expounding was done by Priscilla and Aquila to Apollos. Although one cannot build a system of theological understanding or base a thorough exegesis on the basis of the use of different words or on the nuances of meanings found in those words, one must still consider that the selection of a specific word and the nuances of the meaning of that word are factors to be considered. Nevertheless, there is no one passage, and certainly not one word, that builds a case for ferreting out a theology of what women can or cannot do in the church. The challenge is to fit all the passages together and identify the diverse factors in each so that when jointly understood this Word from God is consistent, free from confusion, and adequate to supply principles needed for faith and practice.

The second prohibition, "not to exercise authority over men" (*authentein*), makes use of a *hapax legomenon* (i.e., the usage of the word appears only in this one place in the Greek New Testament). Egalitarians regularly contend that only a woman's *abuse* of authority is here proscribed by Paul. This argument is of doubtful merit, however. Scott Baldwin has documented the lack of evidence for a negative use of this expression prior to Paul.[40] Furthermore, Andreas Köstenberger has conclusively demonstrated that if, on the highly plausible assumption "teaching" is to be understood as a positive term in 1 Timothy 2:12, the syntax of the verse necessitates that "exercising authority" is to be understood positively as well.[41] Therefore, the prohibition is understood as being general in nature—a woman is not to teach men or to exercise authority over men—and not merely a reference to forbidding the oppressive or improper exercise of these functions by a woman.

Also interesting is the limitation for these prohibitions, which actually serves as further protection for women. The setting is obviously within the realm of religious instruction in the life of the church. However, what is prohibited is not couched in a particular office or position but rather in the exercising of specific activities or functions. The apostle does not mention official positions like pastor or elder or bishop/overseer in these verses directed to women, but he chooses to use functional terms, i.e., "teaching" and "exercising authority." In the process, Paul never states that women should be banned from the work of the church, nor does he suggest that they be denied any leadership roles in the church. In fact, the apostle commends women who are active in church work (e.g., Phoebe, Rom. 16:1; Priscilla, Rom. 16:3). He notes the importance of women teaching other women and describes the *spiritually mature women* (Gk. *presbutidas*), who are to be leaders among women, especially caring for those *new to the faith* (Gk. *neas*; Titus

---

40. See discussion by H. Scott Baldwin, "A Difficult Word: αυθεντέω in 1 Timothy 2:12," in *Women in the Church: An Analysis and Application of 1 Timothy 2:9-15*, ed. by Andreas J. Köstenberger, Thomas R. Schreiner, and H. Scott Baldwin (Grand Rapids: Baker Book House, 2005).

41. See discussion by Andreas Köstenberger, "A Complex Sentence Structure in 1 Timothy 2:12," in *Women in the Church*, 81-91.

2:3–4). He also notes the vital assignment women have to instruct children (as Lois and Eunice were commended for doing in 2 Tim. 1:5; 3:15; see also Prov. 1:8). Paul also records an instance of a woman teaching a man in private conversation (Priscilla and Aquila with Apollos, Acts 18:25–26).[42]

Clearly, then, these prohibitions specifically pertain to the teaching of men by a woman and to a woman's exercising authority over men. The passage is set in a section discussing *church* order and does not specifically address *every* gathered assembly of believers.[43] Nevertheless, one is wise to remember that to live as the scribes and Pharisees with one's heart and mind sold out only to the *letter* of the law is insufficient. Rather, one's desire should be to live life within the *spirit* of the law, looking for ways to bend the will to that of the Father, not for how close one can come to acquiescing to personal desires without outright disobedience. The choice ought to be: How far away can one move from disappointing the Father and marring His clear principles? One's personal testimony must be clear and free from compromise. The most logical application for these prohibitions is to the pastoral office,[44] which in the collective passages describing the pastor combines the activities of both prohibitions. Also under consideration must be either function as it may appear within the work of the church and the

---

42. For additional discussion, see Andreas Köstenberger, "Women in the Pauline Mission," in *The Gospel to the Nations: Perspectives on Paul's Mission* (ed. Peter Bolt and Mark Thompson; Leicester, UK: IVP, 2000), 221–47.

43. Many Christians gather in assembly outside official gatherings of the church. Although the spirit of the passage is important to consider in this regard, the specific mandate is not meant as a blanket for every group of men and women who gather.

44. Some biblical interpreters hold to a division among pastoral leadership, that is, pastors as distinct from elders. As a congregationalist, I do not hold that position but see the different words used as describing one office. Note 1 Peter 5:1–4, where the pastoral office is described with three Greek words: πρεσβυτέρους, translated "elders"; ποιμάνατε, translated as "shepherd" and used as a verb; and επισκοπουντες, translated as "overseers" and used as a participle.

kingdom. Timeless principles are not limited to the terminology unfolding official positions.

Paul does not leave future generations to conjecture that these directives recorded in the first century are for that time alone. Rather, he ties his guidelines to theological foundations, arguing for the man's natural and spiritual headship and the woman's role as his helper by appealing to creation itself (1 Tim. 2:13; see Gen. 2:4–24). To do so is to preclude the view of those who hold that male/female roles are simply a direct result of the fall.

Paul argues from creation in verse 13 and then illustrates this argument, albeit negatively, from the fall in verse 14. Paul appeals to the fall as an event that demonstrates in the starkest terms the dire consequences of a reversal of leadership roles. The apostle moves to the pericope detailing the fall, showing the disastrous effect of the role reversal that occurred in the garden (1 Tim. 2:14; see Gen. 3:1–25). He notes Eve's violation of the divine command and alludes to the ensuing reversal of the divine order prompted by Eve's fateful decision. By her act, Eve took leadership that was not hers, while simultaneously Adam abdicated his divinely assigned spiritual leadership by following the woman in contradiction to the clear directive he personally received from God (Gen. 2:16–17). There is a lesson to be learned: Nothing should be done in the church that undermines God's order in the home.

1 Corinthians 11:3-10

Paul shows that the respective positions of man and woman are like the structure within the godhead: "The head of every man is Christ, and the head of the woman is man, and the head of Christ is God" (v. 3). The Father planned redemption (John 3:16); the Son enacted the plan (John 17:1-5); the Spirit revealed that plan to us (John 16:13). "Without question, the whole framework of the earthly life, work, ministry, and mission of the Son was one in which the Son sought to do the will of the Father."[45] The home and relationships therein serve as the primary metaphors the Lord used to unveil Himself and to describe Christ's relationship to His Church. One cannot separate the home and church in divine order because the underlying principles are the same.

Complementarians hold that man and woman were created equally in the image of God (Gen. 1:27-28); they are equal in their position in Christ (Gal. 3:28), and they are equally responsible before God (1 Pet. 3:7). However, if the equality of personhood and position in Christ mandates uniformity and the erasure of differences in function and role for believers, then relationships within the Triunity of the godhead may also be held as either misleading or erroneous.

> Without question, the whole framework of the earthly life, work, ministry, and mission of the Son was one in which the Son sought to do the will of the Father. Hence, the Son's submission to the leadership, authority, and headship of his Father must be given careful consideration if we are to understand how the Father and Son relate. Here, we'll focus on the headship of the Father over the Son in the Son's incarnate mission, and also in his relationship with the Father in eternity past and eternity future. We'll see, in short, that the Son in fact is the *eternal Son* of the *eternal Father*, and hence, the Son stands in a relationship of eternal submission under the authority of his Father.[46]

For example, the Bible clearly states that Father, Son, and Holy Spirit are equal in being and personhood (Jn. 1:1; 5:23; 10:38; 14:6, 7, 9, 11). Yet Scripture is just as clear that a difference in office and function exists within

---

45. Dorothy Patterson, "Aspects of a Biblical Theology of Womanhood," 71.

46. Bruce Ware, *Father, Son, & Holy Spirit* (Wheaton: Crossway, 2005), 71. See full discussion 71–87.

the Triunity. The Son voluntarily is subject (even subordinate) to the Father (Jn. 5:19-20; 6:38; 8:28-29, 54; 1 Cor. 15:28; Phil. 2:5-11), and the Holy Spirit is sent by and under the direction of the Father with the assignment to glorify the Son (Jn. 14:26; 15:26; 16:13-14).

The structure within the godhead does not rest in the arena of worth—to being more or less God—but rather addresses respective functions within the work of the divine Triunity. The same is true of role assignments for men and women. Just as Persons within the Triunity have separate and distinct functions, according to His design, God gave distinct responsibilities to both men and women: The man is assigned headship in the home; the woman is to be his helper.

Just as Christ is not less than fully God because the Father is His head or "authority" (1 Cor. 11:3; Phil. 2:5-11), the woman is not an inferior person because the man is her head or "authority" (Eph. 5:22-24). The Son's deity is not dependent upon a denial of the Father's headship. God sovereignly set the general boundaries for leadership among men and women without regard for an individual's ability or giftedness to perform the service involved. Note the requirements for Old Testament priesthood (Lev. 10:8-11; 21:1-24). ". . . A priest with a physical defect was unqualified for priestly service [21:17-18a]. . . . he could not approach the   tabernacle. . . ."[47]

Let's be fair: Paul clearly states his commitment to role distinctions (1 Cor. 11:3-10), while certainly indicating that he did not consider the woman to be inferior or less vital to the kingdom (vv. 11-12). This passage allows and affirms, but does not mandate, participation in worship by both men and women. Women are free to pray and prophesy in the church, but they are admonished to do so with an attitude of submission to male leadership. This attitude was illustrated in that culture by the wearing of a head covering.

---

47. Mark F. Rooker, *Leviticus*, in *The New American Commentary*, vol. 3A (Nashville: B&H, 2000), 275. See full discussion, 271-276.

Titus 2:1-5

As a woman, I am astounded and concerned when self-styled "biblical feminists" imply that teaching men has higher value or importance than teaching women, young people, and children! Women teaching women is "spiritual mothering" in which spiritually mature women share through teaching and lifestyle the importance of carrying into daily life an example of holiness as well as voluntarily submitting themselves to God's order for the welfare of the family. The curriculum in Titus 2:3-5 includes the relationships of a woman in the home to her husband and to her children, her personal holiness and character, and the domain of her work and activity. Interestingly the list begins and ends with the relationship of the younger woman to her husband.

Single women are not excluded from this challenge to teach and model Christian character. They can exercise their divinely-given nature by acting as "spiritual mothers" to others, which includes keeping their homes as a refuge for those whom God may send to them. Mary and Martha opened their humble home to the Lord Himself (Jn. 12:1-11) for rest and fellowship. There He found a quiet place to sleep, nourishing meals, and comforting friends with whom to relax. Lydia, a prominent businesswoman, surely must have given money and witnessed verbally to the kingdom cause. Yet, though she was respected and honored in the community for her education, position, and business expertise, she was primarily commended for her hospitality (Ac. 16:14-15, 40).

Woman-to-woman teaching may be described as spiritually mature women sharing, through teaching and lifestyle, the importance of holiness in daily life as well as voluntarily submitting themselves to God's order for the welfare of the family. This divinely planned woman-to-woman mentoring program is one of the most effective tools for winning women to Christ and discipling them in whatever the cultural setting. Women indeed are challenged to share the gospel and to provide nurture in the faith, performing a myriad of kingdom tasks—all within biblical boundaries and in harmony with the creation order. There are a myriad of ways in which women are encouraged to do their work for Christ:

» Older or "spiritually mature" women (Gk. *presbutidas*) are exhorted to instruct the younger or "new-to-the-faith" (Gk. *neas*) women, and they are given specific instructions on what to teach (Titus 2:3-5).
» Mothers share equal responsibility with fathers in teaching their children in the home (Deut 6:7-9).
» Women are to present the gospel (1 Pet 3:15).
» Women may pray and prophesy in the church (1 Cor 11:5).
» Women are uniquely prepared to be guardians of the home and nurturers of the children (Prov 31:10-31).

The New Testament describes women who serve in various ways in the kingdom:

» Priscilla joined her husband Aquila in instructing Apollos (Acts 18:26).
» Women, like Mark's mother Mary and Lydia of Thyatira, opened their homes for meetings of believers, and they practiced hospitality (Acts 12:12; 16:14-15).
» By His own divine fiat, God reserves the right to make decisions, even through the unexpected or extraordinary—such as calling Deborah to be a judge of Israel (Judg 4–5).
» Paul mentions women, like the highly capable Phoebe, with favor (Rom 16:1-2); and he employs women in the service of the gospel (Phil 4:3).
» Women offered themselves in special ministries to Jesus (John 12:1-11).

» Women are mentioned as prophetesses: Miriam, who led the women of Israel (Exod 15:20); Huldah, whose only prophecy in Scripture was to a man who consulted her at home (2 Kgs 22:14-20); Anna (Luke 2:36-40); and the daughters of Philip (Acts 21:9), though the text does not place their prophesying in the assemblies.

Though there are some distinct ways in which women and men relate to one other within the home and church, the biblical witness is clear that both men and women are vital for the task of accomplishing God's Kingdom purposes.

WHY DO GENDER ROLES MATTER?

God *intentionally* created men and women as distinct, yet complementary beings (Gen 1:27, 2:18). He did not create men and women haphazardly with no plan or design. Both men and women are given the responsibility of being God's image-bearers from the very beginning (Gen 1:27). These distinct roles for women and men were a part of God's good plan before sin ever entered the world. Men and women need each other; they are "interdependent" (1 Cor 11:11), but not interchangeable, with one another.

God cares how you relate to one another. Despite shifting cultural and religious norms and values, believers must cling to God's unchangeable standard as recorded in Scripture. Gender roles still matter to you as the creation because they matter to God the Creator. God's reminder is that we are to model distinct gender roles so that the "Word of God will not be blasphemed" (Titus 2:5). What a strong word to use! God's Word is honorable regardless of how His children live, but the testimony of that Word may be marred by the behavior of believers. In an egalitarian society, proclaiming God's Word about His unique design for the sexes will be unpopular to many. However, to be unpopular is a better choice than to live in such a way as to malign and impugn God's Word.

At the end of the day, God's plan will be accomplished whether or not you choose to be obedient to Him. Your focus should be on how amazing it is that He wants to use you! How much wiser to determine to do things His way and to live according to His design for His creation—women and men. God grant to each of us the humility and wisdom to live in obedience to Him and according to His design. In so doing we proclaim His message to all and bring joy to the Creator God.[48]

---

48. My personal gratitude goes to Dr. Candi Finch, whom I consider to be the foremost female complementarian theologian of her generation. I had given up on writing this chapter for a myriad of reasons, but she stepped forward to assist me with research, typing, and editing so that now the chapter is complete!

10

DOES THE RAPTURE STILL MATTER?

MARK H. BALLARD

Announce in the local newspaper that you are going to preach a series of sermons on the Rapture, the Second Coming, the Book of Revelation, or End Time Events, and you will likely gain a few attendees for the series. Human nature drives interest in these topics. I have experienced this reality throughout my forty-one years of preaching ministry. Having preached in churches across almost half of the United States, I have preached on such topics countless times. Nearly every time I have announced preaching on eschatological topics, visitors came for the series. Even unbelievers seem to be curious to know what a Bible preacher has to say about the end of the world.

While interest in the Rapture seems to remain high among people in the pew, and some level of interest can still be found among the general populace, that may not be the case among the clergy. Serving as a president of a Bible college, I have numerous conversations with pastors, professors, authors, and other Bible scholars and theologians each week. While most of these folks are ready to enter discussions of most biblical and theological matters, increasingly, professional clergy resist discussing end times issues, particularly the Rapture. Some of the most common responses are:

> » "I'm a pan-millennialist. I believe it will all pan-out in the end."
> » "I really haven't studied eschatology enough to have an opinion on end times events."
> » "There is so much controversy on that topic that I try to avoid it."
> » "All I know is that one day Jesus is coming back."
> » "I really don't have time to think about that kind of stuff. I am too focused on helping people live the Christian life today to worry about what is going to happen in the future."

Recently, Tyler Ballard, my summer intern, was given a list of twelve conservative evangelical preachers. Each of these men have a public ministry that includes, radio, television, and podcasts. Tyler was asked to research the last three years to find how many sermons about the Rapture were preached by these twelve preachers during that time frame. Three of the twelve preachers had two sermons each on the topic. One of the twelve preached five sermons on the Rapture, four of which were part of a series, and the fifth was preached on a separate occasion. Eight out of twelve had no sermons on the Rapture available. While this research is simply anecdotal in nature, it nevertheless proves interesting that only eleven sermons about the Rapture are available from the last three years from twelve popular, conservative, evangelical preachers.

Considering all the controversy surrounding the topic of the Rapture, and the growing lack of interest in the topic among both professors and pastors, many appear ready to answer the question of this chapter in the negative. This fact is noted by Hindson and Hitchcock who wrote, "More and more believers today appear to be agnostic about issues related to the end times, especially the timing of the Rapture."[1] Despite the increasing avoidance of the topic, the very fact that a book was published on the subject in 2019 reveals that there remains some interest.

During the last academic year, Northeastern Baptist College offered a night class designed to be an intensive study of the Book of Revelation. The class was open to all students, no matter their major area of study. In addition, the class was announced at a handful of local churches. Amazingly, this became one of the largest classes in NEBC History. Despite student's busy class schedules, many took the course as an elective. Despite the busyness of life, several believers from local churches signed up to participate in a 3-hour course that met every week for 15 weeks.

While some are willing to study and discuss end time topics, including the Rapture, others avoid the topic completely. In 2016, LifeWay Research conducted a survey on end time beliefs. Twenty-five percent of those surveyed said they did not believe the Rapture was a literal event.[2] Thus, the question remains, "Does The Rapture Still Matter?"

To this point in the chapter, we have only described anecdotal evidence for "what is" the case among pastors, professors, and people in the pew. However, the more important question remains. In answering the question of this chapter, we must not be satisfied with the state of current thought, even if we could provide solid evidence as to the majority opinion on the topic. Rather, the believer must not only understand "what is" but must seek to know "what ought to be."

The question of whether the Rapture still matters is not really a question of popular opinion. If the Rapture is biblical, it is important whether people like the topic or not. In determining the answer to the question of

1. Mark Hitchcock, *Can We Still Believe in the Rapture?* (Eugene, OR: Harvest House Publishers, 2017).

2. "Belief in the Rapture," *Lifeway Research*, accessed September 11, 2021; https://lifewayresearch.com/search/Belief in the Rapture/.

this chapter, one must consider the biblical data. The reader must ask, "What does the Bible teach about the Rapture?" In attempting to answer this question two things must be examined. First, one must consider the nature of the Rapture as presented in the Bible. Second, one must consider the timing of the Rapture according to the biblical record. Once these two issues are dealt with, the reader will be ready to answer the question of relevance.

THE NATURE OF THE RAPTURE

Before answering the question of relevance, one must understand what is meant by the term. While there is widespread agreement among evangelical believers about the visible, bodily, return of Jesus to the earth, there is disagreement as to the nature of the Rapture. In his systematic theology, Milliard Erickson notes two different understandings of the nature of the Rapture. He states, "A large and influential group of conservative Christians teaches that Christ's coming will actually take place in two stages. These stages are the Rapture and the revelation, or the "coming for" the saints and the "coming with" the saints…In contrast to pretribulationism, the other views of Christ's second coming hold that it will be a single occurrence, a unified event."[3] While Erickson's description assumes some generalizations many pretribulationalists would deny, it proves helpful here simply to show that the nature of the Rapture is not universally agreed upon among conservative Bible scholars.

In seeking to understand the nature of the word *Rapture*, it is important to consider four aspects of the discussion. First, we will define the Rapture. Second, we will respond to those who deny the Rapture. Third, we will defend the biblical nature of the Rapture. Fourth, we will distinguish the *Rapture* from the *Second Coming* of Jesus to the earth.

---

3. Millard J. Erickson, *Christian Theology*, 3rd ed. (Grand Rapids: Baker Academic, 2013).

Defining The Rapture

Concerning the definition of the Rapture one should consider both the meaning of the word as well as the way in which the word is typically used in eschatological discussions. Hindson and Hitchcock present a good working definition. They write, "The word *Rapture* comes from the Latin word *raptus*, meaning 'to snatch up, to seize, or to carry off by force."[4] While this presents the technical definition of the word, other theologians and commentators speak of its usage in theological discussions. In his Systematic Theology Ryrie includes *Rapture* in his list of definitions one should know when studying theology. He writes: "**Rapture**: The catching away of the church from the earth to heaven."[5] Kimball also includes his definition/description of the *Rapture* in his *Index of Terms*. He writes, "**Rapture** – This is a term which is applied to the scriptural event characterizing the translation of the living saints and the resurrection of the dead saints to meet Christ in the air when He returns."[6] In his commentary on the Revelation, Paige Patterson states, "The Latin word Rapture refers to the taking away of every true believer at the time of the *parousia* or the coming of Christ."[7] These authors consistently apply the correct definition, "caught up" to the taking away of the church from the earth.

In his work, *Could The Rapture Happen Today?* Mark Hitchcock argues that the Bible speaks of seven different *Raptures*. He suggests that six have passed and one remains. Further, Hitchcock argues that five of the *Raptures* are physical and two are spiritual. He refers to the catching up to heaven of

---

4. Hitchcock, *Can We Still Believe in the Rapture?*, Kindle Location 667.

5. Charles Caldwell Ryrie, *Basic Theology* (Wheaton, IL: Victor Books, 1986).

6. William R Kimball, *The Rapture, a Question of Timing* (Grand Rapids: Baker Book House, 1985).

7. Paige Patterson, *Revelation*, in *The New American Commentary*, vol. 39, gen. ed., David S. Dockery (Nashville: B&H, 2012).

Enoch, Elijah, and Jesus as past *Rapture* events.[8] Hitchcock also refers to Philip's miraculous "catching up" and removal to a different location in Acts 8:39-40 as a *Rapture*.[9] Hitchcock also speaks of Isaiah's seeing of the throne room of heaven in Isaiah 6:1-8 and Paul's experience of seeing the third heaven recorded in 2 Corinthians 12:2-4 as *spiritual Raptures*.[10] Hitchcock then argues that one *Rapture* remains. The Rapture of the Church is briefly described in chapter four of Hitchcock's book, but it is also the primary subject of the work.[11]

The above review offers a picture of both the technical meaning and the typical use of the term *Rapture* in biblical and theological discussions. For the purposes of this chapter the reader should be aware of this author's definition. Typically, the present author focuses his attention on the definition, *caught up* and demonstrates the connection with the Greek word, *harpodzo*, and the Latin word *raptus*. *Harpodzo* is best translated into English in 1 Thessalonians 4:17 as *caught up*. Consider the verse, "Then we who are alive and remain shall be *caught up* together with them in the clouds to meet the Lord in the air, and thus we shall always be with the Lord."

Beyond the technical definition of the word, this writer typically reserves the use of the word *Rapture* to describe the *catching up* of the church toward the end of the age. While most conservative scholars would agree with this definition and usage, there remains disagreement among scholars as to the timing of the *Rapture*. This issue will be discussed later in the chapter. For now, the reader needs clarity about what the term means both technically and in this chapter's discussions. It is the first step in understanding the nature of the Rapture. However, despite widespread agreement among conservative Bible scholars on this definition, there are those who reject the

---

8. Mark Hitchcock, *Could the Rapture Happen Today?* (Sisters, Or: Multnomah Publishers, 2005).

9. Hitchcock, *Could the Rapture Happen Today?*, 58.

10. Hitchcock, *Could the Rapture Happen Today?*, 57-59.

11. Hitchcock, *Could the Rapture Happen Today?*, 60-61.

definition and deny the existence of an event known as the *Rapture*. This view must be addressed before we can proceed. Therefore, attention must now turn to consider the denial of the Rapture.

Denying The Rapture

On August 1, 2008, Cecil Maranville posted an article titled, "The Rapture: A Popular but False Doctrine." He began, "The Rapture, often called 'The Blessed Hope,' is sadly more hoax than hope."[12] Maranville argues, as many who oppose the Rapture all together as well as many who reject a pre-tribulational Rapture, that the concept of the Rapture was held by no one until John Nelson Darby began teaching it in the 19th century.[13] Francis X. Gumerlock acknowledges that several theologians have made a similar argument. However, in his 2019 article in *Biblio Sacra*, Gumerlock demonstrates that the evidence shows several spoke of the Rapture long before Darby was born. In fact, his article focuses on 11th century discussions of the important event.[14]

Some have argued that since the word *Rapture* does not occur in the New Testament, one should reject the concept altogether. Most scholars,

---

12. Cecil Maranville, "The Rapture: A Popular but False Doctrine," Text, *United Church of God*, last modified August 1, 2008, accessed September 6, 2021, https://www.ucg.org/world-news-and-prophecy/the-Rapture-a-popular-but-false-doctrine.

13. Erickson and Grudem both argue in their respective systematic theologies that the pre-tribulational Rapture is a recent concept and attribute the idea to Darby as well. However, as noted in the paragraph above, Gumerlock has clearly demonstrated that there were indeed advocates of a pre-tribulational Rapture dating back to at least the eleventh century. To have a better understanding of Erickson and Grudem see: Erickson, *Christian Theology*. Wayne A. Grudem, *Systematic Theology: An Introduction to Biblical Doctrine* (Leicester, England: Grand Rapids: Inter-Varsity Press; Zondervan Pub. House, 1994).

14. Francis X. Gumerlock, "The Rapture In An Eleventh-Century Text," *Bibliotheca Sacra* 176, no. 701 (2019), 81.

however, reject that argument on two grounds. First, it must be noted that the word, Trinity, is not found in the New Testament either. However, the concept of the Trinity is throughout the Bible. Second, as noted in the previous section of this chapter, the word *Rapture* comes from the Latin word, *raptus*.[15] The reason the word *Rapture* is not found in our New Testament is because we are reading the text of 1 Thessalonians 4:17 in English rather than Latin. The Greek word, *harpodzo*, is translated, *caught up*, in English and *raptus* in Latin.

One of the most aggressive opponents of the pre-tribulational Rapture, Dave MacPherson, wrote two books attacking the position. The titles of his two works demonstrate his contempt for the pre-tribulational view. In 1975 he authored the book, *The Incredible Coverup: The True Story of the Pre-Trib Rapture*. He continued his attack, publishing *The Great Rapture Hoax* in 1983. Despite his contempt for the *pretribulational Rapture* position, even MacPherson acknowledged the existence of the *Rapture* as a literal event. In the preface to his first book he wrote, "All Bible-exalting persons believe in the 'catching up' of I Thessalonians 4, but there is still disagreement on the timing of this event—chiefly whether it happens before the Tribulation or after."[16] Indeed, most evangelical scholars today acknowledge the reality or the *Rapture*, though many differ on the timing of the event.

One of the reasons I identify as a Baptist is because of the longstanding Baptist belief that the Bible itself is the final authority for all faith and practice. While knowing the history of discussions on the *Rapture* throughout church history can be both instructive and helpful, the bottom line is that one's belief in the *Rapture* should be a matter of studying the Scriptures. The most crucial question is simply, "Does the Bible teach that the *Rapture* is a future event, and should believers look forward to its occurrence?" We now turn our attention to answering this question.

---

15. See footnote 3.

16. Dave MacPherson, *The Incredible Cover-up: The True Story on the Pre-Trib Rapture*, Rev. and combined ed. (Plainfield, N.J: Logos International, 1975), xi.

Defending The Rapture

In his work, *Could The Rapture Happen Today?*, Mark Hitchcock correctly encourages, "Don't let anyone lead you astray. The Rapture is in the Bible. But don't just take my word for it. See it for yourself in the pages of the Word of God."[17] He goes on to suggest that many passages speak to the *Rapture,* but three texts stand out as crucial.[18] I go a step further. While there may be subtle references to the *Rapture* in several Bible passages, only two texts describe the Rapture in detail and one additional text makes a clear reference to the *Rapture.*

First Thessalonians 4:13-18 provides significant detail as to what will happen when the *Rapture* takes place. First Corinthians 15:50-58 describes the physical transformation of believers that will take place at the time of the *Rapture.* The Apostle Paul connects the transformation of believer's bodies at the *Rapture* to the bodily resurrection of Jesus in the past. While conversing with eleven of His disciples in the upper room on the night of his betrayal, Jesus made a clear reference to the *Rapture.* John 14:1-6 records His words. When understood in the grammatical-historical context in which they were spoken, Jesus must have been referring to the *Rapture* of His church. Consider each of these passages.

1 Thessalonians 4:13-18

Paul faced persecution soon after establishing the Church at Thessalonica. He was, therefore, unable to spend an extensive amount of time in the city. Yet, we can observe from reading his two letters to the believers in Thessalonica that he must have taught them about the imminence of Jesus's return. Clearly, the congregation expected Jesus to return at any moment.

As time passed and Christ had not returned, great concerns arose. Fellow believers began to die. While they anticipated the Lord's return,

---

17. Hitchcock, *Could the Rapture Happen Today?*, 17.
18. Hitchcock, *Could the Rapture Happen Today?*, 17-19.

they now wondered what that meant for those who had died trusting Jesus. Did they miss the Rapture? Were they eternally confined to live as spirits? Did they receive a glorified body when their spirit entered heaven? How did their deaths impact their participation in Christ's return? Questions and confusion troubled their minds.

Paul wrote 1 Thessalonians to encourage the believers and answer some of their questions. Every chapter says something about the Second Coming of Jesus. In the final paragraph of chapter four, Paul specifically addresses their concern for their deceased loved ones. He begins by expressing his purpose in writing this paragraph. "But I do not want you to be ignorant, brethren, concerning those who have fallen asleep, lest you sorrow as others who have no hope."[19] Notice he does not chide them for their grief. Grief is a part of life. Rather, he reassures them that their sorrow is not without hope.

Paul begins this paragraph by offering hope and he concludes the paragraph by commanding the believers in Thessalonica to encourage one another in this hope. Note his words. "Therefore, comfort one another with these words."[20] In between offering hope and commanding them to offer hope to one another, the Apostle gives them two specific reasons they could have hope.

Jesus's Promise

First, the Thessalonians could have hope despite the death of their loved ones because of Jesus's promise. "For if we believe that Jesus died and rose again, even so God will bring with Him those who sleep in Jesus. For this we say to you by the word of the Lord, that we who are alive and remain until the coming of the Lord will by no means precede those who are asleep."[21] Notice, Paul begins with a statement that can be understood as a promise. He promised the Thessalonian believers that their loved ones who died in the Lord would return with Jesus and receive a glorified body like unto Jesus's

---

19. 1 Thessalonians 4:13.
20. 1 Thessalonians 4:18.
21. 1 Thessalonians 4:14-15.

resurrected body. He then provides his source of this knowledge. He did not want them to think he was just making this up so they would feel better. Notice his words, *"For this we say to you by the word of the Lord."* This was not a promise from Paul; it was a promise from the Lord Himself.

It is important to understand the meaning of the word translated *precede* in verse fifteen. The New King James parts from the Old King James in translation at this point. The Greek word in question is *phthano*. According to Mounce's Greek Dictionary, the verb means, *"come before, precede."*[22] As is often reported by Evangelical believers, "Context is king." The context demonstrates that Mounce's assessment of Paul's use of *phthano* in I Thessalonians 4:15 is correct. The very next verse describes the order of events at the *Rapture*. God's plan is that the dead in Christ will rise, receiving their glorified bodies, prior to the *Rapture* of the those who are alive at the time of the event. Indeed, the Thessalonian believers could have hope, despite the death of their fellow believers, because of Jesus' promise.

Jesus's Plan

In verses sixteen and seventeen Paul points to the second reason for hope. The Thessalonians could have hope despite the death of their loved ones because of Jesus's plan. Many times I have thought, "Lord, if you would just let me in on Your plan, it would be easier to trust You." Rarely does the Lord share the details of His plan. Most often He calls us to simply trust Him and walk by faith, obeying His Word and the promptings of His Spirit. Yet, on this occasion, the Lord revealed several details regarding His plan for the Rapture. Notice verses sixteen and seventeen.

> For the Lord Himself will descend from heaven with a shout, with the voice of the archangel, and with the trumpet of God. And the

---

22. *Accordance 13 Bible Software* (Oak Tree Software, Inc., 2021), www.accordance.bible.

dead in Christ will rise first. Then we who are alive and remain shall be caught up together with them in the clouds to meet the Lord in the air. And thus, we shall always be with the Lord.[23]

Observe several aspects to Jesus' plan. He tells us who will come, how He will come, and to where He will come. He also reveals who will rise first, what will happen to those who are alive in the Lord, and what the result of this event will be. In contrast to sending his angles to do the gathering,[24] Jesus Himself is coming to do the gathering. The method of how He performs this gathering is three-fold: He shouts, the archangel shouts, and the "trumpet of God" sounds.

Notice in this passage, Jesus comes in the clouds but never touches His feet on the earth. Rather, believers meet Him in the air. In Revelation 19, Jesus returns all the way to the earth; there is no mention of Him coming in the clouds. The contrast will be further discussed below, but one cannot consider this text without noticing the contrast in Jesus coming in the clouds rather than returning to the ground.

Paul then reveals Jesus's plan to receive His church. First, those who have died trusting Jesus will be raised from the dead, receive their glorified bodies, and join Jesus in the clouds. Then and only then will the living believers be *Raptured, caught up,* to meet the Lord in the air. As a final revelation of Jesus' plan, notice the result of the *Rapture.* "Thus, we shall always be with the Lord." Here Paul brings the question of grief to rest. Death does not bring an eternal separation for believing loved ones. There awaits a grand reunion of all those who have trusted Jesus. The best part of the reunion is that not only will we be together, but we will also be together, with the Lord—forever!

---

23. 1 Thessalonians 4:16–17.
24. Compare Matthew 24:31.

First Thessalonians 4:13-18 is one of the clearest passages describing the Rapture! We learn the Lord's purpose in revealing this information is to bring hope and comfort to His followers. We learn of His promise concerning those who "sleep in Jesus." Amazingly, we learn several crucial details of His plan. Certainly, this is a profound and comforting text. It also should settle the issue of whether such a thing as the *Rapture* exists. While this passage uses the term, this is not the only text that speaks of the Rapture.

I Corinthians 15:50-58

First Corinthians fifteen is a foundational and crucial chapter for understanding the Gospel, the Resurrection of Jesus, and the Rapture of the Church. During the Conservative Resurgence of the Southern Baptist Convention (1979-2000), it was learned that some professors denied the resurrection of Jesus.[25] In recent years, some Southern Baptists leaders have sought to add to the Gospel.[26] When it comes to the Rapture, few believers will actually deny the existence of the Rapture today. Yet as previously noted, many avoid talking about eschatology in general and the Rapture specifically.[27] However, Paul dedicated fifty-eight verses toward the end of his letter to the Corinthian believers to defend these three crucial doctrines.

Paul defines and defends the Gospel in the first four verse of the chapter. The Gospel is a threefold message: 1. Christ died for our sins according to the Scriptures, 2. He was buried. 3. He rose again, according to the Scrip-

25. Jerry Sutton, *The Baptist Reformation: The Conservative Resurgence in the Southern Baptist Convention* (Nashville: Broadman & Holman, 2000), 33.

26. Mark H. Ballard and Christian, Timothy K., *Words Matter: What Is the Gospel?* (Bennington, VT: Northeastern Baptist Press, 2020); Ronnie W Rogers, *A Corruption of Consequence: Adding Social Justice to the Gospel*, 2021.

27. David L. Allen and Steve W. Lemke, *The Return of Christ A Premillennial Perspective*, 2011, accessed September 6, 2021, http://www.vlebooks.com/vleweb/product/openreader?id=none&isbn=9781433675812.

tures.[28] Elsewhere the Apostle warns against adding to the Gospel in the strongest possible words. "But even if we, or an angel from heaven, preach any other gospel to you than what we have preached to you, let him be accursed."[29] We must not add to the Gospel.

Beginning in verse five and continuing all the way through verse forty-nine, Paul defends the bodily resurrection of Jesus. He presents names of eyewitnesses and invites the Corinthians to cross-examine them, declaring that many were alive at the time he wrote the letter. He moved on to present additional arguments for the veracity of the bodily resurrection of Jesus. Paul then tied the resurrection of Jesus in the past to the future resurrection and transformation of all believers in the future.

In the final paragraph of the chapter, Paul describes a future moment in time when the dead in Christ will be raised and those alive in Christ will be transformed. While Paul uses different language and provides different details than he supplied to the Thessalonians, it is clear that he is speaking of the same event. Consider his words.

> Now this I say, brethren, that flesh and blood cannot inherit the kingdom of God; nor does corruption inherit incorruption. Behold, I tell you a mystery: We shall not all sleep, but we shall all be changed—in a moment, in the twinkling of an eye, at the last trumpet. For the trumpet will sound, and the dead will be raised incorruptible, and we shall be changed. For this corruptible must put on incorruption, and this mortal *must* put on immortality. So, when this corruptible has put on incorruption, and this mortal has put on immortality, then shall be brought to pass the saying that is written: *"Death is swallowed up in victory. O Death, where is your sting? O Hades, where is your victory?"* The sting of death *is* sin, and the strength of sin *is* the law. But thanks *be* to God, who gives us the victory

---

28. 1 Corinthians 15:3-4.
29. Galatians 1:8.

through our Lord Jesus Christ. Therefore, my beloved brethren, be steadfast, immovable, always abounding in the work of the Lord, knowing that your labor is not in vain in the Lord.[30]

The resurrection of Jesus makes it possible for believers who die trusting Christ to be resurrected at a specific point in time in the future. Jesus' resurrection body is a body that can never again experience pain, death, or even the temptation to sin, yet it can be recognized and touched. The transformation that Jesus experienced from a "corruptible body" into an "incorruptible body" will also be experienced by all believers at a specific point in time in the future. Consider three important truths Paul taught about that transformation in this paragraph.

Resurrection Hope Will Not Be Fully Realized In this Life

Often today when evangelical believers talk about the hope of the resurrection, they are referring to hope in this life. Certainly, since Jesus rose from the dead, He can and will help His followers deal with any trial this life throws at them. However, earlier in First Corinthians chapter fifteen Paul stated, "If in this life only we have hope in Christ, we are of all men the most pitiable."[31] In this final paragraph, Paul explains more about why that is the case. "Now this I say, brethren, that flesh and blood cannot inherit the kingdom of God; nor does corruption inherit incorruption."[32] That is quite a statement, particularly considering the view of the Kingdom of God prevalent in today's evangelical world.

Do a quick search on Amazon for the topic, "The Kingdom of God" and several hundred books appear instantly. Attend an evangelical Christian

30. I Corinthians 15:50-58.
31. I Corinthians 15:19.
32. I Corinthians 15:50.

conference and you are likely to hear quite a bit of talk about the Kingdom of God. You can attend conferences and read books about having a Kingdom focused church, marriage, business, and more. Often today, the focus is on how the believer can experience the Kingdom of God now.

All the talk about the Kingdom of God now has caused many believers to equate the Kingdom of God with the church. However, Wayne Grudem writes, "We should not identify the Kingdom of God and the church, nor should we see the Kingdom of God as entirely future, something distinct from the church age."[33] I agree with the first half of Grudem's statement but I struggle with the second half. Particularly because much of the emphasis today in pulpits, books, seminars, small group studies, etc., seems to so over-emphasize the Kingdom as now. The biblical concept of the Kingdom as future has nearly been lost.

Reflecting Grudem, many Baptists today repeat the statement, "The Kingdom is now and not yet."[34] However, it seems that fewer and fewer sermons are preached about the return of Christ to establish a future Kingdom. In the introduction to this chapter an anecdotal research project was described. The project revealed that of twelve well known Baptist and Evangelical preachers only four had preached a message on the Rapture in the last three years. Out of the hundreds of sermons preached, only eleven focused on this crucial end time event.

This is not a reality new to the present decade. In a sermon at North-eastern Baptist College preached in 2015, Ronnie Floyd noted, "You don't hear many sermons on the Second Coming of Jesus anymore."[35] Writing in 2016, Hitchcock agrees. "More and more believers today appear to be

---

33. Grudem, *Systematic Theology*, 864.

34. This is a very common statement in Baptist life. I do not know the original source of this statement. However, I credit it to Daniel Akin, from whom I first heard the statement in college classes at the Criswell College in the 1980s.

35. Ronnie Floyd, Chapel Sermon at Northeastern Baptist College. Bennington, VT, September 15, 2015.

agnostic about issues related to the end times, especially the timing of the Rapture."[36] Indeed, there seems to be so much emphasis on "the Kingdom now" that very little is said about the coming of Jesus to establish the Kingdom of God in the future.

Despite the realities of the last couple of decades in the Western Evangelical world, Paul, under the inspiration of the Holy Spirit writes, "Flesh and blood cannot inherit the Kingdom of God."[37] While the believer may have a small taste of what is in store, as Jesus reigns in his or her life, the fact remains that we are not living in the Kingdom of God. Flesh and blood cannot inherit the Kingdom. Before we can inherit the Kingdom, there must be a physical transformation. Only a resurrected body can truly enjoy the Kingdom of God. Resurrection hope will never be fully realized until believers receive their resurrected bodies. Resurrection hope will be fully realized at the Rapture. Paul describes that hope in the next seven verses of this paragraph.

Resurrection Hope Will Be Fully Realized at the Rapture

Paul calls the Rapture a mystery. Commenting on this paragraph, Paige Patterson notes, "Mystery (*musterion*) does not refer in the Scriptures to a mystery in the sense of unraveling a criminal plot but rather to an understanding which has been given by direct revelation of God."[38] The word emphasizes something that was hidden in the past but is now being revealed by God Himself. Notice the content of the revealed mystery, "We shall not all sleep, but we shall all be changed."[39] This is it! This is the moment that the corruptible flesh and blood of believers will put on incorruption.

---

36. Hitchcock, *Can We Still Believe in the Rapture?*, Kindle Location 1037.

37. I Corinthians 15:50.

38. Paige Patterson, *The Troubled Triumphant Church: An Exposition of First Corinthians* (Fort Worth, TX: Seminary Hill Press, 2011), 304.

39. 1 Corinthians 15:51.

Notice, this moment in time is similarly described in 1 Thessalonians 4:13-18. To his friends in Corinth, Paul said, "In a moment, in the twinkling of an eye, at the last trumpet. For the trumpet will sound, and the dead will be raised incorruptible, and we shall be changed."[40] As in his message to Thessalonica, Paul tells the Corinthians that the trumpet will sound, the dead in Christ will be raised, and those alive in Christ will be changed. Here however, Paul specifically adds an emphasis on the change necessary to inherit the Kingdom of God. The dead will not only be raised, but they will also receive an incorruptible body. Those alive at the sound of the trumpet will be changed so that they too receive an incorruptible body that is able to participate in the Kingdom of God.

Though Paul has already emphasized the necessity of this transformation, he reiterates this necessity in the next few verses. Consider his words.

> For this corruptible must put on incorruption, and this mortal *must* put on immortality. So, when this corruptible has put on incorruption, and this mortal has put on immortality, then shall be brought to pass the saying that is written: *"Death is swallowed up in victory. O Death, where is your sting? O Hades, where is your victory?"* The sting of death *is* sin, and the strength of sin *is* the law. But thanks *be* to God, who gives us the victory through our Lord Jesus Christ.[41]

The transformation is necessary. It "must" happen for one to inherit the Kingdom of God. Having dispelled the idea that one can really experience the Kingdom of God in its fullness now, Paul takes the opportunity to dispel another misconception.

Sometimes believers speak of death as if it is our friend. Biblically, death is our enemy. In fact, in this very chapter death is called "the last

---

40. 1 Corinthians 15:52.
41. 1 Corinthians 15:53-57.

enemy."[42] Believers do not presently have victory over death. Unless the Rapture takes place first, we will all die. In fact, we will not even have total victory over the full effects of death the moment our spirit wakes up in the presence of God. To be sure, when one's spirit is absent from the body, he/she is present with the Lord.[43] However, the believer who dies remains without total victory until the moment of receiving a resurrected body, like that of Jesus' body. Paul says then, and only then, "shall be brought to pass the saying that is written: *'Death is swallowed up in victory. O Death, where is your sting? O Hades, where is your victory?'*" This moment of victory happens at the sound of the trumpet, when the dead believers arise, and the believers who remain alive are changed as they rise to meet the Lord in the air. This moment is the event called the *Rapture*. Knowing that one's future includes the Rapture brings hope, as we observed in the letter to the church at Thessalonica. Knowing this truth also brings thanksgiving as we see expressed by Paul in 1 Corinthians chapter fifteen.[44] Resurrection Hope will be fully realized at the Rapture but having this hope does indeed impact us today.

Resurrection Hope at the Rapture Calls us to Perseverance Today

The full benefit of the resurrection comes to the believer at the time of the Rapture. However, there is a benefit for today. Notice the final verse of this great chapter. "Therefore, my beloved brethren, be steadfast, immovable, always abounding in the work of the Lord, knowing that your labor is not in vain in the Lord."[45] Believers can persevere today knowing that we will win, knowing that victory is coming, and knowing that victory is assured. We can persevere knowing that one day Jesus will come in the clouds, with a shout,

---

42. 1 Corinthians 15:26.
43. 2 Corinthians 5:8.
44. 1 Corinthians 15:56–57.
45. 1 Corinthians 15:58.

with the voice of the archangel, and with the trumpet of God. Knowing that at that moment the dead in Christ will rise and we who are alive in Christ will be caught up together with them in the clouds to meet our Lord Jesus, and we all will be transformed and given resurrection bodies like unto Jesus's resurrected body; knowing all this enables a believer to persevere today.

With an eye on future glory rather than the temporal grind, we are able to be "steadfast, immovable, abounding in the work of the Lord." No matter how difficult the trial, no matter how long the trial, it will end. But eternal joy and bliss awaits every true believer. We know that our work may be vicious today, but it is not in vain. Our work for Jesus may be accomplished amid great trial, but it will end in greater triumph. It may be hard today, but the reward is heavenly tomorrow. Therefore, knowing the Rapture is coming enables us to persevere in following Jesus today.

Thus far we have considered two paragraphs of Scripture that speak directly to the Rapture of the church. First Thessalonians 4:13-18 is one of the clearest texts on the topic and uses the Greek word, *harpadzo*, which is equivalent to the Latin word, *raptus*, and is translated into English as *caught up*. First Corinthians 15:50-58 connects the Rapture to the resurrection of Jesus and to the ability of one to inherit the Kingdom of God. The truth of this future event was once a hidden mystery, but God revealed it to His children in these two paragraphs of Scripture.

While these two passages are the clearest statements on the Rapture, there remains one more passage that one must consider. This final Rapture text was originally spoken by Jesus Himself to the eleven disciples in the upper room in Jerusalem, just hours before his arrest in the Garden of Gethsemane. Our attention must now focus on this important paragraph.

John 14:1-6

The Gospel of John is a unique book of the Bible. While part of the Gospel genre, the Apostle's presentation of the life and ministry of Jesus follows a different pattern than does Matthew, Mark, and Luke. The first three Gospels, often called the Synoptic Gospels, present Jesus' life and ministry following a rough chronological pattern. However, John presents the Lord's life in a thematic fashion. The Apostle identifies his purpose for writing toward the end of his Gospel. "But these were written that you may believe that Jesus is the Christ, the Son of God, and that believing you may have life in His name."[46]

To fulfill his purpose, John built the first twelve chapters of the book around seven miracles and seven teaching times. The events of these first twelve chapters are taken from the first three and one-half years of Jesus' public ministry. When the reader gets to chapter thirteen, John slows down and provides more detail. Chapters thirteen through nineteen cover less than twenty-four hours.

Chapter thirteen describes a few events in the upper room. While John leaves the description of the Last Supper to the other Gospel writers, he tells of Jesus washing the disciples' feet. Following the foot washing, Judas departs to betray Jesus. John chapters fourteen through seventeen describes an intimate teaching and prayer time between Jesus and the remaining eleven disciples.

Jesus knows that in just a few hours He will be betrayed, denied, tried, beaten, mocked, and then crucified for the sins of the world. He knows His body will be buried in a borrowed tomb and His disciples will hide in the upper room in fear for their lives. His last words to the eleven were designed to prepare them for what was coming and to prepare them to follow Him for the rest of their days.

A Precept to Trust

Jesus began this discourse with a precept, a promise, and a path. The promise is significant to the present discussion because it speaks to the Rapture of the church. Consider how the paragraph unfolds.

---

46. John 20:31.

Let not your heart be troubled; you believe in God, believe also in Me. In My Father's house are many mansions; if *it were* not *so,* I would have told you. I go to prepare a place for you. And if I go and prepare a place for you, I will come again and receive you to Myself; that where I am, *there* you may be also. And where I go you know, and the way you know. Thomas said to Him, 'Lord, we do not know where You are going, and how can we know the way?' Jesus said to him, 'I am the way, the truth, and the life. No one comes to the Father except through Me.'[47]

Knowing the fear and grief that is about to overtake His followers, Jesus offers them a precept: "Let not your heart be troubled...believe in Me."[48] Despite the trials they were about to face, Jesus reminded them that they should trust Him. Jesus is worthy of our trust. We may not understand what is happening in life, but we can be assured that Jesus loves us, He will never forsake us, and He has a plan.

A Promise of Triumph

Jesus moves from His precept of trust to provide His followers a promise of triumph. He says, "In My Father's House are many mansions, if it were not so I would have told you. I go to prepare a place for you, and if I go, I will come again and receive you unto Myself, that where I am, there you may be also."[49] While these words certainly bring comfort to thousands of believers today, they become even more significant when one understands the process of a Hebrew wedding ceremony in the first century.[50]

---

47. John 14:1–6.
48. John 14:1.
49. John 14:2–3.
50. Hitchcock, *Can We Still Believe in the Rapture?*; Shekinah Of Glory Ministries Blogger, "Scripture in Light of '1st Century History': Jewish Wedding Cus-

When a man decided that he had found the young lady he wanted to spend the rest of his life with, he would discuss it with his dad. He and his dad would then enter a dialogue with the young lady's family. At a special ceremony in the presence of both families, as well as friends and witnesses from the community, the man would make his proposal by offering the young lady a cup filled with the fruit of the vine. If the young lady consented to be his bride, she would take the cup and drink from it. Celebration would break forth, and the couple were legally bound together as betrothed husband and wife. Unlike our modern engagements, this agreement was legally binding and could only be broken by a legal divorce or by death. Divorce was generally only granted for the cause of adultery.[51] However, the couple did not live together at this point.

After a short celebration of the betrothal, the man would return to his father's house. Then, under the watchful eye of the father, the son would build a place for him and his bride. Once the son believed everything was prepared, he would seek his father's approval. When his dad agreed that the work was complete, and everything was ready for the son's bride, the work would cease. Then the son would simply wait.

Back at the bride's home everyone lived in anticipation. She made herself ready, preparing herself with beauty treatments, preparing clothing for the wedding night, for the wedding party, and for her new life with her husband. The bride, her family, nor their friends, had any idea when the groom would return for her. Typically, it would be close to a year, but

---

toms," *Scripture in Light of "1st Century History,"* May 15, 2011, accessed September 10, 2021, http://newjerusalemcommunity.blogspot.com/2011/05/jewish-wedding-customs.html; "Ancient Jewish Wedding Customs and Yeshua's Second Coming," *Messianic Bible*, n.d., accessed September 10, 2021, https://free.messianicbible.com/feature/ancient-jewish-wedding-customs-and-yeshuas-second-coming/; "(1) (DOC) Three Foundational Rapture Passages | Robert Dean, Jr - Academia.Edu," accessed September 11, 2021, https://www.academia.edu/42024447/Three_Foundational_Rapture_Passages.

51. Matthew 19:1-10. See also Joseph's consideration in Matthew 1:18-25.

no one knew when it would take place. As time passed, everyone knew the groom's return was nearing. The bride lived in anticipation every day knowing the groom could come for her at any moment.

Back at the groom's house, everything has been made ready. The son is simply waiting for his father to send him to get his bride. The timing of the groom's return for his bride rests only in the father's discretion. Then, at the right moment, the groom's father says, "Son, go get your bride."

With great excitement and shouting the groom, his family, and his close friends would leave the father's house and make their way to the house of the bride. Typically, the ram's horn would be blown as they made their way through the streets of the city. Loud shouts would ring forth. Soon people would gather outside the house of the bride's family. Then the bride would come out with her family and friends. Often the bride would sit on a cart and the groom's friends would lift the cart up on their shoulders and carry her back to the father's house. The entire wedding party would enter the father's house and the doors would be shut. The marriage would be consummated, and a seven-day feast would begin. While first century Hebrew wedding rituals seem foreign to followers of Jesus in the twenty-first century, they were a part of everyday life for the eleven disciples sitting around the table in the upper room with Jesus on the night of his betrayal. As Jesus spoke, there is little doubt that the imagery of the Jewish wedding would have immediately entered their minds. Having a grasp of these facts, sheds light on Jesus's statements for us today.[52]

---

52. For a good docudrama to familiarize oneself with First Century Jewish Wedding Customs see "Before the Wrath," *Pure Flix*, accessed September 10, 2021, https://app.pureflix.com/videos/391012390456/before-the-wrath. Commentary provided by several scholars including: Jay McCarl a Middle East Anthropologist, Jan Markell of Olive Tree Ministries, J.D. Farag a Theologian and Senior Pastor, Jack Hibbs, Theologian and Senior Pastor, Amir Tsarfati of Behold Israel, Scott McConnell of LifeWay Research, and Lizette Dillinger the Qualitative Director at LifeWay Research.

Our Lord promised His followers that while He was going away, He would return. He would return for His bride.[53] This is a unique event. Jesus's focus here is not one of coming in judgment of the world like we read about in Matthew 24. Rather, it is a coming in joy for His bride.[54] Of course, Ephesians 5:22-33 makes it clear that the church is the bride of Christ. This is a word of comfort for the followers of Jesus. This is a word of promise that while He is gone, He is preparing a place in His Father's house for His bride—the Church.

Like a bride waiting on her groom in the first century, believers know that with every passing day the Lord's return is closer than the day before. No one on earth knows when He will come, but He will come. When everything is ready in His Father's house, His preparatory work will cease and He will simply wait for the Father's directive. When the Father gives the word, the Son will shout, Michael the archangel will shout, Gabriel will blow the trumpet, Jesus will descend, the dead in Christ will rise in their brand new resurrected bodies, then we who are alive and remain will be Raptured up to meet them in the air, we will be changed having received our resurrection bodies, and we shall return to the Father's house for the Marriage Supper of the Lamb.

---

53. Not all commentators believe this passage refers to the Lord's return. Borchert notes Dodd and others who suggest this is about Jesus coming to receive a follower at the time of his/her death. Although, he concludes his discussion by acknowledging the likelihood that it indeed has an eschatological view in mind. Gerald L. Borchert, *John 12-21*, in *The New American Commentary*, vol. 25B (Nashville: Broadman & Holman, 2002), 105-106. Merrill Tenney argues that this text cannot be referring to death, but must be focused on the eschatological return of Jesus. Frank Ely Gaebelein, ed., *John - Acts*, in *The Expositor's Bible Commentary*, vol. 9 (London: Pickering & Inglis, 1981), 143. Walvoord agrees that this text has an eschatological return of Jesus in mind and in no way speaks to Jesus coming at one's personal death. John F. Walvoord, *The Rapture Question* (Findlay, OH: Dunham Publishing Company, 1957), 75-76.

54. For a good discussion on the contrast of Matthew 24 and John 14:3 see John F. Walvoord, *The Rapture Question*, 108-111.

A Path to Trod

As exciting as this promise is, Jesus did not stop there. He not only issued a precept to trust and give a promise of triumph, He also explained the path to trod. Notice the balance of the paragraph.

> And where I go you know, and the way you know. Thomas said to Him, 'Lord, we do not know where You are going, and how can we know the way?' Jesus said to him, 'I am the way, the truth, and the life. No one comes to the Father except through Me.[55]

Jesus told the eleven that they knew where He was going. Now, He had just told them He was going to the Father's House and for three and a half years He had been telling them the path to get there themselves. However, Thomas spoke up and expressed his confusion about the matter. So, Jesus explained the path to trod.

There are many paths in life, but most lead to destruction. There is only one path that leads to the Father's house. Jesus said, "I am the path!" Jesus Himself is the way to the Father's House. The Bible is clear, "All have sinned and come short of the glory of God."[56] Not one of us deserve to enter the Father's House. In fact, the Bible tells us what we deserve. "The wages of sin is death."[57] Because of our sin we neither deserve to be in the Father's house nor can we earn a place with Him. We have earned death, separation from God, not just in this life, but for all eternity. Yet, the Bible also tells us that, "The gift of God is eternal life through Christ Jesus our Lord."[58]

---

55. John 14:4–6.
56. Romans 3:23.
57. Romans 6:23a.
58. Romans 6:23b.

Jesus prepared the eleven disciples for the fact that in the next twenty-four hours He was going to die, taking the penalty for their sins, for our sins, and for the sins of every other person who has ever walked or ever will walk on the face of the earth. He was going to be buried, and then three days later, Jesus would rise again, defeating sin, death, and the grave. Jesus explained to His followers that by turning from sin and trusting Him alone to be the Lord and Savior of one's life, one enters the path to assurance that at the Rapture, they will be among those who rise in joy to return to the Father's house for the marriage supper of the Lamb.

These three passages of Scripture speak of the Rapture of the church. There is no question that the Rapture is a real event that is future. It is a joyous event and every believer should look forward to it. We do not know when it will happen, but with every passing day it is closer than the day before. We must be ready. We must be expecting. We must be listening for the shout, the trumpet, and looking for Jesus Himself to come in the clouds, receive us to Himself, and take us to His Father's house for the Marriage Supper of the Lamb.

All three of these passages of Scripture make it clear that the Rapture is real, but not one of them speak directly to the timing of the Rapture—other than that it is imminent. Before considering the timing of the Rapture, one more truth should be noted. The Rapture and the Second Coming of Jesus to the earth cannot be the same event.

Distinguishing The Rapture

One of the main points of contention regarding the Rapture is whether the term is simply another way of describing the Second Coming of Jesus, whether the Second Coming and the Rapture are two separate events, or whether they are two phases of the same event. Those who believe that the Rapture will take place prior to the Tribulation (Daniel's 70th Week), hold to one of the latter views. This is also true of those who hold to a partial Rapture, mid-tribulation Rapture, or pre-wrath Rapture. Those who hold to a post-tribulation view as well as those coming from an amillennial perspective tend to believe that rather than being two separate events, the Rapture and Second Coming describe the same event. However, there are several distinctions between the two events.

Several commentators and theologians have noted differences between the Rapture and the Second Coming that cannot simply be dismissed. Hindson and Hitchcock note, "Similarities exist between the Rapture and the return, but the irreconcilable dissimilarities carry more weight."[59] They go on to describe ten specific differences, noting that these are only some of the more significant distinctions. Consider their list of ten.

1. There is a difference in the signs given for each stage.
2. There is a difference in the place Christ will meet believers.
3. There is a difference in who removes people from the earth.
4. There is a difference in who gets taken from the earth and who is left.
5. There is a difference of when Jesus comes in relationship to the Tribulation.
6. There is a difference as to when judgment takes place.
7. There is a difference in the timing of the resurrection of the dead.
8. There is a difference in the people involved.
9. There is a difference in the mention of the Rapture of living believers.
10. There is a difference in the changes on earth associated with these events.[60]

Hindson and Hitchcock are not alone in noting significant distinctions between the Rapture and the Second Coming. Danny Akin often re-

---

59. Hitchcock, *Can We Still Believe in the Rapture?*, Kindle Location 1726.
60. Hitchcock, *Can We Still Believe in the Rapture?*, Kindle Location 1726-1777.

fers to his own chart to demonstrate some of the distinctions between the two events. Note his chart reproduced here from his chapter in *The Return of Christ: A Premillennial Perspective.*[61]

THE RAPTURE	THE SECOND COMING
Christ comes to receive His church in the air	Christ returns with His bride and angels to the earth
The seven-year tribulation begins shortly after the Rapture of the church	The millennial kingdom (1,000 years) of Christ is established after the Second Coming
The event is imminent; it could happen at any time	Numerous signs precede this event (Rev. 6-19)
This is a message of comfort for believers	This is a message of judgment (and warning) for unbelievers
The church is of primary importance	Israel is of significant importance
The Rapture is a mystery	The Second Coming is predicted in both the Old and New Testaments
The judgment seat of Christ for believers occurs (Rom 14:10; 1 Cor 3:10-15; 2 Cor 5:10)	The sheep-and-goats judgment occurs (Matt 25:31-46); and the Antichrist and the world are judged (Rev 19:11-21)
Only believers are affected	All people are affected

While all the distinctions pointed out by these three scholars are both reasonable and significant, it should be recognized that all scholars do not accept each of the distinctions described above. The present author accepts all the distinctions and the explanations provided by the two works referenced. However, for this writer some of the distinctions carry more significance than others. These include the following.

---

61. Allen and Lemke, *The Return of Christ A Premillennial Perspective,* Kindle Location 1392-1414.

1. At the *Rapture* the saints (dead in Christ first, followed by believers who are alive and remain) will be *caught up* to meet the Lord in the air. In contrast, at the *Return* Jesus comes to the earth bringing both His saints and His angels with him. (1 Thess 4:13-18; Rev 19:1-16).

2. At the *Rapture* the dead in Christ and those alive who are in Christ will be taken from the earth in joy. At the *Return* those who reject Christ are taken from the earth in judgment. (1 Thess 4:13-18; 1 Cor 15:50-58; John 14:1-6; Matt 24:40-44).

3. At the *Rapture* believers are taken from the earth only by the shout of the Lord, the archangel, and the trumpet. At the *Return* the Lord sends His angles with the sound of a trumpet to gather unbelievers from the earth for judgment. (1 Thess 4:13-18; 1 Cor 15:50-58; John 14:1-6; Matt 24:29-31).

4. The *Rapture* is imminent (The entire New Testament from Acts 1:6-Revelation 22:20 emphasizes the expectation of the imminence of the *Rapture*. This imminence is often used as a motivator for the urgency of sharing the Gospel and the urgency of faithful obedience). The *Return* is preceded by many signs. (Note Matthew 24 and Revelation chapters 6-19 just as a starting place).

The bottom line is that while there may be similar language used to describe these two events, there are also significant differences in the Biblical descriptions and the outcomes. Whether one prefers speaking in terms of two events or two phases of a longer event separated by time, the evidence demonstrates that the *Rapture* and the *Return* (Second Coming) are indeed different from one another. One cannot conflate the two and reconcile the Biblical distinctions. Indeed, the Rapture takes place at a distinct moment in time and brings about different results.

Summary

This section of the chapter has sought to discover the nature of the Rapture. First, consideration was given to defining the term. Second, this section sought to answer those who deny that the Rapture exists and demonstrate that indeed the Rapture is real. Third, a defense of the Rapture was given by examining the three clear Rapture texts in the New Testament. Fourth, this section of the chapter examined issues that distinguish the *Rapture* from the *Return* (Second Coming) of Jesus.

While the discussion of the nature of the Rapture demonstrates that the event is indeed a real event that is yet future, the timing of the Rapture has not yet been considered. Indeed, the three Rapture texts (1 Thess 4:13-18; 1 Cor 15:50-58, John 14:1-6) speak to the reality of the Rapture but say nothing as to the timing of the Rapture. The only possible indication of timing may come in the understanding of the cultural background of the Hebrew weddings in the first century. Yet even this does not offer certain clarity on the timing of the Rapture. Before answering the overall question of this chapter (Does The Rapture Still Matter?) one must not only understand the nature of the event, but one must consider the timing of the event as well.

THE TIMING OF THE RAPTURE

When will the Rapture occur? This is one of the most controversial questions discussed by theologians, pastors, and people in the pew. Most self-identified Christians still believe that Jesus is coming back and many of them emphasize the physical return. However, when it comes to the timing of the Rapture, there is widespread disagreement. In 2016 LifeWay Research conducted a survey of senior pastors asking about the timing of the

Rapture. While 36% of those surveyed indicated they believed the Rapture would happen prior to the beginning of the seven-year period known as the Tribulation, as noted earlier in this chapter 25% replied that the concept of the Rapture should not be taken literally. The next largest group, 18%, indicated the belief that the Rapture would happen after the Tribulation. The Mid-Tribulation view and the Pre-Wrath Tribulation view was each held by 4% of respondents. Another 8% of respondents held to some other view.[62] Obviously even senior pastors hold differing views on the timing of the Rapture. This difference is prominent not only among pastors but also among professors, theologians, and the average church attender.

As Danny Akin has noted, there are five main views held by conservative evangelicals and most of these views can easily be found in a gathering of Baptists.[63] These views include, the post-tribulation view, the mid-tribulation view, the pre-wrath view, the partial-Rapture view, and the pre-tribulational view. Each of these views are briefly described below. The reader will be pointed to various evangelical preachers, professors, authors, etc., that hold to the different views. Resources will be noted for the reader to do further research on each view. This section of the chapter will then conclude with an explanation of why I hold to the pre-tribulational view.

The Post-Tribulation View

As noted above, in the LifeWay Research survey 18% of senior pastors responded that they held to a post-tribulation view.[64] For much of the last 50 years this view has been the view most often held by those who reject the pre-tribulation view. Douglas Moo argued for this position in a *Three*

---

62. "Belief in the Rapture," *Lifeway Research*, accessed September 11, 2021; https://lifewayresearch.com/search/Belief in the Rapture/.

63. Allen and Lemke, *The Return of Christ A Premillennial Perspective*, Kindle Location 1332-1343.

64. "Belief in the Rapture," *Lifeway Research*, accessed September 11, 2021; https://lifewayresearch.com/search/Belief in the Rapture/.

Views book published by Zondervan in 1984 and renewed in 1996.[65] Moo is a respected New Testament scholar among conservative evangelical believers. He has authored and co-authored numerous works. At the time he participated in writing the *Three Views* book, he served as the Assistant Professor of New Testament at Trinity Evangelical Divinity School. Today he serves as the Kenneth T. Wessner Professor of New Testament at Wheaton College.[66]

Moo not only argued for his view in the *Three Views* book, he also wrote responses to the other contributors. It is important to note his humble spirit in approaching the subject. He concluded his chapter with the following words.

> The truth of the imminent coming of our Lord Jesus Christ is an important and indispensable element of biblical truth. That this coming is to be premillennial the Scriptures plainly state. That a time of unprecedented Tribulation will immediately precede that coming and the living believers will be Raptured into the presence of Christ at His coming are also plainly stated. But the time of that Rapture with respect to the Tribulation is nowhere plainly stated...What I think the Scriptures indicate about this relationship has been stated on the preceding pages. But...I cannot, indeed must not, allow this conviction to represent any kind of barrier to full relationships with others who hold differing convictions on this point.[67]

While Moo's presentation is charitable, he nonetheless defends the post-tribulation view with vigor. He begins by describing the view. "It is my purpose to present an exegetical and theological argument for the view

---

65. Gleason L. Archer, ed., *Three Views on the Rapture: Pre-, Mid-, or Post-Tribulation ?*, Counterpoints (Grand Rapids, Mich: Zondervan, 1996).

66. "Douglas Moo - Wheaton College, IL," accessed September 14, 2021; https://www.wheaton.edu/academics/faculty/douglas-moo/.

67. Archer, *Three Views on the Rapture,* 211.

that the church, or the saints of the present dispensation, will be Raptured *after* the Great Tribulation."[68] The reader who desires to understand why some hold to this view would do well to read Moo's chapter.[69] To understand how someone holding to a pre-tribulation Rapture may respond to Moo, one could read Paul Feinberg's response in the same work.[70] For the purpose of this chapter it should be understood the this position believes that the seven years of Tribulation should be identified with Daniel's 70th week, is yet future, and that the Rapture will take place immediately following the Tribulation. Those who hold this view believe that Jesus will come and receive the Church in the clouds and then Jesus and the saints will immediately come to the earth and establish the 1,000-year reign of Christ.

The Mid-Tribulation View

The mid-tribulation has never held as many adherents as the pre- or post-tribulation view. As noted above, in LifeWay's 2016 survey only 4% of senior pastors responded that this was their understanding of the timing of the Rapture.[71] However, there has been several significant scholars who held this position.

I have been privileged to learn from professors, pastors, and laymen alike. Indeed, the Lord has used many godly men and women in the pew through the years to teach me invaluable lessons. One of the Baptist men that influenced me was Johnny V. Boley. Johnny served the Lord in any way he could throughout his life. A bank employee by trade, he was proficient in several languages including Greek, German, Spanish, Yiddish, Russian, and more. Indeed, when I was studying first year Greek, Johnny's tutelage proved

68. Archer, *Three Views on the Rapture*, 171.
69. Archer, *Three Views on the Rapture*, 171-211.
70. Archer, *Three Views on the Rapture*, 223-231.
71. "Belief in the Rapture," *Lifeway Research*, accessed September 11, 2021; https://lifewayresearch.com/search/Belief in the Rapture/.

invaluable. Johnny loved the Lord, the Bible, the Church, and enjoyed serving alongside several pastors, missionaries, and professors throughout his life.

One of his favorite things to do was to discuss various biblical and theological issues. However, Johnny rarely discussed the Rapture. He recognized conversations on this topic were often heated. Yet, Johnny wanted to grapple with the topic. He was particularly intrigued by the Pre-wrath position, which is discussed below. So, he set out to settle the issue in his mind once for all. As he studied Johnny ended up writing the book, *Another Look at the Rapture.*[72] Boley argues for a mid-70th Week of Daniel position. However, he also argues that the Great Tribulation only lasts three and a half years. Therefore, he argues for what he calls a "pre-Tribulation, but mid-week view."[73] However, his view of the Mid-Week Tribulation is not the most common view.

To gain an understanding of the typical approach to the mid-tribulation view one should read Gleason Archer's chapter in the *Three Views* book mentioned above. At the time of writing his sections of the book, he served as the Professor of Old Testament at Trinity Evangelical Divinity School. Prior to this appointment Archer served at Fuller Theological Seminary and as pastor of the Park Street Church in Boston, MA. He authored several works and participated in several conservative evangelical projects during his lifetime. Archer went home to be with the Lord on April 27, 2004.[74] Prior to his death, he had a significant influence among many Baptist and evangelical believers.

---

72. Johnny V. Boley, *Another Look at the Rapture* (Unpublished, n.d.).

73. Boley argues that the first three and a half years of Daniel's 70th week should be understood as having taken place during Jesus's public ministry on earth. He then believes there to be a break in the timeline as God begins to deal with the world through the Church, rather than through the nation of Israel. He believes at some point in the future, just prior to the revelation of the Antichrist, the Rapture will take place and the second half of Daniel's 70th week will begin. Thus, he refers to his view as "pre-tribulation but mid-week."

74. A short biographical sketch of Archer's life and works can be found here: https://en.wikipedia.org/wiki/Gleason_Archer_Jr.

Archer introduces the mid-tribulation view on the first page of his chapter. He begins by acknowledging the importance of the subject. He asserts that the Rapture is taught in "1 Thessalonians 4 and related passages."[75] Archer then asks if the Rapture will occur prior to or immediately following the seven years of Tribulation. Responding to his own questions, he writes. "Within the ranks of sincere Evangelicals, who believe in the inerrancy of Holy Scripture and the fulfillment of all biblical prophecy, there is a difference of opinion. There are energetic advocates of each interpretation. Between these two views there stands a third, the view that the Rapture will occur at the midway point between the beginning of the final seven-year period and its end."[76] Archer then dedicates thirty-one pages to defend his mid-Tribulation view.

The Pre-Wrath View

In 1990 Marvin Rosenthal entered the discussion of the timing of the Rapture with a newer view. He argued for a "pre-wrath" Rapture of the church.[77] His work offered an alternative and renewed serious discussions concerning the timing of the Rapture. While his view failed to gain a large following, it did indeed gain some traction. In 2001 Renald Showers published his own work examining and critiquing Rosenthal's position.[78] By the time LifeWay Research conducted the 2016 survey the view reached a stable following. The reader may remember that 4% of senior pastors held to the pre-wrath position at that time.[79] So what is the pre-wrath Rapture view?

---

75. Archer, *Three Views on the Rapture*, 115.

76. Archer, *Three Views on the Rapture*, 115.

77. Marvin J. Rosenthal, *The Pre-Wrath Rapture of the Church* (Nashville: T. Nelson, 1990).

78. Renald E. Showers, *The Pre-Wrath Rapture View: An Examination and Critique* (Grand Rapids: Kregel Publications, 2001).

79. "Belief in the Rapture," *Lifeway Research*, accessed September 11, 2021; https://lifewayresearch.com/search/Belief in the Rapture/.

Showers provides a helpful and accurate summary of the pre-wrath view in the introduction to his book. This position holds that the 70th Week of Daniel is divided into three time periods. The first is referred to as the time of the birth pangs connected to Matthew 24:24-28 and coincides with the first four seals of Revelation chapter six. The second period is viewed as The Great Tribulation referred to in Matthew 24:21 and relates to the fifth and sixth seals of Revelation 6:12-14. The sixth seal then serves as a pre-cursor to the third period according to the pre-wrath position. This final period is viewed as The Day of the Lord. The focus of this period is that of God pouring out His wrath upon the earth.[80]

The pre-wrath view distinguished between the Rapture and the second coming. Unlike the post-tribulation view, this position holds that the church is Raptured out and taken to heaven prior to the opening of the seventh seal, which contains the seven trumpets and seven bowl judgments. Unlike the mid-tribulation view, this view holds that the opening of the seventh seal takes place after the mid-point of the 70th Week. Those who hold this view believe that Jesus and the saints return to earth to set up Christ's millennial reign at the conclusion of the bowl judgments.

The Partial Rapture View

While the partial-Rapture view did not have enough respondents in the end times survey conducted by LifeWay Research in 2016 to garner a separate category, it is, nonetheless, a view that has been held by some over the last one hundred years. Indeed, John Walvoord dedicated an entire chapter to explaining and critiquing the view in his book published in 1957.[81] Walvoord describes the position. "There has arisen in the last century, however, a small group of pretribulationists who contend that only those who are faithful in

---

80. Showers, *The Pre-Wrath Rapture View*, 10-11.
81. Walvoord, John F., *The Rapture Question*, 105-125.

the church will be Raptured or translated and the rest will either be Raptured sometime during the tribulation or at its end."[82] Walvoord goes on to explain that the proponents of this view believe people will be Raptured in groups throughout the Tribulation based on their growth in faithfulness in the midst of the troubles associated with the Tribulation period.

While this view has never enjoyed a large following, occasionally one may come across someone who holds this view today. For a contemporary example the reader could consider Paul Shonebarger and his work, *The Partial Rapture and the Left Behind Church*.[83] This variation of the pre-tribulation position is rarely discussed in other works, although Danny Akin briefly described it in his chapter mentioned earlier.[84] No further description will be presented in this chapter. Rather focus now shifts to consideration of the pre-tribulation view.

The Pre-Tribulation View

Those who hold to the pre-tribulation Rapture position believe that Jesus could return to Rapture His followers at any moment. This position believes that once Raptured, Jesus will take His saints to heaven where they will enjoy the Marriage Supper of the Lamb. They will also stand before the Judgment Seat of Christ to receive rewards for their earthly labors. While worshiping the Lord in their glorified bodies, Jesus will open the scroll described in Revelation chapters five and six. As He opens each seal of the scroll, He is pouring out His wrath on those who remain on the earth. This judgment will last for seven years and is described in Revelation chapters six through eighteen. Jesus will then return to the earth with His saints and His

---

82. Walvoord, John F., *The Rapture Question*, 105.

83. "The Partial Rapture and the Left Behind Church," accessed September 14, 2021, https://www.napabookmine.com/book/9798698152309.

84. Allen and Lemke, *The Return of Christ A Premillennial Perspective*, Kindle Location 1343.

angels. He will throw the Antichrist and the False Prophet into the Lake of Fire. He will bind Satan for 1,000 years and will fulfill the Davidic promises to rule and reign from His throne in Jerusalem.

This view stands as one of the most popular views of the Rapture and related end time events among evangelical believers. D.L. Moody and C.I. Scofield popularized the pre-tribulational view in the late nineteenth and early twentieth centuries. Scofield's study Bible and Moody's worldwide preaching emphasized that Jesus could return at any minute. While Moody never focused on theological nuances, he certainly preached the imminent return of Jesus to Rapture His church, and he preached it often. Many scholars, whether in joy or sadness, have noted the vast influence of the Scofield Study Bible.[85] Scofield's Dispensational theology, including the pre-tribulational, pre-millennial view of the Rapture, influenced countless Baptists and evangelicals through the years.

In the latter half of the twentieth century the preaching of W.A. Criswell, Adrian Roger, Paige Patterson, and many others continued to have a significant influence on Baptists' view of the pre-tribulational Rapture. In addition, Charles Ryrie's works on dispensationalism, systematic theology, and his study Bible influenced countless Baptists and evangelical believers.

In the 1970s a trilogy of movies about the end times had a widespread influence on Baptists, evangelical believers, the American Church in general, and in many cases, even among non-professing Christians. The first movie, *A Thief in the Night*,[86] presented a pre-tribulation Rapture of be-

---

85. C. I. Scofield and Henry G. Weston, *The Holy Bible Containing the Old and New Testaments: Authorized King James Version with a New System of Connected Topical References to All the Greater Themes of Scripture, with Annotations, Revised Marginal Renderings, Summaries, Definitions, Chronology, and Index, to Which Are Added, Helps at Hard Places, Explanations of Seeming Discrepancies, and a New System of Paragraphs*, 1945.

86. Donald W. Thompson et al., *A Thief in the Night* (Mark IV Pictures Incorporated, 1973).

lievers. It was followed up with the movies, *A Distant Thunder*[87] and *Image of the Beast*,[88] both of which focused on the seriousness of the seven years of Tribulation at the end of the age. These movies were shown in theaters, special event venues, and churches across the United States. Many people responded to the Gospel during this era, having become convinced that Jesus could return at any moment.

Also released in 1970, Larry Norman's popular song had a significant influence. *I Wish We'd All Been Ready*[89] played on Christian radio stations across the nation. Secular radio stations picked it up as well. It was sung in Christian concerts and as special music in churches throughout the 1970s. With all this emphasis on the Rapture as a pre-tribulational event, it is not difficult to understand how this view became the prominent view held by Baptists and conservative evangelicals in the twentieth century.

While more than a decade of influence produced positive results, it also produced negative results that eventually hurt the position. On the positive side, countless individuals came to personal faith in Jesus. In addition, many believers moved from being "nominal Christians" to becoming serious about their faith. The negative results can be observed when one examines both the literature and the sermons about the Rapture produced during the final two decades of the twentieth century. Many preachers and teachers began making predictions regarding the Rapture that moved beyond what is revealed in Scripture.

---

87. Donald W. Thompson et al., *A Distant Thunder* (Mark IV Pictures Incorporated, 1978).

88. Donald W. Thompson et al., *Image of the Beast* (Mark IV Pictures Incorporated, 1981).

89. Larry Norman, *Larry Norman - I Wish We'd All Been Ready - [1989]*, 2013, accessed September 15, 2021, https://www.youtube.com/watch?v=aP-JpZdEOILQ.

Space will not allow this chapter to cover all the false predictions of this era. Consider just a few examples. In January of 1988 a self-published book captured the attention of people across the United States. Edgar C. Whisenant's book, *88 Reasons*, claimed the Rapture would happen in September of 1988.[90] Of course in 1989 he followed it up with another work explaining why he was off by one year. By 1990 everyone who was fooled by his predictions realized his folly.

Others also made predictions which included various dates that the Rapture would take place, the identification of the Antichrist, the identification of the "mark of the beast", and many other end times claims to which the Bible simply does not provide details. With each false prediction, more and more people grew cold to the idea of a pre-tribulational Rapture. As the twentieth century gave way to the twenty-first, more and more people lost interest in the Rapture of the Church.

Sensing that the biblical doctrine of the Rapture, and particularly the pre-tribulational view, was beginning to wane in the face of false predictions, Tim LaHaye and Jerry B. Jenkins wrote a series of novels based on the pre-tribulational position. The *Left Behind* series gained a wide audience with over 63 million copies sold.[91] Three movies were produced based on this series that further popularized the concept once again. Coupled with this fictional series, LaHaye and Jenkins also published non-fiction works on the topic.[92] These works began to influence believers once again across the United States. Yet, a significant number of believers remained skeptical.

---

90. Edgar C. Whisenant, *88 Reasons Why the Rapture Is in 1988* (Edgar C. Whisenant, 1988).

91. Tim LaHaye and Jerry B. Jenkins, *The Left Behind Collection* (Wheaton: Tyndale House Publishers, 2014).

92. Tim LaHaye, *No Fear of the Storm* (Sisters, OR: Multnomah, 1992); Tim LaHaye and Jerry B Jenkins, *Are We Living in the End Times?* (Wheaton: Tyndale House Publishers, 2001); Tim LaHaye, *The Merciful God of Prophecy: His Loving Plan for You in the End Times* (New York: Warner Books, 2002).

As Hindson and Hitchcock note, "Every time there is a 'blood moon' or war heats up in the Middle East, there are a number of 'prophetic panhandlers' who assure us this is the Big One."[93] Following this statement, the authors offer a significant list of such predictions through the years. Each time these predictions are made and then fail to come true, the hearts of people grow cold and they ask, "Where is the promise of His coming?"[94] Despite the many distractions from the pre-tribulation, pre-millennial position, LifeWay's 2016 survey of senior pastors across America found that 34% still believe this position best describes what the Bible teaches.[95] I was not questioned as part of LifeWays' survey, however, I am convinced that Scripture presents a pre-tribulational Rapture.

Reasons For The Pre-Tribulation View

It must be acknowledged that Bible believing inerrantists agree as to the reality of the Rapture but disagree over the timing of the Rapture. There is not a verse of Scripture that specifically states that the Rapture will occur just prior to Daniel's 70th week. However, there are significant biblical, theological, and practical reasons to hold to a pre-tribulational Rapture of the church. Consider the following.

Biblical Reasons for The Pre-Tribulational Rapture

1. First Thessalonians 4 clearly teaches the event is real, a source of comfort now, and a source of joyful hope for the future.

---

93. Hitchcock, *Can We Still Believe in the Rapture?*, Kindle Location 425–433.
94. 2 Peter 3:1–7.
95. "Belief in the Rapture," *Lifeway Research*, accessed September 11, 2021; https://lifewayresearch.com/search/Belief in the Rapture/.

2. First Corinthians 15 clearly teaches that at the Rapture, believers who have died and those who are alive at the time will receive a glorified body that will be like Jesus's resurrection body. This must take place for one to inherit the Kingdom of God.

3. John 14:1-6 clearly teaches that Jesus went to His Father's house to prepare a place for His followers, that He would one day come back and receive His followers unto Himself, and that He will take them to the place He has prepared for them. Considering the historical context of the first century Hebrew wedding practices, these promises are best understood as a pre-tribulational Rapture.

4. The church is mentioned repeatedly in the first three chapters of Revelation but is not mentioned as being on earth thereafter until the saints return to the earth with Jesus in Revelation 19.

5. The church is seen in heaven worshiping Jesus in Revelation chapters four and five.

6. Though there are people coming to faith in Christ during the Tribulation, the primary work of evangelism is entrusted to the two witnesses and the 144,000 Jews. The church is never mentioned as being on earth during this time.

7. The church is again observed in heaven at the beginning of Revelation nineteen, and then seen as coming **with** Jesus as He returns to the earth.

8. The pre-tribulation view fits New Testament references to the church being a mystery and makes sense of the time gap between the sixty-ninth and seventieth weeks of Daniel.

9. A clear distinction can be observed between the passages that speak about the Rapture, where Jesus comes in the clouds and believers are "caught up" versus the passages

that speak about the Second Coming where Jesus physically returns to the earth.

Theological Reasons for The Pre-Tribulational Rapture

1. The imminent return of Christ – The early church was unanimous in believing Jesus could return at any moment. This is only possible in three scenarios: a Pre-Tribulation Rapture, a Partial-Rapture, or Amillennialism. Both the partial-Rapture and the amillennial positions are inherently filled with both hermeneutical and theological problems that are insurmountable. Therefore, the imminency of Jesus' return points to a pre-tribulational Rapture.

2. While believers in the time of the Church do indeed experience the discipline of God and will certainly experience both persecution and tribulations, we will never experience the wrath of God (Rom. 8:1). Jesus paid it all! A natural reading of Revelation 4-19 clearly demonstrates that Jesus alone is able to open the scroll and as He does so, the wrath of God is being poured out on the earth.

3. A clear distinction must be made between the nation of Israel and the Church. Romans 9-11 makes it clear that God is not finished with the nation of Israel. Though salvation has always been by grace alone through faith alone, God sent the message of salvation and has dealt with the world in different ways during different times throughout history. In the Old Testament He dealt with the world primarily through the nation of Israel. Today, He is dealing with the world primarily through the Church. However, Daniel prophesied 70 weeks (each week representing a period of seven years)

that God would deal with the world through the nation of Israel. The first sixty-nine weeks concluded with the *cutting off* of the Messiah. This prophecy can be marked in history as having been fulfilled. Following Jesus's ascension and the coming of the Holy Spirit in Acts 2, God has dealt with the world through the Church. Yet, there remains one week – one period of seven years, where God will once again deal with the world through the nation of Israel. At the Rapture the time of the church will be completed and the 70th week of Daniel will be fulfilled. A pre-tribulation Rapture of the church is the best way to understand the fulfillment of Daniel's prophecy of the 70 weeks.

Practical Reasons for The Pre-Tribulational Rapture

1. The pre-tribulational Rapture provides a time and place for the Bema (judgment) Seat of Christ.[96]
2. The pre-tribulational Rapture provides a time and place for the Marriage Supper of the Lamb.[97]
3. The pre-tribulational Rapture does not struggle with the question of how believers could be "caught up" in the clouds, eat the Marriage Supper of the Lamb, and return to the earth in a "twinkling of an eye" (1 Corinthians 15:52).
4. The pre-tribulational Rapture helps explain how the earth will be populated during the millennial reign and over whom Jesus and His Church will rule and reign.
5. The pre-tribulational Rapture provides the opportunity for children to be born during the millennial reign and for the

---

96. 2 Corinthians 5:9-11; 1 Corinthians 3:12-15.
97. Revelation 19:9.

fact that when Satan is released for a short time, some will choose to follow him.[98]

While I am strongly convinced that the Rapture will take place prior to the start of the Seven Years Tribulation, one thing is certain. No matter what one holds about the timing of the Rapture, anyone who takes the Bible seriously must acknowledge the reality of the Rapture.

Summary

We began this section of the chapter by acknowledging that while the reality of the Rapture is widely accepted among both Baptists and conservative evangelical believers, the timing of the Rapture is the source of much disagreement and controversy. We then noted the five most prominent views of the timing of the Rapture among pre-millennialists. Each position was defined, and the reader was exposed to various proponents of each view. The dominance of the pre-tribulation view over more than one hundred years was briefly reviewed. Abuses in this position were acknowledged. I then presented the reader with seventeen reasons I hold to a pre-tribulational Rapture viewpoint. Attention now turns to the main question of this chapter, "Does the Rapture Still Matter?"

DOES THE RAPTURE STILL MATTER?

This chapter began by noting that there appears to be less interest in the Rapture in the days in which we live. While we noted there remains some interest in the pew and in the public to hearing thoughts on matters related to the end of the world, pastors, professors, and other Christian leaders tend

---

98. Revelation 20:7-10.

to focus on issues of living today and avoid eschatological debates. However, we also noted that while this may describe "what is," it does not really speak to "what ought to be." Therefore, we concluded our introduction by asking the question of this chapter, "Does the Rapture Still Matter?"

To consider that question one must understand the issues surrounding the nature of the Rapture and the timing of the Rapture. The chapter grappled with the nature of the Rapture by defining the Rapture, addressing those who deny the Rapture, then by defending the Rapture, and finally by distinguishing the Rapture from the Second Coming of Jesus. In this section we clearly defined the Rapture as a real, future event, where Jesus will descend from heaven with a shout, with the voice of the archangel, with the trump of God, the dead in Christ will rise to meet Jesus in the clouds, receiving a glorified body like the resurrected body of Jesus, and then those who are alive in Christ will also be "caught up" and transformed so that they too receive a resurrected body. Those Raptured will then return with Jesus to His Father's House. As the first section of the chapter came to a close, we noted that the fact of the Rapture is a clear biblical teaching that nearly all conservative evangelicals believe.

When it comes to the timing of the Rapture, particularly its relationship to Daniel's 70th Week or the Tribulation, there remains no consensus. The second section of the chapter explained the five major views on the timing of the Rapture, noting the main emphasis of each view along with some proponents of the position. I then offered biblical, theological, and practical reasons that I hold to a pre-tribulational view of the Rapture. The timing of the Rapture should not be a test of faith issue. While the fact of the Rapture is a clear biblical doctrine, solid Bible believing inerrantists disagree as to the timing of this glorious event.

Considering the Bible's testimony as to the nature of the Rapture and the various texts that do impact the timing of the Rapture, one must conclude that the Rapture is clearly taught in the Bible. Since the Bible teaches that the Rapture is a real event, one must answer the question of this chapter with a resounding, yes! The Rapture does indeed still matter!

The Rapture matters to those who have never turned from their sin and trusted Jesus. If indeed Jesus could return at any moment and take all those who have trusted Him to His Father's House for a joyous reunion, it matters to every person who has not yet been saved. One must not delay. Turn to Jesus today. The Rapture still matters!

The Rapture also matters to those who have turned from their sin and trusted Jesus. At the Rapture believers will joyfully receive their glorified bodies, they will joyfully participate in the Marriage Supper of the Lamb, but they will also stand before the Judgement Seat of Christ to receive rewards for the work done in the flesh. There is coming a day when our work on earth will cease. We will no longer have opportunity to share the gospel, minister to other believers, or serve the Lord in His work on earth. Our opportunity to make a difference for Jesus will be over. Knowing Jesus could return at any moment becomes a strong motivator to serve Jesus now. Tomorrow may be too late. The Rapture still matters!

11

DOES THE CONSERVATIVE RESURGENCE STILL MATTER?

Z. SCOTT COLTER

"The Truth is incontrovertible. Malice may attack it. Ignorance may deride it, but in the end, there it is." – Sir Winston Churchill

---

A recent invitation to speak at a conference brought this author across the country and over the Rocky Mountains to a small community nestled in the foothills. However, the rural location also provided another unexpected but welcome opportunity. Situated in a small community associated with a U.S. Air Force base, the majority of the residents of Mountain Home, Idaho are in some way or another employed by or related to employees of the United States Military.

The proximity to the air base and a few key connections presented the opportunity to receive a private, behind-the-scenes tour of the base operations. The ground vibrated rhythmically near the flight line as some of the world's most powerful aircraft launched into the air—fighter planes that can reach into the heavens and quickly break through the sound barrier. At some point during the afternoon, after having ascended a precariously perched ladder into the cockpit of one of these active fighter jets and observing the intricate controls in the miniscule pod from which two men operate the aircraft while in flight, the question of cost instantly leapt to mind. Leaning over the edge of the plane, this question was raised. "Cost?" responded a young airman on the ground who could not yet have passed his 19th birthday. He smiled. "What price can you put on freedom?" responded the young man in uniform. He was correct in every way. Later, a commanding officer shared that the observed plane rolled off the line fully loaded at just more than $58 million. Straightway, this author was grateful not to have touched any of the controls or switches. But the statement by the young man—who had stepped forward and volunteered to give his service and even his life, if necessary, to protect the principles upon which our nation rests—rang hauntingly clear.

At home in Tennessee, my family rested safe and secure while I traveled. I boarded a commercial aircraft simply by showing identification and traversed the continent without difficulty. I reserved and resided in a hotel room without challenge or trouble. And each evening in the small community, a thriving church gathered together. Laughter rang throughout the hallways, and children ran and frolicked while playing hide-and-seek from their parents. Hugs were exchanged between friends, and smiles greeted all who entered the worship center. However, a quick glance around the room found several wives sitting alone, solo mothers wrangling multiple children, and empty chairs up and down each row—all tangible reminders of so many who were actively deployed at that very moment fighting for the freedom to gather in that church, to preach and teach the Bible, and to practice religion as this group saw fit. The young man told the truth: $58 million is a small price for freedom. Indeed, as many have quipped, freedom is not free.

Those men in active-duty military service are owed a great debt by society. Those who live free lives, and often take them for granted, are the beneficiaries of those who have gone before and established a solid foundation upon which they stand. Looking around the global scene reveals nations enslaving people, dictatorships destroying the nuclear family unit, economic difficulties, starvation, and disease. While America is not perfect, her principles of freedom have provided unparalleled opportunities for success and prosperity. Yes, a great debt is owed indeed.

Akin to the debt Americans owe is the debt we as Baptists owe to those who have come before us—those who have sacrificed much so that others can worship freely and believe freely and those who fought theological battles to keep Baptists foundationally established upon the Bible. This chapter is written from the perspective of one who is a great debtor and who recognizes, at least in part, the vastness of what is owed to others.

America is commonly defined, and correctly so in many ways, as a Christian nation. Recent reports from Lifeway Christian Resources indicate that on average more than 5 million Southern Baptists gather in corporate worship in a denomination that boasts more than 14 million members across nearly 50,000 individual churches.[1] While few may realize it, these people called Baptists also owe a great debt.

A Brief History of Baptists in America

Founded in 1845 in Augusta, Georgia (previously as the Triennial Convention, an apt description derived from the groups assembling once every three years beginning in 1814), the Southern Baptist Convention came into existence for the purpose of like-minded churches cooperating together in a global mission effort. The Home Mission Society was established a few years

---

1. "Annual Church Profile Statistical Summary 2019-2020," Lifeway Research, Lifeway Christian Resources, April 23, 2021, http://blog.lifeway.com/newsroom/files/2021/05/ACP_Summary_2020.pdf.

prior in 1832.[2] The Foreign Mission Board was founded in conjunction with the Southern Baptist Convention in 1845.[3] From their earliest formal existence, Southern Baptists were a people focused on international and domestic missions. Southern Baptists championed Scripture and implemented its precepts through their cooperation in the global mission effort. For more than 100 years, Baptists in America were known as a "people of the Book."

The people of God known as Baptists have left indelible fingerprints on the foundation of America. A look through the history of this nation provides an informational picture of the role of the Baptists and of similar Christian groups. However, Baptists did not begin with the Southern Baptist Convention.[4] Historians trace early roots of the Southern Baptist Convention to the English Baptists as well as to the Anabaptists.

These early Baptists championed faith and repentance as the means by which an individual is saved, and not by his or her works. Baptists also believed in the free church and advocated the separation of church and state.[5] They taught the doctrines of believer's baptism, wherein only a believer in Christ should be presented as a candidate for baptism. Free, local churches gathered together, and leaders ultimately proclaimed baptism by immersion. Baptists followed the biblical model presented in the term *baptizo*, which was transliterated, "baptize," and literally means "to immerse."

In America, early Baptists stood shoulder to shoulder with Congregationalists and Puritans. These groups championed religious liberty with

---

2. Nancy Ammerman, *Baptist Battles: Social Change and Religious Conflict in the Southern Baptist Convention* (New Brunswick: Rutgers University Press, 1990), 26–27.

3. Ammerman, *Baptist Battles*, 32.

4. Jesse C. Fletcher, *The Southern Baptist Convention: A Sesquicentennial History* (Nashville: Broadman & Holman, 1994), 9–14.

5. This government-church relationship was espoused in a way that avoided the government from restricting or delimiting the church and did not prevent in any way but actually encouraged the church and her members to participate actively in the public processes of democracy.

fierceness in churches that gathered throughout cities and dotted the countryside. Parishioners filled wooden pews several times throughout the week as pastors and circuit-riding preachers stood behind the sacred desk and preached from Scripture about Christian responsibility, morality, faith, and obedience to God's desires for his followers.

As America grew, the congregations known to be Baptist grew and increasingly endeavored to fulfill the Great Commission of Christ. As presented in Matthew 28:19-20, the Great Commission is a charge extended to local churches to be about the task of making disciples. The process of making disciples begins evangelistically by sharing the message of Christ as the sole means by which one can believe and be redeemed. Out of this deepening concern, the Southern Baptist Convention and its mission partnerships were born.

As it developed, the Southern Baptist Convention experienced extraordinary growth and quickly found its place as the largest protestant group in existence. Southern Baptists sent thousands of missionaries around the globe and across the North American continent. The convention constructed seminaries to train the next generation of pastors and church leaders, established committees and processes to streamline and enhance the work of ministry, and developed a publication arm to provide trusted, biblical resources for pastors and churches. The Southern Baptist Convention created the Christian Life Commission (later renamed the Ethics and Religious Liberty Commission) to stand against secular culture, to proffer a biblical worldview, and to inform Baptist churches regarding matters of public policy and faith dialogue.

From their earliest existence, Baptists cooperated together in mission efforts both globally and domestically. A core principle of Baptist ministry work has been that more can be accomplished in advancing the kingdom of God by working together than separately. This premise—while elementary—formed the practice of Baptist cooperation.[6] However, believers soon

---

6. Chad Owen Brand and David E. Hankins, *One Sacred Effort* (Nashville:

realized that they could not simply cooperate for the sake of cooperation without establishing a common doctrinal position that the majority of constituents affirm as a sufficient parameter for denominational efforts. In 1925, the first Baptist Faith and Message was adopted as the Convention's statement of faith, which was based on the previous 1833 New Hampshire Confession of Faith. The Baptist Faith and Message subsequently underwent a revision and update in 1963.[7]

THE SHIFT AND THE RESURGENCE

In the middle of the 20th century, many Baptists noticed some uncertain sounds coming from the denominational leadership and Southern Baptist entities. Ralph Elliott, a professor of Old Testament at Midwestern Baptist Theological Seminary, espoused an historical-critical method of interpreting the biblical book of Genesis in which he elaborated that details in the text should not be understood as actual and historical facts, but as allegorical descriptions intended to demonstrate a point. Regarding this publication, James Hefley records what he defines as typical neo-orthodoxy, "Elliott classified as non-historical and error-prone the stories of Adam and Eve, Cain and Abel, Noah and the Flood, the Tower of Babel and some events in the life of Abraham."[8] The extrapolation of this view is that Scripture was neither reliable nor verifiably truthful and provided little guidance apart from demonstrating a particular spiritual element.

Readers of this volume expressed outrage at the argument that the divine Author was able to inspire a book of the canon that was historically

Broadman & Holman, 2005), 62-63.

7. Herschel Hobbs, *The Baptist Faith and Message* (Nashville: Convention Press, 1971), 12-13.

8. James Hefley, *The Conservative Resurgence in the Southern Baptist Convention* (Garland, TX: Hannibal, 1991), 29.

inaccurate. Further, Southern Baptists took notable exception to this resource having been published by Broadman Press, the official publishing arm of the Southern Baptist Convention. The volume's publication through the Baptist Sunday School Board and Broadman Press as well as its authorship by a Southern Baptist seminary professor, whose salary was paid with Cooperative Program funds, led to significant opposition from thousands of grassroots Southern Baptists.[9]

The volume was withdrawn from publication, and the administration of Midwestern Baptist Theological Seminary requested that Elliott not seek to publish it through another avenue. When he refused and considered having the volume republished, he was terminated by the seminary's board of trustees for insubordination.[10] While this termination and removal of the volume from print offered a temporary solution for concerned Southern Baptists, uncertain sounds regarding orthodox doctrinal fidelity quickly returned.

Only a few years after what became known as the Elliott controversy, Broadman Press undertook the publishing of a commentary series carrying the moniker *The Broadman Bible Commentary*. G. Henton Davies authored the first volume in the series addressing the books of Genesis and Exodus. In this volume, Davies dissuaded his readers from accepting a literal interpretation of the account of Abraham offering Isaac, which brought into question the veracity of the narrative account as presented in Scripture. In turn, he advocated for a non-historical hermeneutic. Once again, conservatives expressed alarm with the publication of a Southern Baptist resource that presented doubt regarding the truthfulness and accuracy of the Word of God.[11]

---

9. James Hefley, *The Truth in Crisis: The Controversy in the Southern Baptist Convention*, vol. 3 (Richmond, VA: Hannibal, 1988), 8.

10. Jerry Sutton, *The Baptist Reformation* (Nashville: Broadman & Holman, 2000), 10.

11. Hefley, *The Conservative Resurgence in the Southern Baptist Convention*, 34.

As these issues progressed, conservatives began to raise their voices in opposition to what they saw as a modern-day Downgrade Controversy. K. Owen White published a widely read article entitled, "Death in the Pot," which served as a rallying point for concerned Baptists.[12] Following the Davies commentary, conservatives disrupted the annual meeting of the Southern Baptist Convention and demanded answers regarding the integrity of Southern Baptist publications.[13]

Rumors of theological compromise taking place in Southern Baptist seminaries added to the concerns presented through these publications. In what was later confirmed by Southern Seminary student Noel Wesley Hollyfield, Jr., students at Southern seminary believed fewer and fewer orthodox doctrines the longer they studied at the institution. Hollyfield studied students' beliefs regarding key doctrines such as theology proper, the divinity of Christ, Scripture, miracles, and the necessity of salvation in Christ alone and traced the devolution of orthodox beliefs of Southern Seminary students. While the overwhelming majority of students entered seminary holding to conservative positions on each of these topics, Hollyfield's research demonstrated that the greater amount of time students spent in seminary, the less likely they were to maintain their conservative, orthodox perspectives. At increasing levels, students embraced moderate and progressive ideologies in every category.[14]

While these issues polarized the Southern Baptist Convention and divided various factions from others, few were able to offer tangible solutions or plans toward reconciliation. Some attempts were made at establishing a conservative stronghold in the SBC in response to the various controversies, but disorganization and lack of support caused these efforts to struggle in their early years. In 1967 this changed.

---

12. Hefley, *The Truth in Crisis*, vol. 3, 8.

13. Hefley, *The Conservative Resurgence in the Southern Baptist Convention*, 30.

14. Paul Pressler, *A Hill on Which to Die* (Nashville: Broadman & Holman, 2002), 149-150.

Paul Pressler, a conservative judge from Houston, visited the campus of New Orleans Baptist Theological Seminary in New Orleans, Louisiana. Pressler was aware of many of the perceived challenges facing the Southern Baptist Convention. The concerns expressed by many conservatives rang in accord with his personal views and convictions. Pressler provided scholarships for conservative students in seminary and looked for other avenues to perpetuate conservative theology among a sea of ideas entangled in progressivism. Through various conversations, Judge Paul Pressler, or "the Judge" as friends and opponents know him, heard of a student at New Orleans holding firmly to conservative convictions. That student was Paige Patterson.[15]

Patterson had gained a reputation on the campus of NOBTS as a conservative student unwilling to waver in his beliefs. As students became exposed to moderate teaching and began to question their faith, their calling, and even the central tenets of Christianity; they were often directed to Patterson in an effort to quell concerns and help them endure in seminary. While Patterson refused to abandon his biblical convictions, he understood the importance of theological education and perpetuated the comments of his father who encouraged him to engage and persevere in seminary training to learn all he could for vocational ministry. At the same time, his father admonished him to hold fast to what he had come to believe the Scripture taught.[16]

One evening while he was studying, Patterson responded to a knock on his door and opened it to find the Judge and his wife, Nancy Pressler. The Pattersons and the Presslers met each other for the first time and headed to the well-known Café Du Monde in the New Orleans French Quarter to visit over café au lait and beignets.[17] During this meeting, Patterson and

---

15. Sutton, *The Baptist Reformation*, 74.

16. Paige Patterson, *The Southern Baptist Conservative Resurgence* (Fort Worth, TX: Seminary Hill Press, 2008), 14.

17. Paige Patterson, *Anatomy of a Reformation* (Fort Worth, TX: Seminary

Pressler discussed the state of what was being taught in Southern Baptist theological institutions and their shared concerns about the trajectory of the denomination. Judge Pressler did not feel he had the denominational standing necessary to direct a movement for change, and Patterson did not feel he had the age or position necessary to lead a significant endeavor. These perceived weaknesses were each offset in the other. Patterson and Pressler ultimately agreed to work together in an effort to preserve orthodox, biblical faithfulness in the Southern Baptist Convention. That evening birthed a friendship that would eventually reshape the horizon of the Southern Baptist Convention and conservative evangelicalism at large.[18]

In his aptly titled brief volume, *The Southern Baptist Conservative Resurgence*, Patterson describes the initial strategy and steps they understood were foundational to any grassroots movement in the Southern Baptist Convention. Following an idea first recognized by Southern Baptist pastor William Powell, Patterson and Pressler studied the governing documents of the SBC and confirmed the conclusion that the election of a conservative president provided the key.[19] Each year at the annual meeting of the Southern Baptist Convention, messengers would elect a president who in turn would appoint various committees including members to the Committee on Committees.[20] This committee strategically recommended individuals from each applicable state to then nominate trustees onto the various boards. As has been discussed previously, the concerns of Southern Baptists intersected with the work of the entities—specifically in the realms of publishing and theological education. By electing a conservative president, who would appoint conservative, like-minded members on the Committee on Committees, who then nominated members to the Committee on Nominations,

---

Hill Press, 2011), 2-3.

18. Pressler, *A Hill on Which to Die*, 60.

19. Paige Patterson, *The Southern Baptist Conservative Resurgence*, 21-22.

20. Jerry Sutton, *The Baptist Reformation* (Nashville: Broadman & Holman, 2000), 63.

who ultimately nominated potential trustees onto the various boards governing the SBC entities; the messengers had an opportunity to affect the entirety of the Southern Baptist Convention through continually electing conservative presidents. Southern Baptist polity, and the way the churches and convention are governed, made this movement possible.

The leaders of the Conservative Resurgence also recognized the unique aspects of the Southern Baptist Convention that made such a resurgence possible. The majority of Baptist churches adopted what they believe to be the New Testament form of church government—namely that of congregational polity. In this polity, the gathered congregation is the highest authority and "governs" the church, which can include financial and budgetary decisions, pastoral hiring and termination, and oversight of significant, top-level matters. This form of church government exists differently than in churches that practice elder-ruled polity or other forms of church government. Because of the commonality of this congregational practice among Baptists, a similar form of government was instituted in the Southern Baptist Convention. Within the SBC, churches are permitted to send messengers based upon size and contribution to Southern Baptist ministry causes. These individual messengers vote and determine the official business of the SBC. They approve and adopt annual budgets and expenditures, elect the president, first and second vice presidents, vote on recommendations from various committees including resolutions (statements representative of the positions and opinions of the gathered body), and appoint members to various boards as trustees.

Pressler and Patterson understood from their research and strategic planning that the key to effecting change successfully in the SBC resided with the presidential election—that the first domino in a sequence of events that had the potential to cause significant change in the SBC is the election of a conservative candidate as the president of the SBC.[21] Although he

---

21. Pressler, *A Hill on Which to Die*, 78-80.

holds a position with very little actual authority, the president is afforded these limited but influential appointments which have the capacity to lead to widespread change. Pressler and Patterson agreed they needed to develop a grassroots strategy to elect a consecutive series of conservative presidents.[22]

Concerned members of most other mainstream denominations would have no such opportunity to be represented and effect change in their denomination as was possible through the Southern Baptist Convention. Thus, a stewardship of opportunity exists for Southern Baptists. With the opportunity to guide and influence the direction of the convention of churches according to biblical convictions, the leaders of the Conservative Resurgence and the tens of thousands of pastors and lay individuals who joined them recognized the need of the hour and their responsibility to take a stand for the truthfulness of God's Word.

Once Patterson and Pressler understood the task before them, these conservative leaders divided the country, and each took one half in an effort to build a grassroots infrastructure capable of mobilizing church representatives or "messengers" educated and prepared to vote for a yet-to-be-determined conservative presidential candidate. Strategic leaders in each state were contacted. They were urged to give attention to their own states and make an effort to bring large numbers of conservative messengers to the SBC's annual meeting. Due to some unique aspects of the presidential election in 1977 and 1978, it was determined that the election in 1979 at the Houston meeting of the SBC was the best point to launch such a conservative movement.[23]

Despite significant opposition, the conservatives were successful in 1979. Adrian Rogers was elected president of the Southern Baptist Convention. Rogers served as pastor of the historic Bellevue Baptist Church in Memphis, Tennessee. Bellevue was a leading congregation in the SBC, and Rogers was an influential convention leader with outstanding respect. It is commonly said that even those who disagreed with Rogers convictionally

---

22. Patterson, *The Southern Baptist Conservative Resurgence*, 21-22.
23. Pressler, *A Hill on Which to Die*, 97-98.

respected him as a Christian statesman.

The successful election of Rogers is marked historically as the start of the Conservative Resurgence—the designated effort in the SBC to elect conservative presidents with the intent of placing conservatives in positions of leadership, and eventually onto the trustee boards of the various SBC entities, and to lead the entities to positions of conservative practice.[24] Following the election of Adrian Rogers, an unbroken line of conservative presidents was elected for the next 20 years and beyond.[25] With average length of trustee terms, Patterson and Pressler expected this grassroots effort to take a minimum of a decade to produce tangible results. While in some ways success was felt by conservatives long before the ten-year mark, in other ways the movement lasted well beyond the initial ten years.

The central core in the Battle for the Bible, or the Conservative Resurgence, was the doctrine of inerrancy. Southern Baptist theological institutions had begun teaching that elements of Scripture were not historically accurate and should not be understood factually but allegorically. In these cases, miracles were described as illustrative fictional accounts. Much of Scripture was understood allegorically, and narrative accounts were viewed as historically inaccurate. The Conservative Resurgence sought to restore Southern Baptists to the place from which they came.

There is value in noting that those who led the movement did not initially believe they would be successful in their cause. In spite of recognizing the odds were not in their favor, these leaders nonetheless stood firmly upon their beliefs and convictions and worked to effect change in the Southern Baptist Convention. Patterson did not believe they would prevail. He understood the inner workings of the denominational system they were challenging and the system's natural inclination toward self-preservation.[26] Further, he understood that one of the notably lacking elements present in

---

24. Pressler, *A Hill on Which to Die*, 104.
25. Pressler, *A Hill on Which to Die*, 353–355.
26. Patterson, *Anatomy of a Reformation*, 4.

that period was courage. Patterson and Pressler would describe these early moments as engaging in the battle for the Bible, not because they expected to win but because they believed without doubt that it was what God had for them to do with their lives. They were leaders driven by conviction instead of pragmatism and opportunity.

Culminating with the SBC presidency of Paige Patterson and through the adoption of the revised Baptist Faith and Message 2000, the central tenet of the Conservative Resurgence, the inerrancy of Scripture, was codified as the chief outcome of the movement. Patterson recalls that when the Judge and he first met to share their concerns, only a minute handful of professors in Southern Baptist seminaries advocated for the inerrancy of the Bible, and an even smaller portion of those were willing to state their beliefs publicly. According to Patterson, at the time of the adoption of the revised Baptist Faith and Message in 2000, every member of the faculty at every Southern Baptist seminary affirmed the full inerrancy of Scripture.[27]

THE INERRANCY OF THE BIBLE— THE HEART OF THE CONSERVATIVE RESURGENCE

Countless accounts exist of denominations and institutions that have drifted from the purpose for which they were first established. Tales of Anglicans, Lutherans, Episcopalians and Methodists reveal the tendency of religious organizations to embrace more progressive ideologies over time, including those that contradict biblical positions previously championed.[28] A study of

---

27. Patterson, *The Southern Baptist Conservative Resurgence*, 36.

28. For additional study, see Thomas C. Oden, *Requiem: A Lament in Three Movements* (Nashville: Abingdon Press, 1995). This monograph proffers a lament and post-biblical critique of the mainline protestant movement including a detailed discussion of theological education and church polity that focuses generally on the Methodist denomination.

America's great, stalwart universities details the path by which these schools, originally established for religious and ministerial training, have devolved into institutions hostile toward conservative perspectives, including those of the Christian faith. Students walking along those historic hallways are no longer trained in orthodox theology and the gospel message of Scripture but instead are indoctrinated with the gospel of political correctness and "cancel" culture.

The simple statement that "a boat never drifts upstream," has been attributed to many individuals across the years. This statement's accuracy resounds not only on the riverfront, but also in the evangelical landscape across America and around the world. With previously conservative religious denominations and institutions now leading in embracing LGBTQ+ ideologies, advocating for pro-choice politics, and cancelling speakers and leaders advocating for a literal interpretation of Scripture as those characterized by "hate speech," one does not have to wonder whether or not religious institutions will remain conservative when left to their own tendencies.

At the center of the Conservative Resurgence stood the doctrine of Scripture. Supporters of the controversy established that the essential matter at stake was the inerrancy of the Bible, as they stood against ideas of higher criticism that questioned the veracity of Scripture. Pressler summarized this central issue:

> Conservatives believe the Bible is completely accurate and true because it came from God. A perfect God is able to communicate perfectly. He does not stutter, misunderstand, or miscommunicate. He is not limited by the fallible human beings through whom He gave His Truth. . . . For the liberals, the Bible contains a human element which keeps it from being absolutely perfect in all that it says. Since the views of liberals have a great variance as to how much of the Bible is to be accepted and how much is not, I define a liberal as one who believes the Bible does or could contain errors or make mis-

takes. . . . If someone believes that the Bible does contain an error, a means must exist for that person to determine what portion of the Scripture is error and what portion is not. Some have quipped that the liberals have a Dalmatian theory about the inspiration of Scripture. According to the quip, liberals believe Scripture is inspired in spots and that they are inspired to spot the spots. I think it is dangerous to attempt to edit God. What objective standard exists for doing the editing if a person believes that only portions of the Bible are inspired?[29]

These men understood that the inerrancy of Scripture was crucial and worth the cost of the controversy, not only because of the nature of Scripture but also because of all that an erosion of the standard of God's Word would cause downstream.

Evangelism, Baptist distinctives, religious liberty and the free church, and the moral and ethical virtues of society and culture are all eroded through the downgrade of the doctrine of Scripture. Paul Pressler, Paige Patterson, Jerry Vines, Adrian Rogers, W. A. Criswell, and other leaders of their generation recognized what stood to be lost in the world and determined that standing for the Bible was worth the cost.

The foundation of the inerrancy position is a view rooted in the nature of the author of Scripture. If one accepts a verbal-plenary inspiration of the Scripture, God is the author of both the specific words and the concepts presented in the original autographs. Consequently, a downgrade of the nature of Scripture also infringes on the very nature of the Creator God. For the words of Scripture to include errors or misrepresentations of reality necessitates that the Author made a mistake, an omission, or an error. Theologically, conservatives were unable to reconcile a perfect God with having produced an imperfect and error-filled, divinely revealed manuscript.

---

29. Pressler, *A Hill on Which to Die*, 151.

Southern Baptists during the Conservative Resurgence recognized that to relinquish the doctrine of biblical inerrancy was also to relinquish local and international evangelism, the biblical role and function of the Christian church, and the standard for ethics and morality in culture. For these convictional leaders, the cost of silence and remaining unengaged was simply too high.

Inerrancy was essential to conservatives because it is derived from Scripture itself. The Word of God is self-authenticating; it claims and substantiates its own veracity. To believe Scripture is to accept the claims in Scripture appertaining to Scripture. The Bible assumes its veracity and trustworthiness, as do the original biblical authors. Accepting higher critical perspectives related to the biblical text departs from the textual understanding and practice of first-century readers as well as the biblical writers, as is demonstrated through their approach and references to other canonical texts. To accept the words of Scripture as authoritative is to accept their own reflexive definition.

The leaders of the Conservative Resurgence understood that the significance of the inerrancy of Scripture was not limited to the doctrine itself, but in its informing all other doctrines and Christian practices. If Christianity loses Scripture as its true standard, it becomes a religion guided by opinion, culture, and ideas proffered by flawed individuals. A divine mandate, which is by its nature free from error, sets apart the Christian faith from the ideologies and practices of humanity as expressed through systems of thought and various forms of religion. The authority of the Bible is derived from the divine Author of the canon. To establish the presence of errors in the manuscripts is to erode the integrity of the Author and corrode the veracity of the Word of God. A book that cannot be trusted is not a reliable source for truth in matters of faith and practice. Further, to question the nature of Scripture elevates the reader as the authority above the Scripture. The reader then determines the accuracy and value of the Bible instead of the biblical canon remaining as it historically existed: the external authority above individuals, societies, faiths, and cultures.

The collapse of the view of Scripture is not limited, however, to matters of the doctrine of Scripture alone. The leaders of the Conservative Resurgence understood that evangelism and the public witness of Christ rests upon an unfailing foundation of Scripture. Once the reader is elevated to a position above the Scripture, he or she is then able to determine which precepts and principles should be embraced in his or her individual life. The standard of truth becomes one's ideas or opinions, no matter how informed or educated they may be. If the reader is tasked not simply to read and implement the Word of God in his life, but first to determine which portions of the text are reliable and should be followed, then logic entails that he will be unlikely to embrace commands and aspects which he finds difficult, unpleasant, or challenging. Patterson, Pressler, Vines, Rogers, and many others agreed that one of the first casualties of the collapse of the doctrine of inerrancy would be the practice of evangelism. Once the door is opened to redefining the biblical texts, those practices which are beyond the comfort zone of most individuals are the first from which readers will depart.

Patterson describes himself as foremost an evangelist. Though his ministry career included more than six decades of service in pastoral and presidential roles, he never departed from his primary calling of an evangelist. While the Conservative Resurgence addressed a multitude of concerns in the Southern Baptist Convention, its original architects maintained that the necessity of the movement was due to the focus on evangelism they knew would be lost following a scriptural downgrade in their convention of churches.

Not only does the inerrancy of Scripture affect evangelism, but it influences matters of Baptist distinction. Once again, Baptists are a "people of the Book." Vines emphasized this foundational tenet through his sermon, "A Baptist and his Bible." Baptist ecclesiology is derived directly from the New Testament local church example. Precepts established in the New Testament are the central practices of the denomination. Baptists draw from a rich biblical heritage regarding the doctrines of soteriology and baptism, regenerate church membership, the roles of the pastor, the mission and calling of the local, gathered congregation, and the practice of church ordinances. Baptist ecclesiology is an attempt to replicate biblical ecclesiology as closely as possible. Baptists remain Baptist because of the ways in which this group of churches adheres to the biblical example. Should they forsake that example and standard, many convictional Baptists would depart from this group at points of divergence and align with those more closely adhering to biblical practices.

Proponents of inerrancy also recognized the result that allowing the downgrade of Scripture would have on culture at large. According to Christ's Sermon on the Mount as recorded in Matthew 5, Christians are to be "salt" and "light." These elements are representative of standing for and shining the "light" of truth and also of serving as a moral preservative working to maintain ethical and biblical values in culture and the public square. Apart from an inerrant standard of Scripture, Christians at large are unable to agree on a unified set of doctrinal positions regarding ethics and morality, which are no different in function than those derived from atheism, agnosticism, or competing secular worldviews. However, the Scripture provides sufficient and necessary truth for engaging in the world according to the plans and purposes of God. To lose that standard is to lose the ability to engage society biblically.

While it has been stated clearly that these men did not embark on this process to steer the SBC back towards the right with the expectation of success, their efforts, in actuality, did bring about the necessary results. The original architects of the Conservative Resurgence attribute its success solely to the intervention of God.[30] Through the continual election of conservative presidents of the Southern Baptist Convention consecutively for more than two decades and beyond, the various committees and trustee boards of

---

30. Patterson, *Anatomy of a Reformation*, 6.

the SBC were filled with like-minded pastors and laymen who championed conservative positions.

MODERN SIGNIFICANCE OF
THE CONSERVATIVE RESURGENCE

More than two decades after the adoption of the Baptist Faith and Message 2000, the document displays the achievements of the conservative movement in many ways. Looking to the current state of evangelicalism and the Southern Baptist Convention in particular, concerning issues have returned anew. Uncertain sounds related to the SBC have once again surfaced.

With the recent infiltration into the SBC of Critical Race Theory, Intersectionality, and other secular ideologies, many Southern Baptists recognized the embrace of these systems of thought as a derision toward the sufficiency of Scripture.[31] Similarly, political correctness and "cancelling" conservative speakers and leaders has become pervasive in the convention and in evangelicalism at large. What has been popularly coined as "woke" progressivism and heavy influence from social justice movements now reside within the Southern Baptist Convention.

The question posed by this volume, "Does it Still Matter?" has never been more relevant than it is in this hour.

Reports have led to concern about the funding practices of the various SBC entities and whether or not their ministry work aligns with the Baptist Faith and Message 2000. Perhaps most importantly, the number of individuals being led to Christ and baptized through Southern Baptist efforts is declining in an exponential fashion. Prior to the COVID-19 pandemic,

---

31. "On Critical Race Theory and Intersectionality," Resolution 9, Southern Baptist Convention Annual Meeting, Birmingham, AL, June 1, 2019, https://www.sbc.net/resource-library/resolutions/on-critical-race-theory-and-intersectionality/.

Baptists reported in 2018 a total baptism number of 246,442. One must go back to 1944 to find a time when Southern Baptists historically baptized fewer individuals, and at that time, the number was on the increase with significantly fewer churches working in cooperation.[32] Currently, reported statistics trend sharply downward.

Many among the SBC are recognizing that current efforts, including attempts at popularizing the gospel, modernizing the church, and embracing progressive ideologies, are simply failing to reach more people for Christ. Conversely, these strategies seem to be having an adverse effect. If current trends do not soon reverse, the group known as Southern Baptists will functionally cease to exist in the not-so-distant future.

Once again, conservative Southern Baptists are rising to this call and standing for the inerrancy and sufficiency of Scripture among other concerns within the SBC. Just as Paul Pressler and Paige Patterson sat late one evening discussing over powdered sugar-clad beignets at the world-famous Café Du Monde whether or not they had a sufficient reason to stand for truth in the SBC, the same question once again has emerged. As each generation accepts the baton of leadership from their predecessors, they must answer this question afresh. Regarding the Scripture, each generation must consider for themselves the way in which they will view the Bible.

The Conservative Resurgence conserved the Word of God and preserved an inerrant understanding of this divine communication from God to his people. How will the current generation respond, now presented with the same inquiry? How will they view the Bible? While previous generations had to consider the question, "Is the Bible true?" the question today presents as, "Is Scripture sufficient and authoritative?" Will the Southern Baptist Convention, and the broader evangelical community, accept and

---

32. Bob Allen, "Southern Baptist baptisms at lowest level in 74 years," *Baptist News Global,* May 28, 2019, https://baptistnews.com/article/southern-baptist-baptisms-at-lowest-level-in-74-years/#.YSfSJy2ZPOQ.

continue to follow Scripture; or will they turn unto themselves, believing that they have a better way, forever departing from the precepts once and for all delivered to the saints of God?

Few know the cost of championing conservative values as Paige Patterson. His family was threatened, he lost employment opportunities and positions, and he has been attacked, ridiculed, misrepresented, slandered, and mocked. Patterson, aware that many individuals found his positions polarizing, has often quipped about the way in which he is viewed by moderates and progressives in evangelicalism. When asked more than two decades after the fulfillment of the Conservative Resurgence if he felt it was worth it, his response was resolute: absolutely. Despite the difficulty and challenges that ensued in standing for the Bible, the benefit and necessity of this movement far outweighed the negative consequences. Was it worth it? Most certainly yes.

In his concluding chapter and account of the Conservative Resurgence, Patterson wrote:

> Every generation has its own battles, and not infrequently, resurrects conflicts from the past. The next few generations of Baptists, being a free people, will debate fiercely. But the reliability and authority of God's Word that guided Baptist life for the first 100 years of the Southern Baptist Convention will likely now guide the next 100 years if Jesus delays His return. Those who led the movement are retiring or transferring residence to a happy clime where God's Word is never contested. None to my knowledge regrets what was done, though hindsight might dictate some changes of method and action. Pastors, evangelists, and missionaries determined to get the saving gospel of Christ to all people will never consistently emerge from the framework of those who question the truthfulness of the Bible, whatever their virtues. We have given our children, grandchildren,

and sons in the ministry a chance to live under and to proclaim the unsearchable riches of Christ by preserving the doctrine of biblical inerrancy. May the grace of God attend them and keep them faithful. We gladly pass the torch to the next generation![33]

Grassroots movements are awakening across the SBC as men and women of the next generation answer this call. History has shown that when a group of Christians depart from these orthodox positions, they depart never to return. The question posed in this chapter, "Does the Conservative Resurgence still matter?" cannot be answered in isolation. This question must be answered in a broader sense. Does global evangelization matter? Do local and international mission efforts matter? Do biblical, moral, and ethical values expressed in culture matter? Does religious liberty and the free church pattern of the New Testament matter? Does understanding and living according to God's ways in one's life matter? If so, then the very conservative movement that preserved these positions most certainly does matter.

The truthfulness of Scripture is not up for debate; this issue is settled in the very nature of the inspiration of the Bible. What humanity does or does not do will not affect the veracity of God's Word. The matter for consideration is not whether the Bible is true. The matter is simply what God's people do with it. In the nation and the denomination, freedom and specifically biblical freedom is certainly not free. Only the actions and decisions of the current generation, measured years from now and looking back historically will be able to answer accurately the posed question. "Indeed, does it still matter?"

---

33. Patterson, *The Southern Baptist Conservative Resurgence*, 46.

Epilogue

WHERE DO WE
GO FROM HERE?

TIMOTHY K. CHRISTIAN

"Ready or not, here I come!" I am sure you remember those words. They began a game of "hide and seek." They warned all those hiding that "It" had counted to one hundred and was coming to find them. At least that is the way we played the game in east central Alabama back in the 1960's.

I never cared much for the game. I did not like to be "It"; I seldom found anyone. Nor did I enjoy hiding. Being an insignificant part of my peer group, when I hid, they did not always bother to look for me.

I do not know if Jesus ever played "hide and seek" during His childhood in Nazareth. However, I do know that He said, "Ready or not, here I come!" In fact, He said it three times in the last chapter of the Bible.

Jesus said, "Behold, I am coming quickly!" (Rev 22:7). Would you agree that means the same as, "Ready or not, here I come"? Again, Jesus declared, "And behold, I am coming quickly" (v. 12). Finally, He promised, "Surely I am coming quickly" (v. 20). The Bible concludes with a simple statement of fact: Jesus is coming soon. Ready or not.

I believe Jesus is coming quickly. The confession is based on a firm belief in the inerrancy of Scripture and in the consistent practice of literal, grammatical-historical interpretation of Scripture. Inerrancy affirms that the Scripture's content is true. Grammatical-historical interpretation affirms its clear declarations. Without these, believing that Jesus is coming soon is indefensible, wishful thinking. With these, it is a confident confession of truth. It encourages us in troubled times and transforms our lifestyles. Therefore, inerrancy and grammatical-historical interpretation still matter.

In the thrice-repeated statement, "I am coming quickly!" I hear Jesus's answer to the question, "Where do we go from here?" With each of His three statements (*precious promises* if you are ready, *stern warnings* if you are not), Jesus called for three corollary responses.

As I understand the book of Revelation from a dispensational premillennial perspective,[1] the book opens with the Apostle John's post-resurrection vision of our glorified Savior, Jesus Christ (Rev 1). He sent a message to seven churches in Asia (Rev 2-3). They were real churches, and He addressed their real needs. He praised their faithfulness and corrected their sins and failures. We need those seven messages. The same kinds of good and bad characteristics are in our churches today.

Jesus told John, "What you see, write in a book and send *it* to the seven churches which are in Asia" (1:11). John did, and that is how we got the book of Revelation.

Our Lord Jesus outlined His Revelation. Again, He directed John to write it down (1:19). "Write," He said:

> » The things which you have seen [Rev 1][2], and
> » The things which are [Rev 2-3][3], and

---

1. Charles C. Ryrie, *Dispensationalism Today* (Chicago: Moody, 1965), 43-47. Ryrie states the three-fold *sine qua non* of dispensationalism: (1) Literal, historical, grammatical interpretation of Scripture, (2) A distinction between Israel and the church, (3) A doxological view of history.

2. Jesus is alive and well, glorified, and in the midst of His churches (note 1:13, 20).

3. The seven churches in Asia Minor are: Ephesus, Smyrna, Pergamos, Thy-

» The things which will take place after this [Rev 4:1-22:5][4]."

That is the general outline. The Revelation concludes with an action plan that we can follow (22:6-21). Jesus promises, "I am coming quickly! You can count on it. But in the mean time, here is what I want you to do." That answers, "Where do we go from here?" Or, "What does Jesus want His followers and churches to do until He returns?" For the sake of this volume we can add, Jesus also declares what He wants the SBC to do until He returns. Notice the three-fold answer.

OBEY THE BIBLE

First, since Jesus is coming soon, obey God's Word. Jesus said, "Behold, I am coming quickly! Blessed *is* he who keeps the words of the prophecy of this book" (Rev 22:7). The one who "keeps the words" keeps an attentive eye on God's Word to be sure he or she is obeying it.[5] It describes the active, not passive, obedience of one who chooses "to persist in obedience."[6] The NASB translates it, "Blessed is he who heeds the words of the prophecy of this book."[7] It describes one like Joshua who daily chose to "fear the LORD, [and] serve Him in sincerity and in truth" (Josh 24:14).

---

atira, Sardis, Philadelphia, and Laodicea.

4. The 7-year tribulation unfolds (Rev 4-18); Jesus Christ returns to earth (Rev 19); Jesus establishes His Millennial reign on earth (Rev 20); Heaven, our eternal home is revealed (Rev 21:1-22:5).

5. Spiros Zodhiates, *The Complete Word Study Dictionary: New Testament*, electronic ed. (Chattanooga, TN: AMG Publishers, 2000), s.v., τηρέω, *tēréō*.

6. Frederick William Danker, ed., *A Greek-English Lexicon of the New Testament and other Early Christian Literature*: BDAG, 3rd ed. rev. (Chicago: The University of Chicago Press, 2000), s.v., τηρέω.

7. *New American Standard Bible: 1995 update* (La Habra, CA: The Lockman Foundation, 1995), Rev 22:7.

The first corollary response to Jesus's promise to return soon is: obey God's Word. In our thoroughly secularized culture, many ask, "Obey the Bible? Why would I do that?" Mockery is in their tone and in their hearts. Believers, however, have a different perspective. We have a different source of authority. We are under God's authority as revealed in the Bible.

The call to obedience in Revelation 22:7 specifically refers to "the words of the prophecy of this book." Jesus promised to bless—pour out His supernatural favor upon[8]—those who obey the book of Revelation. That sounds appropriately pious, but what does it mean? How does one obey prophecy? We cannot "will" prophecy into fulfillment. We can only wait for God to fulfill it in His way at His time. So, how can we obey prophecy?

For one thing, we can respond to prophecy with a proper attitude. We can believe it. We can expect God to do exactly what He promised. Several texts point to the life transformation that results when we live out genuine faith in Christ's promised return. We will:

» Trust that God is wisely working according to His schedule (1 Cor 15:24-25).[9] The book of Revelation reassures us that present day rebellion does not diminish His sovereignty.
» Evangelize the lost (2 Pt 3:3-4a, 9).[10]
» Love one another (1 Thess 3:12-13).[11]

---

8. Definition of "blessed" stated in Bruce Wilkinson's 2005 book, *The Prayer of Jabez: Breaking Through to the Blessed Life.*

9. Then *comes* the end, when He delivers the kingdom to God the Father, when He puts an end to all rule and all authority and power. For He must reign till He has put all enemies under His feet (1 Cor 15:24-25).

10. "Knowing this first: that scoffers will come in the last days, walking according to their own lusts, and saying, 'Where is the promise of His coming? ... The Lord is not slack concerning *His* promise, as some count slackness, but is longsuffering toward us, not willing that any should perish but that all should come to repentance'" (2 Pt 3:3-4a, 9).

11. "And may the Lord make you increase and abound in love to one another and to all, just as we *do* to you, so that He may establish your hearts blameless

- » Faithfully attend and be involved in a local, Bible-believing church (Heb 10:24-25).[12]
- » Be patient (Ja 5:7-8).[13]
- » Live a pure life (1 Jn 3:2-3).[14]

Let us, however, focus on our Lord Jesus's Revelation. In the immediate context (vv. 6-11), He specified three obedient responses He desires. These three responses bring God's blessings and also bring the meaning of Revelation 22:7 into sharper focus. Notice *why* and *how* we can obey God's Word until Jesus returns.

Why Obey?

The angel that communicated the Revelation to John noted why we should obey God's Word. He reassured John and us, "These words are faithful and true" (v. 6).

We can trust and obey God's written Word because it is "faithful"—dependable and trustworthy. We can believe the words because they are "true" and life transforming. Therefore, obey God's "faithful and true" Word.

---

in holiness before our God and Father at the coming of our Lord Jesus Christ with all His saints" (1 Thess 3:12-13).

12. "And let us consider one another in order to stir up love and good works, not forsaking the assembling of ourselves together, as *is* the manner of some, but exhorting *one another,* and so much the more as you see the Day approaching" (Heb 10:24-25).

13. "Therefore be patient, brethren, until the coming of the Lord. See *how* the farmer waits for the precious fruit of the earth, waiting patiently for it until it receives the early and latter rain. You also be patient. Establish your hearts, for the coming of the Lord is at hand" (Ja 5:7-8).

14. "Beloved, now we are children of God; and it has not yet been revealed what we shall be, but we know that when He is revealed, we shall be like Him, for we shall see Him as He is. And everyone who has this hope in Him purifies himself, just as He is pure" (1 Jn 3:2-3).

A few years before penning the Revelation, the apostle John reported Jesus's High Priestly prayer (Jn 17). As His arrest, trial, and crucifixion drew near, He interceded for His disciples. "Sanctify them by Your truth," He prayed. "Your word is truth" (v. 17). The statement is loaded.

God's revealed Word is absolute and certain "truth." In other words, it is equally true for all people in all places at all times. "Forever, O LORD, Your word is settled [stands firm] in heaven" (Ps 119:89). "The entirety of Your word *is* truth, and every one of Your righteous judgments *endures* forever" (Ps 119:160). The Apostle Peter, quoting and affirming Isaiah 40:8, said, "But the word of the LORD endures forever" (1 Pt 1:25).

Not only is the Bible true, it is also transforming. Jesus asked the Father to "sanctify them by Your truth" (Jn 17:17). He fully expected that the Father would use His Word to sanctify believers—to make us progressively more like Him.[15]

John's declaration about the "faithful and true," sanctifying Word is not limited to the books of John and Revelation, of course. The same is said for every word of every verse in every chapter of the sixty-six books of the Old and New Testaments. For example, "The law of the LORD *is* perfect, converting the soul; the testimony of the LORD *is* sure, making wise the simple" (Ps 19:7). It has transforming power because "all Scripture *is* given by inspiration of God" (2 Tim 3:16). "Thus Paul reminded Timothy that **all Scripture is God-breathed** (*theopneustos*, "inspired"), that is, God's words were given through men superintended by the Holy Spirit so that their writings are without error."[16] "Holy men of God spoke *as they were* moved by the Holy Spirit" (2 Pt 1:21). We can trust and obey our Bible because the God who inspired it is "the Holy One *who is* faithful" (Hosea 11:12). And that is why inerrancy still matters.

---

15. D. A. Carson, *The Gospel According to John*, in *The Pillar New Testament Commentary*, gen. ed., D. A. Carson (Grand Rapids: William B. Eerdmans, 1991), 565-66.

16. A. Duane Litfin, *2 Timothy*, in *The Bible Knowledge Commentary: An Exposition of the Scriptures*, vol. 2 (Wheaton: Victor Books, 1985), 757.

Chapter 1 of this volume affirms that the entire Bible is the fully inspired and inerrant Word of God. As the *Baptist Faith and Message 2000* states, "It has God for its author, salvation for its end, and truth, without any mixture of error, for its matter. Therefore, all Scripture is totally true and trustworthy."[17] Further, it is infallible; it "will never lead us astray in what we are to believe or obey."[18] It is also sufficient. The same text that declares the Bible's inspiration also declares its sufficiency. "All Scripture *is* given by inspiration of God, and *is* profitable for doctrine, for reproof, for correction, for instruction in righteousness, that the man of God may be complete, thoroughly equipped for every good work" (2 Tim 3:16-17). It has been noted that the Bible is profitable for:

» "Doctrine"—it shows us what is true
» "Reproof"—it shows us when we are wrong
» "Correction"—it show us how to get right
» "Instruction in righteousness"—it shows us how to stay right

Therefore, the inspired Word, your Bible, is sufficient to fully equip you to accomplish every assignment He gives.

Returning to our text, John noted, "And the Lord God of the holy prophets sent His angel to show His servants the things which must shortly take place" (Rev 22:6b). Here is another affirmation of inspiration. "The Lord God" who inspired "the holy prophets" (cf. 2 Pt 1:20-21) of the Old Testament, sent His angel to speak to John. The angel did not originate the message; he mediated God's message.[19] Again, this is why the "words *are* faithful and true"; they are from God.

---

17. See article 1, "The Scriptures," in *The Baptist Faith and Message*; https://bfm.sbc.net/bfm2000/#i-the-scriptures.

18. Wayne A. Grudem, "Scripture's Self-Attestation and the Problem of Formulating a Doctrine of Scripture," in *Scripture and Truth*, D. A. Carson and John D. Woodbridge, eds. (Grand Rapids: Baker Books, 1992), 58.

19. William R. Newell, *The Book of The Revelation* (Chicago: Moody Press, 1935), 357.

Further, the message is urgent. It is about "things which must shortly take place." Some, noting the repetition of "shortly ... quickly" (vv. 6, 7, 12, 20), have questioned the veracity of the book of Revelation and of Christ's promised return in particular. "It's been nearly 2000 years," they say. "That doesn't sound very quick to me." The prevalence of such scoffers is, in fact, a sign that Jesus's return is drawing near. The apostle Peter said, "Knowing this first: that scoffers will come in the last days, walking according to their own lusts, and saying, 'Where is the promise of His coming? For since the fathers fell asleep, all things continue as *they were* from the beginning of creation'" (2 Pt 3:3-4). The *"parousia"* mockers miss the point. "The emphasis is not on the fact that all of these things recorded in the book would take place within a few months or years but rather that they will happen certainly and quickly when the eschaton ['the events described in the Apocalypse'] begins."[20] Rather than being scoffers or doubters, let us believe and obey God's faithful and true Word.

Therefore, Jesus said, "Behold, I am coming quickly! Blessed *is* he who keeps the words of the prophecy of this book" (v. 7).

How to Obey?

We noted *why* to obey. Next, Jesus tells us *how* to obey.

Worship God

First, we can worship God. The apostle John's response to Jesus's promise is instructive. "Now I, John, saw and heard these things. And when I heard and saw, I fell down to worship before the feet of the angel who showed me these things" (v. 8).

---

20. Paige Patterson, *Revelation*, in *The New American Commentary*, vol. 39, E. Ray Clendenen, gen. ed. and David S. Dockery, assoc. gen. ed., NT (Nashville: B&H Publishing Group, 2012), 378.

Worship acknowledges the superior worth of the one worshiped. John bowed to worship because he was overcome by the glorious, humbling, awe-inspiring visions that the angel unveiled to him. He was thankful and thrilled that Jesus would soon return to claim His throne. His heart leaped in anticipation of joining the saints and angels around heaven's throne. The emotional experience overwhelmed him. John fell before the messenger to worship. We have often heard, "Don't kill the messenger." Equally important is, "Don't worship the messenger."

John's angel worship was a colossal error. "Then he said to me, 'See *that you do* not *do that*. For I am your fellow servant, and of your brethren the prophets, and of those who keep the words of this book. Worship God'" (Rev 22:9). Emotional intensity, good intentions, or even personal sincerity do not justify false worship. True worship, acceptable worship, must be directed exclusively to the one true and living God.

Early in His ministry, Jesus used a 'worship seminar' to lead a Samaritan woman to trust in Him. She, in turn, led many others to Jesus. Initially, Jesus drew the woman-at-the-well into a conversation. He loved and accepted her as a woman created in God's image. He asked her for a drink of water, and then offering her an internal spring of "living water" (Jn 4:7-14). She was surprised that a Jew would speak to a Samaritan woman, and even more surprised He would drink water from a vessel she had touched (v. 9). Still, she wanted the spring of water Jesus offered. She hoped it would satisfy her thirst and reduce her workload (v. 15).

Jesus went to the heart of her problem (Jn 4:16-18). Notice, Jesus did not use Critical Race Theory and Intersectionality to diagnosis her need, understand and identify with her cultural perspective, and formulate an effective ministry response. He did not acknowledge that she was socially ostracized, had personally encountered Jewish racial prejudice, was a victim of a patriarchal system, and had been coerced by gender oppression. These were not her real problems; correcting them would not have satisfied her spiritually parched soul. Her problem was not that others around her were insufficiently "woke." She did not need for Jesus to confess and perpetually repent of His obvious Jewishness. The heart of her problem was not her grievances but her personal sin. Knowing "the truth" was the only thing that would "set" her "free" (Jn 8:32). The solution was genuine repentance and faith in the true Messiah. Nothing else could satisfy the thirst in her soul.

Convicted and uncomfortable, she tried to redirect the divine search-light toward a debatable religious question: the place and practice of wor-ship. Surely a prophet could clarify her confusion (Jn 4:19-20). The woman was closer to the bullseye than she realized.

Jesus led her gently. He explained to the immoral woman that genu-ine worship pleases God. He desires true worshipers, and she could qualify. Worship is more than a time, a place, and a ceremony. It is more than emo-tion and sincerity (Jn 4:21-22). Genuine worship is inspired and informed by reveled truth—truth revealed in both the written Word and the incarnate Word. God's revelation of Himself is both propositional and Personal.[21]

Jesus said to the woman, "The hour is coming, and now is, when the true worshipers will worship the Father in spirit and truth; for the Father is seeking such to worship Him. God *is* Spirit, and those who worship Him must worship in spirit and truth" (vs. 23-24). "This is what matters, not where, but how (in reality, in the spirit of man, the highest part of man, and so in truth). All this is according to the Holy Spirit (Rom. 8:5) who is the Spirit of truth (John 16:13)."[22]

Since "God *is* Spirit," true worship must be spiritual. He "can be wor-shipped only *in spirit and truth*. Both in v. 23 and in v. 24, the one preposition 'in' governs both nouns. … There are not two separate characteristics of the worship that must be offered: it must be 'in spirit and truth', *i.e.* essentially God-centered, made possible by the gift of the Holy Spirit, and in personal

---

21. See Hebrews 1:1-2.

22. Archibald Thomas Robertson, "The Fourth Gospel," in *Word Pictures in the New Testament*: vol. 5 (Nashville: Broadman Press, 1933), 66-67.

knowledge of and conformity to God's Word-made-flesh, the one who is God's 'truth'."[23] "Only those who have the indwelling Holy Spirit, and who obey the truth, can worship God acceptably."[24]

Is your worship God-focused or mere religious entertainment? True worship may include Spirit inspired emotion, but fleshly emotion to impress fellow congregants is false worship. True worship in the human spirit, empowered by the Holy Spirit[25] is regulated and informed both by God's Word and God's Son. Do you worship "in spirit and truth"? God seeks such worshipers. Are you one whom God seeks?

The woman thought she was speaking to a prophet of God. She soon discovered she was speaking to God. "I believe the Messiah is coming," she said. "When He comes, He'll explain it all." I suspect Jesus answered with a smile and a twinkle in His eye, "I who speak to you am *He*"[26] (v. 26). For her it was a lightning-bolt revelation.

Returning to Revelation 22:9, we are reminded how quickly we can forget. John had made the same error a short time earlier (cf. 19:10). Now he blunders again, bowing to worship the angel. Furthermore, John had written his gospel a few years earlier. He remembered and was inspired to record Jesus's encounter with the woman at the well. He knew not to worship an angel. He already believed the angel's command, "Worship God." But in the emotion of the moment he again needed correction. At times, we do too. And that is one vital reason the local church still matters. We all need spiritual direction, and sometimes correction, to faithfully worship the true and living God.[27]

---

23. Carson, *John*, 225.

24. Warren W. Wiersbe, *The Bible Exposition Commentary: New Testament*, vol. 1 (Wheaton: Victor Books, 1996), 300.

25. The Holy Spirit is the "Spirit of truth" (Jn 16:13).

26. Do you see the "I AM" (cf. Ex 3:14) in the verse?

27. See Chapter 5.

Spread the Word

There is a second way for us to obey the Word. We can spread the Word. The angel said to John, "Do not seal the words of the prophecy of this book, for the time is at hand" (Rev 22:10). The admonition is in contrast to Daniel 8:26. The angel Gabriel interpreted Daniel's vision, which in part concerned the end times. He concluded, saying to Daniel, "but the vision … is true; therefore seal up the vision, for *it refers* to many days *in the future*." The fulfillment of Daniel's prophecy was distant, but John's was "near at hand,"[28] "meaning the imminent arrival of the **Parousia** (1:3; 22:6)."[29]

Instead of sealing the news of Christ's return, we are to spread the Word. Why?

On the one hand, we spread the Word *to believers* for an obvious reason. How can believers keep "the words of the prophecy of this book" if they are sealed and therefore unknown? Christian obedience demands that we spread the Word.

On the other hand, we spread the Word *to unbelievers* that they may "heed the warnings,"[30] turn to Christ through faith, and be saved. Christ's imminent return, shared with compassion and wisdom, can be an effective part of a gospel invitation.

The biblical gospel, as emphasized in Chapter 2 of this volume, is: Christ's vicarious death, necessary burial, and bodily resurrection—and it still matters. The imminent return of Jesus Christ is a convicting and convincing reason for a sinner to believe the gospel and receive Jesus Christ today. Certainly, it is also an urgent reason the rapture still matters.[31] The

---

28. Patterson, *Revelation*, 280.
29. Grant R. Osborne, *Revelation Verse by Verse* (Bellingham, WA: Lexham Press, 2016), 365.
30. Osborne, *Revelation*, 365.
31. See Chapter 10.

rapture, rightly understood, is a powerful motivation both for sharing and for believing the gospel.

Obedience is Urgent

Finally, recognize that obedience is urgent. In light of Christ's soon return, the angel noted this third way to obey the Word. "He who is un- just, let him be unjust still; he who is filthy, let him be filthy still; he who is righteous, let him be righteous still; he who is holy, let him be holy still" (Rev 22:11). If this verse is uncoupled from the previous verse—"Do not seal ... the prophecy ... for the time is at hand"—and from its place as the con- clusion of a thought-paragraph (vv. 6-11), we may misinterpret the verse.

Reading verse 11 out of its context may lead one to conclude that God sovereignly wills for many sinners to remain unjust, filthy, and hell-bound, while He wills for others to be righteous, holy, and heaven-bound. With such an interpretation, one's present spiritual condition appears to be the foreordained plan and purpose of God. It appears there is nothing one can do about it, nor should one try.

There is a serious problem with that interpretation. We are familiar with God's urgent call for the wicked to repent. "'*As* I live,' says the Lord God, 'I have no pleasure in the death of the wicked, but that the wicked turn from his way and live. Turn, turn from your evil ways! For why should you die, O house of Israel?'" (Ezek 33:11). God does not want any sinner to continue in an unrepentant lifestyle. Nothing could be clearer. His urgent call is, "Repent! Choose life. Why should you die?"

Jesus made similar appeals during His ministry. "I have not come to call *the* righteous," Jesus said, "but sinners, to repentance" (Luke 5:32).

Likewise, the early church proclaimed the hope-filled message: repen- tance is possible. Preaching on Mars' Hill to the men of Athens, Paul pro- claimed, "Truly, these times of ignorance God overlooked, but now commands all men everywhere to repent" (Acts 17:30). Peter added, "The Lord is not slack concerning *His* promise, as some count slackness, but is longsuffering toward us, not willing that any should perish but that all should come to repentance" (2 Pt 3:9).

This is good news. Repentance and redemption are possible. But do the verses that declare a possible repentance contradict Revelation 22:11?

We scratch our heads at this conundrum and wonder what we have missed. Thus, we are reminded that both grammatical-historical Bible interpretation[32] and carefully prepared, Spirit-anointed expository preaching[33] still matter. Yet, having said all of that, we still have not answered the key question. What is the meaning of Revelation 22:11? Seen in its context:

> Here is ... a powerful warning against putting off one's decision to become a faithful follower of the Lamb. The time remaining is short, and once it is up, no more opportunity to change remains. Because of the imminence of Jesus' coming to initiate the events of this book, the response of a person to this message may very well be the decision that will carry him to this eternal state, whatever that may be.
>
> ... The lesson is, "Change while there is time."[34]
>
> Those who reject God's warnings will fix their eternal destiny in hell, where they will retain their evil and filthy natures for all eternity. Those who respond to the warnings will fix their eternal destiny in glory and realize perfect righteousness and holiness in heaven.[35]

---

32. See Chapter 6.

33. See Chapter 7.

34. Robert L. Thomas, *Revelation 8-22: An Exegetical Commentary* (Chicago: Moody Press, 1995), 502.

35. John MacArthur, ed., *The MacArthur Study Bible* (Nashville: Word Publishing, 1997), 1426.

Since Jesus Christ's return is imminent, being ready for death or the rapture is urgent. Death is final. And for the vast majority of earth's population, the rapture will be as well. It will seal the fate of most who are left behind.[36]

EARN REWARDS

Second, since Jesus is coming soon, you can earn rewards. Jesus said, "And behold, I am coming quickly, and My reward *is* with Me, to give to every one according to his work" (Rev 22:12). When He comes, and He's coming quickly, He will give rewards. Why did Jesus mention rewards? Rewards are a motivation for obeying the Word.

Certainly, Jesus was not encouraging a mercenary, 'play for pay' attitude toward Christian service. 'Balanced-ledger Pharisees' do not please Him. Our service has a higher motivation. We love and appreciate our Savior because He sacrificed His life for us. Further, as we abide in Him, He lives His resurrection life through us by the power of the Holy Spirit. Gratitude for all He has done and is doing in and through us motivates our service.

------

36. A plan to remain skeptical now, with the hope of having a post-rapture responsive and repentant heart, is a fool's plan. Revelation teaches that there will be a host of tribulation saints (Rev 7:9, 13-14). They were unconverted at the Rapture; they will receive Christ during the tribulation period. Some Bible teachers believe the tribulation saints will include the entire unconverted Jewish population on earth at the time of the Rapture (Rom 11:25-27). Most of the saints, however, will be persecuted and martyred for their faith (Rev 6:9-11). The coming Antichrist will rule through pervasive Satanically-empowered lies, sinful deceptions, and crushing coercive force (2 Thess 2:9-10a; Rev 13:5-8, 16-17). It is possible that those who rejected Christ pre-Rapture—they "did not receive the love of the truth, that they might be saved" (2 Thess 2:10b)—will face an even greater obstacle for a post-rapture salvation. "And for this reason God will send them strong delusion, that they should believe the lie, that they all may be condemned who did not believe the truth but had pleasure in unrighteousness" (vs. 11-12).

Our Lord is gracious and generous. Though Jesus deserves all of the praise for our Spirit enabled service, He will reward us. He wants us to know that, even if our service is unheralded now, it is not unnoticed. He sees. He knows what we are doing and why, and He will reward us accordingly.

Rewards Based On Works

Jesus said that future rewards are based on our present works. He will give rewards "to every one according to his work" (Rev 22:12b). In light of the larger context, as we obey God's Word, worshiping and witnessing with urgency, our works will please God. In fact, David spoke of God's Word, and noted the connection between obeying the perfect "law of the Lord" (Ps 19:7) and receiving rewards. He said, "Moreover by them Your servant is warned, *and* in keeping them *there is* great reward" (Ps 19:11). From David's perspective, rewards were both in time and eternity.

Jesus will present the rewards when we "appear before" Him[37] at "the judgment seat of Christ" (2 Cor 5:10a). Our appearance is not optional; it is a "must" appearance for "all." On that day, each one will be rewarded "according to what he has done, whether good or bad" (2 Cor 5:10b).

Jesus is vitally interested in our local churches, which is the ultimate reason the local church still matters.[38] He is the church's true foundation. We build the church on the foundation, "which is Jesus Christ," with either good quality works or poor-quality works. He knows if they are good—"gold, silver, and precious stones"—or bad—"wood, hay, straw" (1 Cor 3:11-12). Organization, activities, enthusiastic crowds, or the lack thereof, do not tell the whole story. But the story will be told, and the truth will be revealed. "Each one's work will become clear; for the Day will declare it, because it will be revealed by fire; and the fire will test each one's work, of what sort

---

37. "For the Father judges no one, but has committed all judgment to the Son" (Jn 5:22).

38. See Chapter 5.

it is. If anyone's work which he has built on *it* endures, he will receive a reward. If anyone's work is burned, he will suffer loss; but he himself will be saved, yet so as through fire" (1 Cor 3:13-15). Is your 'Christian service' accumulating rewards or building a bonfire?

> **The day** of judgment is when Christ will judge the quality of His servants' **work** (2 Cor. 5:10). It is not a question of salvation which is a gift (Rom. 6:23), or a matter of individual deeds (Eph. 2:8–9), but of service which is judged on the basis of quality not quantity. Considerable apparent success can be had by dint of human effort and wisdom (cf. 1 Cor. 2:4), but unless it is empowered by God in accordance with His plan it cannot last (Ps. 127:1).[39]

Jesus Knows Our Works

Jesus knows the true character of our works because He is the all-knowing God. He said, "I am the Alpha and the Omega, *the* Beginning and *the* End, the First and the Last" (Rev 22:13). With this symbolic language, Jesus declared Himself to be the God of the Old Testament who spoke to Isaiah. "Thus says the LORD, the King of Israel, and his Redeemer, the LORD of hosts: 'I *am* the First and I *am* the Last; besides Me *there is* no God'" (Isa 44:6).

The Bible describes believers' future rewards with at least two vivid images: "garments (Rev 3:5, 18; 19:7, 8) and crowns (see 1 Cor 9:25; Rev 2:10, 3:11)."[40] In heaven, we shall receive beautiful white robes. "After these things I looked, and behold, a great multitude which no one could number,

---

39. David K. Lowery, "1 Corinthians," in *The Bible Knowledge Commentary: An Exposition of the Scriptures*, vol. 2, John F. Walvoord and Roy B. Zuck, eds. (Wheaton: Victor Books, 1985), 512.

40. Earl D. Radmacher, gen. ed., Ronald B. Allen, OT ed., and H. Wayne House, NT ed., *NKJV Study Bible, 2ⁿᵈ ed.* (Nashville: Thomas Nelson, 2007), 1970, n. 1:12.

of all nations, tribes, peoples, and tongues, standing before the throne and before the Lamb, clothed with white robes, with palm branches in their hands, and crying out with a loud voice, saying, "Salvation *belongs* to our God who sits on the throne, and to the Lamb!" (Rev 7:9-10). The beautiful garments are wedding garments, for all believers together will be Christ's bride. Therefore, Scripture says:

> Let us be glad and rejoice and give Him glory, for the marriage of the Lamb has come, and His wife has made herself ready." And to her it was granted to be arrayed in fine linen, clean and bright, for the fine linen is the righteous acts of the saints.
>
> Then he said to me, "Write: 'Blessed *are* those who are called to the marriage supper of the Lamb!'" And he said to me, "These are the true sayings of God" (Rev 19:7-9).

The bride is the church (2 Cor 11:2; Eph 5:22-33), and the Bridegroom is Jesus Christ, the Lamb (John 3:29). ... The Lamb's bride is dressed in "the righteous acts of the Saints." When the bride arrived in heaven at the judgment seat of Christ, she was not at all beautiful (in fact, she was covered with spots, wrinkles, and blemishes, according to Paul in Eph 5:27), but now she is radiant in her glory.[41]

A second observation has to do with the bride making herself ready. She has clothed herself in fine linen, which is bright and clean, and this fine linen stands for the righteousness of the saints (v. 8). How radiantly beautiful the bride of Christ appears as she has prepared yourself to be presented to the Lamb. However, her beauty is bestowed beauty, for John is also informed that the clean, bright linen she is wearing "was given her to wear." Again the emphasis on grace and redemption is brought to the fore. ... The righteousness of the

---

41. Wiersbe, *Study Bible*, 1873, n. 19:7-10.

church and those who make up the bride of Christ is not an acquired righteousness but a bestowed righteousness.[42]

Crowns are another reward Jesus will give to the saints. Traditionally, five categories of crowns have been named. Perhaps the judgment seat of Christ will include an awards ceremony where the crowns will be awarded and distributed. The different categories of crowns indicate the faithful works believers do to earn their rewards. The supporting Scriptures, however, may not fully support the tradition, though they in no way diminish the reality of rewards.

For example, the Crown of Rejoicing (1 Thess 2:19; Phil 4:1)[43], also called the Soul-Winner's Crown, is said to be the award for faithful soul-winners. However, when Paul mentioned the crown, he said those he had led to Christ would be his laurel wreath crown—*stephanos*—the award given to the winner in an athletic event such as the Olympics or the Isthmian Games. His converts' personal presence in heaven would be Paul's "hope, … joy" and "crown of rejoicing" (1 Thess 2:19). In this passage, the *stephanos* "represent not what Christ will give to Paul but what Paul will offer to Christ in joyous tribute to Him at His return."[44]

Also, the Crown of Life (James 1:12; Rev 2:10)—is given to those who continued to be faithful, serving through life's trials. These include martyrs for Christ who were "faithful until death."

Some challenge this understanding. "This 'crown' consists of life, that is, the crown *is* life (cf. Rev. 2:10). 'The life which is promised is probably life here and now, life in its fullness, life in its completeness' (cf. James 1:4)."[45]

---

42. Patterson, *Revelation*, 344.

43. "For what *is* our hope, or joy, or crown of rejoicing? *Is it* not even you in the presence of our Lord Jesus Christ at His coming?" (1 Thess 2:19) "Therefore, my beloved and longed-for brethren, my joy and crown, so *stand* fast in the Lord, beloved" (Phil 4:1).

44. Spiros Zodhiates, *Word Study Dictionary*, s.v., στέφανος; *stéphanos*.

45. J. Ronald Blue, *James*, in *The Bible Knowledge Commentary: An Expo-*

I respectfully disagree. In Revelation 2:10, "the crown of life" is promised after martyrdom. That is not "life here and now." So, it seems to me that Jesus' promise of a reward in heaven for faithful service under the fire of life's trials, includes some who remain faithful until martyrdom. The text states the reward is a *stephanos*. That is good enough for me. When the plain, literal sense makes good sense, I seek no other sense.

Whether or not this crown refers to a physical *stephanos* given at Christ's judgment seat, it reminds me of our Baptist and Anabaptist forefathers and mothers who shared the gospel and were true to the Word despite intense persecution. Many were martyred, often by drowning, to mock their unflinching belief in believer baptism by total immersion. Discussing the crown of life is a vivid reminder of why the 'term Baptist' and the 'doctrine of believers Baptism' still matter.[46]

Further, Christ will give the Crown of Righteousness (2 Tim 4:8)[47] to all who "love Christ's appearing, live in obedience to His will, and do the work He has called"[48] them to do. Again, some question whether it refers to a physical *stephanos* or if righteousness itself is the reward. No one will go to heaven without Christ's imputed righteousness (Rom 4:5-8). Litfin summarized the question:

> "Crown of righteousness" can mean either that righteousness itself is the crown or reward, or that this crown is the reward *for* righteousness (cf. 2 Tim. 3:16). In favor of the first view is the fact that James 1:12 and Revelation 2:10 seem to say that the "crown of life" means

sition of the Scriptures, vol. 2, John F. Walvoord and Roy B. Zuck, eds. (Wheaton: Victor Books, 1985), 821.

46. See Chapters 3 & 4.

47. "Finally, there is laid up for me the crown of righteousness, which the Lord, the righteous Judge, will give to me on that Day, and not to me only but also to all who have loved His appearing" (2 Tim 4:8).

48. Warren W. Wiersbe, gen. ed., *The Wiersbe Study Bible* (Nashville: Thomas Nelson, 2018), 1782, n. 4:8.

that life *is* the crown, not that a crown is given because one has life. In either case Paul expected to receive his reward **on that day** (a reference to Christ's return, not Paul's death), side by side with the rest of the faithful **who have longed for His appearing** (cf. Phil. 3:20–21; Titus 2:13).[49]

As I indicated in the "crown of life" discussion, I respectfully disagree with Litfin's supporting defense for "righteousness itself" being the crown instead of the crown being the reward for one's righteously lived life. As I will indicate under the final section of this chapter, our Lord Jesus takes special pleasure in those who love and live with vigilant expectancy for His return. They are watching and ready to welcome Him. They faithfully and consistently stay with the assignment God gives, whatever it may be. The great news is, any believer can earn this reward. In God's eyes, simple faithfulness is irreplaceable and pleasing.

The Imperishable Crown (1 Cor 9:25) is for one who, like an Olympic athlete in training, denies and disciples himself that he might persevere in faithful service for Christ (cf. vs. 24-27). Lowery states:

> The prize for Paul was not the temporary **crown** (*stephanon*) bestowed by men (in the biennial games near Corinth the "crown" was a pine wreath) but the eternal **crown** bestowed by Christ (3:13–14; 2 Cor. 5:10). Paul's crown would be the consummation of the reward (1 Cor. 9:18) he partially enjoyed, the opportunity to glory before Christ in those he had been able to win (2 Cor. 1:14; Phil. 2:16; 1 Thes. 2:19).[50]

The Crown of Glory (1 Pt 5:4) is for pastors who have fulfilled their calling. These servants were faithful to humbly feed and lead their congre-

49. Litfin, *2 Timothy*, in *The Bible Knowledge Commentary*, 758.
50. Lowery, *1 Corinthians*, in *The Bible Knowledge Commentary*, 525.

gations for Christ's glory (1 Pt 5:1-5). Whether the congregations were large or small, the Lord knows about their service and will reward them. "When Christ returns, His faithful undershepherds will share in His glory (1 Peter 5:1) and receive unfading crowns (cf. 1:4)."[51]

The contemporary cultural climate is at war with the Christ-centered, Bible focused churches, and faithful, biblical pastoral ministry. One of the primary attacks on the church concerns God's simple and good requirement that pastors be biological males who actually know they are males. The issues are not insignificant; they are urgent. If a church rebels against God about the gender of its pastor, it will soon spiral downward in an avalanche of disobedience. Faithfulness to God and His Word declares that gender roles and gender identity still matter.[52]

Revelation 4 records an awe-inspiring heavenly throne room scene. John saw twenty-four elders seated before God's throne. Each one wore a white robe; a golden *stephanos* was on each of their heads. Who are these elders? Are they twenty-four angels who hold special leadership responsibilities? Are they the twelve patriarchs of Israel and the twelve apostles representing the Old and New Testament saints united as one glorious Christo-centric family in heaven? Or, since under Mosaic Law there were twenty-four orders of the priesthood, do the elder represent the church, "the royal priesthood" (1 Pt 2:9), i.e., the entire church after the judgment seat of Christ, now judged and rewarded, gathered around the throne? "While scholars differ on this point, it would seem that since the elders are on thrones and are crowned as victors, they represent the church rather than angels. Angels have not been judged and rewarded at this point in the program of God."[53]

51. Roger M. Raymer, *1 Peter*, in *The Bible Knowledge Commentary: An Exposition of the Scriptures*, vol. 2, John F. Walvoord and Roy B. Zuck, eds. (Wheaton: Victor Books, 1985), 856.

52. See Chapters 8 and 9. Editors note: In my opinion, these two well-written and carefully researched chapters are worth more than the price of the book.

53. John F. Walvoord, *Revelation*, in *The Bible Knowledge Commentary: An*

As we have noted, while the traditional interpretation of the five heavenly crowns may not be fully accurate, it does not deny the reality of rewards in heaven.[54] Whether the reward is a symbol of unique blessings or an actual *stephanos* placed on a recipient's head at the judgment seat of Christ, one thing is certain. All will recognize that Jesus Christ is the worthy recipient of all rewards. He is the one who created and redeemed us. His death and resurrection made the difference. He was the one who did the worthy works through His obedient servants. He alone deserves, and will ultimately receive, all the glory. Therefore, "the twenty-four elders fall down before Him who sits on the throne and worship Him who lives forever and ever, and cast their crowns before the throne, saying:

'You are worthy, O Lord,
To receive glory and honor and power;
For You created all things,
And by Your will they exist and were created'" (Rev 4:10-11).

Jesus knows what we have done and are doing. He is the all-knowing God. Our service for Him will not be forgotten or ignored. He will reward His children and His children will cast their crowns at His feet. He alone is worthy of all rewards.

Since Jesus is coming soon, rewards encourage us to obey God's Word thereby pleasing God and earning rewards. This is not a mercenary idea. Some say, "I don't care about a reward. I just want to make it into heaven." However, rewards will matter to us at Christ's judgment seat. We will be glad we served Him and now have something to give back Him. After all, our Savior is the one who told us about the rewards. Obviously, they are important to Him.

Exposition of the Scriptures, vol. 2, John F. Walvoord and Roy B. Zuck, eds. (Wheaton, IL: Victor Books, 1985), 946.
    54. Zodhiates, *Word Study Dictionary*, s.v., στέφανος; *stéphanos*.

Jesus is Lord of Rewards

Fortunately, we are not left to wonder what we should do. In the last of the seven beatitudes in the book of Revelation,[55] Jesus tells us what to do. "Blessed *are* those who do His commandments, that they may have the right to the tree of life, and may enter through the gates into the city." (Rev 22:14) The answer is simple enough. "Do His commands"; obey your Bible.

The Bible everywhere confirms that those "who do His commands," and as a result, "have the right to the tree of life," and the right to enter the gate of heaven, did not earn their salvation by good works. Salvation is by grace through faith, not by works. So how should we respond to verse 14? We should obey God. "And this is His commandment: that we should believe on the name of His Son Jesus Christ" (1 Jn 3:23). Faith in Jesus is the Father's foremost command. Jesus is "the door" to heaven (cf. Jn 10:9).

One day, a spokesman in a large crowd asked Jesus, "What shall we do, that we may work the works of God?" (Jn 6:28). They wanted to know what they could do to please God. First century Judaism had largely degenerated into a "try harder, do better" religion. Not unlike the religious scene in our day, a personal relationship with God was broadly missing. But notice Jesus's response. "Jesus answered and said to them, 'This is the work of God, that you believe in Him whom He sent'" (v. 29). The priority-obedience that God desires is faith in His Son whom He sent. If we receive Him, trust Him, and know Him, we will love Him. That will inspire all other obedient acts. In fact, obedience is the true test of genuine love. Jesus said, "If you love Me, keep My commandments" (Jn 14:15).

Another day, several Pharisees approached Jesus. Their intentions were nefarious. A lawyer among them asked:

Teacher, which *is* the great commandment in the law?"

---

55. The other six beatitudes are in 1:3; 14:13; 16:15; 19:9; 20:6; 22:7.

Jesus said to him, "'*You shall love the* Lord *your God with all your heart, with all your soul, and with all your mind.*' This is *the* first and great commandment. And *the* second *is* like it: '*You shall love your neighbor as yourself.*' On these two commandments hang all the Law and the Prophets" (Matt 22:36-40).

God does not desire religious obedience from us. He desires an active, responsive love relationship with us. Such a relationship will lead us to obey Him.

A textual variant reading in Revelation 22:14 is noteworthy. Instead of "do His commandments," the variant, as noted in most modern translations, reads "wash their robes." As I understand it, this is a distinction without a difference. The saved in heaven are those who "washed their robes and made them white in the blood of the Lamb" (Rev 7:14). Jesus makes the difference. Love Him, obey Him, walk with Him, abide in Him, and He will reward you accordingly. He is Lord of all, including rewards.

Rewards Not For Everyone

Some, however, will not receive a reward; they are not for everyone. We are not playing under T-ball or Kids' Soccer League rules. Everyone does not get a trophy. "But outside *are* dogs and sorcerers and sexually immoral and murderers and idolaters, and whoever loves and practices a lie" (Rev 22:15).

Adam and Eve sinned. They ate the forbidden fruit (Gen 3:1-6). Consequently, they were turned out of the Garden of Eden to prevent their eating from the "tree of life" (Gen 3:22-23). They brought death into the human race (Rom 5:12). All people are now under the curse of sin. When saved people get to heaven, however, the curse will be removed (Rev 22:3) and we will be welcomed to the tree of life and into the heavenly city. But that welcome is only for those who receive, know, and love Jesus Christ (Jn

1:12). Those outside love and practice lies; those inside love and practice the truth. "If you love Me, keep My commandments" (Jn 14:15).

Receive A Reward

You can receive a reward. Respond to His wonderful invitation. "And the Spirit and the bride say, 'Come!' And let him who hears say, 'Come!' And let him who thirsts come. Whoever desires, let him take the water of life freely" (Rev 22:17). Notice, the Holy Spirit and the church extend the invitation. Southern Baptist churches need to be reminded that a major part of our ministry in the world is offering free water to thirsty people.

Many will not go to heaven, but all could. One needs only to act on his or her desire. That is the wonderful invitation and assurance. The best way I can explain the invitation is by quoting one of Charles Haddon Spurgeon's appeals to the lost. It was based on Revelation 22:17. He said:

> This is the last invitation to sinners in the Word of God. ... May all who have not yet accepted this invitation do so now, lest it should never again be uttered in their hearing.
>
> You might say, "Shouldn't I pray?" It does not say so. It merely tells you to "take the free gift of the water of life."
>
> "But shouldn't I go home and get better first?" No, just take the water of life. "But I must wash my glass." No. Just drink. ... The text does not say, "whoever understands, let him take the free gift of the water of life," but whoever wishes. Are you willing to be saved? Then come with Christ's welcome!
>
> Some say, "But my heart is so hard, I cannot bring a tear to my eye. I cannot feel my sins as I think I should." But this text has nothing to do with your heart. It concerns your will. Are you willing to receive new life? It is "whoever wishes," not whoever feels. Others may say, "I cannot come to Christ. I wish I could, but I am unable."

But this verse does not say, whoever is able may come, but "whoever wishes." Do you want salvation? Then take it!

"Yes," someone says, "God knows I want it, but I'm not worthy." But the invitation is not to whoever is worthy but to "whoever wishes." All you must do is act on your desire, and Christ will save you.[56]

Will you take the water of life? You may. It is a free gift. Do not, however, add any requirement to Jesus's invitation. The results will be disastrous.

> For I testify to everyone who hears the words of the prophecy of this book: If anyone adds to these things, God will add to him the plagues that are written in this book; and if anyone takes away from the words of the book of this prophecy, God shall take away his part from the Book of Life, from the holy city, and *from* the things which are written in this book (Rev 22:18-19).

The plagues in the book of Revelation are many and horrible—far worse than COVID-19. You do not want to face even one, let alone all of them. Do not try to add to or take away from God's Word. Jesus and Jesus alone is the way to heaven (Jn 14:6). He will save anyone who will receive Him (Jn 1:12).

We are seeking to answer the question, where do we go from here? What does God want His people and churches to do until He returns? Our text (Rev 22:6-21), notes that in light Jesus Christ's three-fold promise to return quickly, God desires three responses from each of us.

First, He wants His disciples to obey His Word. We noted three specific ways we can obey. We can worship God, spread the Word, and recog-

---

56. Charles Haddon Spurgeon, *Spurgeon's Commentary on Great Chapters of the Bible*, Tom Carter, ed. (Grand Rapids: Kregel Publications, 1998), 330-31.

nize that obedience is urgent. The response we make, as well as the response of those to whom we spread the Word, may very well seal our condition for eternity. We many die, or Jesus may return. Game over. If these responses were taken seriously, (worship, witness, and urgency) I believe our lives, churches, and denomination would be transformed from the inside out.

Second, in light of Jesus's soon return, God wants His disciples to earn rewards. Obviously, rewards are important to Jesus. He tells about them. Future rewards are based on our present works. We certainly want to have something to return to Jesus when we stand before Him. Jesus knows our works and is Lord over the rewards. Some will not receive a reward, though they would qualify if they responded in faith to the Spirit and the church's wonderful invitation. Now we can come in for a final landing.

WELCOME JESUS WHEN HE COMES

Third, since Jesus is coming quickly, be watching and ready to welcome Him when He comes. The Bible closes with the final promise: "He who testifies to these things says, 'Surely I am coming quickly'" (Rev 22:20a). The watchful and ready respond, "Amen. Even so, come, Lord Jesus!" (v. 20b).

The welcome mats of our hearts can always be out for Jesus. It does not require an eschatological obsession. We do not interpret prophetic Scriptures by the latest newsfeed and make foolish predictions. But we do seek to live with vigilant expectancy. We faithfully, steadily, consistently do what He called us to do, and that will please our Lord when He returns.

Jesus told a parable about His pleasure in those who are waiting, watching, and ready for His return (Luke 12:35-40). In Jesus's story, a man went to a wedding. His servants knew he would return home soon, but they were unsure when. Since they were faithful servants, they stayed dressed and ready. When daylight turned to darkness, they lit the lamps. Through the evening they continued to wait, watch, and listen. They knew their master could arrive at any moment. Finally, when he knocked in the wee hours of the morning, the vigilant butler immediately opened the door to welcome the master home. All of his servants rushed from their duties to join the welcome.

Up to that point, Jesus's parable is routine, unsurprising. But then He purposely gives us a jolt. The unexpected happens. "Assuredly, I say to you that he will gird himself and have them sit down *to eat,* and will come and serve them" (v. 37b). Do you see it? The master was so proud of his vigilant servants, he put on an apron, had the servants sit at his table, and he personally served them a feast. "Jesus startles us as he depicts the master's exuberance on finding wide-awake servants. ... He wants us to sense how delighted He is when His servants are fully focused on His coming."[57]

Jesus's conclusion brings the meaning of the parable into focus. "Therefore you also be ready, for the Son of Man is coming at an hour you do not expect" (v. 40).

Are you waiting and watching for His return? Are you ready to welcome Him if He comes today? Have you responded to His wonderful grace-filled invitation? If so, "The grace of the Lord Jesus be with you all. Amen" (Rev 22:21).

Hide and seek has different rules in different places. My friend, Phil Young, who grew up in Chittenango, New York, told me of a rule they used in upstate New York that was different from our rules in Alabama. He said, "If 'It' couldn't find everyone and was tired of looking, he or she called out, 'Olly Olly in come free!'" That meant, "Game over. Everyone can come home free. You win."

That's what Jesus said when He died on the cross for our sins, was buried, and rose again. "Olly Olly in come free!" Come to Jesus. There's no penalty to pay. He paid your debt; all will be forgiven. "The blood of Jesus Christ His Son cleanses us from all sin" (1 John 1:7).

---

57. Dale Ralph Davis, *Luke 1-13: The Year of the Lord's Favor* (Geanies House, Fearn, Ross-shire, Scotland: Christian Focus Publications Ltd., 2021), 230.

"Whoever desires, let him take the water of life freely." Receive Jesus. Drink by faith. And having drunk, share the good news with someone who needs to hear, "Olly Olly in come free!"

* * * * *

We have asked and attempted to answer a question about eleven doctrinal issues considered vital during the Conservative Resurgence of the Southern Baptist Convention. The overarching question is, "Does it still matter?"

1. Does inerrancy still matter?
2. Does the gospel still matter?
3. Does baptism still matter?
4. Does the term Baptist still matter?
5. Does the local church still matter?
6. Does grammatical-historical interpretation still matter?
7. Does expository preaching still matter?
8. Does gender identity still matter?
9. Do gender roles still matter?
10. Does the rapture still matter?
11. Does the conservative resurgence still matter?
12. Epilogue: Where do we go from here?

Each reader will personally answer the questions. It is our prayer that these chapters will be instructive, inspiring, and encouraging. We want this volume to be a tool that helps you to stand strong and give a worthy defense of your faith in these challenging days. I pray that we Southern Baptist will be less "woke" and far more "spiritually awakened" (2 Chron 7:14).

CPSIA information can be obtained
at www.ICGtesting.com
Printed in the USA
LVHW101219280422
716406LV00001B/1/J